The Best American Travel Writing 2006

The Best American Travel Writing 2006

Edited and with an Introduction
by Tim Cahill

Jason Wilson, Series Editor

HOUGHTON MIFFLIN COMPANY
BOSTON · NEW YORK   2006

Visit our Web site: www.houghtonmifflinbooks.com.

ISSN 1530-1516
ISBN-13: 978-0-618-58212-9   ISBN-10: 0-618-58212-6
ISBN-13: 978-0-618-58215-0 (pbk.)   ISBN-10: 0-618-58215-0 (pbk.)

Printed in the United States of America

MP 10 9 8 7 6 5 4 3 2 1

"A Shared Plate" by Chitrita Banerji. First published in *Gourmet*, November 2005. Copyright © 2005 by Chitrita Banerji. Reprinted by permission of the author.

"The Selling of the Last Savage" by Michael Behar. First published in *Outside*, February 2005. Copyright © 2005 by Michael Behar. Reprinted by permission of the author.

"How to Sail Across the Atlantic" by Paul Bennett. First published in *National Geographic Adventure*, February 2005. Copyright © 2005 by Paul Bennett. Reprinted by permission of the author.

"After the Fall" by Tom Bissell and Morgan Meis. First published in *The Virginia Quarterly Review*, vol. 81, no. 4, Fall 2005. Copyright © 2005 by Tom Bissell and Morgan Meis. Reprinted by permission of the authors.

"The Discreet Charm of the Zurich Bourgeoisie" by Alain de Botton. First published in *FarFlungMagazine.com*, July 2005. Copyright © 2005 by Alain de Botton. Reprinted by permission of Alain de Botton and Aragi Inc.

"Ain't It Just Grand?" by Kevin Fedarko. First published in *Outside*, June 2005. Copyright © 2005 by Kevin Fedarko. Reprinted by permission of the author.

"The Price of Paradise" by Caitlin Flanagan. First published in *The New Yorker*, January 3, 2005. Copyright © 2005 by Caitlin Flanagan. Reprinted by permission of the author.

"Where They Love Americans . . . for a Living" by Sean Flynn. First published in *GQ*, October 2005. Copyright © 2005 by Sean Flynn. Reprinted by permission of the author.

"Out of Ohio" by Ian Frazier. First published in *The New Yorker*, January 10, 2005. Copyright © by Ian Frazier. Reprinted by permission of The Wylie Agency, Inc.

Contents

Foreword

THE SLIPPERY NOTION of authenticity — The Authentic Travel Experience — is something that people in the travel-writing business endlessly wring their hands over.

Just pick up any travel magazine and you'll find boasts of authenticity on the cover: "Insider's Istanbul"; "In Search of the Real Umbria"; "The True Taste of Thailand."

The message seems clear: if you're not traveling to see our "hidden gems" or dining on our "local secrets" — well, you're hopeless. Worse than hopeless. You're a *tourist*.

Travel Weekly, the national newspaper for the travel industry, hosted a roundtable discussion in early 2006 and invited top editors from seven of the nation's leading travel publications. They gathered in the Ed Sullivan Room at the Friar's Club in New York and discussed a variety of pressing issues, such as: *"What are the ingredients that create buzz for a destination?"*

The issue of authentic travel experience was quickly raised.

The editor-in-chief of one of the nation's largest travel magazines explained: "That new adventure traveler is the person who wants to fly to India first class or business class. They want to stay in a great hotel. Then they want to be taken to a small village where they meet the rug dealer. Then they want to buy the rug. But the thing is, they want the genuine, authentic experience, and they're willing to pay to get there."

"That doesn't sound authentic at all to have someone take you to a rug dealer," said the editor of a more budget-conscious magazine.

"I don't agree," the first editor persisted. "You can go there and find someone who can take you into the mountains. I have a story in the works on just this thing. They will take you to the guy who will sell you the rug. And it is real, and when they return, it is what they're going to talk about when people come over for dinner."

This assertion was pushed into the realm of the absurd by the editor-in-chief of another big travel magazine, who said, "The adventure traveler is not necessarily the one out there climbing rocks. There's also the adventurous traveler who's Donna Karan's friend, searching for a new experience."

"A new nirvana?" someone else hopefully suggested.

"A new nirvana — or a new thing to buy."

I live in a three-hundred-year-old town called Haddonfield, New Jersey. In the 1850s, Haddonfield served as a vacation spot for well-heeled Philadelphians who made the short trip across the Delaware River to escape the city's stifling summer. Tastes changed (perhaps the travel editors of the era started sending people to hipper, cooler destinations). Anyway, Haddonfield's days as a vacation destination are long gone, and now the town resembles many other colonial-era hamlets throughout the northeastern United States.

A certain type of travel writer might call Haddonfield "charming" or "quaint." It is the kind of place with a main street where — besides law offices, banks, and churches — you'll find stuff like quilting shops, a hospital for dolls, and a bakery for dogs. It's the kind of place where houses have name tags: "Charles French, 1758"; "Methodist Parsonage, 1857"; "Birdwood Tenant House, 1783." There's a Quaker school, a chocolate shop, a grandfather-clock repairman, a sports memorabilia dealer, three ice cream parlors, a violinmaker, a harp store, and a cobbler. The dress shop posts snapshots in the window of local girls wearing their gowns at prom. A photography studio displays portraits of people's pets. There is a novelty shop called Jamaican Me Crazy, a jeweler called The Family Jewels, and a toy store called The Happy Hippo. There is a barbershop that claims to be "the oldest in New Jersey." One of the town's two skateboard shops recently advertised an "all-girl skateboard camp." On summer evenings, you can gather around the gazebo and listen to the town's official brass band perform. Of course, just like every other small American town, we have a volunteer fire station and a Fourth of July parade and a Starbucks.

We boast one small bed and breakfast. We don't really have any tourist attractions to speak of, though on special days the docents in period costume will happily guide you through our historic Indian King Tavern, an important meeting place during the Revolutionary War.

Our major claim to fame — relatively speaking — is that the world's first complete dinosaur skeleton was discovered here in 1858. A National Historic Site plaque marks the spot. Our dinosaur is actually named the Hadrosaurus, and we've erected a huge bronze sculpture of him in the middle of downtown. He now goes by the nickname "Haddy."

We have several cafés and restaurants, though you'll have to bring your own bottle of wine to dinner. That's because Haddonfield is a "dry town," meaning the sale of alcoholic beverages is strictly prohibited. There are no pubs or liquor stores to be found within the town's borders. (Even the Indian King Tavern isn't allowed to serve drinks anymore.)

What I hope to convey here is that, although Haddonfield is a lovely place to live, and to raise children, it is . . . well, to use another travel writing euphemism, it can be "sleepy."

Suffice to say that no American travel editor will be commissioning a travel feature about Haddonfield any time soon.

In fact, many upscale Americans — particularly those who live in major cities and travel abroad and worry about whether they are tourists or travelers — will grow downright cynical or hostile when confronted with a suburban place like Haddonfield. Over the years, we've heard every inevitable snide comparison to places like Mayberry, Stepford, and that town where Jim Carrey lived in *The Truman Show.*

When we moved here, an acquaintance from Manhattan came to visit. After several days and countless eye rolls, she cracked. "I cannot believe you live here! It's, like, a fake town! It's so authentic, it's like inauthentic!" She insisted we move immediately.

I should mention that, at the time, this woman was at work on a lip-smacking *Under the Tuscan Sun* rip-off about a year she spent living in a small town in a popular region of a Mediterranean country, one with lots of lemon trees and vineyards and salt-of-the-earth peasants who deeply understood life's simple pleasures.

In contrast, last summer we hosted some foreign friends who

stopped on their way from New York toward points south. These friends live in a city that is usually dubbed one of the "hottest" in Europe, a place where history is centuries older and design is "cutting edge" and supermodels supposedly roam the clubs.

It's fascinating then that when these stylish Europeans visited, they simply loved small-town Haddonfield. They wandered the main street and hobnobbed with locals. They bought knickknacks. They hung out in the local coffee shop and ate Italian water ice and cheese steaks. They brown-bagged wine into restaurants.

Philadelphia (recently declared "the next great American city" by one major travel magazine) conveniently lies fifteen minutes to the west by train, but my friends took little advantage of this. I tried to present them with my "Insider's Philadelphia" tour, but after a few hours they said, "Let's go back and hang out in Haddonfield."

At first, I just thought I had strange friends. But after a few days, I clearly understood what was going on.

"This is America just like we imagine it!" they said. To them, like it or not, Haddonfield was exactly the vision of the United States they were searching for. Which isn't actually that strange when you think about the way a hill town in Tuscany or a fishing village in Norway or a settlement in the South American jungle appears to the American traveler on an endless quest for the authentic.

In Alain de Botton's essay on Zurich included within these pages, he writes: "We normally associate exotic with camels and pyramids. But perhaps anything different and desirable deserves the word."

All of which means, of course, that there cannot possibly be a single Authentic Travel Experience to be found in any place. Great travel writers know this, and this is why excellent, noteworthy travel writing is always done in the first person.

"The misperception is that the travel book is about a country," Paul Theroux once said. "It's really about the person who's traveling."

The stories included in this anthology are selected from among hundreds of pieces in hundreds of diverse publications — from mainstream and specialty magazines to Sunday newspaper travel sections to literary journals. I've done my best to be fair and representative, and in my opinion the best one hundred travel stories from 2005 were forwarded to Tim Cahill, who made our final selections.

I now begin anew by reading the hundreds of stories published in 2006. I am once again asking editors and writers to submit the best of whatever it is they define as travel writing. These submissions must be nonfiction, published in the United States during the 2006 calendar year. They must not be reprints or excerpts from published books. They must include the author's name, date of publication, and publication name, and must be tear sheets, the complete publication, or a clear photocopy of the piece as it originally appeared. I must receive all submissions by January 1, 2007, in order to ensure full consideration for the next collection. Further, publications that want to make certain their contributions will be considered for the next edition should make sure to include this anthology on their subscription list. Submissions or subscriptions should be sent to Jason Wilson, The Best American Travel Writing, P.O. Box 260, Haddonfield, NJ 08033.

It was an honor to work with Tim Cahill, one of my favorite writers, on this excellent edition. I would also like to thank Nicole Angeloro and Will Vincent, among others at Houghton Mifflin.

JASON WILSON

Introduction

SEVERAL DECADES AGO, when I first started publishing travel books, it was necessary to look for a knowledgeable clerk to help find my tomes when they hit the stores. I might find my latest darlings under "current events" or "new nonfiction" or "humor." There weren't "travel writing" aisles in major bookstores. You could find travel guides, but not "travel writing."

All that has changed in the last dozen years or so. Bookstores have discovered that there are such things as the travel essay, the travel book, and now some stores actually specialize in travel writing. This has led me to conclude that there are now a lot more writers who specialize in travel, and, concurrently, many more readers interested in reading those writers. We seem to be in a golden age of American travel writing and may actually be closing in on some of the great English travel writers who wrote timeless books and essays in the age of Empire and just after. (This is an arguable proposition and one that, I admit, may well be an inexcusable overstatement.)

There was, of course, a hiccup in demand and production just after the events of September 11, 2001, but I sense that, lately, both output and demand have picked up considerably. Magazines are once again assigning writers to seek out remote and sometimes dangerous locations, or to come back with new insights concerning more familiar areas.

In the magazines that assign such work, the word "article" is never used. One writes a "piece" or sometimes, "a story." It is the latter definition that I prefer.

My own opinion is that "story" is the essence of the travel essay. Stories are the way we organize the chaos in our lives, orchestrate voluminous factual material, and — if we are very good — shed some light on the human condition, such as it is.

I realize that there are many very good travel writers, people who interview this person and that, eliciting contrasting views in the manner of a good daily reporter, and those fine writers did not find their way into this book, due entirely to my own prejudice in the matter. Information is of immense value, but if I can't find a story, I often feel I'm being beaten over the head with an encyclopedia. Stories are the sole written instruments that can bring tears to our eyes, or make us laugh, or even — God forbid — compel us to think, and thereby perhaps even take a position.

Additionally, they're generally more fun to read. (In my entirely biased opinion.)

So in choosing "pieces" for this anthology, I've looked for the best stories I could find and was brutal in eliminating purely informational material. There is a controversy in the travel writing community concerning such matters. One argument has it that "the reader wants to read about his trip, not yours." I'm not so sure. Readers want to read, which means they want something that holds their attention. They want to be entertained and informed and amused. If they are reading for information only, modern travelers are blessed with any number of guidebooks, and these volumes seem to become better and more informative every year.

But in travel writing, story is of the essence. And if the narrative in question inspires the reader to visit the destination in question, so much the better. I know from letters I've received, from conversations I've had at writing seminars and book signings, that some of my own stories have inspired readers to undertake journeys similar to my own. Hell, certain adventure travel companies have made places I've written about long ago catalogue destinations, and at least one guidebook followed a trip I took years ago, informing independent travelers how to emulate that peculiar journey without encountering the multitude of dead ends and frustrations that my own party encountered. A hearty traveler, book in hand, could in ten days make the trip that took my party the better part of a month.

Guidebooks are about logistics; stories arise from the heart, and are the essence of travel. Ask anyone who has just returned from a trip how it went, and you are not likely to get directions. You'll hear stories.

In this book, our storytellers have blundered across the globe and come back with essays and articles that I hope will make you laugh, cry, think, and perhaps dream. Or at least that is what we as travel writers like to believe, and often state aloud in the many conferences devoted to travel writing that take place across the United States every year. New such workshops and seminars are springing up like mushrooms after a rainstorm.

These are generally invigorating for both the writers and the attendees who would like to be travel writers. The established writers are forced to think about how and why they do what they do, matters I generally never contemplate. As a matter of fact, most writers, meeting casually, do not talk about "the process," or "narrative arch" or the complications of carpentering together a scene. What we talk about is how we were financially sodomized by this publisher or that, and how the latest editor went goose-stepping through our sinuous prose.

I suspect the conferences are the only time we think about what we do, and in the dozens I've attended, it is instructive to watch established literary travel writers oscillate between self-congratulation and self-hate. On the one hand, there is a tendency to imagine that what we do is important and that encouraging people to travel promotes tolerance and understanding. As Mark Twain, who spent much of his early newspaper career as a "foreign correspondent," said, "Travel is fatal to prejudice." My sense is that most of the writers here would be in agreement.

So we like to think of ourselves as emissaries for world peace, for the convergence of cultures, for international harmony, and, by extension, the end of cultural disharmony and even war. If folks are encouraged to travel our route, so much the better; but if they choose to experience the culture from the comfort of a La-Z-Boy, it is of no matter.

We, as travel writers, will pat ourselves on the back. Maybe we haven't cured cancer or come up with an AIDS vaccine, but we've gone to the ends of the earth, almost always on OPM (Other People's Money: the only good-sized hunks of cash most travel writers get to see), and we can congratulate ourselves that we labor in the cause of understanding and world peace.

The fact that cultures are still in mortal conflict and that world peace is yet a fantasy suggests that either we are dead wrong, or that we still have a lot of work to do.

On the other hand, many of us are consumed with a sort of gentle self-loathing and generally bristle at being called *travel* writers. Most of the writers you will read here did not aspire to travel as a career. I didn't. We like to think of ourselves as writers first, travelers second. We started out as novelists, narrative nonfiction writers, creative journalists, daily journalists, technical writers. And somehow, one day, in the midst of a personality profile or political piece or the explication of a current crime, some trick of fate, generally in the person of a cruel editor, sent us on an assignment that required travel, and we nailed the story. And that led to a second such assignment, and a third. And suddenly, much to our mystification, we became known as travel writers.

The majority of those in my occupation, I imagine, would rather be known as writers who, for reasons not totally explicable, find their best subject matter somewhere beyond the front door.

In contrast, the persons we teach or speak to at various seminars actually *want* to be travel writers. They ask if you need to be in impressive shape to write well about physically difficult assignments, or whether it is necessary to speak several languages, or to be of this gender or that to accomplish certain tasks.

And what we tell them is: no, you have to want to be a writer and you have to write. Period.

Now, it might be supposed that people who attend such workshops, are, on the whole, hopeless wannabes. This is decidedly not the case. I am literally astonished at the number of people who've absorbed the message and gone on to a career in publishing. Indeed, I can think of one such former student whose last book was a national bestseller. I know doctors, judges, plumbers, and airline stewards — all former workshop attendees — who publish travel material regularly in a variety of venues.

Maybe these are the folks who will truly generate the golden age of American travel writing, bring harmony to the world, put an end to ecological devastation, and make bagloads of money in the process. God knows their teachers haven't accomplished these things.

So, what is it I tell prospective travel writers? The rules are simple enough: get your facts straight and tell us a story. Facts first: I was once taken to task by a reviewer who felt "literature" did not define my work. I was instead, he proclaimed, "a high-level journalist," in the manner, I suppose, that certain mentally or physically challenged individuals function at a high level. In point of fact, I found the charge flattering. A high-level journalist is one whose facts are unassailable.

That is our job, but it goes further. To enter into the realm of literature — or even aspire to it — requires that the writer present a coherent narrative of value and insight. There is a story to be told, a bit of the world to be organized in a fashion that can make us laugh or cry, or preferably both.

The differences are easy enough to see. When I was an editor at a travel magazine, I could generally tell when a piece would be a storyless compendium of facts, like a ship's log. They usually began with the date, and a plane landing on a quaint runway somewhere all to hell and gone. It seemed to me that the writer had simply submitted his or her journal, and I knew that I'd be reading facts and observations entirely devoid of story. It is story that elevates the material. By contrast, a manuscript that is, in essence, the traveler's journal is one in which the writer has failed to analyze the material. Reading these manuscripts is like those interminable nights spent at your neighbor's house viewing several hundred unedited slides of his latest vacation.

I should say that there were many well-written Internet pieces among the stories I was asked to review here. Those that were written on a daily basis — reports from the field — were often impressively literate, nimble, and highly immediate. But the writer had no time to contemplate the entirety of the experience. Such reports, written daily on a tight schedule, may have risen to a high-level journalism, but they necessarily lacked narrative. I have written such pieces myself and wish now that I could go back and "write" them, because there was often an overarching story that I wasn't aware existed until I studied my notes.

This volume contains a few "pieces" that might be termed adventure travel. Kevin Fedarko's piece on the Grand Canyon comes to mind. There are those who consider outdoor literature a separate genre. Not travel writing at all. I believe that writing about nature, or exploration or adventure in all its guises, can, in fact, be compelling and literate. This was not always the case in America. In 1975, I and several others were asked to come up with an idea for an "outdoor" magazine. We reviewed all potential competitors and found that — with the exception of a magazine called *Mountain Gazette* — outdoor writing was confined to what is called service articles: a canoeing magazine might tell its readers how best to paddle a canoe. Twelve times a year.

Adventure articles were the province of magazines with titles like *Saga* or *Man's Adventure* or *Adventure for Men,* and the stories themselves — titled "I Survived the Savage Coyotes of Montana" — seemed, well, subliterate and written to appeal to a barbershop clientele. Kira Salak proves here that adventure is not the sole province of men, and that an adventure can be not only exciting but also evocative, literate, and informative. Oh yeah, and true.

Back in 1975, other outdoor magazine startups, now defunct, were firmly based in an earnest ecological niche, and the writers for those sincere efforts tended to elucidate issues by shaking their fingers in the readers' faces. Pieces consisted of facts devoid of story all wrapped around the idea that an ecological Armageddon was just around the corner, and *it was your fault.*

The magazine I was involved with did not have a particular horse to flog. Our idea — simplicity itself — was to produce a periodical that contained *literate writing* about the out-of-doors. This was considered a moronic idea by journalism pundits who explained, in critical articles, that people who went out-of-doors were, by their very nature, subliterate, knuckle-dragging mouth-breathers.

That was largely my fault, I think. Early on, I had argued that adventure could be part of the mix. My colleagues demurred. Adventure was in the realm of barbershop reading. My response was that outdoor and adventure literature is, in fact, American literature, and always has been. James Fenimore Cooper, Herman Melville, Faulkner, Thoreau, Hemingway were all outdoor writers of a sort. It is a great stain that runs through classic American literature. The stories in *Adventure for Men* did serve this tradition well.

So we had adventure stories in the new magazine, and we took a little heat for it. An unintended, but important, side effect was that we were also able to write about ecological issues, but in a story form that held the reader's interest and enlisted him or her in a conspiracy of caring. No finger shaking.

There is another sort of adventure included in this volume. You don't see a lot of erotica in travel writing. In fact, you don't see any. My friend, Don George, the global editor at Lonely Planet, once asked various writers to contribute to a book he wanted to call *The*

Erotic Traveler. Few of us were able to dredge up a suitable story. Nobody wants to get naked in front of several hundred thousand strangers, for one thing. For another, sexual encounters between well-heeled travelers and impoverished people in developing countries feels . . . well, wrong.

This year, someone got it right, as you will see in Rolf Potts's story about Tantric yoga for dilettantes.

Other stories here literally take place in the writer's neighborhood, which validates several points I've been trying to make. Several years ago, Bill Bryson made the point that travel writing is a forgiving genre: once you walk out the front door, you're traveling. And I have an ongoing preference: I'd rather read a well-written piece — a story — about a picnic in the back yard than another addled account of someone's attempt to do cartwheels across the breadth of Turkmenistan.

More to the point: Ian Frazier's memoir about leaving home draws a picture of a midwestern town some forty years ago. Such stuff may be exotic to a person living in Japan, but it was very close to my own experience growing up in my own midwestern town. Despite my familiarity with the subject, the piece is so gracefully written, so spot-on accurate, that I felt that pleasurable prickly sensation that I believe academics call the "shock of recognition."

Meanwhile, Pico Iyer writes, charmingly, about his own neighborhood, which happens to be in Japan and is totally foreign to me. Both writers simply stepped out the front door: Frazier figuratively, Iyer literally.

I'm sure some may argue that various pieces here are not precisely "travel writing." I'm thinking of Michael Paterniti's story, which does, indeed, take us to the Ukraine but is what many might consider a personality profile. The personality in question is what we used to call "a trip" in itself. The author takes us to a very sad and strange place, and if someone wants to argue about whether this story is indeed travel writing, they're too late. It's too good. I've already claimed it for the genre.

Among the stories I read in compiling this anthology, there were many about airplanes. David Sedaris expresses the majority view. Air travel these days is a dreaded abhorrence, especially for those of us who suffer in these flying metal cattle cars for a living. I felt that too many of the airplane pieces were merely foul-tempered rants. Not that Sedaris's effort isn't as well. The saving grace is that it is very funny indeed.

I've included Sally Shivnan's piece on getting a window seat because it was the sole contrarian view of air travel, and because it was written in such a lovely manner that I almost swallowed my own biased opinion. (Note to airline executives the world over: I'm sending each of you a packet of stories, all written by professional travelers, and all suggesting that your industry is in deep trouble.)

One more note on air travel and humor: P. J. O'Rourke can take us to an airplane-manufacturing company and make us see dozens of things we didn't think we were much interested in, not because of the narrative thrust in the story — there is almost none — or his inner journey (he says certain issues make him question his free-market principles, but clearly the question dies). No, we read and learn because P. J. makes us laugh. That's his virtue, and that's why you will read, with unexpected pleasure, about how French people make a real big airplane.

There are, I hope, unexpected pleasures here. Caitlin Flanagan's understated humor compels us to read about a place I could not have imagined could have produced such a lively and charming story. We follow Mark Jenkins on what appears to be and is a pure adventure and yet we end up learning something very valuable about education in what has become a war of cultures. Tom Bissell and Morgan Meis give us a shivery tale of justified paranoia; Chitrita Banerji explicates Indian culture for us using food as a focus; Patrick Symmes writes about fishing in Mongolia but the story turns intensely personal. Alain de Botton encourages us to see the bourgeois of Zurich as admirable and somehow makes what is generally considered boring, fascinating. Calvin Trillin discusses language school and soup in such a manner that you'll want to try both.

So what we have here is a collection of twenty-six stories, all of which touched me in one way or another, changed an attitude, made me laugh aloud, or provided fuel for my dreams. I wish the reader similar joys.

TIM CAHILL

CHITRITA BANERJI

A Shared Plate

FROM *Gourmet*

"THE *TATTO* IS HERE, THE *TATTO* IS HERE!" Bare feet rush down the stairs and out toward the front door as the house resonates with the blowing of conch shells and loud ululation — auspicious sounds believed to scare away evil spirits.

Staying with a friend in Calcutta to attend her daughter's wedding, I am caught up in the excitement. The *tatto* whose arrival is causing such a commotion is a collection of gifts — clothes, cosmetics, decorative objects, food — that the bridegroom's family sends to the home of the bride on the morning of a Bengali Hindu wedding. I haven't attended such an event in many years, but my memory flashes to long-forgotten images of the gifts sent to our house for an aunt's wedding. As a small child, I had been particularly awed by one item — an enormous carp, its silvery scales gleaming with an undertone of pink, its head patterned with turmeric and vermilion, a double garland of tuberoses twined round its ample belly. Is such a princely fish still part of the Bengali wedding *tatto*?

I move forward to look at the trays being unloaded from the car. Yes, one does contain a carp, although its dimensions fall short of those I remember. But the family seems pleased, to judge from their gleeful comments about the *muror dal* to be made with the head at lunchtime. For us fish-loving Bengalis, this is a cherished delicacy. The fish head is fried, broken into pieces, and added to roasted *moong dal*, its copious brain matter (like the marrow from beef bones) giving a baroque note to the redolence of turmeric, ginger, cumin, cinnamon, cardamom, and green chilies.

But amid the happy exuberance, I feel a deep sadness as I think of my own family. My mother was the eldest daughter among many siblings, and her wedding was a lavish affair. The legendary chef my grandfather hired for the occasion transformed the entire roof of the ancestral house into an enormous kitchen for three days. It was said that he prepared an *akhni* water — a stocklike decoction of the various spices used in making pilaf — so fragrant that the entire street was enveloped in its aroma. Every item of the spectacular meal he served was described in excruciating detail whenever any wedding was discussed in our family. It sounded like a golden affair, burnished with each retelling.

By the time I was a teenager, though, these narratives evoked only a bitter irony. The golden couple of the wedding were unrecognizable in the two adults who were my parents. A terrible sense of grievance and letdown seemed to consume them much of the time, and the most unlikely event, topic, visit, or comment could precipitate a marathon session of loud arguments and bitter reproaches, scorching words that walls and doors could not keep out. And then there were the silences — long, throbbing interludes of absolutely no conversation that lasted for hours, even days.

Joy, however, was not totally absent in our family. My conflicted parents shared one enthusiasm — food. She was a fabulous cook, a true artist, and he had a rare and subtle palate. He also enjoyed shopping for the season's best produce, fish, and meats. Through my school and college years, I took for granted the delectable offerings on our table — slow-cooked potatoes with tamarind and asafetida, carp in yogurt sauce, shrimp with ground coconut and mustard, and so many others.

Despite their constant discord, my parents were also extremely hospitable, and friends and family were frequently invited to our home for meals. Among the many classic dishes for which my mother was justly famed was *muror dal*. Each time she made it, she waited intently for my father's reaction. Even if they were not speaking to each other, the appreciative sniff that greeted the serving of the *dal* on his plate and the zestful way he sucked the juices from the head were the accolades she really looked for.

Not having the maturity to sense the complex emotions that underlaid my parents' endless conflict, I blamed the Indian system of arranged marriage that allowed families to match incompatible duos for life, since Hindus do not believe in divorce. Never, I resolved, would I be trapped like that. The only way to avoid it was to escape — and I did, as far away as the United States. I also exercised choice in my marriage.

But I could not escape destiny. In the late 1980s, I found myself, the first divorcée in my orthodox Hindu family, back in Calcutta, living with my parents in their rambling three-story house. Once again, the erupting arguments and conflicts made me ponder the nature of the marital bond that held them together. But with older eyes, I could see the deep attachment below the surface. How had it developed when they seemed to have disappointed each other right from the beginning?

One evening, when I came home from work and found them bickering viciously over a particularly insignificant matter, I lost my usual restraint. "Why didn't you get a divorce years ago?" I burst out. "At least I would have had some peace!"

Immediately, I was overcome with shame and regret. Didn't I know how impossible it was for people of their generation to even think about divorce? Hadn't I shamed them enough with mine? Guiltily, I fled upstairs. But my mother followed me. With surprising calmness, this habitually no-nonsense, even prosaic woman sat down and explained her conception of marriage.

"You didn't care for our rituals," she smiled sadly, "you married outside our religion, you had a civil marriage in America. But you've seen many Hindu weddings. You know the ceremony requires the couple to feed the fire, and then feed each other. Food is life, and by eating together, the pair bonds for life. We did that. How can you talk to us about getting a divorce?"

She spoke of ceremony and bonds. But looking at her face, and listening to her voice, I heard only the word *love*. I thought back to the long years of conflict, but also to the deep, shared passion for the art of cooking, eating, and offering hospitality. That daily tableau of the table, I now saw, was neither duty nor obligation — it was love, but a tormented version that found no expression except through food.

Soon after, I went away again — back to America. After my father's death, I decided to bring my mother over to join me, and for ten years I watched as time and distance failed to wipe out her regrets and sorrows. In the absence of the one person with whom she had argued and fought and eaten, she totally lost the pleasure she once took in cooking. Even her enjoyment of food seemed sadly diminished.

The wedding I am attending in Calcutta — an arranged marriage — is in the evening. By now, I am in a pensive mood. The *tatto* has been put away, the fish consumed by the family. In the large rented hall, a canopied enclosure has been decorated with red cloth and tuberose garlands. In front of the chief actors, seated on a carpet, is an array of items necessary for the complex Hindu ceremony. I see the bowl of snowy white popped rice, the bunch of ripe bananas, the conch-shaped sweets on a terra-cotta plate — and my mother's words ring vividly in my ears: "Marriage is a lifelong undertaking to eat together."

First the bride's father has to give her away. The priest guides him through the Sanskrit mantras, while he holds his daughter's hand and places it on top of the groom's. It is a solemn undertaking, since the "gift" is not simply a daughter but also a woman now endowed with her share of the family property. The pinched look on the father's face demonstrates the effects of a daylong fast. Earlier, I had seen him at home, closeted with the household gods and one of the priests, making sacred offerings to both gods and ancestors, asking them to bless his daughter and son-in-law.

In my mother's time, the bride, too, had to fast all day. But this twenty-first-century bride had been allowed a little snack in the middle of the day. Wrapped in a gold-embroidered red silk sari (red being an auspicious color in Hindu culture), decked out in intricate gold jewelry, her forehead decorated with patterns of sandalwood paste, she seems an icon of happy expectation. Had my mother, too, looked like that on her wedding day?

Once the bride has been given away, the father leaves the scene — a symbolic gesture of renunciation. Now it is the couple's turn to wind their way through further intricate rituals, guided by two priests. Several times they make offerings to the gods: flowers, leaves, unmilled rice, a type of grass called *durba*. But the crucial — and most spectacular — part of the ceremony comes later. The pair rises and stands, she in front. His arms come around her and he places his palms underneath hers so that they can jointly hold a plate laden with foods. One of the priests quickly builds a fire in a large copper vessel and the couple pours offerings into it. The popped rice is the first. As it falls, the flames rise up with a whooshing sound, as if Agni, the god of fire, is welcoming the tribute. Item by item, all the food is submitted to the flames. Finally, the two walk around the fire seven times, the shoulder end of her sari knotted to his shawl, reciting the Sanskrit couplets that express the undertaking of a lifelong bond. But this first day's ceremony (weddings are not complete until the end of the third day) is not over yet. Tradition requires them to feed each other sweets from the same plate. As they do so, I am struck by the tenderness with which he brushes the crumbs from her mouth.

Throughout the long ceremony, guests have come and gone, sampling the wedding feast in another room. When most people have left, the bridal pair sits down to dinner at a large table with a group of friends. I wish them happiness and say goodbye to the family. From the landing, I look back one last time. Amid the laughter and chatter of the friends, the groom is placing a spoonful of pilaf on the bride's plate. She, still feeling shy, looks down, but the flush of pleasure on her cheeks and the upward curve of her mouth are unmistakable.

Suddenly, I imagine my parents in place of this couple. In my vision, their faces are fresh, expectant, and youthful, instead of marked with half a century's wear and tear. I see my father, his handsome face topped by the conical groom's hat, serving portions of food onto his new bride's plate. I watch my habitually stern mother transformed into a bashful bride who smiles with happiness under cover of her veil.

I walk away, but as I go I wish for the young couple that today's shared communion will be allowed to blossom, that the shining bride will have the uninhibited freedom to say she loves her husband and children every time she serves a meal, and that the groom will find a way to reciprocate. I wish for them a home where two people live an ordinary life, its disappointments made bearable by the leavening of laughter and the communion of food. It does not seem too much to ask.

MICHAEL BEHAR

The Selling of the Last Savage

FROM *Outside*

I'M SOMEWHERE in a godforsaken rain forest on the north coast of West Papua, Indonesia, and I'm ready to get the hell out of here. I'm five days into a three-week jungle trek with forty-three-year-old Bali-based outfitter Kelly Woolford, and things have gotten both weird and dangerous. Now I'm scared and confused, and I've lost all faith in my guide.

"We'll meet 'em, share a little tobacco, chill for a bit, and then move on — like passing nomads," Woolford had said. But five minutes ago we encountered bow-and-arrow-wielding bushmen who were so angry that they charged our camp, lobbing three arrows high above our heads. To avoid puncture wounds, I ran straight for a nearby river and almost swam across it, until I remembered that it contained crocodiles that might have torn me to shreds.

Despite all the chaos, Woolford seems detached, remaining calm and puffing a cigarette as our porters grapple for their machetes and bows. I ask for reassurance that I'm not about to get skewered, but his answer isn't very soothing: "If they want to fill our asses full of arrows, there isn't much we can do about it." True enough. Plus, Woolford already told me that if these men wanted to kill us, they would have done so by now.

When I originally heard about First Contact, a trip offered by Woolford's trekking company, Papua Adventures, I couldn't believe he was really doing what he claimed to be doing. An easygoing American expat from Springfield, Missouri, who jokingly describes himself as a "hillbilly," Woolford marches into the jungle in search of uncontacted native tribes who have never seen outsiders — and who aren't supposed to mind tourists barging into their lives. I had trouble buying the idea that, in the twenty-first century, there were still nomadic hunter-gatherers out there using stone tools and rubbing sticks together to start a fire. But there are, Woolford assured me. From his home in Ubud, Bali, he explained the strategy behind his First Contact trips.

"There are a handful of places in West Papua that are untouched — still Stone Age tribes, still cannibals," he said. "It's just that a lot of people are too scared to go look for them."

Despite my initial reservations, when Woolford asked me to join his next trip to this easternmost province of Indonesia, which shares the island of New Guinea with the nation of Papua New Guinea, I decided that eighteenth-century philosopher Jean-Jacques Rousseau might have had a point: seeing a "noble savage" would rouse my spirit and reveal the primordial essence of my being. Of course, this outdated and arguably racist view ignores the fact that first contact has historically resulted in a deadly tsunami of disease, war, famine, slavery, and proselytization like those that engulfed nearly all of the world's tribal societies following the arrival of European explorers. But I signed on for the three-week trip anyway. Someone needed to check out Woolford's First Contact experience, which he was selling on the Web for $8,000.

Right now, though, I'm regretting my eyes-wide-open approach, wondering if I'll end up like Alejandro Labaca, the Spanish Catholic missionary who made first contact with a remote Peruvian tribe in the 1970s. Labaca was later discovered, as Joe Kane wrote in his 1995 book *Savages,* "pinned to the ground, spread-eagled, by seventeen palm-wood spears, which jutted like porcupine quills from his throat, chest, arms, and thighs. His corpse was punctured in eighty-nine places."

Whether these natives are really "savages" or this whole encounter is some sort of bizarre put-on, I don't know. But I do know this: I'm freaking out.

Nearly a year ago, I happened across Woolford's Web site, Papua-Adventures.com, while searching for outfitters in Indonesia. The site featured half a dozen tantalizing trips, but one in particular caught my eye: the First Contact expedition, billed as a "full-on exploratory" trek to find indigenous tribes, which Woolford defines as people who have not only never met or seen outsiders but are not even aware of their existence.

"According to anthropologists the best place . . . to make a 'First Contact' is indeed Papua," Woolford writes on the site. (Like many people, Woolford uses the province's official name, "Papua," interchangeably with "West Papua," a more specific name favored by academics.) "In fact there are unexplored areas which harbor truly 'stone age' tribes."

This sounded incredible, so I started asking around and got different opinions on the likelihood of Woolford's claims.

"I don't believe there are any 'uncontacted' people, nor that anyone has to worry about making a 'first contact,'" Marshall Sahlins, professor emeritus of anthropology at the University of Chicago, told me. But Miriam Ross, a researcher at Survival International (SI), a London-based nonprofit that works on behalf of indigenous people, estimated that at least seventy tribes — mostly scattered throughout the Amazon — remain uncontacted, entirely cut off from the outside world. After checking with other anthropologists, I learned that, based on word-of-mouth reports and the occasional sighting by a local villager out hunting, it's believed there may be a few uncontacted tribes still roaming the foothills, inland swamps, and low-lying jungle along West Papua's north coast.

"But how do you know where they are?" I asked Woolford.

"I study missionary literature," he said. "I study maps. I have good contacts in all the regions."

Woolford, who made his first trip to West Papua in 1989, led his inaugural First Contact trek in November 2003 with two paying clients: a retired sixty-six-year-old Dutch orthopedic surgeon named Herbert Schrouff, and Robert Ferdiny, a forty-nine-year-old veterinarian from Austria. The men were a week into the jungle when eight tribesmen emerged and pointed arrows at their heads, before calming down and allowing them to take a few photos. Ten minutes later, the encounter ended when Woolford's camera startled the natives. "They saw the flash and started to shoot their arrows," says Woolford. He and his group quickly beat it.

Woolford's next trip was scheduled for September 2004, and I signed up. Ferdiny had already reserved a spot — his second trip — so he obviously had faith that Woolford wouldn't get us killed. As he described it, the lure of these trips was perfectly suited to his interests. "I like to see things that other people haven't — I guess that's a problem I have," Ferdiny told me later. "My wife tells me to leave the natives alone. Sometimes I wonder why I go."

I asked Woolford to arrange my *surat jalan*, a $12 special permit, with the West Papuan police — mandatory for all foreigners traveling outside West Papua's larger towns. He'd also assemble a team of nine Papuan porters and arrange a boat to pick us up near Nabire, a scruffy port town of twenty-six thousand on West Papua's Cendrawasih Bay, where we would begin our journey. To "protect the natives" and "keep out the idiots," Woolford forbids clients from carrying GPS devices and insists they keep the exact location and geographical markers of their treks secret. "We don't try to corrupt [the natives]," he said.

So how does he justify going at all?

"People are always looking for the latest thing. I wanted to see these tribes, but I couldn't afford it on my own. So I figured, why not get the experience, take some other people, and make money, too?

"Besides," he joked, "I'm not giving 'em a Mini Maglite, and they're not gonna go out and get a plasma TV after we talk to 'em. Five minutes is all we do. My clients understand that."

Anthropologists I spoke with questioned these tactics. Intruding on uncontacted natives, they warned, is a recipe for disaster. And even though Woolford has experience in the field — he's made twenty-six trips into West Papua — he has no official scientific credentials, just a 1985 bachelor's degree in criminology, with a minor in sociology, from Springfield's Drury University.

"First-contact tribes in West Papua have typically been forced into marginal areas by more aggressive neighbors," warned William A. Foley, head of linguistics at Australia's University of Sydney, who has done field research in both West Papua and Papua New Guinea. "They don't have a positive view of people coming to see them, because in the past it has not led to positive results — i.e., people have been murdered, heads taken, eaten. So they shoot first and ask questions later. You can't just march in, because you could easily be shot at and somebody killed, and it can't be done for some bored Westerner who wants a thrill."

First contact, especially with the wider outside world, has rarely been a pleasant business. When the earliest European explorers headed for new lands, they often traveled with a throng of soldiers in tow, just in case. For more than three hundred years, from the late 1400s through the early 1800s, first-contact encounters were usually synonymous with swords, guns, and violent conquest. From Columbus to Captain Cook, the clash of modern and primitive has almost always led to disaster for native people, in the form of warfare, colonization, disease, and economic exploitation.

More recently, even distinguished anthropologists have been criticized for wreaking havoc on primitive tribes. In his 2000 book *Darkness in El Dorado: How Scientists and Journalists Devastated the Amazon,* author Patrick Tierney alleged that anthropologist Napoleon Chagnon, then a professor at the University of California at Santa Barbara, and University of Michigan geneticist James Neel conducted unethical research in the sixties and seventies on the Yanomamö, an indigenous group residing along the Brazil-Venezuela border in the Amazon. Tierney argued that Chagnon intentionally incited battles between the Yanomamö and neighboring tribes to study the relationship between aggression and reproductive success. Many anthropologists and scientific organizations feel that Tierney's criticisms of Chagnon were inaccurate or overstated, but whether the charges are true or not, they address an important dilemma: does making contact with native tribes inevitably do more harm than good?

"If people are really a first contact, they don't even have resistance to colds," says Foley. "It is a big risk to their population — you're talking about small groups, no more than one hundred people. You get a case of flu going through and you could wipe them out."

According to Fiona Watson, who coordinates field campaigns for Survival International staffers, in the years following first contacts, tribal populations can plummet by as much as half "purely because of disease." SI estimates that, stemming from this and other causes, several hundred tribes have gone extinct in South America alone since the era of colonization began in the 1500s.

This is one reason anthropologists increasingly shun the notion of first contact in favor of a more subdued approach. These days, a lone anthropologist will typically live with a known group for several months, chronicling cultural and social customs. In West Papua in particular, solitary surveys are also necessitated by government regulations: Indonesian officials — wary of foreign journalists and scientists who might publicize the mounting separatist movement being pushed by the Organisasi Papua Merdeka, or Free Papua Movement — have drastically limited permits for formal research in the province.

So how is Woolford able to operate? As an independent tour guide, he can move around the country more freely with clients who are on less-regulated tourist visas. Also, over the years he has befriended many of the officials in the regions he travels. But as much as anything, it's because West Papua is still a wild place.

I first meet Woolford at Bali's Ngurah Rai Airport on September 5, 2004. He's wearing an orange Patagonia T-shirt, cargo shorts, and Fila sneakers. He bears a startling resemblance to the actor Willem Dafoe; his reddish-blond hair is shoulder length, his face rugged and angular, with a thick brow and deep-set hazel eyes.

Woolford has lived in Bali since 1997. He rents a cramped cottage for $70 a month in Ubud, a quaint Balinese village set amid rice fields and crumbling Hindu temples. To raise extra cash between treks, Woolford gives tennis lessons at the five-star Maya Ubud Resort. He doesn't drink and is a strict vegetarian, but he can't seem to get enough *kreteks* (clove-laced cigarettes), which he smokes throughout most of our hour-long drive to Ubud.

As the minivan weaves through traffic, Woolford lays out our game plan. In the last two weeks, his porters have made two trips to the outskirts of the region we intend to visit. They've taken rice, gasoline, and money to pay off a tribal native named Hiri Didat — the *kepala desa*, or regional chief — whose permission we need to travel inland and who will accompany us on our trek.

While Woolford talks, he frequently interrupts himself with accounts of calamity in the jungle. One time in Papua New Guinea, he tells me, "I saw several tribal fights and even walked through the middle of one. They saw me coming, and both sides stopped shooting arrows so I could pass. When I passed the very last man, they resumed shooting." More recently, Woolford claims, he's visited tribes that practice cannibalism, a ritual that many experts say ended decades ago.

Later, over dinner in Ubud, I press Woolford for assurances about our upcoming trek. What exactly are his plans if we find a tribe that turns out to be hostile?

"The strategy is to approach the same men we saw last year," he explains.

"But weren't these the guys who chased you out of the jungle?"

"Yes, but the hope is we can soften them up with tobacco, then convince them to take us farther upriver to the next tribe."

Three days later, we fly to Nabire, then drive forty-five minutes to meet our boat at a small, seldom-used harbor north of town. William Rumbarar, thirty-five, Woolford's local Papuan go-to guy, and six porters are already on board the thirty-foot canoe, called a *prahu*; three more will meet us at base camp. Woolford, Ferdiny, thirty-seven-year-old Australian photographer Stephen Dupont, and I climb atop a heap of supplies shoved into the hull. I notice that the only potential weapons Woolford has packed are a few machetes, which we'll use to cut a path through the rain forest. He tells me the porters upriver have bows and arrows and a BB gun but that these are strictly for hunting crocodiles and birds.

We follow the coast north, cruising at about fifteen knots. An unvarying coat of green stretches twenty miles inland, then vanishes under a low curtain of mist. Through the fog we see the distant peaks of the Kobowre Mountains, part of New Guinea's east-west backbone, which thrusts sixteen thousand feet skyward.

As one descends either north toward the South Pacific or south to the Arafura and Coral seas, the mountains yield to alpine grasslands, montane forests, and, finally, lowland jungle and mangrove swamps. The island's topographic diversity harbors more than twenty thousand plant species and a panoply of birds, insects, reptiles, mammals, and marsupials: tree kangaroos and giant butterflies, flying foxes and spiny anteaters. One particularly nasty beast, a bird called the cassowary — the largest land animal in New Guinea — has been known to fillet trespassers with the flick of a giant claw.

And then there are the rumors of cannibals, which have resounded for decades. On November 18, 1961, twenty-three-year-old Michael Rockefeller, son of New York governor Nelson Rockefeller, was in the province on an expedition sponsored by Harvard University. The team discovered a previously undocumented tribe, part of the Kurelu people, in West Papua's Baliem Valley. Rockefeller remained in Papua to collect native art, but his boat overturned one day while he was traveling along the coast, and he was last seen, swimming for shore, by his colleague René Wassing, an anthropologist. Years later, rumors surfaced that Rockefeller had been captured, killed, and perhaps eaten by cannibals.

Papua has always been mysterious. Tales of black-sand beaches strewn with gold nuggets lured some of the earliest explorers. Portuguese mariners, eager to expand their empire east to dominate the legendary Spice Islands, reportedly first spotted New Guinea's coast in 1511. In 1526, Jorge de Meneses, the Portuguese governor of the Spice Islands, made landfall on the northwestern tip of what is now West Papua and christened it Ilhas dos Papuas, or "Island of the Fuzzy-Haired People." (Until 2002, the province was called Irian Jaya. *Irian* is a Papuan word meaning "hot land rising from the sea," and *Jaya* is Indonesian for "glorious." The name was changed to Papua by former Indonesian president Abdurrahman Wahid, mainly to appease West Papuan separatists.)

For two centuries, Portugal and Spain vied for authority of New Guinea. Neither succeeded. Under the Treaty of Utrecht, in 1714, Holland and Britain gained control of the island. In 1895, New Guinea was split at the 141st parallel: the Dutch staked claim to the western half, calling it Dutch New Guinea, and the Brits and Germans acquired the eastern territory. It wasn't until the early twentieth century that, as one historian I spoke with put it, "the Dutch finally decided to see what they got out of the deal." In the first half of the last century, more than 140 expeditions were mobilized to survey the territory.

It's hard to believe that after such intense scrutiny, there would be any tribes left in West Papua that qualify for Woolford's definition of first contact. During World War II, Allied bombers pounded the Japanese holed up on neighboring Biak Island between May and August of 1944. Natives living anywhere along West Papua's north coast would have seen and heard the bombers and realized there was a world beyond the jungle.

"[West Papuan] tribes are not uncontacted in any absolute sense," argues Paul Michael Taylor, an anthropologist and curator at the Smithsonian National Museum of Natural History, in Washington, D.C. "They've been trading crocodiles and bird of paradise feathers and have had access to metals and tobacco for a long time. So they've always been in contact; it's just a question of degree."

Before leaving Nabire, Woolford agrees that his definition of first contact may need to be modified. Should we actually encounter a tribe in the jungle, he says, it might be impossible to determine whether they have ever set eyes on an outsider. But there are certain clues to watch for.

"One is to see what kind of body decoration they're wearing.

Check for plastic, metal, and synthetic materials," he says. "Another thing is to look at their tools. Do they have metal knives or a machete?"

Lastly, Woolford adds, we should watch their facial expressions to see if they appear unusually frightened or nervous. "Papuans are scared of the unknown."

By late afternoon on September 12, we've covered roughly seventy miles of virtually uninhabited coastline. That's not surprising, considering that West Papua has about 2.2 million people in an area slightly larger than California. When we finally reach our base camp, a large clearing in the jungle next to the river, the remaining porters are waiting for us. They've been fishing and croc hunting for the past couple of days from a tiny *prahu* anchored in the reeds. In the clearing there's a rain shelter, called a *pondok*, about forty feet long and fifteen feet wide, with bouncy bamboo floors, roofed with palm fronds, and open on all sides. Next to it is a small cooking hut where one of the porters is roasting an emerald dove he shot with the BB gun.

Rain pummels us all night. It's unbearably humid, and the air in my tent is thick and stifling. I wake up soggy and cursing, having to mop up water pooling under my sleeping bag. The next morning my mood is worsened by Woolford's ability to survive off little more than cigarettes and coffee. We eat just two meals a day. Breakfast is always the same: instant oatmeal, coffee, and stale biscuits. Dinner typically consists of freeze-dried noodles or fried rice smothered in ketchup and chili sauce, sometimes with cabbage thrown in.

Gnawing on hard biscuits and gulping down watery coffee, I listen to Woolford.

"If we make friends with these first guys from last year," he says, "they will be able to take us to the location of the other guys. The way in Papua is that you gotta go slowly, slowly. You can't just barge right in and bust into their camp. They'll be angry and we'll lose everything."

We enter the jungle shortly before noon, walking south, away from the river. The forest's canopy is nearly solid; only the faintest spears of sunlight penetrate the crown. Some of the tallest trees, called matoas, soar over a hundred feet. As our group spreads out single file, I lose sight of everyone except the porter directly in front of me. There is no discernible trail, and when he gets too far ahead, swallowed by the jungle, I become totally disoriented and have to call out for directions.

"How do they know where they're going?" I ask Woolford when we stop to wait for the porters to stuff betelnut — a mild stimulant extracted from the betel palm — into their cheeks.

"They're Papuans, man. This is their turf. They just have a sense about which way to go."

At one point I stumble and come within inches of stepping on a death adder — "one of the deadliest snakes in Papua," Woolford tells me later. A porter sees me staring at it, grabs a stick, and clubs it to death.

Aside from the stinging clouds of mosquitoes, the jungle is nearly motionless. Unseen parrots, cockatoos, and hornbills cry out from above. Invisible cicadas screech. After four hours of walking, we decide to set up camp next to a shallow creek. Our porters grab machetes and hack down brush and spindly trees. Within minutes they've cut a swath for our tents. Using the fresh-cut timber and vines, they assemble a large eating table, a long bench, a cooking hut, and a shelter roomy enough for all fourteen of us to huddle under when the afternoon rains commence.

Dusk descends on the jungle, and depth, color, and texture slowly fade away. Then something strange happens: seemingly out of nowhere, an unknown man starts calling from the darkness. His voice is shrill and quivering. It's not anybody from our group. According to my map, we're nearly a hundred miles from any significant settlement or village. One of our porters, a twenty-five-year-old Papuan named Yakobus, grabs a pouch of rolling tobacco and wades through the creek toward a rustle in the trees.

"*Tsabat! Tsabat! Tsabat!*" he hollers, holding the tobacco in his outstretched hand. "*Tsabat! Tsabat! Tsabat!*"

"What's Yakobus saying?" I ask Woolford.

"I think it means 'tobacco,' " he says.

"In what language?"

"Burate, the language of the region. About one hundred people speak it."

The figure passes between two trees, and I catch a glimpse of his grass skirt and an enormous longbow, which looks to be six feet tall. As Yakobus gets closer, the man's shouts get louder — now coming in short, angry snorts. Whoever this guy is, he's not too thrilled we're here. After Yakobus makes a few more attempts to give him tobacco, the stranger slips into the jungle, his shouts fading as he recedes.

Yakobus returns, wide-eyed and frightened. He thinks the man might be a chief of some sort. He tells Woolford that earlier, while the porters prepared our dinner, he went to scout our route for the next morning and stumbled across seven tribesmen crowded in a tiny bivouac about a mile from our camp. Initially Yakobus thought he recognized the men as members of the Keu tribe, who are known to hunt in the area, but he couldn't be sure. He'd tried giving them several packets of loose tobacco as an offering. "But they started reaching for their bows," Yakobus says to Woolford, who translates the news to us. "I tried to give them the tobacco again, but they hit it out of my hand and ran into the jungle."

At first Woolford seems bewildered, which makes me nervous. But then he says this kind of aggressive behavior is normal and that it sometimes takes several days of approaching and retreating before a new tribe will allow outsiders to sit with them. I try to relax.

"At least they know we're here," Woolford says, lighting up a *kretek*. "Tomorrow we'll try again."

Early the next day, on September 14, Woolford, Dupont, Ferdiny, Yakobus, and I set out from camp with three other porters. Everyone else stays behind. I'm wishing I could do the same. Something just doesn't feel right. The jungle is claustrophobic and, at times, maddening — the incessant rain, heat, and mud, the screeching of cicadas, the eerie sensation we're being watched.

We've walked for hardly fifteen minutes when I smell smoke. It's the campfire of the native party. Yakobus calls out, "Whooo-ahhh, whooo-ahhh," warning of our approach. Another porter beats the trunk of a matoa with a walking stick, sounding a booming thud so intense I can feel the thump on my chest. We're all bunched together about twenty yards from what appears to be the entrance to a three-sided bush shelter or bivouac. Nobody speaks.

Then all hell breaks loose. There's hysterical screaming and shouting. It's the natives, who leap through the back of their bivouac. Twigs are snapping in every direction. I hear bare feet slapping the mud, more yelling, and bursts of frantic, hyperventilated babble. Within seconds the natives have surrounded us, almost entirely camouflaged by the jungle. They're about forty feet away. To my right, I see one lean out from behind a tree, then pull his bowstring taut and release it. I wince, then exhale. The bow is empty: no arrow. Another man does the same to my left. Then two others move to within twenty feet and twice more pull and release their bowstrings. It's a show of force — they could have shot us dead already if that was their goal.

Yakobus tries to lure the natives back to their bivouac, repeating, *"Tsabat! Tsabat!"* and holding his hands above his head to show that he's unarmed. Twice he coaxes the men closer, but they panic when they see us and disappear into the jungle, whooping and yelping. After several minutes, Yakobus succeeds in calling all the natives to their bivouac. I grab the video camera we've brought and start shooting. There are eight of them: seven younger ones, possibly in their teens or early twenties, and one older man, likely the person who came near our camp the night before.

The men are wearing black headdresses that resemble chin-length dreadlocks. Made from cassowary feathers, the headdresses cover most of their faces. Some have tied the feathers into a kind of ponytail, and one has painted a pair of parallel white stripes down the center of his forehead. Strips of bright-yellow leaves are wrapped around their biceps. Each is wearing a skirt constructed of the same leaves, with a long strip of brown bark holding it in place. They stand motionless and silent in the bivouac just long enough for Dupont to click off a few photos.

That's when I notice that their hands are trembling. They look absolutely terrified. A wave of guilt washes over me. One of the men barks a command, and once again they dash into the jungle.

"This is very wrong," I snap at Woolford. "We need to leave right now. We shouldn't be doing this. They're really freaked out."

Yakobus makes a few halfhearted attempts to bring the men back but then suggests we return to camp and try again in the morning.

"Try again?" I mutter, still amped and jittery. As we retreat, I hear one of the tribesmen chant, "Wu-hu-hu, wu-hu-hu," in the distance. The others join in, repeating the phrase in haunting tones and in syncopated rhythm. It's hypnotic and beautiful — a show of solidarity, perhaps, to celebrate their having chased us off.

In the morning, we set off toward the natives' bivouac once again. But this time their shelter is empty, their fire cold. On the walk back to our bush camp, the porters smoke *kreteks* and mumble quietly to one another. When we rejoin the others at camp, the *kepala desa*, Hiri Didat, hears our story and starts pacing back and forth. "I'm afraid that they might still be around here, circling the place," he warns Woolford.

Woolford mentions that the older man might have been the chief he encountered last year. But he's not certain about the others and has no idea what they'll do next.

"There are three possibilities," Woolford surmises. "They've gone farther away, they're circling around, or they've gone for reinforcements and might come back to attack us."

"Attack us?" I whimper.

"That means we are not safe," says Ferdiny.

"No shit," I say, noticing that the porters have already started to pack our gear, scurrying around camp at twice the speed I've seen them move before.

"The natives can follow our footprints and come attack us at base camp later," says Rumbarar, the local guide, who has barely uttered a word the entire trip. "But if they come back, it'll be more than eight people." Rumbarar then tells Woolford that the tribesmen were responsible for triggering the rainstorm last night, so they could abscond in the dark without being followed.

"The rain covers their footprints in the mud," says Rumbarar.

"Yeah, they made the rain," says Woolford. "They can do that. I've seen it happen in other parts of Papua."

"They can't make it rain," I interject. "So stop saying that."

"You don't believe me?" says Woolford. "It's true — I've seen it with my own eyes."

"I think this is a good note to leave on," says Ferdiny.

During the hike back to base camp, Dupont, Ferdiny, and I stick close together. Woolford is ahead of us and out of earshot. For the first time, we discuss the possibility that he might have sent word ahead that he was bringing Westerners into the jungle expecting to see wild, uncontacted tribes, and made arrangements for a staged encounter with our group.

"I think it might be a trick," Ferdiny whispers to me.

"I'm having a hard time believing that only a four-hour walk from the river, these tribesmen are so close by," I say.

"I'm really suspicious, too," says Dupont. "But I'm just not sure if it's a hoax, either."

We walk quietly but quickly. Every pop, screech, chirp, and whir

— the sounds of the jungle — causes me to corkscrew my head in all directions, certain we're being followed.

Back at camp that night, it's nearing sunset and the sky is alive — drenched in shifting hues of fiery orange, crimson, and violet. We've been in the jungle for four days now, and I'm wiped out. I decide to take a nap in my tent before dinner. Minutes after dozing off, I hear shouts and someone yelling, "They're coming, they're coming! They've stalked us to the river!" I shove on my hiking boots and scoot backward out of my tent. Then I see eight burly natives charging straight at me — bows and arrows at the ready.

Adrenaline kicks in and, without thinking, I break into a full sprint, then lunge headlong over a near-vertical embankment that drops nearly twenty feet into a gurgling river. I land on a narrow, vine-snarled ledge a few inches above the water. Only later will I find out that arrows were flying over my head.

For the moment I'm safe. I claw halfway up the slope, and thorns slice my arms. Squatting in a thicket of ferns, I glance upward and catch sight of two natives peering over the edge a few feet above. They're probably wondering who would be foolish enough to jump into this river. I hold my breath and keep silent.

The tribesmen lose interest. I inch a bit farther upslope and watch the men hustle through camp and toward our porters, who are barking orders and scrambling for their machetes and bows. Crouching in the bushes, bruised and scared, I envision death by wooden arrow. Then I see a porter looking for me. So I hop over the riverbank and reveal myself to the natives, who, to my astonishment, are standing in front of Dupont for an impromptu photo shoot. At that moment, in a way I can't really explain, it all starts to seem absurd.

"Oh, please," I hear myself saying. "Give it a rest . . . lose the bows and arrows and phony outfits. This is a hoax, right?"

No reaction. Maybe it isn't a hoax.

About ten feet to my right, the *kepala desa* grabs his bow. Two of the other porters are clutching machetes, and the rest of the men are cowering near the back of their *pondok*.

The natives stand shoulder to shoulder, glaring at us from beneath their cassowary headdresses, then abruptly look away, as if embarrassed. One of the porters has brought along his dog, which begins to yap loudly, startling the tribesmen, who dart into the

jungle. The *kepala desa* and Yakobus chase after them, hollering
"Tsabat! Tsabat!"

Five minutes later, the natives return, looking calmer, and march
in line into our campsite. Dupont gets within a few feet of the chief
and continues snapping photos. Another five minutes pass. Then
one of the natives shouts an order that prompts them to scurry into
the jungle. One last time, Yakobus cajoles them back. By now it's
dark. The tribesmen watch us from the edge of the forest, but when
one of the porters ignites our kerosene lantern, the flash of white
light scares them off for good.

Rumbarar suggests we pack all our gear in case we need to make
a quick getaway in the night. We agree that it's too late to navigate
the boats downriver in the dark. But everyone is afraid — Rumbarar, the porters, even the *kepala desa*, who Woolford claims has
killed foes in tribal skirmishes. We speculate about how best to protect ourselves, and our words sound like dialogue from a cornball
zombie flick:

Ferdiny: "Should we sleep here in the *pondok* or in the tents?"
Dupont: "Maybe they only kill at night?"
Ferdiny: "Maybe they only kill people wearing headlamps?"
Dupont: "I'm quite serious, Robert. They shot three arrows."
Ferdiny: "If they come in the night, we can use our camera flashes in
           their eyes."
Woolford: "Yeah, we'll flash 'em and back onto the boat."

It's beginning to rain. Ferdiny drags his tent from the edge of the
jungle closer to the river. Dupont and I decide to sleep under the
pondok with the porters. I spend the night fully dressed, boots on,
heart racing, transfixed by the jungle. The rain is torrential and un-
relenting. Lightning explodes above us. For a split second, the
flashes illuminate everything in a blaze of white. The next bolt, I'm
convinced, will reveal our attackers bounding toward us in the
downpour.

At dawn, everyone is awake and scrambling to pack up and get
out. By 7:30, our *prahu* is roaring downriver toward the open sea,
toward Nabire and safety.

Six days after our river escape, I part ways with the group in the
Papuan highland town of Wamena, where we've come to hike and

decompress in the tranquil Baliem Valley. I'm due back in the States, but Dupont and I, still suspicious and troubled by our surreal sighting, decide that Dupont should interview Woolford on videotape when the two return to Bali, away from the distractions of West Papua.

During that session, Dupont mentions that some of us had doubts about the authenticity of our encounter. Woolford, not surprisingly, insists it was genuine.

"So nothing was arranged in advance?" asks Dupont.

"Oh, no, not at all. I couldn't do that. That's beyond me," Woolford says. "Papua is so weird, you don't need to stage anything. It's the land of the unexpected."

Two weeks later, back home in Virginia, I send three hours of our video footage to several anthropologists familiar with West Papuan tribes. None of them is convinced by it.

"I'm 95 percent sure it is a hoax," the University of Sydney's William Foley declares after watching it. He's struck by the fact that the natives didn't appear to have any skin diseases, which are endemic among bushmen. "This is unheard of for people living in the forest," he says. "The guys are too clean. Secondly, their dress is far too elaborate. That's the kind of dress they wear when doing a ceremony. That's not what they wear when they go out hunting and collecting food. All those headdresses — no way."

Other anthropologists have similar reactions. Paul Taylor, at the Smithsonian, adds that it wouldn't be too difficult to hire local villagers to stash their Western garb and don traditional dress, then pretend to be "discovered" as Woolford's clients plod through the jungle. "The big question in my mind," says Taylor, "is whether this is something he's paid these people to do over and over again." Whatever is going on, Taylor doesn't like it. "If it's not a first-contact situation, then it's fraudulent. And if it is a first-contact situation, then it's an insensitive way to go about it."

When I play the video for Eben Kirksey, a doctoral candidate at the University of California at Santa Cruz and one of the few scientists who has been granted permission to conduct research in West Papua, he notices many of the same suspicious details as Foley did — elaborate clothing, lack of skin diseases — but he also sees details that make him think some of what we experienced was authentic.

"The *kepala desa* looked really scared," he says.

The video footage supports this. I decide to have more of the *kepala desa*'s and the other porters' dialogue translated. Some of their talk is captured on camera when they don't know they're being filmed. In one scene, after the tribesmen storm our campsite at the river, the *kepala desa* says to Woolford, "I was so scared, I wanted to attack them when they shot the arrows."

I also interview several of Woolford's friends, curious about whether they think he'd deliberately dupe his clients. They unanimously insist that he wouldn't. They cite his "obvious love for the Papuan people" and call him "a stickler for being a man of his word." Laurence Livingston, a forty-three-year-old commercial beer brewer who lives in Homer, Alaska, roomed with Woolford in college, and the two have remained close ever since. "He is not into bullshit and scams," Livingston says. "The guy's for real."

Livingston suggests one possibility that I'd also been contemplating: if the trip was a hoax, then one of the locals might have set it up, unbeknownst to Woolford and the other porters. It's at least a plausible theory — if a First Contact trek turned up nothing, Woolford would not return to that area of West Papua, and the porters would be out of a job.

Woolford, for his part, fires right back when I run the anthropologists' remarks by him, starting with a comment that anyone who doubts his word should come along on a trip. "Some of these people are just lecturers at nice universities who have tenure and cushy jobs," he says. "If they think I've staged this, then come with me. I give them an open invitation to see for themselves. They can feel the energy of these guys, see them run around, see them barreling down and pointing arrows at them."

As for the appearance of the tribesmen, Woolford says the abundance of freshwater streams in the area means that the men we saw can bathe regularly. He chalks the elaborate ceremonial dress up to adolescent preening.

"Anywhere you go in the world, New York City or wherever, teenagers are always dressed to the hilt," he says. "In Papua's Lani country, the young guys wear *kotekas* [penis gourds] so big that it's obscene. I think that's the case with the guys we saw."

First contact or hoax? I may never know. The last time I speak with Woolford, in December 2004, he's almost positive that the older man we came across was the same tribal chief he saw last year, but he's still uncertain about the rest of the men. He's already scheduled his next First Contact trek for August 2005, based on information he's gathered about an unknown tribe sighted in an area roughly one hundred miles north of where we trekked. Woolford says this could be one of his last First Contact expeditions.

"People pay a lot of money for this trip, and I want to try to find them something," he says. "But locating new tribes is getting harder and harder — and who knows what you are going to come across, if anything."

As I listen to Woolford, he seems heartfelt and sincere, like a man who really wants to give his clients their money's worth. His love of the province is obvious, and he treats his porters exceptionally well, paying them generously and often buying them rubber boots and clothing.

Nevertheless, I can't stop feeling like I've done something wrong by participating in the First Contact experience, even if Woolford is correct in his belief that his treks are helping redefine exploration in a positive manner. The way Woolford sees it, the scholarly elite, once the gatekeepers of discovery, are having to make room for any adventure seeker who can pay for the experience. To him, the First Contact expedition is a means to further democratize the process.

"If a postal clerk is interested in primitive times," he argues, "who am I to say, 'Oh, you only graduated from high school — you don't have a degree in anthropology; therefore, you're not qualified to see these people'? If you are fit, and you want to pay, then you should have the right to go."

Perhaps Woolford has a point. I confess that, a week after returning home, my reaction against what I see as his risky, exploitative style starts to fade. My intuition tells me that what I saw on our trek can't possibly exist. But what if it does? What if West Papua is the last place on earth where ghosts of the past still thrive in the present — where the surreal becomes real?

Now all I want to do is go back. But I don't know if I should.

PAUL BENNETT

How to Sail Across the Atlantic

FROM *National Geographic Adventure*

OUT THERE, SOMEWHERE, moonlit swells are rolling through the darkness over a point I have dubbed "The Spot": 2,700 nautical miles equidistant from Cape May, New Jersey, and Lisbon, Portugal, and roughly 1,290 miles southwest of Newfoundland. The Spot marks the halfway point on our journey and is, by definition, the farthest we'll stray from land on our voyage across the Atlantic Ocean. I plotted it before we set out. But now, on watch at 4:00 A.M. in the predawn cold with nothing to do but stare into the dark and fiddle with my new LED headlamp (on, off, on, off), I've become much more intimate with this invisible point. I've measured it twelve times in the past two hours, and I'm pretty sure that at this moment, The Spot is lurking 2.3 nautical miles dead ahead.

To go up on deck, I have to concoct an excuse. Several months ago, after hearing a gruesome story from fellow cruisers about a husband tripping overboard on watch — and his wife waking hours later to find herself alone, surrounded by empty ocean — my wife, Lani Bevacqua, and I made a pact that neither of us steps out of the cockpit when alone on watch. But this is important. The idea of The Spot has become my personal "heart of darkness," and the urge to be on deck staring at the black sea around us when it arrives is impossible to ignore. So I tell myself that the jib, which in all truth is perfectly trimmed, needs some adjustment. It could be chafing against a shroud. Better check.

I click my life harness into the jackline, a web strap with a ten-thousand-pound breaking point that runs to the bow, and I step up to the bowsprit, which despite Leonardo DiCaprio's screeching in the movie *Titanic*, has not lost its exhilarating sense of freedom.

The moon is beginning to set, and the sea is turning absolutely dark. But if you peer long enough into the blackness you can make out shapes. You think you see a fin. You look for the glowing swoosh of bioluminescent plankton just below the surface. You hope that a bunch of lights on the horizon isn't an oncoming tanker. One night, I mistook a rising Venus for a masthead light and spent several minutes trying to hail the planet on the VHF radio.

Conditions are calm right now: twelve knots of wind, two-foot seas. *Lucy* bounds forward with an easy motion that tells me everything is OK. Standing on the deck of a thirty-eight-foot sailboat in the absolute center of the Atlantic in the middle of the night feels more mundane than I had assumed it would. When I imagined this moment months ago from my leather chair in New York City, it was much more Byronic. I was the plucky adventurer thousands of miles from anywhere, alone with the sea, like the people I read about in books and magazines. Instead, as I look out at the barely discernible line of the horizon, I see the concrete facts that led me here: the engine we repaired in Virginia, the rub rail we replaced in Rhode Island, the mortgage, the dodgy ports whose officials we've grown adept at bribing. I see weather faxes predicting approaching storms. I am not surprised. When we began this journey eighteen months ago, concocting our dream to sail around the world on a thirty-eight-foot sailboat, we were hopeless romantics. It didn't take long for the details of staying alive to overwhelm our dreamy fantasies of balmy islands and fruity rum drinks. "My main goal here is to not die," Lani blurted out one afternoon during a frenzied weekend of prelaunch repair work on our boat. It was a primal concern, but one that summed up pretty much everything we had done to that point and everything we intended to do from there forward.

And so, The Spot is a heroic benchmark to contemplate while killing time on watch, but it's less a romantic accomplishment than a logistical one: we managed to organize our lives in such a way as to make it this far (without dying). And now, closing in on The Spot, I realize that the greatest achievement of our voyage is that it was accomplished by us — nautical amateurs — and that anyone who wants to make their own ocean crossing can accomplish the same feat, provided they have a grasp of basic seamanship and are aware of these twenty-five fundamental precepts.

1. A Bluewater Boat

For us, the task — as decided over martinis one cold February evening in 1999 — was to set off on an ill-defined ocean-crossing voyage that might, or might not, take us around the world. Long-distance ocean voyaging begins and ends with the boat. It's your house, your shield from the weather, and what keeps you from swimming all that way. And after thousands of miles of late-night watch, alone in the cockpit of *Lucy*, I began to appreciate all the superstitious anthropomorphizing that seafarers and sea poets have done over the centuries. At some point, your boat becomes a part of you.

But a boat is also a piece of equipment; and as with anything else, you need to find the one best suited to the task at hand. We knew we needed an ocean-capable boat — what's known in the business as a "bluewater yacht."

What exactly constitutes a bluewater yacht — as we learned over the first six weeks of our adventure, which we spent poking around marinas from Annapolis to Boston and consulting pretty much every book, Web site, and magazine article we could find on the subject — depends on two competing schools of thought. One school holds that the proper craft for crossing oceans is a heavy, strong, traditionally designed sailboat. The philosophy here is that if you get into a storm you want a boat that is built like a safe and has a proven track record. You want something heavy that won't break up when it gets battered by fifty-foot waves. And you want something that lets you hunker down — the nautical term is "heave to" — in a really bad storm to wait it out.

The diametric view holds that, with the technology at our disposal — specifically weather faxes, relatively accurate satellite weather charts that can be downloaded from the sky mid-ocean — having a strong boat that can withstand tough weather is less advantageous than having a fast one that can outrun it. The theory is that if you can see a perfect storm gathering five hundred miles away and marching toward you, wouldn't you rather race southward at ten knots and suffer little more than some gray skies and choppy seas?

It had been more than a decade since I'd been on a boat, and my experience coastal cruising with my parents in Connecticut, where the only time we'd been out of sight of land was on foggy days, hardly qualified me for open-water adventure. Lani's experience — a few summers on Sunfishes at YMCA camp — had been even paltrier. So, a few weeks later we settled on an old, neglected Shannon 38, one of the toughest, most conservatively designed sailboats in the world, made to bob through storm after storm without a scratch. Although we'd planned to buy a cheap fixer-upper in the $30,000 to $40,000 range, the boat ended up costing nearly $85,000. We rationalized this, and the mortgage we had to secure, by the fact that she came equipped with some critical pieces of offshore equipment — like a single side band (SSB) radio, a radar, and a life raft — and that she was generally in good shape. In the end, we wound up exceeding our repair-and-equipment budget by about 300 percent.

But such was the fortitude of our spirit that, employing the tools at our disposal, we financed the balance on credit cards and, playing a shell game of balance transfers, housed the deficit of our lives (about $20,000 over eighteen months). On the eve of our departure, we were broke, and in debt. But as true Americans, we felt that this was not only acceptable, but thoroughly normal, and off we sailed.

2. Don't Worry About Superstitions

Sailors consider it bad luck to change the name of a boat. But *Rolling Home*, the moniker of our chosen vessel, fell into the unacceptable marine-pun category alongside *Seaquel*, *The Seven C's* (for a large family with the surname Christian or Callaway), *Sea Ya Later*, *Nautomatic*, *Yacht Sea* (with a picture of dice), and so on. As we'd learn, your identity on voyage becomes inextricably entwined with your boat. Plus, we liked the name *Lucy*.

3. Embrace the Gearhead Within

When I look back and tally up all the time spent fixing *Lucy* as opposed to sailing her, I am astonished by the fact that over 70 percent of our cruising time was consumed by me hanging upside down in the bilge or scraping my knuckles trying to tighten a hose clamp behind a bulkhead. Erase the images of palmy islands, crystalline waters, and warm sun and replace them with oil-covered gaskets, sulphurous water hoses, bloody knuckles, and the sensation (strangely titillating) of twelve volts of electricity coursing through your body, and you'll begin to get an idea of what it's like to go voyaging.

The most rugged thing I had accomplished prior to our trip was hanging some sheetrock in our apartment. But by the time we sold *Lucy* in Toulon, France, I could bleed a diesel engine in the dark in rolling seas. In the process, I collected a cool set of tools, a nifty tool bag, and something called a bosun's chair, which can take you to the top of the mast as the boat heels and bucks fifty feet below. Still, my evolution from effete New Yorker to greasy, low-slung handyman was slow, gradual, and painful. For the first six months, it seemed like everything I tried to fix only got worse.

4. Sweat the Specs

Displacement: Lucy was a moderately heavy vessel — 18,500 pounds empty, 24,000 pounds when we loaded her up with stuff. A typical racer/cruiser of the same length, built for ocean sailing, might weigh 12,000 pounds unloaded; a very heavy boat, 20,000.

Rig: Lucy was a ketch, a two-masted yacht, and was rigged forward with a small jib and a staysail, which meant that she could fly four small sails at once (from aft, or rear: mizzen, main, staysail, and jib) rather than just two very large sails, as is typical of sloops, the most common boat on the water. There are two advantages to this: the smaller sails on a ketch are easier to handle — a consideration for two shorter-than-average people like Lani and me — than those on a sloop. A ketch rig also has the effect of lowering and spreading the center of thrust in the boat, which makes the vessel more balanced, if slightly slower. But when you are sailing a boat shorthanded across an ocean, balance — which translates into the ability of a boat to sail itself — is very important.

Hull Shape: Lucy had a traditional V-shaped hull with a full keel stretching from bow to stern. The keel contained 7,300 pounds of lead, which made her very stable in heavy seas.

Construction: One of the greatest dangers offshore is hitting something (flotsam, a whale) that puts a hole in your boat. *Lucy*'s hull was built with solid fiberglass, which achieved a one-inch thickness below the water line, making it very strong.

5. The Joys of Plumbing

A few months after buying *Lucy*, we made a twenty-three-mile "shakedown" sail from Stonington, Connecticut, to Block Island. This trip was marvelous: clear skies and steady ten-knot winds. We'd invited Lani's parents and brother, David, a college student. *Lucy* was majestic with her twin headsails and gentle, even motion through the water. Although Block Island can be overrun with tourists, we found a patch of empty harbor near the docks to anchor.

The next morning I awoke to the sound of the electric toilet cycling endlessly. "I think the toilet's clogged," my mother-in-law, Marilyn, announced as she came out of the head.

I leaped confidently into action. When I pressed the button on the electric pumping mechanism in the toilet, it sounded funny, like it was spinning but nothing was moving. I pushed once more. Certainly what I heard was the sound of a clog somewhere in the line — probably toilet paper. I traced the outflow line to the probable source of the clog, a Y-valve, and proceeded to loosen the hose clamp and pull open the line. I was very careful to close the Y-valve first, based on the articles and books that I had read. I didn't want seawater to come flooding into the boat, getting everything wet.

As I pulled the hose free from the valve, I learned two very important lessons about repairing things. First, that pressure accumulates in a closed system (and, being clogged, the outflow line was a closed system) in equal proportion to how much pumping you do — between Marilyn and myself there had been a lot of pumping so far. And second, that a crucial component of any repair is acquiring all the facts, which in this instance included the following: my father-in-law had also used the head at some point during the night, he had probably done quite a bit of pumping himself, and it was far more than toilet paper clogging the system. In the next moment, the obstruction in question shot out of the line with fire-hose ferocity. It caked the walls, the ceiling, and the floor. It covered me completely from head to toe. I can say, unequivocally, that being showered with another person's crap has been the single worst experience of my life.

That's when I dedicated myself to becoming a much more careful and analytic mechanic.

6. Zen and the Art of Diesel Repair

At some point, after a period of mechanical struggle, you will achieve enlightenment. You will realize that your diesel engine is subject to change, and that your suffering and discontent are the result of attachment to the circumstances of your diesel engine and its nature as an impermanent thing. By ridding yourself of this attachment, including attachment to the notion that you are not mechanically inclined, you can be free of suffering.

Add to this a set of head-gasket spares, a torque wrench, and a copy of *Troubleshooting Marine Diesels* by Peter Compton (McGraw-Hill), and you are on your way to complete happiness.

7. Weather Is Everything

The most essential component of cruising is, and must always be, weather. The chance that you might run into a storm informs everything you do, from boat choice to equipment to the chitchat between sailors. (Some basic knowledge about low-pressure systems and the movement of fronts goes a long way on the dock.)

Granted, few run-of-the-mill cruisers ever encounter seriously dangerous weather at sea. The reason for this is that they follow a standard set of cruising routes around the world designed to avoid storm seasons. This is sort of disillusioning. You imagine that you'll simply sail wherever you want, whenever you want. Instead, if you want to avoid storms — and, trust me, you do want to avoid storms — the path around the world is pretty well circumscribed.

8. Go with the Flow

The correct way around the world follows the trade winds and predominant ocean currents as they move through the tropical latitudes from east to west. Timing is everything. You want to leave one part of the globe as hurricane season begins and enter the next part as it's ending. A typical circumnavigation with a departure from the east coast of the United States goes something like this.

Hurricane season in the Caribbean lasts from June to November, so either you embark before this and spend those months in some relatively safe harbor just south of the hurricane belt (which lies roughly between fifteen degrees north and thirty degrees north), usually in Trinidad, Venezuela, or Colombia, or you try slipping south after hurricane season in December (attempting also to avoid the onset of winter). In any case, you want to arrive at the Panama Canal around March.

Cyclone season in the Pacific Ocean lasts from December until April or May. This is about the time you want to be exiting the other side of the canal. You now have about eight months (from April to November) to cross the Pacific and find a safe spot on the other side before cyclone season begins again. A lot of boats divide the trip in half by heading to New Zealand for the austral summer there, and then sailing back north to tropical climes the following May. Others push on directly to Australia.

After transiting the Torres Strait between Australia and Indonesia sometime in June, you can go north of the Equator and cross the Indian Ocean to the Red Sea, and then move on to the Mediterranean; or you can push south, staying below the Equator, to South Africa. For the former, you can make your transit anytime between November and March — so it's a little more leisurely with several months in late summer to kick about Indonesia. (Of course, there are pirates to contend with; read on.) On the southern route, cyclone season in the Indian Ocean starts up again in late October, so you need to scoot from the Pacific in July or August and get across that ocean as quickly as you can.

Beyond the Cape of Good Hope (which is anything but), it's usually a cakewalk up to the Caribbean, as the South Atlantic is the one ocean on earth without a tropical storm season.

9. . . . *Or Don't*

The wrong way around the world goes west to east in the temperate latitudes. Going this route, you don't enjoy the benefits of following trade winds and are often forced to buck currents and flukey headwinds. From the United States, you cross to Europe at forty degrees north, stopping at the Azores. Next comes a transit of the Mediterranean, then down the Red Sea with the wind at your back. In the Indian Ocean the winds are largely on the nose, though you can hug the edge of the Arabian Peninsula and Indian subcontinent and eventually make your way to Malaysia. From here, you shoot through the archipelagoes of the western Pacific, getting northward whenever you can, until you eventually make Japan. Then comes your transpacific cruise, maybe stopping in the Aleutians, down the west coast of the United States and Mexico, through the Canal, and home.

Our route followed neither of these because we weren't committed to a circumnavigation. We left New York City in September 2000 and hugged the U.S. shore until hurricane season was over. In mid-November we pushed to the Caribbean and Central America, where we made a clockwise circuit of its northwest reaches, from Jamaica to Honduras's Islas de las Bahías, then up to Rio Dulce of Guatemala, and on to the barrier reef of Belize, through the Yucatan Channel, and then to Havana.

In early June, when the normally tempestuous North Atlantic is at its calmest, we set out for Europe, stopping in Bermuda and the Azores, eventually landing in Gibraltar. But I'm getting ahead of myself here.

10. *About Time*

Unless you're sprinting around Antarctica in a tricked-out maxi catamaran (fifty-eight days is the record, held by Steve Fossett), it'll take you at least two and a half years to sail around the world following the seasons. Add to this the rule that everything takes doubly long in sailing; the average completion time among circumnavigators we met was four and a half years. Considering our rate of progress, if we'd gone all the way around, it would have taken us nearly seven years.

11. *Watchman Fundamentals*

"So, where will we pull over to sleep at night?" Lani asked one afternoon as we were driving back to New York from a weekend aboard *Lucy* shortly after we bought her.

You don't. In the middle of the ocean there are no rest stops. And unless you carry ten thousand feet of chain (twenty thousand when sailing over a trench), you're not anchoring anywhere. Someone had better be awake at all times when you're under way.

We began our trip following a standard four hours on, four hours off watch rotation. But we soon discovered that anything less than six hours of sleep a night had adverse effects on mental acuity. (I started seeing some strange things.) Lani found sailing at night "a cold, dark, and lonely business." I, on the other hand, got a kick out of the stars and the darkness. So, after a couple of weeks, we devised our own lopsided schedule centered around the key hours between midnight and noon. I took the nighttime half, from midnight to 0600, and Lani took the morning from 0600 to noon. We divided up the remaining hours into segments organized around naps and meals.

12. *Love and Marriage*

Very early in our trip (Jamaica) we realized that 95 percent of the cruisers we met were traveling as couples, and that of these there were essentially two types: those who seemed to be at the point of implosion — snapping at each other publicly, visibly unhappy together, visibly happy apart — and those who seemed blissfully content. And a short time later (Honduras), we discerned the root cause of this division. In the troubled relationships, the men were absolutely driven by some tangible goal, usually to complete a circumnavigation, and the women seemed dragged along on the scheme rather unthinkingly.

The happy couples, by contrast, were strikingly goalless. A kind of therapeutic laziness pervaded their anchorages. So, somewhere in the lower part of the Belize barrier reef we decided to pursue, stubbornly, one goal above all others: to keep our marriage intact. And as February passed into March, we happily turned our backs on the possibility of a circumnavigation for the more-marriage-preserving plan of simply sailing "about" the world.

13. *The Pink and the Blue*

After a couple of weeks aboard *Lucy*, we woke up one morning to find that we'd divided all the onboard duties into pink tasks and blue tasks. It was as if we'd sailed back in time forty years. And it was this way for nearly every other boat we ran into. The woman aboard was in charge of organizing and cleaning and maintaining the living space below decks; the man was in charge of making sure everything worked. She was June Cleaver and he was Mr. Goodwrench — even if in real life she was a trial lawyer and he was a science teacher. The division left us constantly bewildered. Were we more content in these traditional roles? It was a somewhat unsettling idea.

14. A River in the Ocean

A hundred miles or so off the East Coast, lying perpendicular to our progress like a stone wall, was one of the most powerful forces on the globe. The Gulf Stream is formed by a warm-water current that flows up from the Caribbean, sweeps past the east coast of the United States, and then spindles out into swirling tentacles in the North Atlantic. The Stream, as it is called by sailors with a kind of knowing nod, can move as fast as five or six knots, pushing a boat sideways and, during the time it takes to traverse the current, miles off course. It also acts like a magnet for inclement weather, and a kind of all-around badness clings to it like lampreys on a fish. One way to tell you're about to enter the Gulf Stream is that a distinct band of rain squalls will appear on the horizon on an otherwise sunny day.

If you're smart and lucky, it's possible to plan your route to actually take advantage of the Stream — you might cross at a point where the Stream veers a little southward and toward Bermuda, or you might try to hit an eddy on the right side and let it kind of fling you southward. Our test-run passage down to Bermuda was textbook perfect. We hit an eddy on the correct edge and made Bermuda in five and a half days. If you're unlucky, you can also get screwed by the Stream. Our trip back took twice as long.

15. Survival 101

During a night watch about two hundred miles off the coast of Bermuda, I reread (by headlamp) *Adrift*, Steve Callahan's famous account of hitting what he suspects was a whale, watching his boat sink in the middle of the Atlantic, and spending seventy-six days at sea on a life raft fighting off sharks, catching dorados, and flirting with insanity. His survival depended on the singular fact that he'd prepared very well for this type of emergency by carrying a life raft and packing a ditch bag. I had tried to imitate Callahan's preparations as much as possible. *Lucy* had a ditch bag and, mounted on her foredeck, a six-man life raft in a pressure-release canister.

Ditch-bag gear can be divided into different categories. The first is stuff that will help you get rescued, like flares, mirrors, and an emergency position-indicating radio beacon (EPIRB), which, when activated, sends out a distress signal with your GPS coordinates. The second category is stuff that will help you get by until you get rescued. First aid kit shares top billing with water, or some kind of apparatus for making potable water. Callahan had some old rubber stills, in which water evaporated and then condensed in a little cup at the bottom. They were ingenious in their simplicity, but Callahan spent most of his time drifting across the Atlantic repairing the rubber as it quickly degraded in the tropical sun. In the past ten years, the technology of drawing freshwater from saltwater has evolved by several magnitudes; for $500 we purchased a handheld reverse-osmosis "watermaker" that fit into our ditch bag. You also need some way of getting food, which when you're in a life raft in the middle of the ocean pretty much comes down to catching fish. To this end, we packed a fishing line, hooks, lures, and several knives. There were also a couple of radiant blankets, to prevent exposure, and a bunch of water jugs and Luna bars. The kit itself sat on the shelf behind the navigation station, theoretically impossible to miss in a catastrophe.

Occasionally, while on watch during our voyage, I ran through the abandon-ship scenario in my head: grab ditch bag, go forward to release the raft. I was supposed to heave the canister over the side and let the natural motion of it floating away tug the tether and release the raft. But the last time I moved that thing, to paint the teak cradle underneath it, I was surprised to discover it weighed more than a hundred pounds. With adrenaline pounding through my body I could probably do it quickly. But what about 105-pound Lani? Such questions are easy to ponder onshore, less so when you're standing in the cockpit of a rocking boat in the empty ocean.

16. Mal de Mer

Comanche flu, getting green about the gills, motion maladaption syndrome — whatever you call it, seasickness is a major hazard in voyaging. Making a passage of more than three days with a partner who is incapacitated is equivalent to setting off single-handedly without preparation.

Lani battled mild seasickness throughout our trip, but it never became a serious safety concern on long passages because she was able to control it pretty well through a careful combination of drugs (scopolamine patches and Stugeron, an antihistamine widely used in Germany and the U.K. but not approved in the United States) and homespun preventatives (favorites include ginger ale, ginger tea, ginger gum, and arrowroot). We once read that lettuce is good for seasickness, but since it wilts and turns to soup in a matter of days, we never relied on it.

17. It's Different in the Tropics

One afternoon in the Bahamas, we took a stroll along a quiet beach on the ocean side of Exuma Island. The place was deserted. Nothing but seaweed, seashells, sea-tossed tree trunks — whatever had been lifted onto the sand during the most recent rough weather. After a while, we noticed a strange lump in the distance, and as we got closer we recognized the sad figure of a sailboat lying on its side in the sand. We learned the story later in town while lifting pints at the Two Turtles Inn: some guy had gotten all turned around in the waters here a few weeks past and ran over the barrier reef offshore, tearing up his hull. Once caught inside the reef, he tried frantically to extricate himself, but kept bashing into the coral until eventually, with water flooding the bottom of his boat, he turned and drove onto the beach.

Making your way around tropical waters is an entirely different game from navigating in northern waters. For one, in places like the Bahamas, which is riddled with reefs and sandbars, the waters are largely uncharted. One key skill to master, if you're going to spend any time in tropical areas, is the ability to read the color of the water for signs of reefs or hazards. Remember these dicta: blue (deep) water is good; green (shallow) water is not so good; white (very shallow with sand) is even worse; and brown (fiberglass-chewing coral extremely close to the surface) water is disastrous.

18. Tankers Are Real

Late one night in 1995, Judith and Mike Sleavin and their two young children were on their way from Tonga to New Zealand aboard their Compass 47, *Melinda Lee.* Judith was on watch. Down below, the two kids and their father slept. Judith had just made an entry in the logbook and was climbing out of the cabin into the cockpit when a thousand-ton freighter sliced through the *Melinda Lee*, sending her to the bottom in a matter of seconds. Their son, Ben, who was sleeping in the forward berth, died instantly. Somehow Mike and daughter Annie crawled out of the cabin as the boat sank and were able to join Judith on a half-inflated dinghy that bobbed to the surface. But within a day, both father and daughter succumbed to hypothermia and died. Judith alone survived, floating for more than sixty hours and eventually landing on a beach in New Zealand's Bay of Islands.

On the open sea, cargo ships and tankers usually travel at about twenty knots. The horizon, on a clear day or night, might be seven nautical miles away, which means that if that ship is coming directly toward you, you have about twenty minutes to get out of its way. Therefore, the rule of thumb is that the person on watch has to stand up and methodically scan the horizon for any signs of life every fifteen minutes.

To put this in perspective, twenty minutes is about the time it takes a person to boil some ramen, slice a few vegetables for a salad, run a little seawater over the dishes to clean them, and climb out of the cabin into the cockpit. Those were Lani's actions on a calm evening during the return leg of our shakedown cruise to Bermuda. I was awake in the cockpit with a book, lying down on the lazaretto. Technically, Lani was on watch, but since we were both awake no one was really paying attention. Not until she came up with our noodles and salad, and then, glancing over my shoulder toward the water, began stammering "uh, uh, uh . . ."

When I turned around, I had trouble craning my neck far enough to look up at the thousand-ton container ship barreling past us. It might have been a hundred yards away, which, given the size of the ocean, is distressingly close. So close that if it had been heading one degree farther south there would have been nothing to do except watch as it sliced through *Lucy*.

After that, Lani and I became religious about scanning the horizon regularly. Despite this, we were surprised quite often by tankers sneaking up on us from nowhere. According to Lloyd's, the insurance giant that maintains a register of oceangoing ships, there are nearly ninety thousand ships (in the hundred-gross-ton category) currently plying the ocean. The problem is that these vessels stick to the same seasonally advantageous shipping lanes favored by oceangoing sailboats. This is one of the great shocks of offshore passagemaking. You assume that when you get two thousand, or even two hundred, miles away from land that it will be just you and Mother Ocean. Then the sun goes down and you see the horizon dotted with lights. In eight thousand miles of sailing we had two nights (one in the middle of the Atlantic and one off Honduras) during which we didn't see a single ship. Forget also the idea that the crew of the ship is looking out for you and that they will nudge their behemoth one way or the other to sidestep a thirty-eight-foot sailboat. The crew is most likely watching videos or sleeping. And even if alert to your plight, don't assume they'll launch a rescue. Judith Sleavin recounts that after her boat was sunk, the freighter circled back and watched them for a few minutes before inexplicably sailing off.

19. Pirates Are Also Real

Piracy still poses a regular danger to voyagers. The worst parts of the world for this are the narrow straits of Indonesia and the Gulf of Aden, where the Arabian Peninsula and the Horn of Africa pinch together at the mouth of the Red Sea. These tight squeezes, lined by poor countries, are geographically favorable places for pirates to attack. There have also been reports of sailboats being boarded in Venezuela, Nicaragua, and on the Rio Dulce in Guatemala (where we ventured). Usually, thieves sneak aboard in the evening (if no dinghy is hanging off the back, they assume the boat is empty), break in, and take things that are useful to them such as outboards, fishing tackle, and liquor. There are stories of pirates passing over laptops in favor of a set of oars.

There are also organized crime rings — mostly in the Gulf of Aden — that track sailboats on radar and attack them suddenly and violently. One such story came to mind while I was on watch in the Windward Passage between Cuba and Haiti. A family sailing past here many years back was surprised by armed speedboat bandits who boarded them, forced the family into their dinghy, and set them adrift. The family survived, but only after watching the pirates loot and then burn their boat to its water line.

Which is why talking about pirates always brings up the most contentious question in cruising — whether to pack a gun on your boat. The argument for carrying a gun is cynically straightforward; sailing a yacht in the vicinity of poor countries is like walking through the zoo's polar bear exhibit wearing a seal-skin suit.

The arguments against guns are just as forceful. As a former policewoman (now gun-toting ocean cruiser) explained to me in St. George's harbor in Bermuda, the first question you need to ask yourself is whether you could actually kill another person. If you're not ready to do that, then you'd better not even think of bringing a gun onboard. Lani knew there was no way she could ever take someone's life. As for me, I could imagine some pretty horrific scenarios that would make me pull the trigger.

Not that a gun guarantees anything. In 2001, Sir Peter Blake, the New Zealander who twice captured the America's Cup, was attacked by pirates in the mouth of the Amazon. He reached for his rifle, but one of the robbers shot him dead. The policewoman pointed out that wielding a gun is not as Hollywood portrays it. "There's this false idea that if an intruder comes aboard your boat in the middle of the night that you're going to wake up and come out shooting like Dirty Harry," she explained. "That's just wrong. If you're inexperienced then you'll probably never hit anything."

In the end, we decided not to carry a gun.

20. Look! No Hands!

Whether you let your sailing be dominated by gadgets is a stylistic choice. We met cruisers who had everything from a clothes dryer to an electric winch that lowered their dinghy into the water. We met others who peed in a bucket. Since we departed in debt and money was an issue, I tried to acquire only equipment that would make our trip safer.

That said, I've never made a better purchase in my life than our Monitor wind vane. In an age of electronic autopilots that track to a course line, the mechanical wind vane, which steers a boat according to the wind direction, is a bit of a relic. But considering that the average autopilot has only four thousand miles of life in it, any serious ocean cruiser needs to think about using a wind vane.

Moe, as we called our wind vane, sailed *Lucy* for nearly 95 percent of our trip. He was unflagging, capable, and loyal — like a stainless steel border collie. I couldn't have sailed without him.

21. *Here Comes the Bribe*

I didn't understand why the Jamaican port captain was sweating. It
wasn't that hot. And we couldn't figure out why he wouldn't leave.
All our papers were in order. He'd stamped our forms. We'd paid
the boat tax. He'd given a cursory look over our cabinets to make
sure we weren't smuggling any fruits or livestock. But then he just
sat there tapping his fingers.

"He wanted a tip," Hulk later explained. Hulk lived on a house-
boat in the middle of the lagoon, and he saw the port captain visit
boats every day. By tip, of course, he meant a bribe.

We eventually learned how to spot this. The sad *federalistas* tending the customs house in Livingston, Guatemala, definitely wanted
one. So did the sweaty doctor who spoke flawless English in Havana; his eyes gave him away.

Bribing is an acquired art. Dollars are accepted everywhere.
There's the obvious wadding and passing of bills across the table.
Or the sly slipping of money into a stack of papers you have to fill
out. Then there are the subtler techniques of serving tea or having
a cold American beer at the ready — which may not be a bribe per
se, but can still lubricate the bureaucratic machine. Neither of
us smokes, but we carried several cartons of Marlboros. Any nice
thing that you can share gets counted against your baksheesh lia-
bility.

22. *Sea Food*

The bulk of our provisioning was done en route in the local markets. Certainly we visited places with little in the way of interesting
local cuisine — four weeks in the Bahamas was bland as hell — but
for the most part, eating our way around the world proved to be as
much of an adventure as sailing. There was *feijoada* (black bean and
pork stew) at an all-night beer fest in the Azores, lime soup in Mexico, some mysterious rum concoction in Bermuda. We reached the
zenith in Port Antonio, Jamaica, where we ate goat's head soup
with a veterinarian whose skill in identifying the skull parts was
phenomenal.

On passage, we'd feast on fruit and greens for the first few days
out of port, then potatoes and carrots, and eventually rice and

beans. (Unless you're a rabid carnivore, meat is best avoided on long voyages — it spoils quickly.)

Oh, and fish aren't as easy to catch as you'd think. In eight thousand miles, we caught four.

23. *Wildlife*

One time I went snorkeling in eight feet of murky water around a mangrove key and came nose-to-nose with a small shark. It terrified me. On the way back from Bermuda, off New Jersey, Lani was peering over the stern of *Lucy* to check the exhaust and saw a huge shadow of a shark swim out from under the boat. We saw a lemon shark in the Bahamas; another bull shark in the Bahamas; some kind of gray shark in the Bahamas; and then another unidentified shark in the Bahamas.

Three things: sharks are a part of voyaging. I hate sharks. The Bahamas are Shark Central. Ergo, I am not that fond of the Bahamas.

Whales, likewise, made me nervous our entire trip. A tanker, at least, could be dodged. But whales have been known to attack — and sink — sailboats. How would *Lucy* fare if a mammoth creature double her size decided to ram her, repeatedly? Not well, I imagined. These fears only mounted as we made our way from Bermuda to the Azores, through an area so rife with whales that it's known as Whale Alley.

For days we'd been hearing reports about whales from other boats in the vicinity. Someone saw a spout; the next day a tail. Finally, on the afternoon of June 28, after nine hundred miles and seven days at sea, we met our first leviathan. We were on a broad reach with twelve knots of wind, and I was taking advantage of the heel of the boat by lying on the leeward (or lower) cockpit lazaretto. I was completely in tune with the rhythmic motion of *Lucy*. And then the rhythm stopped. We heeled quickly, another five or ten degrees, in an awkward and unnatural motion, and slid back to flat. I shot upright, and there, not three feet from my face, was the large, slick, brown head of a sperm whale. He (she?) exhaled and seemed to sink in the water slightly. I had the distinct impression that we'd awakened it. It took several seconds, until we were a hundred yards away, before the head disappeared below water and the tail came up in classic, photogenic fashion.

24. Perfect Enough Storm

Our first gale arrived the day after we passed The Spot. As the weather fax had predicted, the winds picked up out of the southwest through the night and then settled at thirty-five knots for an entire day. Our anemometer was broken at this point in the voyage, so we couldn't measure wind speed precisely, but we heard from another sailor in our area (maybe twenty miles away) that he'd recorded gusts of forty-five knots, which is damn high. The waves reached twenty feet by noon; and with the wind blowing in the opposite direction of them, the waves looked like large, square teeth chomping at *Lucy*'s stern.

When conditions get very rough on a sailboat, you have two options: to turn into the waves and heave to until the storm passes, or to turn away from the wind and run with the storm. In our case, since we still had six hundred miles to go and the storm was running in our direction, I turned *Lucy* and went with it.

Eventually, we disengaged Moe, our wind vane, who seemed to be struggling as *Lucy* surfed down the waves at seven knots. At some point — you lose sense of time — I emerged from the cabin to see a medium-sized humpback whale breach from the white froth in our wake. Or at least I think I saw it. Your sense of reality starts to get lost as well. Once, when *Lucy* rose high enough on a wave, we were able to catch sight of a large tanker nearby that had somehow escaped both naked eye and rain-choked radar.

Weather like this has the effect of stripping everything to its essentials: sails reduced to mere scrap, technological doodads rendered useless, sleeping in our rain gear and peeing in the cockpit, holding on and waiting it out.

25. Landfall

Because of all the variables — weather, seasons, currents, alluring harbors — cruising stories tend to have no real beginning, middle, or end. We met sailors, such as Lin and Larry Pardey, who'd set out for a nice sail one day and were still at it over thirty-six years and 180,000 miles later. We met others who'd had very definite plans to circumnavigate in three years and hadn't managed to extricate themselves from the northwest Caribbean yet. Many, like ourselves, found their course altered on a daily basis. A cold front from the north approaches, and suddenly you're off to Cuba rather than Honduras.

In the autumn of 2001, we found ourselves crossing the Mediterranean. After a brief stop in Menorca in the Balearics, we pressed on to Sicily and the stinking cesspool of Palermo harbor, and from there, to little Cefalu on the north coast of the island. We stayed for a week trying to figure out the next step; whether to stay put and winter in Sicily, or make a late-season run to Greece, say, or maybe Israel.

I returned from an Internet café in Cefalu one day with these possibilities bobbing in my head to find Lani standing in the cabin, beaming. In her hand lay an obviously positive pregnancy test.

So, pregnant and broke, we sold *Lucy* in Toulon for a meager profit, which just about covered our credit cards.

From everything I hear, the adventure of parenting will make sailing across the Atlantic seem like a breeze.

TOM BISSELL AND MORGAN MEIS

After the Fall

FROM *The Virginia Quarterly Review*

Morgan — *2:30 A.M., April 25, 2005, Ho Chi Minh City*
(Née Saigon), Thi Minh Khai Street

CERTAIN PARTS OF LATE-NIGHT Saigon have a windy quiet that
seems almost pastoral. Maybe it's the closeness of the city, the
fortresslike squatness of its blocks, the numerous trees, or the way
that the nighttime pinches out the faraway headlights and brake
lights of the evening's last scooters and taxis. I don't much care for
the pastoral, typically. I like pavement and noise. But this was different. The night that lay upon this massive, malfunctioning, astonishing city was vast, starless, as warm and secret as an embryo. Unlike
many cities, Saigon seemed to welcome us into its secrets, not keep
them from us.

This was my second trip to Vietnam. The first had been alongside my wife, while on honeymoon last year. Here I met Tom, who
was making his third trip. We shared many things: an approximate
age, a New York City residency, an interest in the intersection of the
literary and the political, and most importantly the war in Vietnam.
Tom's father had served with the marines in Vietnam from 1965 to
1966. My father had dodged the draft, providing me the lifelong
conversation piece of having been born in Montreal. When my father had returned to the States, to take up the cudgels against President Ford's strings-attached amnesty program for draft dodgers,
he was prosecuted. The case ultimately went to the Illinois Supreme Court. My father won, and the decision became the basis for
the no-strings blanket pardon President Carter granted all draft

dodgers in 1977. In real ways, then, Vietnam helped make us both who we are.

We stuck to the emptier side of the street while along the opposing sidewalk a half dozen lipstick-wearing skeletons stood in their high-heel shoes and tight jeans lifting their hands halfheartedly at an occasional passerby. Behind the prostitutes, in shadows relieved only by the moving orange penlight of cigarette embers, were rough-looking men with dirty baseball caps sitting astride their Chinese scooters. Neither of us could get over the heat. Was it really nearly three in the morning? Impossible. It felt as though we were moving through oxygen chowder. The weather was clearly a subject of no complaint for the many cyclo drivers asleep or passed out along the street. Some were pouched in crudely strung-up hammocks, some were athwart doorjambs, some curled into child-like balls in the cockpit of their cyclos. The cyclo was a bicycle-wheelbarrow hybrid that carried human cargo. Their drivers tended to be some of the poorest men in urban Vietnam. Many of these men spoke English because they had been soldiers in South Vietnam's military and, after the collapse of South Vietnam in 1975, were punished by the victorious Communists and forbidden any but the most menial work.

The collapse was why we were here. Six days from now the Socialist Republic of Vietnam would celebrate the thirtieth anniversary of the day the North Vietnamese Army formally accepted South Vietnam's total surrender. South Vietnam, the most augmented, defended, and bled-over client state in the history of American foreign relations, ceased to exist on April 30, 1975. But the story of Saigon's fall, once well-known, is being forgotten — even among young Vietnamese. With the world as it is, it seemed useful to contemplate the fates of nations that fail despite foreign aid, good intentions, countless deaths, and human will.

What did the failure of an American client state ultimately mean, three decades on? Although the personnel and leaders of South Vietnam are today dismissed by the rulers of Vietnam as "puppets," there were many in South Vietnam who resisted the Communists precisely because of their patriotism and their wish to lead lives free of Communist dogma. At the same time, the ranks of the South Vietnamese government, as well as its military, the Army of the Republic of Vietnam (ARVN), were thick with former French collaborators, gangsters, cowards, and buffoons. The insolvable corruption of South Vietnam was a problem throughout the entire course of the war. In this way, Nguyen Cao Ky, one of the war's most fascinating characters, also serves as a perfect lens through which to approach the whole story.

In 1965, with American backing, Air Marshal Ky had been made premier of South Vietnam at thirty-five years of age. The months leading up to Ky's ascendancy had been some of South Vietnam's most difficult and bizarre. During his first ninety days in office, Lyndon Johnson had witnessed three full changes of government in coup-struck South Vietnam. One American during these days suggested changing South Vietnam's coat of arms to a turnstile. Ky, part of a cabal of ambitious military upstarts known as the Young Turks, seemed a promising leader to spearhead the rescue of the floundering effort against South Vietnam's insurgency. The United States liked Ky because of his vicious anti-Communism, his French-trained background, his brilliance as a pilot, and his neon personality. Ky's problems had been his unpredictability and arrogance, and he eventually alienated all but a few of his supporters. In 1967, he was made vice president of South Vietnam, beneath General Nguyen Van Thieu, and then was forced out of power altogether by Thieu in 1971. For the remainder of the war, Ky schemed to get back into power. He was never able to. As South Vietnam collapsed, he flew himself out in a helicopter.

Ky is the only prominent living member of South Vietnam's benighted government. A longtime resident of California, two years ago — in a turn of events barely noted in the United States — Ky put in a request with the Vietnamese government to return to Vietnam. For the first time in Vietnam's post-1975 history, a major figure from the South Vietnamese government appeared in public and spoke of the past on Vietnamese television. It would be hard to overstate the importance of this for the millions of Vietnamese who had supported ARVN, lost husbands and sons, and then suffered reeducation; it meant that their lives had not been, as they were told, a lie and a mistake. It meant that there was another version of the story that the Vietnamese Communists relied upon and manipulated for their prestige and authority. It also meant that the authorities were finally willing to allow the former elite of South Vietnam a place, however restricted, in contemporary Vietnam. Ky and his wife were going to be in Vietnam for the anniversary of what its Communist government has always called the Liberation of South Vietnam. After a few guarded conversations with Madame Ky, as she is known, it was agreed: we would meet General Ky — for that was what he now wished to be called — in Saigon, tomorrow, and see what happened from there.

Filled with anticipation, Tom and I couldn't sleep, so we decided to walk instead. We saw up ahead some evidence of the celebration that would commence in a few days' time. First was a large, circular, inflated red archway over Le Duan Street, formerly known as Thong Nhut Boulevard. Across it was written what translated as "Enthusiastically Welcoming the Thirty-Year Anniversary." Thong Nhut Boulevard had been the street down which North Vietnamese tanks rumbled before smashing in the gates of the Presidential Palace on the morning of April 30, 1975 — one of the war's most famous images. In actual fact, the gates had been opened for the tanks. When an Australian cameraman was found waiting inside the compound, the North Vietnamese — mindful, as ever, of propaganda's potential — asked the Australian if he would film them coming through the gates again. Tank 844 came in first. One could find Tank 844 on the grounds of Reunification Palace today. One could also find Tank 844 a few blocks away at a war museum. And one could find Tank 844 in Hanoi. Here it was not the artifact that mattered but the event the artifact commemorated. The Trinity of Tank 844 provided holy, if not entirely coherent, testament.

And here was the palace itself. We gazed upon the building through the bars of its front metal gate. Long, splendidly terraced, and mostly eggshell-colored, the palace, awash in orange spotlight, stood about one hundred yards back from the gate. It had a Frank Lloyd Wright-ish look to it, notwithstanding the large banner of Ho Chi Minh currently flying above the balcony where Viet Cong insurgents had joyously rushed to run up their flag.

We crept away from the palace along the eastern edge of a nearby park, noting within its grounds the empty bleachers specially erected for the celebration, the scaffolds of klieg lights, the trees draped in red bunting. We passed Notre Dame Cathedral, the most peed-upon structure in Saigon; the impressively tall HSBC building; and, a few blocks later, on Hai Ba Trung Street, one of

Saigon's several Kentucky Fried Chicken (or *Ga Ran Kentucky*) restaurants, outside of which loomed a life-sized statue of Colonel Sanders, whose uncanny resemblance to one Ho Chi Minh was almost certainly being exploited. We were making our slow, ambling way toward the heart of foreigner's Saigon, District 1, the only part of the city still officially called Saigon, and with excited comment walked passed Graham Greene's old hotel, the Continental. Across the street from the Continental was an opera house, completely obscured by a massive stage littered with empty chairs and music stands for an orchestra, all of it lit by a score of ghostly, shadow-fattening low-wattage bulbs. Rolling up to the stage's edges, weirdly, was a fringe of grassy sod, and at the base of the stage was what looked to be a modestly approximated Vietnamese village, replete with thatch huts, wheelbarrows, and carts. I wondered if, during the celebration, these huts were intended to be torched by a squad of American GIs.

Tom and Morgan — 8:06 A.M., Chancery Hotel

"Are you awake?"

"I don't think I ever fell asleep."

"You did. You were snoring."

"I don't snore."

"True fact: everybody snores. But you know what? The thought of talking to General Ky today is actually making me nervous."

"We're meeting him at eleven-thirty?"

"At the Sheraton."

"So who do you think picks up *that* bill?"

"His wife, probably."

"She nice? When you talk to her on the phone is she nice?"

"She's nice to me."

"That's good. So don't be nervous."

"But then why wouldn't she be nice? Think about it. We're here to watch a ceremony that means very little in a country that's no longer that significant while trying to talk to a man whose moment in time is long gone. Face it. No one cares about any of this today but the people who experienced it firsthand. And *us*. That's why Madame Ky is so nice. We appreciate her husband's role in history."

"Yeah, as a nutty charismatic."

"But when he took power he actually managed to unite the military and put an end to all the coups. He executed people for corruption. He was one of the only ARVN leaders who didn't escape with a fortune in stolen gold."

"He's also been accused of having personally run heroin for the CIA out of Laos."

"But at the end he got in his plane and fought. When all the other generals took off, Ky stayed and fought."

"To a point."

"Sure, to a point."

"You admire him."

"I do and I don't. I doubt I would have admired him at the time."

"I heard that the reason the regime softened up to Ky was because when China invaded Vietnam in 1979, he volunteered to fly attack runs against the Chinese."

"Is that true?"

"I have no idea."

"Do you think he's watched by Vietnamese intelligence?"

"I assume so."

"Do you think we'll be watched if we talk to him?"

"I heartily doubt that."

"So what do we ask him?"

"I don't know. How about asking him about his comment as Saigon was falling that 'I will stay here until my last blood, until I'm dying.' "

"Sure. Great. That's a good one: 'So why did you run away, you fucking pussy?' "

"Goddamn it — now *I'm* nervous."

Tom — 11:25 A.M., *Sheraton Hotel*

We walked through a near-noon heat so overwhelming it had a sort of oceanic weight. But for the green lushness of the trees, the city looked scalded and colorless; I imagined I could hear the sidewalks sizzling. By the time we approached the Sheraton, in District 1, we looked as though we had showered in our clothes. The attentive Vietnamese men and women manning the Sheraton's glass doors were decked out in strange hybridized costumes that looked part

Nguyen Dynasty functionary, part *Star Trek* alien diplomat. A pneumonia-inducing blast of air conditioning met us as we walked inside. Indeed, the lobby felt not unlike the world's biggest, most handsomely decorated storage freezer. We strode across its buffed floor and took our seats upon a comfortable backless couch near the check-in desk. Soon my foot was nervously tapping out an endless string of Morse code. Morgan looked over at me and asked, "I wonder if we'll even recognize him."

Of that there was no danger. With a resonant ding, one of the many lifts in the Sheraton's elevator bank whooshed open, and, as though he were leaving a cryogenic chamber, out strolled General Ky. Somehow you could tell that Ky walked slowly not because of limited mobility — he was seventy-six years old — but because he was used to having people wait for him. He wore a peach-sherbet linen shirt, cream plaited pants, sockless loafers, sunglasses, and a black wristwatch that must have cost at least $5,000. After a tentative series of handshakes, Morgan blurted, "Wow. You look great!"

Ky smiled indulgently. "Your father was here?" he asked Morgan.

"No, it was Tom's father — a marine. My father was a draft dodger."

Ky's tan, moley scalp glowed beneath a thinning black combover, his skin as drum-tight as that of a fifty-five-year-old soap opera star. I, too, had to admit it: the man looked terrific — spa-kissed and fabulous — exactly as he had thirty years ago. Only Ky's famous pencil-thin wartime mustache, which numerous South Vietnamese men had once grown in imitation of him, was different, much fuller than before. General Ky motioned toward the open dining area right off the lobby and led us to a corner table. One of the waitstaff hurried over before he could seat himself. It was hard to tell if anyone else here in the Sheraton knew who he was. He produced a gold lighter, lit up the first of several Marlboro Lights, and ordered a cappuccino.

Morgan started with the obvious: How did it feel to be back?

It was General Ky's third time back. Did we not know? General Ky liked coming back to Vietnam very much. All of Vietnam, yes. Even the North! As he began to talk, Ky puffed at his cigarette delicately. In between drags he waved the cigarette around with an artist's extravagance, as though painting a portrait in smoke.

"They love me in the North — even though I bombed them!"

Morgan, in spite of himself, laughed warm, spontaneous laughter.

Ky went on: "My face is everywhere again. The young people here like me especially." He described going to a Saigon clothing store and being mobbed while he shopped. He leaned toward us; some of his cigarette's ashes flaked into the table's sugar-packet dish. "They called me 'Uncle Ky' — like Uncle Ho!" But then he waved this away. "Whatever the reason for the war — who's right or wrong, who's a puppet or a patriot — the war was the darkest time in Vietnamese history. One hundred percent of the young Vietnamese people agree with this. That's why I'm so popular."

Morgan took this in without affect. In fact, since arriving Morgan had been asking every young person we met if they knew who General Nguyen Cao Ky was. Most seemed to think Ky was "one of those famous California singers." Ky's daughter was the singer; among California's Vietnamese expatriates — or Viet Kieu — she was famous, and her variety show, *Paris by Night,* which typically featured her singing in exotic locations around the world, reached Vietnam in the form of pirated videocassettes. Others had known that Ky was a famous politician from the pre-1975 years, but no one so far had connected him to the South Vietnamese government. One of the strangest things about contemporary Vietnam was the dearth of young Vietnamese who knew much of anything about the war. One young woman we spoke to shared news of a terrible documentary she had recently seen on television. It was about the war, people getting killed, really terrible, and America was involved. Can you imagine?

"How about the government?" Morgan asked. "How have they been?"

Ky puffed away at his cigarette. "I'm the unofficial expert on the United States. After all, the leaders of Vietnam are all dead now. I'm the only survivor." Ky was referring, of course, to his military and political colleagues in South Vietnam. But he might have also been talking about the North Vietnamese. Of them only General Giap was still alive. I stopped writing for a moment, struck by the reality of General Ky. The men he had been a direct contemporary to, the men with whom Ky had spoken. Lyndon Johnson (whom he called "Lyndon"), Richard Nixon, Zhou Enlai, Mao, Ho Chi Minh, William Westmoreland, Pham Van Dong, Ngo Dinh Diem.

How, Morgan wondered, were his relations to the current regime? Ky laughed. All the Party's young Communists today wanted
to talk to General Ky, a man who personally strapped himself into a
fighter plane and bombed his northern brothers. And General Ky,
who during the war had taken personal satisfaction in killing all the
Communists he could get his hands on, got what you could only
call a twinkle in his eye when he reflected on this strange fact.

"I can yell at the Party members," Ky said, chuckling. "I'm older
than they are, so they respect me. Leninism is stupid." He pro-
nounced *stupid* wonderfully: *stew*peed. "You know, I also suggested
to the Party leadership that they replace all this talk of the 'liberation' of Saigon with the 'reunification' of Saigon." Ky plowed
on, saying that "many" imprisoned religious and political activists
in Vietnam had been freed because of his advice. "I said to the
Party, 'Why do you do this?' It's stupidity! Police cutting Buddhists'
phone lines? It's *stew*peed!"

"Why," I piped up, "history aside, do you suppose the Communists are so eager to talk to you?"

Ky blinked. "Because they don't have any idea what they are
doing."

"And they know that?"

"They know it. They admit it to me all the time. They know they
have nothing. They want my help."

"Have you met Prime Minister Pham Van Khai?"

"Yes."

"Were you impressed?"

Ky smiled. It was a remarkable state of affairs. If what General Ky
was saying was true, the Party had been reduced to turning to a
man who represented the government that their fathers fought
and despised. The imperialist stooge! The running dog puppet!

"How," I asked, "do you feel about this week's festivities?"

Ky snorted. "I feel nothing! They have to do it. It's ceremonial
only. The Communists realize they are today at — what do you call
it? — an impasse. Nobody here believes in the leadership of Vietnam."

"So you think that you'll play a role in politics again?"

"My destiny is firmly attached to Vietnam's. I know this. My
mind is still OK. People here still love me." His biggest plan of the
moment was to open an American University in Saigon for "all
Asians," not just Vietnamese.

That, for the moment, was what motivated Ky. He would be plotting until he died. It was his nature. But he was no longer plotting to defeat anyone; he was only plotting to matter. Perhaps, in an odd way, a stray bit of Confucianism was seeping in through the cracks and fissures of a moribund ideology. Ky was a link to revered fathers from an esteemed generation of heroes. It was hard to point to any heroes like that in contemporary Vietnam, whose politicians were an anonymous, uninspiring lot. Few believed the slogans anymore. They had ceased to be human language. There was something very powerful about Ky. The power of confidence, of adaptability, of patience. Despite all evidence to the contrary, the man still believed that his own personal narrative and the history of Vietnam would thread themselves together again. Perhaps it was this kind of deathless cultural optimism that allowed the Vietnamese to win the war.

"General Ky, are you watched?" Morgan asked.

Ky's head bobbed back and forth in deliberation. "'Watched' is not the right word. They protect me. Some of the authorities are nervous about my presence here. Not all, but some. They realize I'm not the enemy."

But Ky would not go out and about the city with us, for I had asked, and Ky flatly refused. He was very conscious of making the authorities nervous, or of embarrassing them. "It's not appropriate," he said simply. Morgan asked if General Ky would be around during Saigon's reunification ceremony — which both he and I had been counting on — and we were crushed to learn that Ky and his wife would be spending it in Hanoi golfing. Then Ky's face changed.

"Perhaps you could come to Hanoi."

Tom — 2:00 P.M., April 27, 2005, On the Road to Hanoi

We passed over the Red River upon the massive Paul Doumer Bridge, built by a French governor-general of Vietnam — and one of the most-bombed structures during the war, even though it was protected by three hundred antiaircraft guns and dozens of surface-to-air missile batteries. Something about going to Hanoi, the mental anticipation of it, never ceases to electrify me. It's purely conceptual, I know, but there is little in life more fascinating than visiting an erstwhile enemy capital.

The night before, Joe, our photographer, had arrived in Saigon and was noticeably worse for the transoceanic wear. When he was not photographing the sopping jade countryside of penumbral Hanoi, he was fighting off sleep. When we picked him up at the airport, Joe had been wearing an MIA/POW T-shirt under his sweatshirt, which I suggested may not have been such a smart idea. Joe had looked down at his shirt and said, "Oh, yeah," with such sweet surprise that I burst out laughing. It was Joe's first trip to Asia since being born in South Korea. *So these are my people,* he had thought, while waiting for his connection in Seoul. Then he went off to find the smoking room.

While Joe photographed, Morgan and I discussed the many famous instances of Western writers and artists visiting Hanoi during wartime. Mary McCarthy, for instance, who was completely gulled by the North Vietnamese. Susan Sontag, who was more reticent during her trip but still mainly positive. Finally, there was the slippery old linguist Noam Chomsky, whose book *At War with Asia,* recently reissued without one whit of circumspect revision, I was currently reading.

I flipped through and found a passage I wanted to read to Morgan: "The most striking difference between Hanoi and the countryside is, of course, the destruction and ruin caused by the 'air war of destruction.' Hanoi itself, so far as I could see, was not badly hit, except near the Red River, where the bridge and surrounding areas must have been heavily bombed. But as soon as one leaves the city limits, the destruction is enormous." I asked, "Did you know that only seven percent of the bombs used in Vietnam fell upon the North?"

Morgan shrugged. "Seven percent of a lot of bombs is a lot of bombs."

I looked out on the rice paddies. Some conical-hatted farmers were out working them. I had once spent half a day poking around in a rice paddy with a Vietnamese friend. It was insanely difficult work. I imagined the conical-hatted men and women being blown to pieces. Morgan was, of course, right. Seven percent of hell was still hell.

We had left for Hanoi in such a hurry that we had not thought, until too late, to call ahead to reserve a hotel room. A friend of mine in Saigon had recommended a small new hotel near St. Joseph's Cathedral, but when we arrived we found the hotel was full.

We stood outside and looked down the street. The air smelled of gas fumes but also of pollen and chlorophyll. Hanoi was a great city for trees and greenery, far more than Saigon, and over many of its low, dingily pretty buildings hung a leafy ceiling of branch and vine, which, combined with Hanoi's cooler weather, made for a city that rewarded exploration. But it was never a comfortable thing to be a Westerner hauling huge amounts of luggage — Joe's equipment alone took two of us to carry — through an unfamiliar city with no place to stay, and we quickly ducked into another smallish, new-seeming hotel called the Golden Buffalo. The two young men manning the desk enthusiastically welcomed us. It appeared we were the hotel's only current guests.

After checking in, we took a cab to Ho Chi Minh's mausoleum. The mausoleum, which Ho did not want (he had asked in his will to be cremated, though the Party edited that request out of the published version of Ho's will), was centered within a great complex of French-colonial-era buildings. All the old French buildings shared the same Cheez Whiz color. The last time I had visited the mausoleum, its endless concrete plaza had been crowded with tourists, Western and Vietnamese, but today it was so postapocalyptically empty that you half expected a tumbleweed to blow by. In designing Ho's mausoleum, Soviet and Vietnamese architects looked at everything from the Pyramids to the Lincoln Memorial to Lenin's Tomb and ended up with a massively boxy marble eyesore. Nonetheless, Joe marched off into a nearby park to get a better angle.

Moments later I began to undergo gastrointestinal Chernobyl. I had my day-to-day problems in this area, it was true. I had thanked Imodium AD in the acknowledgments of my first book, after all. Nothing that could be deemed a true solid had passed through me since the Clinton administration, but the rifling pain I felt now was of a different caliber altogether. My stomach burbled out some many-syllabled sound that was loud enough for Morgan to hear, my eyes filled with stunned tears, and I began walking toward the bathrooms around the mausoleum's corner.

Morgan kept pace beside me. "Hey — are you OK?"

"I don't think so."

"Is it your stomach?"

"Right now it's my whole body."

"What about Joe? I don't know if he saw us leave."

"*Fuck* Joe."

When I, drained in every sense of that word, stepped out of the restroom half an hour later, Joe and Morgan were sitting on a nearby strip of grass. Morgan suggested the restorative power of some more sightseeing.

"I have to go back to the Golden Buffalo," I said.

Morgan — 11:00 A.M., April 28, Hanoi

Tom soon developed a fever and spent the rest of the day in bed, in the bathroom, or somewhere within the twenty feet of space that separated them. The next day was no better. Joe and I realized that we had best figure out something to do until he grew well. Ky, after inviting us here, was inexplicably unavailable, but a friend in New York had provided me with the contact information of a Vietnamese artist named Nguyen who lived in Hanoi. In the past, Nguyen had gotten into trouble with the authorities over simple matters, such as not consistently vetting his work through the proper censors. He was not notably political, but he was unwilling to complete the various moral and ethical somersaults expected of Vietnamese artists during the course of their careers. In whatever ways Vietnam had opened up in the last decade, and they were many, I knew, the government was still nervous about civil society, nervous about art and literature, nervous about popular expression. Thus, they were nervous about Nguyen. And Nguyen was nervous about the authorities, but in the indulgent, wearied way of a man who knew he was right and recognized his opponents as philistines and morons. I called Nguyen, and he seemed willing to talk. "Come by," he said. "We'll have tea."

Nguyen was sitting in his living room when we arrived. His apartment had an interesting green tinge to it, and for unknown reasons his living room smelled vaguely of dirt. As we talked — about art, about the government, about the government's interference with art, about the clandestine exhibits he was forced to engage in — Nguyen got up and sat down a hundred times, pacing his living room and grabbing at various objects, pictures, and documents in order to illustrate his points. I envied him. All the American artists I know, men and women, worry about grants and reviews and attracting the right gallery owner's attentions. I couldn't help wondering if Vietnamese artists were not somehow more emotionally

invested in their work than my American friends. When the consequences were so huge, the spiritual payoffs had to be equally gar-
gantuan. The things Nguyen was doing were important for the
sheer reason that they were being resisted. It meant that his work
stood for freedom, and it gave him an aura of importance.

The phone rang. Nguyen went upstairs. We could hear him speak
in growingly agitated Vietnamese, then he came down in a state of
even greater agitation. "You're being watched," he told us. "Followed."

Joe and I looked at each other. For some reason Joe was smiling,
and then, even as the word *followed* stabbed at me with a little shiv of
fear, I was smiling. There was a sense of converse accomplishment
that the things we were doing here could matter enough for government tails to be dispatched, papers filed, operatives consulted.
This feeling did not last long. Minutes later, eight Vietnamese men
— five in drab olive uniforms that looked shipped from Leningrad
in 1974, three in plainclothes, looking like anyone you might pass
in the street — burst into Nguyen's house and rushed into his
living room. One man was videotaping the whole thing. They ordered Joe to stand back from his mounted camera and began ques-
tioning us. In an instant, the room was rich with the faintly stupefying air of bureaucratic wheels turning. God only knew what button
of paranoia had been pushed, what man at what Party level in what
city in what office had decided that some unknowable line had
been crossed.

I tried to stand up and make the transition from feeling I had
been caught doing something wrong to projecting a sense of out-
rage and indignation at a plainly absurd state of affairs, but the fact
is Joe and I were terrified. These officials were the kind of officials
who were good at being officials. They exuded officialness. They
had a cool stance of authority, conducting themselves with an air of
simultaneous annoyance and triumph. As it quickly became clear,
their goal was to intimidate us into revealing our purpose, CIA- or
Viet Kieu-dissident-related or otherwise. I looked over at Nguyen,
an expert in affairs of storm trooper management, and noticed a
distinct glaze of concern on his face. Was Nguyen scared too?

"What are you doing here?" one of the storm troopers asked. It
was the fifth time he had asked this question. Not waiting for an answer, he asked another.

"How do you know Nguyen?"

"Through a friend in New York."

"Who?"

I was utterly in the thrall of saving myself; I suddenly understood why captured revolutionaries ratted out their fellow insurrectionists, however beloved they might have once been. "Sam Henderson," I said, and felt the disgrace in my throat.

"Where are your passports?"

My passport was in my pocket. But I had an idea. "At the hotel," I said.

Tom — 12:30 P.M., Fevered, Golden Buffalo Hotel

I was in bed when Morgan entered, panic-eyed and fidgety. I sat up. "Listen," Morgan whispered, "the Vietnamese secret police or something has said they're going to take us downtown — it's possible they're arresting us." I laughed and returned my head to the pillow. "And, Tom, you have to fucking *listen* to me when I say I'll need you to call the embassy if we're not back in two hours."

I looked at Morgan for a moment. Then I sat up again. "You're serious?"

"They're downstairs."

"Wait. What?" I was whispering now, too. "Who is downstairs?"

Heavy, sinister footsteps clomped up the stairway. Morgan's eyes widened, and then he was walking out of the room — furiously. It was the fastest I had ever seen him move. "They said I could come up here!" I heard him complain the moment he pulled the door shut behind him.

I did not go downstairs until I was certain all of the Golden Buffalo's mysterious visitors were gone. I wandered down the stairs in my T-shirt and boxer shorts, both still damp from the day's fever. The two hotel attendants were standing in the front doorway, shaking their heads and looking down the street.

I approached them. "What the fuck happened?"

The younger of the two spoke: "I don't know."

"Who took my friends away?"

"I don't know."

"Was it the police?"

"I don't know."

"What should I do?"

"I don't know."

Tom — 3:30 P.M., Conversation with Anonymous Friend,
Golden Buffalo Hotel Phone

"The important thing is for them to smile a lot and not act guilty. I mean, you guys have done nothing wrong, right?"

"Well, I think they were seeing a dissident painter."

"Do you know which one?"

"I don't, actually. Morgan has the name with him."

"It would help if you knew the name of the painter."

"I imagine it would."

"And then there's the whole General Ky thing."

"How so?"

"You've been pretty visibly meeting with a man history knows as one of the most strident anti-Communists South Vietnam ever produced."

"Looked at from that perspective, I guess that's true."

"But when I think it over, my mind goes in the general direction that everything will be fine."

"OK. So what do I do?"

"All the advice I really have concerns their behavior, not yours. Let me think. You guys came on journalists' visas, right?"

"Uh. No."

"You didn't."

"We didn't. We came on tourists' visas."

"*Why* didn't you come on journalists' visas?"

"I admit that this is a good question."

"That right there could be a huge problem. They could be asked to leave."

"You mean they could be forced to leave."

"And you, too. And they'd have a leg to stand on, technically."

"For seeing a *painter?*"

"Call me if you haven't heard from them by 5:30."

Tom — 5:00 P.M., Conversation with U.S. Embassy
Official, Golden Buffalo Hotel

"You should be aware that, in the eyes of Vietnamese law, what you've all done is illegal. They could hold Morgan and Joe for days."

"Days."

"For as long as they like, actually, but I don't think that will happen."

"OK. Good."

"I'd also recommend that, if you want a good night's sleep, you check into another hotel."

"You're saying the authorities could come back here and rustle me up?"

"I don't think anything will come to physical force."

"Not *rough* me up. *Rustle* me up."

"In the eyes of Vietnamese law, yes, they could. And there'd be nothing we could do about it other than make phone calls."

Morgan — *Time Unknown, Place Unknown*

We were taken to a nondescript room somewhere in a pinkish nondescript government building on a not-too-noticeable street in centralish Hanoi. Outside the room, in a concrete courtyard, were eight or nine people, intelligence officers of some kind, playing badminton in the lazy leftover of a hazy day.

A three-star general was led into the room. Everyone sat down on knock-off imperial Chinese armchairs. The general and his staff and a number of other unidentified people began to question us about everything. Why were we here, what had we done, where had we gone, what were we doing, who had we met with? Why, if we were so innocent, was our friend Tom at this very moment checking into another hotel? An old fan swung around in a meaningless loop on the ceiling. Joe kept repeating that he was simply a tourist, simply a tourist, sir. I just fed them the facts. The facts will save us, I thought, because the facts are so simple, so utterly dumb.

It ceased being a real interrogation at all soon after I, in a moment of inspiration or desperation or both, said, "I just want the General to know that my father left the United States so that he didn't have to fight an unjust war. The war was, you know, a crime against your country." This was something that I believed, though it came out essentially as shameless pandering. The general loved it; the military men nodded and smiled.

"Very interesting. But why do you care about this artist Nguyen? He makes art that the people have rejected."

"His art is appreciated around the world."

"But the people reject it."

That was the aesthetics portion of the interrogation. Next, the officials watched all of Joe's video footage, but it was mostly Tom and me sitting around in different hotels yammering endlessly about the Vietnam War, Communism, and Tom's diarrhea. The footage did not exactly constitute a smoking gun. By this point, several people in the room had drifted to watching the events in the badminton game still going on outside. One of the secret policemen had a pretty devastating serve that included a little two-step approach and then a jumping whacking motion that sent the shuttlecock into a crazy, spinning dive over the net.

Two young women were brought in from the travel agency that sponsored our visas. They were not pleased to be in this situation, but they were now responsible for making sure that we were out of Vietnam within twenty-four hours. The general made jokes about how one of the young women was very pretty and Joe was single. She smiled obligingly. Joe smiled obligingly. Everyone was chuckling knowingly as if all this statecraft had come down to making sure Joe got laid before sundown tomorrow. I wished them all a happy reunification ceremony. But an air of menace lingered. It was clear that there would be unpleasant consequences for the women and their travel agency, and some dire, unnamed penalty for us, if the twenty-four-hour deadline were missed.

Morgan — 4:00 A.M., April 29, En Route to Ho Chi Minh City from Hanoi

It was a strange and melancholy predawn. Dark and quiet, too early even for the activity of the group exercises and games that animate Vietnam's mornings. And it was cold. A car was waiting downstairs with the young women from the travel agency and an unidentified plainclothes official. We drove to the Hanoi airport in silence. Being in Vietnam had ceased to be fun. The adrenaline from the day before was gone. All that remained was a dull sense of urgency that came from the deadline and from being surrounded by people who were clearly taking that deadline extremely seriously.

A few hours later we were landing back in Saigon, where we were met by another group of officials charged with the solemn duty of getting us the fuck out of Vietnam for good. It's a strange thing to be an object of concern to large groups of men in military uniform. They told us where to go and when to go there. When we were hungry they brought, fittingly, some bread and some water. The head of airport security informed us that the only sure way to make it out on time was to take an available flight to Singapore. Doing this would force us to finance our own expulsion. I brought up the idea of waiting and using the tickets we already had for a later flight to Tokyo. The security chief looked at us in disbelief, then his jaw hardened. "You'll go to Singapore," he said.

And so we waited to do exactly that. We were held until the plane had been fully boarded by all the other passengers. We were then marched through the airport with a full phalanx of military guards surrounding us on all sides. Conversation died as we passed. Who were these international men of intrigue and danger? We were marched that way all the way to the mouth of the plane. We turned and bowed slightly to our unrequested escorts and entered. A few minutes later, Vietnam was little more than a rapidly receding swath of green through an ovular window.

Tom — 9:30 A.M., Hanoi

I rode on the back of a moped, flying along Hanoi's majestic embassy row. Small brown leaves were falling from the trees overhead, the whole street shade-dimmed. I had received a call from the U.S. embassy asking me to "come in." Last night's good-bye with Morgan and Joe had been rushed and comic, heartbroken and frightened. I wondered where they were now.

I was expecting the U.S. embassy to be handsomely located here among these gray and gated mansions, but when the canopied street ended, we turned off onto another, far less grand street. The U.S. embassy was housed within a tall building along a row of taller buildings and had the assailed dignity of an insurance company headquarters in downtown Omaha. I had heard that, when the United States moved in ten years ago, theirs was the tallest building on this street. The U.S. had wanted to swap embassies for several years now, but the Vietnamese were resistant. After all, they had worked out all the best nests and nooks from which to spy on this embassy and did not much feel like scrapping a decade of work.

I was greeted by an official and quickly taken to an embassy break room. He was surprised to learn that Morgan and Joe were meeting with a painter when they were detained; he had assumed they were nabbed for talking to a writer. It was all a big misunderstanding, I explained. My embassy friend nodded sympathetically. He described the dilemma of Vietnam's security services: the intelligence branch had some rough customers in it, some beaters and disappearers, but it was mostly staffed with holdovers from the Soviet-influenced period. So the intelligence service in Vietnam was addicted to information. They did not necessarily ever *act* on it; they just wanted it. The Foreign Ministry, on the other hand, was filled with many young men and women of purer motive, more worldly perspective, and more nuanced understanding. Our problem was that, by not registering as journalists, we had become an intelligence problem, not a Foreign Ministry problem. I needed to watch my step. Soon I was again hurtling toward my hotel on the back of another moped.

My flight out of Hanoi left at 4:00 P.M. It was now just after eleven. I checked out, stored my bag, and decided that if I indeed had a tail then this tail of mine was going to get a fucking workout. He would walk around Hanoi's Lake of the Returned Sword again and again and again. The Lake of the Returned Sword was where the fifteenth-century patriot Le Loi was given a Vietnamese Excalibur that he shortly used to chase the Chinese out of Vietnam. The provider of this sword was not some watery Vietnamese sylph but a turtle. The turtle, and its sword, were still waiting at the bottom of the lake. Or so it was said. It was also said that the day Ho Chi Minh died, Ho's spirit, which had taken the form of a large turtle, crawled out of the lake, basked in the sun for a few minutes, and then returned to its depths. I loved the Lake of the Returned Sword. How could one not? It was the prettiest part of Hanoi. Perhaps I would even see a turtle. The Vietnamese government was said to dump a few of the beasts in the lake from time to time, to keep hope in its vision alive. Which was either beautiful or insane. Vietnam was either beautiful or insane.

I walked, cherishing the loneliness of wandering aimlessly and alone around a lake in this city in which I knew no one. I circled the lake several times. At various stations around the lake were inviting little tents that advertised trips to Sapa in the high north, trips to Nam Dinh (one of the poorest parts of Vietnam, and one that had been virtually destroyed during the war), trips to Nha Trang, trips even to India. I hoped that this circling of the lake, its sheer mind-numbing repetitiveness, had discouraged my tail.

On my eighth or ninth time around the lake, a Vietnamese man wearing a gray suit and noticeably well-combed hair approached me and introduced himself. He said he hoped I still planned on leaving Hanoi today at 4:00 P.M. He said he hoped I would not practice any more journalism while I was here. Then he bid me good day. I in return thanked him and said I hoped the man would enjoy the reunification ceremonies. At this, the man smiled. Various things may have happened next. I may have sat down on a bench and held my leaden head in my hands. I may have tried talking to a pretty young Japanese woman, frightened her, and stood there reaching out into the air after nothing. I may have found an isolated corner of the lake, knelt beside it, and believed, in my heart, to have seen the flash of a turtle shell discus through the water.

Tom, with His Anonymous Friend — Nearing Midnight, April 29, Ho Chi Minh City

Q Bar looked busy, and a chatty and photogenic assemblage of Vietnamese swans and Western wolves had spilled out onto the patio, ten-dollar drinks in hand. It looked like a swell party at Q Bar. Just before leaving my friend's apartment, he had pulled from his pocket a tiny Ziploc bag of Ecstasy. Within minutes we had ingested the first bits of the stash, the little yellow pills, about the size and texture (but not the taste) of a yellow Flintstones vitamin, bitten in half and chased with Tiger beer, the other half swallowed moments after that.

We wended through the palm trees wrapped in Christmas lights and sat at an outside table with a stunning young Vietnamese woman dressed in spidery black and sporting a scorpion tattoo on her shoulder. I recognized her instantly as Viet Kieu. She was an acquaintance of my friend. Sitting with her were Mike and Sean, a writer and photographer, respectively, working in Vietnam. Journalists — real journalists! I was introduced, first as who I was, then as what had happened to me — that I was, in other words, part of the contingent that was thrown out of Vietnam this morning.

Mike, who was shaven-headed and mutton-chopped, looked at me disbelievingly before blurting, "I just wrote a story about you guys!"

I took this in. My thoughts were not making much sense to me. "How," I finally managed, "do you know what happened?"

"There were plenty of whispers about it last night at a diplomatic cocktail party. Respect!" Mike suddenly thrust out his hand. I shook it, smiling, feeling how nice it was to smile, how interestingly flesh changed its mold. But Mike's story, as it turned out, was far from complete. He had to work with only last night's rumor, a near no-comment from the U.S. embassy, and the confirmation of the Vietnamese Foreign Ministry that American journalists on tourists' visas had been expelled from the country. Mike had assumed (though did not write) that these Americans were "Viet Kieu muckers" troublemaking in Hanoi, not American journalists. Now that he had learned the truth, Mike admitted, "You kind of fucked up things for us here. They're clamping down. It's total lockdown."

It took various forms, apparently. All foreign journalists in Vietnam had to live in Hanoi, for instance, though many had dummy apartments there and spent their time in Saigon. They were watched, and sometimes bugged. Mike went on to explain that he had been trying to interview a dissident Buddhist leader for months and nearly got himself in serious trouble scraping around in the Central Highlands a few months ago, where unrest still exists. There had been a brief, ill-planned, and speedily crushed attempt to overthrow the Vietnamese government in the Central Highlands as recently as the late 1980s. Much of the resistance was run, Mike said, out of North Carolina by a Viet Kieu with the unfortunate name of Kok Ksor. But everyone had been talking about the expelled journalists. Mike's news service had reported it, *Time*'s Vietnam correspondent was gabbing about it. This suggested to me several things, none of them good: that this was actually a bigger deal than I knew, that I was almost certainly being watched right now, and that the expatriate community in Vietnam desperately needed TiVo.

Someone handed me a salty, olivey martini, and I heard my friend discussing the possibility of staying up all night and attending the reunification ceremony while still stoned. The idea, I have to admit, made a weird kind of sense. *I am Michael Herr,* I thought to myself. The beautiful raccoon-eyed Viet Kieu woman cunningly asked what I was on. I told her. "The X here is cut with a lot of speed," she said, and she looked like she would know.

"How do you feel?" asked Sean, the photojournalist.

I sat there, thinking. The night breeze was so cool. "I feel," I said, "a weird mix of euphoria and paranoia."

Sean nodded. "That sounds like life."

And then, because it was late, and more drinks had been sent for, emptied, and replaced, and because they were journalists talking to journalists in a place that was magical, Mike had the idea to sneak me into the ceremony tomorrow morning.

"Is that wise?" I asked.

"No!" Mike said joyfully. "It could be a complete fucking disaster! So, do you want to do it?"

I nodded, enjoying how it felt to nod.

"Meet me outside the ceremony," Mike was saying, "at 5:40 A.M. You can't be late."

It was now just past two. Not a problem, I thought, and we shook on it.

Tom — 5:45 A.M., April 30, Hai Ba Trung Street

The morning sky was some color between black and orange. The sky was Neapolitan ice cream, I thought. White, black, pink. I walked past Vietnamese families sitting in lawn chairs blocks and blocks away from the celebration. They were just going to sit here and enjoy their independence. I passed through a fish market, its washtubs filled with penny-colored carp. Nearby a woman was peddling fish and cow innards, including a plate of shiny brown calf livers. There was an aquarium of eels, as shiny as wet rubber, all squirming around one another. I was clearly still too high to be in a fish market.

It soon became equally clear that not only was I late in meeting Mike, but I was on the opposite side of the festivities that I needed to be. Maybe this wasn't such a bad thing. Last night I had thought it was a great idea to sneak in with Mike, but if I was being watched — and I was certain I was — then those watching me knew I had no journalist visa. Walking into the restricted parade area with a journalist who had already had minor but persistent troubles with the authorities was to beg for expulsion for both of us. Mike had been so excited, but it didn't matter. I was now well aware that I was not getting into the festivities, I was too far away, I had not navigated this well at all, I had not gotten authorized. I had completely fucked everything up.

At last I reached good old Thi Minh Khai Street, where the crowd was thickening like batter as more people were poured into it from feeder streets. I came to the first group of celebration-bound Vietnamese: about one hundred children in white shirts, white ball caps, blue trousers, holding little red Vietnam flags. They marched in a gentle way, as though they were not taking this too seriously. It was already so hot. The euphoria of Q Bar was gone. I was trying not to take notes, because I did not want to be noticed. I was being followed. I was in the kingdom of paranoia now, but the feeling of my pen in my hand was exquisite. I passed the marchers and saw they were not children at all but fully grown adults. These small people, this small country. They beat us. They beat us.

The first blocked-off street I happened upon was near the French Consulate, the building where thousands were turned away the night of the U.S. evacuation thirty years ago. Each roadblock was a series of angled metal gates striped barbershop red-and-white and manned by ten Vietnamese in felt-green uniforms and red-striped green caps. Meanwhile, patrolling the streets were hundreds of Vietnamese in cigarette-filter-brown uniforms and red-striped caps. I looked in vain for an unblocked street, some place I could slip inside. Once-familiar blocks were now utterly alien with floats, single-file crowds of choreographed marchers, and surprisingly few soldiers. In fact, there were no soldiers I could see. I was exhausted. My legs were tingly saplings. I had not slept for close to forty hours.

Down Thi Minh Khai Street I went, the same street I wandered with Morgan on my first night in the country. Roadblock, roadblock, roadblock. There was something so outlandish about celebrating the liberation of a people that the people could not take part in. Many Vietnamese were sitting along the curbs. The morning haze hovered above the pavement like . . . serpent's breath, I thought. Yes. I wrote that down. *Serpent's breath.* I was sweating so much I could have, and probably should have, wrung out my clothes. I was wide-eyed, breathing audibly out with each exhalation, not because I was physically tired but because the mere act of forcing air out of my lungs felt orgasmically good. I was strolling beneath the same red hammer-and-sickle banners that days ago Morgan and I had laughed at. Who was laughing now?

A trumpet blast from inside the sealed area. Children were singing what were invariably referred to in Vietnam as "patriotic songs." I finally could not hold it anymore — the wrongness of my situation, my morning, my trip, my life — and waited until I came across a blockade manned by officers who looked to be roughly my age. "*Toi la nha van*," I said to one of the officers. *I am a writer.* Let me inside. The man scanned my body for a pass, which was white and laminated, and which had emblazoned upon it "Tank 844" (one of them), and which it suddenly seemed everyone but me was wearing. When he found no pass, the man's demeanor darkened.

"Where is your pass?" he asked in English.

"I lost it," I said.

The man looked over to someone else, and there was something beckoning and consulting about this, something frightening, and I apologized and quickly rushed away. I was expecting footfalls behind me, hands around my arms, breath sweetened by Vietnamese coffee upon my cheek. But nothing. I had escaped. Desperate, I lingered longingly at each roadblock, making notes, putting my notebook away, storming to the next roadblock, making notes. If I was being followed, I was fairly certain that word was going back to Communist Party headquarters about now that I was insane. The circling-the-lake business was one thing, but now he had completely lost it.

Approaching were more single-file lines of smiling, marching Vietnamese on their way into the parade. All were grouped together by, to say the least, oddly arbitrary-seeming distinctions: here was the group dressed like judo masters, here were the young men in the same shade of collared blue shirt and black baseball cap, here were the women in red T-shirts emblazoned with a yellow star, here were the robots. I stopped. Yes, there really were robots approaching. Or men dressed as robots. They wore shiny silver pants and some strange Tin Man–type hat. I ran across the street, away from the celebration. I was near my hotel, but when I got there I didn't go in.

I could not stop thinking about this city, what had happened here. The people who had died in these streets. I felt magnified. I was not where I needed to be, where I should be. The sky was slate blue. I had promised I would get into the ceremony, and I failed. Mission failure. I was a failure. Within the hour, I was far away from the celebration, walking down streets I had never seen before. Mechanics squatted beside half-pulled-apart scooters, women boiled soup on the sidewalk, these routines unchanged. And here I was to see them.

Had I been only a few blocks away, I could have seen former Prime Minister Vo Van Kiet wave to the crowd. I could have seen General Vo Nguyen Giap and Cuba's vice president Raul Castro, like some time capsule mailed from 1959 to 2005, shake and raise their joined hand-mass to the cheering crowd, near a banner that read, "Long live the Vietnamese Communist Party!" I could have seen the expected sight of marching Vietnamese soldiers — the twenty-fifth anniversary parade had been nothing but soldiers and hardware — but then seen the marching electricity workers, the marching teachers, the marching factory workers, the marching youth union, the doddering old veterans of the North Vietnamese Army. But I would have seen no tanks. No missiles. The Vietnamese Communist Party had apparently realized that their countrymen no longer cared if they had missiles and tanks. I could have then seen the float that triumphalized "Saigon's port facilities." I could have seen the float shaped like an ATM, sponsored by Vietbank, draped with the national flags of Visa, MasterCard, and American Express. I could have seen the men and women dressed up as fruit, marching on behalf of the agricultural workers of Vietnam. I could have seen the marchers pushing shopping carts. I could have seen Vietnam's Motorbike Club of Liberation. And, yes, I could have seen the robots. Marching in the parade were several dozen robots. The long, sad story of Vietnam's revolution had begun with Ho Chi Minh's "Nothing is more precious than freedom and independence." It had, apparently, drifted into its strangest and probably terminal stage, for nothing now was more precious than fruit and robots.

But I was too far away from the celebration to be thinking of any of this. I had been taking every turn, not wanting to walk straight anymore. It was too difficult to go straight. It was too difficult to walk toward what I expected. Had I really watched Nguyen Cao Ky sip cappuccino? The heat came down on me like a curse. The city I thought I knew well was alive; it was breathing on me. The people I thought myself comfortable with eyed me with no motive I could name. I thought about Vietnam, and I thought about how truly far away from home I was. My friends had left me. I did not know what I was doing, or where I should go. As helpless as an army, I no longer had any idea even where I was.

ALAIN DE BOTTON

The Discreet Charm
of the Zurich Bourgeoisie

FROM *FarFlungMagazine.com*

1.

THE MOST SINCERE compliment you could pay Zurich is to describe it as one of the great bourgeois cities of the world. This might not, of course, seem like a compliment — the word *bourgeois* having become for many, since the outset of the Romantic Movement in the early nineteenth century, a significant insult. "Hatred of the bourgeois is the beginning of wisdom," felt Gustave Flaubert, a standard utterance for a mid-nineteenth-century French writer, for whom such disdain was as much a badge of one's profession as having an affair with an actress and making a trip to the Orient. According to the Romantic value system that today still dominates the Western imagination, to be a bourgeois is synonymous with laboring under an obsession with money, safety, tradition, cleaning, family, responsibility, prudishness, and (perhaps) bracing walks in the fresh air. Consequently, for about the last two hundred years, few places in the Western world have been quite as deeply unfashionable as the city of Zurich.

2.

Attractive girls born outside Switzerland are particularly against going to Zurich. Such girls (and modern science has proved this) prefer Los Angeles or Sydney. Even if they are looking for something

Protestant and homey, they choose Antwerp or Copenhagen instead.

I've always tried to interest girls in Zurich. I've always thought that a girl who could like Zurich could like important recesses of me. But it's been hard. I recall a trip with Sasha. She was an artist, she was beguiling, she was tricky. We'd have furious arguments, often in the middle of the night. Sometimes the argument went like this:

She: You don't like intelligent women, that's why you're
     disagreeing with me.
He: I do like intelligent women, but sadly you're not one of
     them.

Neither of us came out of this sort of thing very well. It's a reminder (were one to need it) that lovers practice a form of rudeness that is generally impossible outside of open warfare.

One weekend, Sasha and I flew to Zurich (we lived in Hackney in London, we were bohemian, we had views, evolved ones, about Habermas). I tried to point out how exotic Zurich was. Trams were exotic, as was the Migros supermarket, and the light gray concrete of the apartment blocks and the large, solid windows and the veal escalopes. We normally associate the word *exotic* with camels and pyramids. But perhaps anything different and desirable deserves the word. What I found most exotic was how gloriously boring everything was. No one was being killed by random gunshots, the streets were quiet, everything was tidy and, as everyone says (though you don't see people trying), it was generally so clean you could eat your lunch off the pavement.

But Sasha was bored. She wanted to go back to Hackney. She couldn't bear the tidiness. On a walk through a park she told me she wanted to graffiti insults on the walls — just to shake the place up a bit. She did a little mock scream, and an old lady looked up from her paper. Her boredom reminded me of my friend Gustave Flaubert, who'd grown up in Rouen, which is perhaps a little bit like Zurich minus the lake. "I am bored, I am bored, I am bored," Flaubert wrote in his diary as a young man. He returned repeatedly to the theme of how boring it was to live in France and especially in Rouen. "Today my boredom was terrible," he reported at the end of one bad Sunday. "How beautiful are the provinces and how chic are the comfortably off who live there. Their talk is of taxes and road improvements. The neighbor is a wonderful institution. To be given his full social importance he should always be written in capitals: NEIGHBOR." Sasha was bored with Flaubert (she'd tried *A Sentimental Education,* but got bored halfway), but she and Flaubert at least agreed on how boring it is to live in a boring place.

However, as mother tends to tell you near the end of the school holidays, it's mostly boring people who get bored — and I began to lose patience with Sasha's boredom. I wanted someone interesting enough inside not to ask of a city that it also be "interesting"; someone close enough to the wellsprings of passion that she wouldn't care if her city wasn't "fun"; someone sufficiently acquainted with the darker, tragic sides of the human soul to appreciate the stillness of a Zurich weekend. Sasha and I weren't an item for much longer.

3.

But my attraction to Zurich continued. What most appealed to me about Zurich was the image of what was entailed in leading an "ordinary" life there. To lead an ordinary life in London is generally not an enviable proposition: "ordinary" hospitals, schools, housing estates, or restaurants are nearly always appalling. There are of course great examples, but they are only for the very wealthy. London is not a bourgeois city. It's a city of the rich and the poor.

According to one influential wing of modern secular society, there are few more disreputable fates than to end up being "like everyone else"; for "everyone else" is a category that comprises the mediocre and the conformist, the boring and the suburban. The goal of all right-thinking people should be to mark themselves out from the crowd and "stand out" in whatever way their talents allow. But the desire to be different depends on what it means to be ordinary. There are countries where the communal provision of housing, transport, education, or health care is such that citizens will naturally seek to escape involvement with the group and barricade themselves behind solid walls. The desire for high status is never stronger than when being ordinary entails leading a life which fails to cater to a median need for dignity and comfort.

Then there are communities, far rarer, many of them imbued with a strong (often Protestant) Christian heritage, where the public realm exudes respect in its principles and architecture, and where the need to escape into a private domain is therefore less intense. Citizens may lose some of their ambitions for personal glory when the public spaces and facilities of a city are themselves glorious to behold. Simply being an ordinary citizen can seem like an adequate destiny. In Switzerland's largest city, the urge to own a car and avoid sharing a bus or train with strangers loses some of the urgency it may have in Los Angeles or London, thanks to Zurich's superlative tram network — clean, safe, warm, and edifying in its punctuality and technical prowess. There is little reason to travel alone when, for only a few francs, an efficient, stately tramway will transport one across the city at a level of comfort an emperor would have envied.

4.

There's something faintly embarrassing about loving the Dutch seventeenth-century painter Pieter de Hooch deeply, so deeply that one would include him among one's favorite painters of all time. Of the 170 works assigned to him, most are plain mediocre, overly coarse in the early years or mannered in the later ones. He is operating in a minor genre, his pictures are too pretty and yet not quite pretty enough, not as pretty as a Raphael's or Poussin's, and compared to his countrymen, he lacks the inventiveness of Jan Steen, the grace of Vermeer, or the density of van Ruisdael. His morality can appear reactionary, a celebration of the most banal human occupations: delousing and cleaning the patio. He doesn't even paint people very well; look closely at his faces and they are no better than sketches. And yet I've long loved him for reasons very similar to why I love Zurich: because he understands and celebrates bourgeois life, without sentimentalizing it. The world he paints, despite the differences, seems in essence identical to the Zurich I grew up in.

De Hooch is often described as fitting into a tradition of Dutch art and literature which sermonized about the virtues of domesticity. Although de Hooch's paintings do look positively on domestic pursuits, although one would be unlikely to come away from them emboldened to break up one's marriage or leave the kitchen dirty, it seems unfair to label him a crude moralist of domestic virtue. He never tells us that it is important to love one's children or keep the house tidy, he merely provides us with such evocative, moving examples of maternal love and ordered rooms that we would be unlikely to disagree.

Furthermore, his art has none of the smug tone of much overt propaganda of domestic virtue. The simple pleasures of home come across as highly vulnerable achievements. Critics might argue that de Hooch was not painting seventeenth-century Holland the way it really was, they could point out that many women were abused by their husbands, many houses were dirty and primitive, there was a degree of blood and dirt and pain that de Hooch chose not to represent, idealizing matters instead. And yet his art is never sentimental, because it is so infused with an awareness of the darker forces liable at any point to vanquish the hard-won serenity. We don't need to be told that the whole of Holland was not spotlessly clean, we have enough suggestion of it through the many windows at the ends of corridors in de Hooch's canvases. We don't need to be told that the order achieved by women in their homes might be destroyed by war or feckless husbands, we can feel the danger, too.

In *A Woman with a Young Boy Preparing for School,* a mother butters some bread for her son, he stands dutifully beside her, a little man holding his hat, dressed in a neat gray coat and polished shoes. If the scene is both unsentimental and moving, it is because we are made to feel the evanescence of these intimacies of mother and son. To the left of the canvas, a corridor leads to an open door and out to the street, where there is a large building marked Schole. The boy will soon disguise his debts to his mother who has over the years buttered him loaves and checked his head for lice.

De Hooch's art helps us to recover positive associations of that word with which we may have deeply ambiguous relations: *bourgeois*. It seems laden with negative connotations; it can suggest conformity, a lack of imagination, stiffness, pedantry, and snobbishness. But in de Hooch's world, being bourgeois means dressing in simple but attractive clothes, being neither too vulgar nor too pretentious, having a natural relationship with one's children, recognizing sensual pleasures without yielding to licentiousness. It seems the embodiment of the Aristotelian mean. His works perform the valuable task of reminding us of the interest and worth of modest surroundings, quelling vain ambitions and temptations to disengage snobbishly from ordinary routines: the evening meal, the housework, a drink with friends. By paying attention to the beauty of brickwork, of light reflecting off a polished door, of the folds of a woman's dress, de Hooch helps us to find pleasure in these omnipresent but neglected aspects of our world.

5.

Some seventy years before Pieter de Hooch painted his greatest works, in a passage in his *Essays*, Michel de Montaigne expressed thoughts that appeared to capture in words some of the atmosphere of de Hooch's art — and, in turn, the qualities upon which the greatness of Zurich is in my view founded. Seeking to remind his readers of the adequacy of ordinary lives, Montaigne wrote: "Storming a breach, conducting an embassy, ruling a nation are glittering deeds. Rebuking, laughing, buying, selling, loving, hating and living together gently and justly with your household — and with yourself — not getting slack nor belying yourself, is something more remarkable, more rare and more difficult. Whatever people may say, such secluded lives sustain in that way duties which are at least as hard and as tense as those of other lives."

Unfortunately, the point keeps getting lost. We keep forgetting that buttering bread for a child and making the bed have their wondrous dimensions. Sir Joshua Reynolds clearly didn't understand. Writing of Jan Steen in the next century, he remarked that though Steen's work was wonderful, "he would have ranged with the great pillars and supporters of art" had he been able to live in Rome, the greatest city in the world for artists, rather than Leiden, a depressing Zurich-like backwater. In Rome, he would have been inspired to paint really great canvases, he would not have had to limit himself to beggars and merchants, provincial towns, and the clutter of daily existence. It is one of the glories of Dutch seventeenth-century art that it proves Sir Joshua Reynolds conclusively wrong. Alongside Steen and Vermeer, Pieter de Hooch and his housewives cleaning the patio deserve much of the credit.

6.

Zurich's distinctive lesson to the world lies in its ability to remind us of how truly imaginative and humane it can be to ask of a city that it be nothing other than boring and bourgeois.

KEVIN FEDARKO

Ain't It Just Grand?

FROM *Outside*

NORMALLY, THE RIVER down here is restless and kinetic, sluicing along with a muscular roll of its shoulders. At the moment, though, the current has mysteriously disappeared, and the water's surface has taken on the heavy, sullen stillness of a polished green gemstone.

Litton strokes his beard thoughtfully, then casts a glance behind the *Sequoia* to the boat I'm in, a yellow supply raft manned by a nervous-looking fifty-seven-year-old named John Blaustein. J. B., as everyone calls Blaustein, is sporting hipster shades and a cocoa-colored cowboy hat.

"You know, J. B.," Litton calls out, "when things get all calm like this, it means the river's backed up by something. And in this case, what it's backed up by is an absolutely terrifying pile of boulders called Dubendorff."

"Jesus, we're coming up on Dubendorff?" Blaustein yells back. A former Grand Canyon guide, J. B. now lives the agreeable life of a Berkeley-based commercial photographer, but once every summer he allows himself to be dragged down the river again. During these ordeals, he spends half his time pretending to complain about absurdly minor discomforts, the other half awash in a lather of angst over rapids like the one we're about to enter.

"I'm afraid it is," replies Litton, who's clad in a straw hat, an indigo shirt, and black suspenders — an ensemble that makes him look like an Amish farmer gone to sea. "This is a terrifying place, J. B. Absolutely terrifying."

"Absolutely terrifying" is Litton's favorite expression, a phrase he invokes several times an hour to describe everything from shifting weather patterns to the possibility that the six liters of Sheep Dip Scotch stowed in his hatch might run dry before the conclusion of this 280-mile odyssey through the rapids of the Grand Canyon.

There are eighty of these named rapids, a dozen of which serve up some of the biggest white water in North America. And though Litton and Blaustein know that Dubendorff, which marks the mid-point of most canyon trips, doesn't rank among the worst, it's not to be taken for granted. The run is a maelstrom of huge waves and sharp pour-overs that sound like the afterburners of an F-16. In the brief cushion of tranquillity before all hell breaks loose, Litton has a final thought to share.

"J. B.!" he barks.

"Whaddaya want now?"

"Do you know what the greatest pleasure in life is, J. B.?"

"No, Martin. But before we enter the mother of all rapids here, I'm sure you're about to tell me."

Among a few other small vices, Litton delights in reciting scraps of literature; today's offering comes from Kenneth Grahame's 1908 classic, *The Wind in the Willows*.

"There is *nothing*," he declares, "absolutely nothing, half so much worth doing as simply messing about in boats."

Well, damn. As every Grand Canyon guide knows, this pro-nouncement by the river-loving Water Rat is potent stuff: the clos-est thing dirtbag boatmen have to an Apostles' Creed. Which is why Blaustein can only sit there looking trumped as Litton — who is currently eighty-seven years old and may be making the last of his many, many runs through the canyon — lets fly with a wicked peal of laughter that booms off the soaring walls.

"Touché, Martin," replies Blaustein, touching the brim of his hat as Litton and the *Sequoia* are seized by the current and abruptly dis-appear over the edge of Dubendorff.

And with that, we follow the old man into the thunder.

Every trip down the canyon is special, but this trip is particularly fine because the man at its center has no antecedent. In the annals of Grand Canyon boating and conservation, Martin Litton is a unique force of nature, a tornado of ungovernable passions, soar-ing eloquence, and stiff-necked defiance quite unlike anything else that's ever blown through one of the most storied locales in Ameri-can adventure.

Born in Gardena, California, in February 1917, Litton grew up exploring the California wilderness, served as a glider pilot in World War II, and started taking trips down the Colorado back in the fifties, eventually becoming the only outfitter to guide the river's ferocious rapids exclusively in the frail wooden boats known as Grand Canyon dories. These double-ended, flat-bottomed craft, which he played a key role in designing, are radically different from the ponderous oar boats that Major John Wesley Powell used during the first descent of the canyon, in 1869. Beautiful, delicate, and graceful, Litton's dories became — and remain — the sacred craft of the canyon.

Along the way, in his roles as a freelance writer for the *Los Angeles Times*, an editor at *Sunset* magazine, and a board member of the Sierra Club, Litton also elbowed into some of the most important environmental battles of his time. In 1956, he helped block two dams inside Utah's Dinosaur National Monument, and in 1967, he and others thwarted several dams on Idaho's Snake River. Thanks to Litton's years of public drumbeating on behalf of California redwoods, he's sometimes called the Father of Redwood National Park, which was signed into being in 1968. In that same year, he helped lead what is probably the biggest of all his crusades: a successful campaign to kill a pair of dams that would have stilled the Colorado as it winds through the Grand Canyon.

Today, Litton merits double-barreled distinction as one of the founding commercial river runners of the Colorado and one of America's greatest living conservationists: a man who, after seventy years of both reveling in and battling to preserve a treasure trove of natural wonders, has become something of a national treasure himself.

For all his accomplishments, though, there have always been contradictions, mostly in the form of Litton's puzzling personality quirks. He has fought for all sorts of restrictions to protect fragile landscapes, yet he loathes any government agency that musters the temerity to tell him where he can go and how to behave when he gets there. He inspires great loyalty, but his former employees describe him as the sort of mercurial boss who could switch in a heartbeat from charming to curmudgeonly to nitpicking. He bemoans the loss of solitude in wilderness but made his living by encouraging millions of people to go out and discover it. He's a paragon of environmental rectitude, and yet, throughout the sixties, in what

Litton says was an action suited to "different times," he concluded his twenty-one-day canyon trips by dumping nearly a month's worth of empty beer cans and liquor bottles into the Colorado, telling his guides that "studies have shown the river to be deficient in silica and aluminum."

"A very, very complicated person with deep flaws who has done extraordinary things," says Brad Dimock, a river guide who's known Litton since 1973 — and who, like everyone close to Litton, harbors sentiments colored equally by affection and exasperation. "I don't think you'd find a single heroic figure who isn't also burdened with contradictions. And when you look at the Grand Canyon today, it's impossible to say that Martin didn't make one hell of a difference."

Perhaps Litton committed himself to the nation's most spectacular waterway because this landscape mirrored some of his own paradoxes. The canyon's signature attribute is a frigid river tumbling through a savage furnace of sun-blistered rock — a theater of hellish beauty whose sublime charms are matched only by the concussive force of its harshness. Held up as the supreme example of nature's forces laid bare, it is also a labyrinth of abiding mystery that's best grasped by traveling in the company of a man whose character, like the canyon itself, defies any attempt to contain it.

"There's just no explaining the old fart," Dimock concludes. "He's still out there fighting his battles and rowing his frickin' boat. I just want to know when his last river trip's going to be."

Last spring, Litton's former guiding company invited him to return for one more run. And so Litton duly presented himself before a group of bright-eyed passengers who'd paid up to $4,314 apiece to float alongside the most notorious boatman and rebel ever to drift the Colorado in a cloud of rapture.

"The Grand Canyon is America's greatest scenic treasure — an experience made to order in wonder," Litton told the clients the night before they hit the river, congratulating them on having the good sense to join him. "Floating a boat down the Colorado River? Why, it's simply the best thing one can do."

We begin where all Grand Canyon journeys begin: at Lees Ferry, fifteen miles downstream from Glen Canyon Dam. Gathered at the put-in ramp around three bulbous baggage rafts and six elegant, scimitar-shaped dories are eighteen passengers from all over the United States, among them Duane Kelly and his wife, Cosette, a pair of retired teachers from Kansas City; Pat Newman, an accountant from Golden, Colorado, here with her husband, Dennis, who invents devices to monitor medical patients; and Devon Meade, a singer from Los Angeles, who used to perform backup vocals for Alice Cooper. An eclectic hodgepodge, the clients are united by the simple fact that all of them want to see the canyon and the river through Litton's eyes while it's still possible.

The trip has been outfitted by OARS, the Angels Camp, California, company that now owns Litton's old guiding concession, and it's being led by Bill "Bronco" Bruchak, a barrel-chested former beer distributor from Pennsylvania who's been running the canyon for twenty-eight years. Bronco is joined by Rondo Buecheler and Eric Sjoden, who have worked the river for nearly three decades, along with three members of the "Dale dynasty," the most illustrious family in Grand Canyon dory guiding. Sue "Coyote" Dale — whom everybody calls 'Ote — is here with her son, Duffy (who started rowing a dory at the age of three while perched on his father's lap) and Duffy's uncle, Tim. Rounding out the crew are the baggage boatmen: Curtis Newell, Ryan Howe, and their grumpy court jester, Blaustein, who has known Litton since 1970 and collaborated with him on *The Hidden Canyon*, a 1977 book that stands as the definitive tribute to boating on the river.

While the crew rigs the boats, Litton sits quietly in the *Sequoia*, his physical appearance bespeaking both weightiness and mileage. The skin on his face, framed by a thick white beard and mustache, is creased with wrinkles and flecked with broken veins. His eyes are a startling shade of blue. The backs of his powerful hands are covered with liver spots. Together, these features make him endearing and intimidating all at once — part Santa Claus, part Old Testament prophet.

Litton has been through the Grand Canyon at least thirty-five times, but even he doesn't know the exact number. In 1997, then eighty, he set a record, which still stands, as the oldest boatman ever to run the canyon, rowing every rapid himself. But recently his age has started taking a toll on his reflexes, which is why the setup on this trip is a bit different.

Litton will spend the better part of each day rowing the *Sequoia*, but when we hit some of the more technically challenging rapids, Tim Dale will have to dance out of the stern and try to convince Litton to hand over his oars. It's an arrangement that will force Litton to take a back seat just as the action gets good — something that cuts directly against his grain. Over the years, Litton has won his share of victories and also tasted some bitter defeats; but in conservation battles and on the river, he has held steadfastly to the idea that you never compromise and never surrender.

"People always tell me not to be extreme," Litton declares. "'Be reasonable!' they say. But I never felt it did any good to be reasonable about anything in conservation, because what you give away will never come back — ever. When it comes to saving wilderness, we can't be extreme enough. To compromise is to lose."

For a man like Litton, relinquishing control is an onerous thing. "Try not to write too much about Martin not rowing all the rapids," Tim whispers to me as the boats are being loaded. "This is the stuff that just breaks his heart."

When the last of the drybags are finally stowed, Bronco gives the word and we shove off. As we drift downstream, the cliffs soar upward in a layered tapestry of pastels: pinkish limestone, buff-colored sandstone, and deep-red shale. The combination contrasts well with the brightly painted hulls of the dories.

Along with their colors, the most noteworthy features of these boats are their sharply pointed bows and sterns and their "rocker" — that is, the way their bottoms flare up quickly at the front and back. The design enables a dory to ride dry in all but the roughest water and to pivot with extraordinary quickness, because only part of the hull is touching water at any moment.

Bronco, Litton, and the other pilots send their eleven-foot oars planing through the water with smooth, powerful strokes. As the blades emerge at the end of each stroke, the boatmen rotate their wrists with a subtle snap — a technique known as "feathering," which turns the blades parallel to the river's surface and sends droplets flicking off the ends, flashing in the canyon light. The rhythm is crisp, silent, precise.

Feather . . . flick . . . flash . . .

Breaking the water into V-shaped ripples, the dories achieve a visual alchemy seen nowhere else. They appear to be suspended partly on the surface of the river and partly — through a trick of the rocker and the magic of their radiance — on the air itself.

We won't see a horizon line again until we emerge from the canyon, in three weeks.

Over the next few days, a routine sets in. In the mornings we make our miles, pausing at side canyons for lunch and hikes. (Litton always skips the hikes but demands detailed field reports on which flowers are blooming.) By late afternoon we've usually reached camp. While the guides make dinner, the passengers gather around the *Sequoia*, break out cocktails, and listen to Litton hold forth. Our nights are dark and silent and studded with stars.

On the afternoon of the third day, we pull over at a beach where Bronco points to several large bore holes that, back in the fifties, were dynamited into the cliffs lining both sides of the river. This is where the U.S. Bureau of Reclamation once proposed anchoring the Marble Canyon Dam, a concrete wall that would have created a lake stretching all the way back to Glen Canyon Dam. A second structure, Bridge Canyon Dam, just above the edge of Lake Mead, nearly two hundred miles downstream, would have drowned the bottom portion of the canyon. The spot we're standing on would have been submerged beneath a three-hundred-foot-deep lake.

Back in the sixties, when construction was slated to begin, the Sierra Club was prepared to accept these monoliths as a necessary evil, a concession Litton deemed ludicrous. By 1963, he'd goaded David Brower, the Sierra Club's executive director and a man who once called Litton "my environmental conscience," into waging an all-out war against the scheme. When the dams were finally stopped cold, in 1975, the environmental movement that Litton had played such a central role in creating — usually without taking any credit — had scored one of its greatest victories.

Standing here, it's hard to imagine a better illustration of the impact one person can have. But the sight of the holes appears to send Litton wandering off into a more sobering mental landscape: the wilderness of his own regrets. "In so many ways, the American West really was a paradise, but look at it now," he tells the clients, who've gathered around him. "All you see are places that have been ruined because of greed. Ugliness. We had a paradise, and we lost it."

One of the passengers asks Litton if he thinks he made a difference. "I don't know," he says quietly, staring at his feet. "I suppose I never really succeeded in much of anything."

The passengers find Litton's comments disconcerting. But to boatmen like Blaustein — who know the full scope of what Litton achieved — his words just seem dead wrong.

Litton made his first trip down the Grand Canyon in 1955 with an early guide named P. T. Reilly, a venture that inspired him to start putting his own trips together. This was at the dawn of commercial river running, when pioneering outfitters like Georgie White and the Hatch brothers were experimenting with army-surplus pontoons, which would morph into the thirty-foot motor rigs and eighteen-foot oar rafts that are now the mainstays of Grand Canyon guiding. But for reasons of tradition, aesthetics, and stubbornness, Litton was determined to stick with wood.

The most promising design was a modification of a Grand Banks cod-fishing dory called a McKenzie driftboat. In the early sixties, Litton purchased a handful of these craft from two Oregon boatwrights and began taking friends down the Colorado. Every summer, more people signed up. And every winter, Litton dashed back to Oregon for more boats, ordering up design changes with each batch.

It was all pretty much a lark until 1968, when a story Litton had written at *Sunset* about threats to the California redwoods was spiked and Litton, in a fury, resigned. Within a few years, he'd become both a full-time wilderness activist and the admiral of a tiny navy of commercial dories, each painted in a distinctive hue and christened after a natural wonder that, in Litton's eyes, had been heedlessly ruined by man. Names included *Hetch Hetchy* (a valley just north of Yosemite that was flooded by a dam in 1914) and *Music Temple* (a feature in Glen Canyon, drowned beneath Lake Powell in the sixties).

Litton recruited his earliest guides from California — most were ski instructors who couldn't tell a gunwale from a chine but were willing to fling themselves down the Colorado armed with little more than cut-off jeans and toothbrushes. Together, Litton and this ragged platoon dedicated themselves to the idea that providing cheap, no-frills trips to high school teachers, Boy Scouts, and housewives would build a constituency of citizens willing to fight to protect the canyon.

During the earliest trips, everybody had to follow the boss. At the approach to each rapid, the boatmen would scramble to clip the passengers into their life jackets while Litton stood, waved his arms, and explained what needed to be done. "This is Sockdolager — for God's sake, pull left at the tongue!" he'd scream. Each oarsman would relay the message back to the next, then pray he wouldn't screw up too badly. The results were often spectacular.

One summer at Crystal, a rapid Litton's rookie guides were too terrified to row, he took three dories down by himself — hiking up the shore after each run — and flipped them all, shearing off hatch lids, splintering sterns, shattering oars. At Bedrock, the *Bright Angel* (named for a creek inside the canyon) was sucked beneath a boulder that raked off its entire side. And in 1970, Blaustein managed to ram the *Hetch Hetchy* into a rock in a rapid called Unkar, splitting the hull from oarlock to oarlock.

"I basically broke the boat in half," Blaustein recalls glumly.

After each disaster, the guides would repair the worst of the carnage with plywood, duct tape, marine putty, and even driftwood. Then they'd go out and break everything all over again. "That was definitely the golden age of Grand Canyon boating," recalls Rondo Buecheler. "And what made it golden was there were absolutely no rules, and we had no idea what the hell we were doing."

When his crew finally started getting the hang of things in the late seventies, Litton stopped leading every trip and instead kept tabs using his company's vintage Cessna 195. He'd load up the plane with blocks of ice and cases of beer and then roar down the canyon at 150 miles an hour, buzzing the tops of the tamarisk trees and looking for his camps.

"We'd hear his approach and it'd be like 'Here he comes; *everybody run!*'" laughs Andre Potochnik, a veteran dory guide. "Pedal-to-the-metal Martin. He'd strafe us with supplies, then fly off to Washington to lobby for whatever wilderness issue he was fighting at the time."

By the 1980s, the dory fleet had become the envy of the river, and its oarsmen sat at the pinnacle of the guiding hierarchy. Whenever Litton returned to the canyon on a trip, boatmen working for motor and raft companies would pull alongside him in the eddies, or stroll over to his camp at night, and beseech him for a job. Around this time, however, Litton's abysmal business instincts — which included giving away trips to virtually anyone interested in conservation — began driving his company to the edge. In 1987, he was finally forced to sell Grand Canyon Dories to George Wendt, the president of OARS. The National Park Service approved the transaction on the condition that Wendt would devote two thirds of his trips to dory ventures for ten years — a commitment that Wendt has maintained ever since, in honor of the heritage Litton created.

"What Martin did was just nuts," says Blaustein. "I mean, here was this guy who wanted to run this great big river in these itty-bitty boats that broke every time they hit a rock. But, God, they were beautiful, and riding in them somehow made you feel very humble and pure and connected. And so Martin made it work. That was his vision for the Grand Canyon. It was the way he knew it should be done."

All along the canyon, news has spread that Litton is on the river. One morning, a party of boaters pulls over to listen while he tells off-color jokes. A few days later, a crew of archaeologists beaches their powerboats, whips out a banjo and fiddle, and performs an impromptu riff called "The Martin Litton Breakdown." Another night, a fleet of rafts pulls into an eddy just so the trip leader can toss Litton a bottle of Bombay Sapphire gin. "Well, wasn't that nice?" says Litton, studying the label like it's a lost page from the Talmud. "Who in the world was that fellow?"

Toward the end of our first week, the canyon begins to change. First, the space between the cliffs opens up, letting us see all the way to the South Rim, more than five thousand feet above. A day later, the walls narrow dramatically, and as the dories enter a ferocious rapid called Hance, the gates slam shut on the Inner Gorge.

This is the subbasement of the canyon. The walls are blacker than coal and the rapids feral. Every day they hit us with staccato bursts. Sockdolager, Grapevine, Horn Creek. Granite, Hermit, Crystal. Waltenburg, Bedrock, Upset. The huge boulders lining these cauldrons create deep, recirculating holes into which the entire river seems to disappear. The current seethes and churns, folding back on itself to form whirlpools, boils, and massive eddies. The rides are fierce, furious, and shockingly cold.

A half-century after Litton's first expedition, these waves are still enormous and their hydraulics explosive, but the challenge is not quite the same. The dories are now made from sturdy, closed-cell foam instead of wood, and oarsmen like Bronco have run the river so many times that it's rare to see them even flirt with a submerged rock. But while much of the carnage has faded, the dories' power over the guides endures.

A typical dory apprenticeship can last nearly a decade, longer than any other in the canyon. By the time a boatman has earned his place, his attachment to these custom-made craft — which cost up to $17,000, more than a season's salary for most guides — is absolute. You can see it in the way the boatmen fret over their dories: spit-polishing microscopic scratches on the hulls, glowering when passengers track dirt onto the decks. Perhaps the deepest evidence of their incorrigible love, however, comes out during the winter, when they're off the water.

Back home in Flagstaff, Duffy spends hours carving miniature replicas of his craft, the *Paria*, and his mom, 'Ote, touches up the stern of *Dark Canyon*, which she has decorated with a hand-painted scene of a butterfly landing on a wildflower. In Mesa, Colorado, Rondo tromps across the street to Bronco's driveway, where the men climb into Bronco's boat, the *Yampa*, wearing their down jackets while they drink Scotch and reminisce about rapids. As for Eric Sjoden, a few years ago he built a scale model one third the size of his dory, the *Virgin*, and converted it into a bathtub at his cabin in Whitefish, Montana. He spends winter evenings soaking and dreaming about returning to the river.

"The dories have a grace in design that is astonishing — they're just so fucking gorgeous," says Brad Dimock, who is coming out of retirement this season because he can't bear to be away from the boats. "The first time I ever rowed one, I was just stunned. And that feeling never really left. They're that cool."

"What's so appealing about a dory?" says Bronco one afternoon, borrowing a line from Litton. "It's pretty simple. Rafts are ugly. Dories are beautiful."

By our second week, the canyon isn't the only thing changing: the wind and water have started to peel back the more constrained layers of people's personalities. Doug Vavrick, a political consultant from Seattle, and his wife, Kathleen, frolic naked in the shallows during the evenings. And Pat Newman, who started the trip shy and withdrawn, has turned giddy. Each morning, she dashes around camp giving everyone a hug.

"Hugging's done an awful lot around here," Litton observes after accepting a postbreakfast embrace. "It's what the younger generation seems to like to do." (Newman is sixty.)

The only person who hasn't transformed is Vernita Allen, but that's because she doesn't need to.

A seventy-three-year-old retiree from Kansas City who's been down the river three times, Allen has undergone extensive cancer treatments and is now so weak that every day the guides have to set her in and lift her out of the boats. She knows this is her last trip. And in the process of bidding farewell to each feature of the canyon, she long ago arrived in the cerebral zone that the other passengers are just now discovering.

"I've seen a few people go down this canyon and not get changed, but not many," she said to me one day. "There's just something about how minuscule you feel compared to how long it took to put this place together. It seems to put things in balance. It wakes you up. It opens your eyes. And afterwards, things are not the same. It's that space in the middle — that's why I come here."

When Allen said this, I had no idea what she meant. But then, below Dubendorff, something happens and I do.

While floating along and staring up at the pinkish rock walls, it suddenly seems as if the canyon has reached out and cupped me lightly in the palm of its hand. Part of the sensation has surely come from bobbing down a current of warm air on the surface of a cool, green river. More than that, though, the feeling of languorous buoyancy has arisen from where I find myself in time. The circumstances I've come from seem irretrievably far behind: things that weighed on me at work are now irrelevant. Yet I'm also far enough from the end — of the trip, of the canyon, of this particular moment — that it's unnecessary to brace for reentry. I am suspended in a state of betweenness, not unlike the rocker of a dory. A state in which I can pivot and float in the luminous embrace of a pink-and-emerald haze that — right here, right now — strikes me as our true destination, the marrow of the journey.

A few minutes later, we pull over for lunch. After finishing my sandwich, I spot Litton sitting in the shade of a tamarisk and wander over to ask if he's gotten something to eat. He looks up at me, his blue eyes momentarily vacant, still lost in his thoughts.

"Thank you for asking," he replies after a long pause. "I've had everything I could ever wish for."

*

That, as it turns out, isn't entirely true.

For more than two weeks, Litton has graciously resigned himself to his subordinate role, cheerfully needling Blaustein while Tim Dale gets the *Sequoia* through the worst white water. But as the trip enters its final phase, the frustrations bottled up inside Mr. No Compromise are about to collide with the biggest obstacle on the river.

Just below the Toroweap Overlook, 179 miles downstream from Lees Ferry, the Colorado drops off a ledge and detonates. This is Lava Falls, a chaos of water and rock that, over the years, has ravaged more boats than any other rapid in the canyon. Even today it's a gamble, and when things go wrong, the results can be frightening: boatmen blown from their seats, oars cartwheeling through the air, passengers swimming for their lives.

The night before we reach Lava, Litton has a message for Bronco: "I've never been a passenger through Lava, and I'll be damned if I'm going to start now," he declares. "I'll walk around."

The next afternoon, the river is flowing at nine thousand cubic feet per second, not a bad level for running Lava. We'll go down the right side, a route whose entrance is extremely hard to judge. The tongue runs just to the right of a massive ledge hole that claimed the life of a client named Norine Abrams in August 1984.

A boatman who threads this entrance perfectly has just enough time to square up his bow before the current drives him directly into the center of an enormous, V-shaped standing wave. The hope is that this wave will push the boat slightly to the left. If it does the opposite, the boat rockets right and washes alongside a glistening slab of lava called the Big Black Rock. The rock is where Lava's other victim, a client named Andalea Buzzard, was stripped of her life jacket and drowned in August 1977. (Neither fatality occurred on an OARS or Grand Canyon Dories trip.)

After the crew ties the boats off to the right-hand bank and scouts the rapid, Litton and Bronco put their heads together for a powwow. Then Litton returns to the *Sequoia* and, without any ceremony, takes his seat at the oars.

"Let's move," he says quietly.

As we drift into the current, things suddenly get very quiet. Sitting in the *Sequoia*'s bow with Curtis Newell, I can hear only the creak of the oars and the muffled roar of the falls. "Well," Litton announces, "here we go."

He handles the entrance flawlessly: you could spit into the ledge hole as we flash past it and slice down Lava's incline toward the V-wave. Litton gets in two good strokes, lining up the dory. Then the V-wave smashes us with the force of a runaway coal truck. The river gathers into a fist and punches straight over the bow, a haymaker of solid water as thick as wet cement. The decks and the footwells are swamped. The boat reels.

In the midst of this mess, I turn to see that one of the *Sequoia's* oars has been wrenched out of its oarlock. I also can't help noticing that Litton — who's been drenched and spin-cycled like a cat in a washing machine — looks happier and more alive at this moment than any sane eighty-seven-year-old probably should. The old fart is actually grinning.

Then I face forward to see that we're sluicing directly toward the Big Black Rock. Litton heaves on his remaining oar with everything he's got. No dice: the rock's coming up fast, and we're about to hit it.

As the river rolls around the massive rock, it tends to create a pillow of moving water that rises and ebbs with each surge. Through a combination of angle, timing, and Littonian luck, the *Sequoia* arrives just as this pillow is building. Instead of slamming us into the rock, the water cradles the boat for a second, then gives it a nudge and washes us around the left side. The rock's dripping surface races past, almost within reach, and we find ourselves back in the main current, bucking through the tail waves.

"You did it, Martin! You did it!" the boat's four passengers yell.

"I didn't do anything at all!" he protests. "I was rowing shabbily. Very shabbily."

"Jesus, Martin," someone calls out, "if you didn't do it, who the hell else did?"

"Why, the boat, of course," he says, indignant at having to spell out something so obvious. "It was the dory that did it."

Two days later we make our last camp, on the edge of Lake Mead.

The next morning, Vernita Allen, Pat Newman, and the rest of the passengers bid farewell and board a blue jet boat that will connect them to city-bound shuttle buses. The guides lash the dories and rafts together and, with help from an outboard, begin motoring toward the gates of the Grand Wash Cliffs, where the land flattens and the river sprawls into the slack water of Lake Mead.

Eric Sjoden and Ryan Howe set up a faded purple lounge chair so Litton has a place to sit. Bronco hands him a sandwich that Rondo prepared the night before. While Curtis sets a bottle of cold Dos Equis into the cup holder of Litton's chair, Tim unfolds Duffy's teal-colored umbrella and holds it over the old man's head. Then, as the rig drifts toward the lake, everyone gathers around and sits at Litton's feet. For the boatmen, it's a chance to relish this last bit of river with their old boss and to think about his place in the canyon.

What will probably endure most in the minds of these guides is the memory of how, against all logic and common sense, Litton launched a fleet of frail boats bearing the haunted names of vanished wonders. They'll also remember him as a warrior cut from the same cloth as Ed Abbey and David Brower: a fighter who turned the tables on stronger adversaries. And they'll remember that Litton, at eighty-seven, insisted on rowing himself through the fury of Lava Falls.

"He taught us about belief and how to make a stand," Bronco says to me quietly as we pass through the Grand Wash Cliffs. "He showed us that when you really believe in something, you don't ever compromise. Compromise is what you let the other guy do."

All those things are surely worth remembering. But what I'll remember from this journey is something different.

I never knew Litton during his period of towering strength, so I won't be able to recall his victories, his militancy, or his fire. Instead, what will stay with me is the memory of how he conducted himself as he confronted forces that can never be defeated — age, infirmity, and time — and how his conduct illuminated the Grand Canyon in an unusual way.

These days, a Grand Canyon river trip is no longer the same pioneering quest it was when men like Powell and Litton first took it on. But what remains is, in some ways, even bolder and more challenging: an odyssey that offers incontrovertible evidence of how small we are — not much different, really, from the fossils laid down 340 million years ago in the Redwall limestone above the Marble Canyon dam site. By imparting this sense of almost overwhelming humility, a trip down the canyon opens the door to insights about the place's deeper relevance.

When you row the river with Martin Litton, you come to understand that the Grand Canyon is "America's greatest scenic treasure" not simply because of the thrills and the fun — which are tremendous — but because it reminds us of who we are, and who we are not, and of what we most need to become. This isn't something Litton ever said to me directly, but I think he knows it in his bones. He knows it because the elements of his legacy — his dories, his canyon, his river — all come together to underscore one emphatic little parcel of truth.

Which is what, exactly?

Well, as it happens, the Water Rat nailed that one, too. "It's my world, and I don't want any other," he said of the river. "What it hasn't got is not worth having, and what it doesn't know is not worth knowing."

CAITLIN FLANAGAN

The Price of Paradise

FROM *The New Yorker*

WHEN I WAS TWO YEARS OLD, I traveled across the country by train from New York to Oakland with my mother and my seven-year-old sister. In the observation car on the first morning, we fell into company with an older gentleman who was journeying slowly home to Honolulu, and who had just suffered a considerable misfortune: he had lost his glasses, only a few hours into the first day of a long trip that he had intended to spend reading. While my mother commiserated with him, I thrust an investigating hand into the crevice between the seat cushions and, to everyone's astonishment, pulled out the glasses. I remember the episode — the bristly prickle of velour on my soft fingers; the stunned delight of the grownups — in the vivid, dreamlike manner of most invented memories. But for years afterward I was in possession of the two gifts the man sent me in thanks: a six-inch-tall hula girl and a plastic charm bracelet with a dangling pineapple and palm tree.

The hula girl became the queen of the souvenir shelf, a location littered with trinkets acquired on my family's edifying vacations, and to me she represented a different kind of holiday altogether: one that was undertaken on purely hedonistic impulses, responding only to the deep human need for sand and sea and tropical fruit punches. I was the daughter of an academic whose field was Irish history, and while I had known the thrill of jet travel (that is what it was called in those days, and the very words suggested money and comfort), our airplane trips had always dumped me at the same unromantic port of call: the Dublin airport, where sheep grazed beside the runway and international travelers were sometimes herded into a drafty immigration hall and sprayed down with pesticide to prevent the spread of hoof-and-mouth disease.

On the other hand — aloha. The very notion of a lei greeting — beautiful girls with lush flowers on a balmy tarmac — drove me wild with longing and frustration. My sense that Hawaii was a destination of singular allure was reinforced by a childhood heavily invested in watching television. The C & H Sugar Company had a riveting advertisement that featured a little girl running through a field of sugarcane, a hibiscus blossom tucked behind one ear. Oahu was the destination of an unprecedented three-part *Brady Bunch,* a kind of extended advertisement for United Airlines and the Sheraton Waikiki. When I was a bit older, I began reading Joan Didion's famous essays on the islands, with their mesmerizing descriptions of the Royal Hawaiian Hotel, a palace in Honolulu where wealthy Californians sat on a roped-off beach and took the sun together. It was "an enclave of apparent strangers ever on the verge of discovering that their nieces roomed in Lagunita at Stanford the same year, or that their best friends lunched together during the last Crosby. The fact that anyone behind the rope would understand the word 'Crosby' to signify a golf tournament at Pebble Beach suggests the extent to which the Royal Hawaiian is not merely a hotel but a social idea." This was a degree of glamour that threatened to overwhelm me; my experience of sunbathing had been at the community pool, an enclave of housewives ever on the verge of discovering that pork chops were on special at Safeway. The honeymoon following my first wedding was to have consisted of two weeks in Hawaii (at last!) but was then downgraded to a more financially prudent week at an all-in resort in St. Martin, intensifying my fierce, indignant resolve to visit those sun-kissed islands.

And so, inevitably, my first trip to Hawaii (undertaken at the advanced age of thirty-four, with husband No. 2 and my aged parents in tow) was disappointing. I had by then ventured far beyond what had once been the twin poles of my existence, California and Ireland. But Hawaii, I unhappily discovered, wasn't so different from California (palm trees, blue water, Tony Roma's). Worse, because of the intense green and the sheer, mist-shrouded mountains, much of it looked an awful lot like Ireland. I was eager to feel far-flung; the islands of the Hawaiian archipelago are, after all, some of the most remote in the world. Among the many captivating details in Didion's essays from the seventies was a description of the mainland newspapers arriving a day or two late, lending "the events of the day a peculiar and unsettling distance." But, modernity being what it is, we weren't in the condo five minutes before someone zapped on CNN. In a rude twist of fate, we happened to be there on St. Patrick's Day, the night of which we spent not basking in the trade winds beneath a canopy of stars but hunkered down watching a PBS documentary on the potato famine.

The strange thing about this episode was not that I had a disappointing time; the cost of seeing the world is often disillusionment. What's curious is that I've repeated the experience five times. It seems that I have scarcely unpacked my bags from one dispiriting visit before I start dreaming about going back. I've wondered if I should stay at one of the famous resorts, or on a different island. When I was a girl, the precise locations of my schoolmates' enthralling stories of Hawaiian vacations changed with such regularity that I feared there wouldn't be any Hawaii left for me to go to. Just when I had a grasp of the geography and the principal delights of Waikiki — Diamond Head looming at the end of the crescent beach; the string of white high-rises; the Kodak Hula show; the moan of the conch shell signaling luau time — kids started saying that Honolulu was too crowded, too common. Luaus? Those were for grandmas. It was now about catching a wave, it was now about Maui — unspoiled, wild. Then it was Kauai, the Garden Isle, so unvisited that you might find yourself the only person on the beach.

Perhaps the sweetest and most gently misguided impulse of parenthood is to give one's children precisely the thing most yearned for in one's own youth. One Christmas when I was small, my father gave me a model-train set, and he lay on his tummy all day switching tracks and humming happily to himself, while I tiptoed around him with my Barbies. In the same spirit, I resolved long ago that my own little boys' holidays would not be spent in Irish B & Bs redolent of turf fires and rashers. I would give them Hawaii. And I would not stint.

A travel guide published in 1930 advised, "If you're going to be very grand, stay at the Royal Hawaiian." This is no longer true. Today, if you are going to be very grand you must go to the place where grandness, in its every possible connotation, is king. You must go to the Grand Wailea.

*

The Grand Wailea, which is situated on a blamelessly beautiful stretch of beach on the leeward side of Maui, has 780 guest rooms, six restaurants (one of them floating), numerous boutiques, more than a thousand full-time workers, a private medical practice, a wedding chapel, a business center, the largest spa in the state, an art gallery that includes four Picasso monotypes and eighteen Léger bronzes, a kids' camp, a seasonal children's concierge, a night club, and the largest ballroom on the island (twenty-eight thousand square feet, not counting the contiguous, twelve-thousand-square-foot Haleakala Gardens, which serve as the ballroom's "pre-function" area). Arguably the hotel's most famous feature — in a tight race with its legendary prices — is the Canyon Activity Pool, a two-thousand-foot-long complex of interconnected swimming pools, water slides, waterfalls, grottoes, raging rapids, and the world's only "water elevator," all of which can be traversed in a ten-minute "swim ride."

The notion that a Hawaiian hotel might be a residential amusement park with a South Seas theme has been steadily evolving since the fifties, when the industrialist Henry Kaiser opened the Hawaiian Village at Waikiki. It had thatched huts and a man-made lagoon, and guests were transported from the airport in an open-air bus with a grass roof. The hotel's slogan — "The Fun Resort" — was a rebuke to the Royal Hawaiian, with its afternoon teas and formal dinners. The resort begat the "mega-resort," which, in turn, begat the Grand Hyatt Wailea, which opened its doors in 1991 and on which the Japanese developer Takeshi Sekiguchi spent $600 million — reportedly the largest amount of money ever invested in a hotel at the time — mere months before the crash of the Japanese bubble economy. The hotel struggled along — changing management, dropping the "Hyatt," and eventually being sold in 1998 at a loss of more than $200 million — but the developers' hunch that its commanding magnitude would excite considerable curiosity proved accurate. Indeed, the hotel is often completely booked months in advance. It was to this supercharged pleasure zone that I recently repaired with my husband and our six-year-old twins.

The family vacation, as it is now experienced by many members of the upper middle class, is marked by numerous and often conflicting desires. Busy parents want to spend some uninterrupted time with their children, but they also crave a substantial break from those children. Dad wants sex, but Mom has envisioned an interlude of near-monastic solitude. The intention is to leave work worries far behind, but modern telecommunications have become so advanced, and the contemporary workplace so fast-paced, that the inclination is often to stay in regular contact with the office. The Grand Wailea seems to have an uncannily precise grasp of each of these competing goals, and to have found a way to make money on all of them. When I mentioned to some acquaintances that we were planning a visit, a woman whipped around and said with astonishing vehemence, "Don't!" She had recently been there, and added in disgust, "They charge you for every single thing." She suggested that we change our reservation to the Four Seasons, which is just down the beach and which she described almost as a Communist collective compared with the gouging Grand Wailea.

But when we arrived at the hotel we were received graciously: wreathed in orchid leis and encouraged to help ourselves to cups of tasty iced guava juice. Only much later, while reading some very fine print, did I learn that we had actually bought both treats. The sixteen-dollar-a-day "resort fee" covers one lei greeting per guest and a "Welcome Mai Tai punch (nonalcoholic)." Our room was like a little shop. In addition to the standard mini-bar setup, there was a basket of suntanning products ($70), shrink-wrapped bottles of Evian, playing cards, and children's shampoo for sale. We begged the kids not to touch any of the merchandise.

"Don't forget anything when you go to the beach," the bellman said after dropping off our suitcases. "It's a long way back."

We didn't doubt him, because we could sort of see the beach from our room. I had been persuaded by several members of the pro-Grand Wailea faction back home to ante up for a room in the Napua Tower, which a promotional brochure described as "our hotel within the resort" and an article in *TravelAge West* called "a 100-room oasis," separated from the main grounds by a locked gate. These descriptions made the rest of the outrageously expensive resort seem like a kind of Calcutta-by-the-sea, from which one would crave sanctuary and safety. But the Napua Tower turns out to be one of the greatest marketing innovations of all time. With an audacity that would have impressed P. T. Barnum, the Grand Wailea has managed to turn the concept of "exclusivity" into a plausible excuse for charging some of its highest rates for some of its worst rooms: those with only a partial view of the distant sea. Ours, attractive though unremarkable — except for its majestic marble bathroom — cost $590 per night.

It was time for our first swim ride, and we needed to make haste; the water slides closed at six o'clock each evening, and it was already past four. First, a walk through the lobby — as vast as several football fields, open-air, very pleasant. Then a descent down a sweeping marble staircase, followed by circumnavigation of the adults-only Hibiscus Pool, at which the main pastime seemed to be baking like an oiled capon in a hot oven and reading *The Bourne Supremacy*. At last, the Activity Pool. You register for its use as you would for surgery, by identifying yourself, having your records checked on a computer, and holding out your arm so that you can be tagged with an identifying wristband. The pool is loud and enormous, and hard to figure out. From where we stood, clutching our newly issued towels, we could see a scuba-diving pool, a man-made beach, a lagoon with a volleyball net, and a grotto containing the egress of two long slides, into which riders landed with a scream every minute or so. Despite the noise and confusion, I found the place inviting, if for no other reason than the water's dazzling blue translucence.

The four of us climbed up a long flight of stairs constructed from ohia wood that had been lashed together, *Gilligan's Island* style. At the top was a small pool poised high above the complex. Here we had a choice: we could cheat death on a slide so long and dangerous that we would have to be cleared for departure by an attendant — she wielded a walkie-talkie and was in constant contact with someone at splashdown — or we could take a far shorter slide that led through a series of meandering rivers and bays. We opted for the latter, shooting down the little slide and landing in a second, slightly larger pool, with another slide at its far end. And then we got the hang of it, crashing down longer watery tunnels, careering in rapid currents past statues of the old Hawaiian gods, emerging in tiny, tranquil pools, and then lurching eagerly through chest-high water to the next slide. At one point, we ducked under a waterfall and found ourselves in a cave containing a swim-up bar, where the atmosphere of good, clean fun suddenly vanished. Somehow, people had managed to get cigarettes in there, so it was smoky and close; booming, drunken voices reverberated off the rock walls. The boys immediately apprehended that the bartender could produce milk shakes. When I handed my son Conor an Oreo smoothie, he accidentally sloshed half of it out of the cup. Normally, we would have scrambled for napkins, but in the swim-up bar there was nothing to do but watch the slick of goo dissipate and drift away. We swam onward, plummeting down white-water rapids, and then letting the current take us to a deep pool with a Tarzan swing. We were chatting with another set of parents when my husband saw a small opaque object bobbing in the water. He reached out and picked it up; it was an empty tube of "personal feminine lubricant." We all stared. "Makes you want to keep your head above water," the other dad said. I looked warily upstream for what might be coming next, but I could see nothing except the sparkle of sunlight on the bright water.

For what we were spending on our room at the Grand Wailea, we could have stayed at one of the famous hotels of Europe, or at one of the grand old American resorts — the Broadmoor, say, or the Breakers. But these places were not specifically designed to allow us to have our children at our side virtually around the clock, while simultaneously — and guiltlessly — enjoying some of the adult pleasures that we deny ourselves back home. When a parent bellies up to the Napua Tower bar for a stiff one, his child is just across the room, bellying up to the knee-high Shirley Temple bar and mixing a virgin highball of his own. At the Grand Wailea, children and parents exist in a kind of ageless Neverland, in which grownups spend hours happily splashing in kiddie pools and children climb into booster seats at a restaurant where adult entrées cost $40 or $50.

The older hotels, moreover, tend to be haunted by disapproving characters with long memories. A woman who has been visiting the Breakers for fifty years recently carped to a reporter from the *Los Angeles Times* that the children there are "out of control." But at the Grand Wailea there are no censorious blue-hairs bumming you out for your lax parenting techniques. In fact, the most "adult" presence is that of the hotel management, which, like an indulgent but watchful parent, at once coddles and scolds its guests. During our first night there, a letter from the concierge was slipped under the door, informing us of the next day's roster of fun and also instructing us not to go to breakfast in bare feet or to the Napua cocktail reception in a bathing suit. The fine print on the sumptuous Spa Grande brochure forbids "ladies on their cycle" from sullying the Jacuzzi. An army of workers is employed to pick up after the guests who litter the place like careless children, dropping their plastic cocktail glasses wherever they happen to drain them, and leaving behind a trail of pineapple rinds and flower garnishes.

At the Royal Hawaiian, where we stopped for a couple of nights before going to Maui, the prices are steep but not exorbitant, and old-fashioned proprieties continue to exert themselves. The question of whether it would be appropriate to sashay through the magnificent lobby in swimsuit and flip-flops is answered before it is asked — the bellman advises guests of the location of the old Bathers' Elevator, which lets you out in an underground corridor buzzing with the secret, purposeful commerce of the hotel: waiters rolling trays for room service, pink-uniformed maids delivering loads of pink towels and sheets to the laundry. Waikiki Beach is as crowded as ever, a restless parade of people on the march: honeymooners and sunburned families and tough-looking teenagers with boom boxes. But they still give a wide and respectful berth to the ribbon of sand behind the low-slung pink chain that marks the private beach. In the open-air Surf Room, the food is terrible and the service indifferent, but diners sit patiently under pink-and-white awnings, sipping restorative mai tais and talking in soft voices.

The pace of life at the Royal Hawaiian is slow and almost somnolent. Indeed, the principal activity is remembering — or, more accurately, imagining — what it was like in the old days, when children, if they were brought along at all, were accompanied by a starched nanny and were rarely a nuisance. In the cool shadows of the lobby facing the Coconut Grove, there are photo displays of the famous opening-night dinner, and in a glass-topped case there are some battered silver serving pieces and china place settings from that evening. Beside each elevator there are desks with heavy black Bakelite telephones, still operational. When the maids turn down the beds at night, they leave behind vanda orchids and pink cards bearing a tidbit of historical information for you to ponder — thirty-five thousand barrels of cement were used in the hotel's construction; in the days before air conditioning, guest rooms were cooled via louvered doors — before lights-out.

None of this, of course, appeals much to children. Nor does the hotel seem eager to encourage their patronage. The Surf Room offers a children's menu, but trying to cajole hungry children through its de facto cocktail hour and the interminable wait for food is a fresh hell, mai tai or no. The pool is small and plain, and few kids will be stoked to learn that they can borrow a cribbage set from the attendants.

When traveling with small children, it is a good idea to head in an easterly direction, for the time change will work in your favor. Head west and you're doomed. Our first morning at the Grand Wailea, my boys were awake by 4:30 — entirely, deeply awake. This might not have been so unpleasant were we not all sharing the same room.

As thrifty as my parents were, it would not have occurred to them to save money on a holiday by bunking with their children. For them and for many of their friends, the economics of travel were simple: if you couldn't afford two rooms at the good hotel, you took two rooms at the modest one, and if you couldn't afford two rooms there, you stayed home. Even as a young child, I had a sense that my parents had a private life in which (how maddening!) I figured not at all, and in which they indulged in various puzzling adult pleasures, involving gin-and-tonics, and cigarettes, and perhaps my mother's silky negligees. A tropical vacation was once so thoroughly associated with pleasures of the flesh and a promise of marital renewal incompatible with childcare that little ones, on whom fine linens and outdoor dance floors would be wasted anyway, were often left at home with a sitter. But now, in the frantic attempt to fuse sophisticated recreation with familial duty, entire families often occupy a single room at the toniest places. So there we all were, watching cartoons at minimum volume and waiting for daybreak. After breakfast, we would be springing some unwelcome news on the children: they were going to spend the morning at kids' camp.

Resorts, of course, have not always had kids' camps. A century ago, several of the older ones had schools on the property that young guests attended, and also children's dining rooms, to which the commotion of nursery suppers could be confined. Such amenities were not dedicated to the entertainment of the little ones; they existed so that parents on holiday might seamlessly re-create the habits of home, which involved seeing as little of one's children as possible. Times have changed. Fifteen years ago, the Hyatt Corporation opened the first Camp Hyatt, an idea so perfectly of its time — providing guests' children with lots of organized fun and close supervision — that it has been widely copied by resorts all over the world.

The problem is that children often don't want to go to these places. We had tried to rally enthusiasm the night before by taking the boys on a field trip to the camp, but we got stuck in an elevator with a man and his small son, who was screaming, "I won't go! I won't go!" and it had seemed best to abort the mission. The boys sensed that we were equivocal and guilt-ridden about sending them — even for a short morning session — and they attacked our vulnerability with gusto. "We just want to be with *you,*" my son Patrick said with a heart-piercing sweetness.

Nonetheless, we took them to Camp Grande, uneasy in the knowledge that the best parents don't drop their kids and run — they go to camp with them, taking hula lessons and racing around the hotel grounds on scavenger hunts. We needn't have worried: as soon as we got there, the boys ran off to learn more about Hawaiian culture and to play Nintendo. After filling out a series of forms that were both reassuring and disturbing — requiring the names of primary-care physicians and health insurance, making provisions for emergency medical treatment — it seemed possible to slip out, so we did.

We had spent the previous seventy-two hours entertaining our children on the flight, persuading them to use seat belts in the taxi, shushing them in the room, settling their quarrels, confiscating their Game Boys, finding their sandals, encouraging them to eat some fresh vegetables, wrestling them down for sunblock application. Walking along the corridor, suddenly liberated from this round-the-clock burden, we felt stunned, weightless. For three hours, we could do anything we liked.

My husband headed up to the room to call the office, and I hurried off to the spa.

Spas promote themselves as purveyors of novel physical sensations — the seaweed wrap, the salt scrub — but many of their clients, harried middle-aged women like me, are drawn to them for the sensory deprivation they offer, the dim lighting and warm fog, and the solicitous, murmuring voices. Still, each establishment must have its signature attraction, and Spa Grande's is called Termé Wailea Hydrotherapy, a complex of Jacuzzis, chilly plunge pools, specialty showers, and — the centerpiece — a set of five "aromatic baths." In the brochure, these five tubs are attractive; in reality, they are smallish and filled with murky water. One is the color of sludge (healing mud); another is the rich, organic green of pond water. Visitors are instructed to shower after using each one, to prevent cross-contamination, an unpleasant reminder that the tubs are essentially filled with cloudy, used bath water. Also included in the price of admission to Spa Grande is a procedure that calls for you to lie on a metal table in a room that has tiled walls and a drain in the floor and be scrubbed down by an attendant with a loofah and a hose. The only thing to do is yak away, as one does during the most unpleasant parts of a gynecological exam.

After my scrubbing, I felt thoroughly clean — nakedness itself seemed to have been brought to a tender new level — and I couldn't imagine spending another moment in one of the hot tubs or showers without dissolving like an Alka-Seltzer. I wandered around the facility, and thus accidentally discovered Valhalla: a shaded lanai with two neat rows of lounge chairs, none of them occupied.

Somewhere else, this might not have been such a remarkable sight, but at the Grand Wailea one of the hardest things to lay claim to isn't an oceanfront suite or a private butler but a lowly deck chair. Getting a good one at the Activity Pool, which is ringed by countless hundreds of them, involves strategy and determination. It also requires a ruthless disregard for one's fellow guests — most of the chairs spend their days reserved but unoccupied. Some guests get up at dawn and stumble down to the pool to spread towels across a few prime seats, and then head back to their rooms to sleep for a few more hours. The hotel polices against such practices; a special team of poolside "maitre d's" clears off possessions that are left unattended for more than three hours, but guests find countless ways to get around the authorities. Families traveling with nannies sometimes send them down to the pool before sunrise, where they are charged with guarding the real estate.

Reserving a chair is rude, yet most of the people I encountered at the hotel were not rude. The husbands were gregarious to a fault; the wives were quick to take an interest in one another's children. But something about the hotel's prices occasionally causes a breakdown in the social order; the thought of spending so much money on a tropical vacation and not even getting to sit in a deck chair produces a kind of madness. The hotel capitalizes on this by charging rent on the best chairs — those shaded by umbrellas or cabanas. Just as dieting produces an instant fixation on food, the chair situation seemed to be a preoccupation all over the hotel; friends who stayed at the Grand Wailea last winter remember their chair struggles more vividly than anything else. I lay down on the best of the lanai deck chairs, closed my eyes, and rested in the filtered light.

The short holiday wore on, and the days quickly developed a pattern: morning and afternoon visits to the Activity Pool, an off-site lunch somewhere cheap, dinner cobbled from the Napua Tower's "hearty hors d'oeuvres" spread, and a nighttime walk around the hotel's capacious gardens, which were lit by tiki torches and almost deserted. With each visit to the Activity Pool, the boys' passion for it swelled, as did my dread. Just walking onto the wet flagstones at its outermost edge, hearing the yelps of delight and the roaring waterfalls and piped-in music, and seeing the personal grooming services — pedicures, hairstyling, temporary tattoos — offered poolside, I became tense. Excursions took on the nature of a prison break. Indeed, a high point of the trip occurred when we loaded our bag of dirty laundry into the minivan and escaped to a Laundromat, where we spent a happy hour eating Doritos and watching a TV that had been chained to the dryers.

Only when we got home did I realize that we had never ventured onto the famous beach. There is a town in Wisconsin that is apparently composed of nothing but water parks; we could have gone there for a tenth of the price. This thought discomfited me for a while, but as the weeks passed I began to indulge in something that academics who study vacations call "rosy retrospection." The photographs came back, and we all looked very jolly in them. I propped one up on my desk. It wasn't the most flattering shot of us, but the sea and the sky are the make-believe blue of a picture postcard, and it stirred something in me. We plan to return in March.

SEAN FLYNN

Where They Love Americans . . .
for a Living

FROM *GQ*

THERE'S AN EXPAT in a bar called the Blue Marlin, which is on the ground floor of a pink hotel in downtown San José, Costa Rica. He used to be a detective, did a bit of vice, enough to know how the world works, how people think. It's late, and he's drinking gin.

"These girls," he says, waving his glass at the *chicas*. The place is packed with *chicas*. "They average out at, what? An eight and a half? Nine?"

He's partial to Latin women. Make it seven.

"OK, seven. But, c'mon, a *lot* of them are beautiful."

Conceded, assuming your taste runs to python-tight clothing. And, you know, prostitutes.

"Now look at the guys." Another sweep with the glass. Almost every man in the place is a gringo. "Guys like them, to get a girl like one of these in the States, they've gotta have three things. They've gotta have a good job. They've gotta have a lot of money. And they've gotta be a nice guy."

The expat takes a drink, studies the gringos again. "All these guys," he says, "they've probably got one of those things. They might even have two of those things. But I guarantee you, none of them have all three."

When you're not drunk and the place is almost empty, this is what it looks like: there are tables just inside the door to the right, three rows of them between the windows fronting the street and the

wooden rail that keeps people from tumbling off the raised platform that holds the main bar, which is huge, two peninsulas poking
out in the shape of an upside-down U. There are TVs bolted to
the walls and tuned to sports channels, because this is ostensibly
a sports bar, and there are fish — stuffed fish, carved fish, and
sculpted fish — mounted above the liquor shelves and dangling
from the ceiling, because the "World Famous" Blue Marlin is also
ostensibly a fisherman's bar, even though it's hours away from any
place where you might actually catch a fish. Also, it's a gringo joint:
There's a crinkled American flag, like the ones newspapers printed
after September 11, taped to one wall, and dozens of shoulder
patches, left behind by American cops and firemen, tacked up behind the bar — San Francisco, Chicago, Detroit, New York City,
Boynton Beach, Waynesboro, a hundred other little towns you've
never heard of. Eleven o'clock on a Monday morning during the
Costa Rican rainy season and it's all white boys at the bar, eight of
them, except for one wobbly local named Fernando that the security guys keep trying to pour out the door.

Seven girls sit on stools in the back corner, smoking cigarettes
and looking bored. Six more are off to the left, just beyond the casino, in the lobby of the Hotel Del Rey. They're working, but not
very hard. Not much to choose from this early — not for them, not
for the men.

Wait a little while — say, 5:00 — when the sun's still clawing
through the rain clouds over San José and before the streets are
lousy with beggars and peddlers. By cocktail hour, the place is
jammed. There are a few *ticos* and the biggest Asian kid you've ever
seen, but the rest of the men here are gringos. There are young
guys in tank tops and old guys wearing socks in their sandals and a
whole mess of graying middle-aged guys in polos and floral-print
shirts. They've got the bar surrounded three deep, and most of the
tables are gone, too.

And they're not even half the crowd.

The *chicas* — Christ, there's a lot of them. Black girls and brown
girls and beige girls and even a couple of white girls, brunette and
blond and redheaded and skinny and chubby and tall and short
and stacked and not-as-stacked, and every one of them single.

Are they looking at you? Hell yes. A hundred brown eyes turn on
you the second you walk through the door, trying to catch your

attention before you even get past the security guard with the metal detector, like you're Brad Pitt or something. When's the last time that happened at the Bennigan's in Parsippany? Never, that's when.

Which is exactly why all these men are here. "San José: the very best place in the world to get laid, I am convinced," an aficionado who calls himself La Muerte (literally, Death) wrote a few years back in one of the bajillion or so field reports that pop up when you search "Costa Rica sex" on the Internet. Even then, in 2001, the Blue Marlin was legendary among a certain sort of gringo tourist — the sort who likes a wide selection of pretty, inexpensive women in a safe place where the bartenders speak their language. But why stop at the Blue Marlin? That's just one joint in a city of 300,000. There's Key Largo and Atlantis and all the other bars, and the strip clubs that hang billboards — THE NEW NIGHT CLUB KUMAR: OH, YES! — in English along the highway from the airport, and the street corners and parks parceled out by gender and age and fetish. Cheap blow jobs from old whores with drug problems? The Red Zone, a few dirty blocks around the Central Market. Teenagers? There's four by the pay phones at the edge of Parque Morazan. Transvestites, transsexuals, queers? They've all got their own turf close by, and the cabbies all know exactly where they are. "It's very easy to become like a kid in a candy store when you first go to San José," as Death says. "There's so much available talent down there, and it's all done in wide-open public spaces. That's a great feeling, but don't lose your good sense in the original bliss."

Yeah, don't lose your good sense. Get a seat — one of the high-tops by the bar rail is open. Have a drink. Take your time. The girls aren't going anywhere. Sure, every few minutes one leaves with a guy, wiggles out the back toward the hotel lobby or out the front to a cab, but the selection never noticeably thins. The *chicas*, all freelancers and all eighteen (or at least with papers to prove it), always outnumber the gringos. That's the point.

They won't pester you if you don't want them to. They're not like those girls in the Philippines who swarm your table, jabbering in broken English. *You buy me ladies' drink? You bar-fine me?* Or the ones in Thailand. They'll grab your junk right out on the street. *You ready? Oh, you feel ready.* Total whore scene. No, at the better bars in

Costa Rica, at the Blue Marlin, you've got to give a girl a signal, make eye contact, let her know you're interested. When she slides up next to you, she'll ask if you're alone or if you want some company. She'll be charming and gently aggressive, in a way you only wish the women back home would be. So talk to her. She's not going to ask you for any money, not right away. "Take your time, be selective, and get to know the *chica* before you do any negotiating," Death says. "Look for someone with a personality to go along with the looks — someone who smiles and seems to enjoy being around you."

Thing is, they *all* seem to enjoy being around you. Prostitutes are good like that. The best ones make you forget they're even prostitutes, make you think you've stumbled into the greatest singles' bar in the world. That girl you're talking to, she'll tell you that you're handsome and sexy and intelligent, and she'll make you believe it no matter how fat or dumb or ugly you are because she knows you've got a hundred bucks burning a hole in your pocket. Back home, you'd spend that on dinner and a movie, and for what? A kiss on the cheek? Down here, that gets you laid, and by a woman who pretends she doesn't think you're a pig.

Have a few more drinks, let it get late, way into the early morning. The gringo crowd is clearing out now. Too many *chicas* and not enough customers. The tall one in the tight white pants, the one who's been eyeing you for the past hour, she's at the table asking for a light, but she's speaking in Spanish, so you don't realize what she wants until she grabs a pack of matches from the ashtray.

"Where you staying?" She knows a little English, enough to get by.

"Why?"

She smiles. Bad teeth, but otherwise pretty: slender, long dark hair, coppery skin that makes her halter top seem even whiter.

"Where?"

"Holiday Inn."

"Nice hotel."

No, it's an average hotel with an intermittent ant problem. What's nice about it, though, is that it's a Holiday Inn. If you're coming to Costa Rica to hump prostitutes, a room in the world's family-friendliest hotel is good cover. Tell your wife or girlfriend you're staying at the Hotel Del Rey and you might as well be sleeping at Heidi Fleiss's offshore discount whorehouse. The Del Rey's Web site is respectable enough — "Children under 12 stay free" is a nice touch — but the bad shit, the stuff that'll get you in trouble, starts on the first link that comes up on Google. ("Hotel Del Rey and Blue Marlin Bar, the best known Sport-Bar and Casino of Costa Rica, are San José's number one meeting spots, specially for single men looking for sexy girls, and night live activities.") No, better to stay at the Holiday Inn. It's just on the other side of the park, and the staff doesn't care who you bring back. They see it all night, every night, gringos tottering in with hookers.

The girl keeps talking, asking questions. Small talk. Where you from? Married? Girlfriend? Want one? Lie to her. Or not. Like she cares. Ask her questions. Where's she from? Cuba. How old? Twenty-one. What's the tattoo, the one crawling up the small of her back?

"It's a panther," she says. "But the little girl kitty is lonely, and she needs a big, strong male tiger." She means you, even though you're neither big nor strong and have never been mistaken for a tiger.

It sounds better in Spanish.

The Costa Rican government, of course, would prefer that its wedge of the Central American isthmus not be so well regarded among American men trolling for sex. The tourist board is much more enthusiastic about their beaches, rain forests, and volcanoes, and the country's official slogan — NO ARTIFICIAL INGREDIENTS — would seem to have nothing at all to do with picking up prostitutes in bars. True, every horny American who comes down here is renting a hotel room, eating in restaurants, probably drinking, maybe gambling, and definitely paying the $26 departure tax on his way out; at least some of the money he's spending on sex goes back into the local economy. But what self-respecting country wants to shill for those dollars? "You might be sure that this type of tourist are not wanted here," says one Costa Rican official. "We only want the people that want to spend a *'Pura Vida'* time."

Yet the whoremongers came in droves anyway. And by the early 1990s, they'd branded Costa Rica with a reputation as a sex haven — a reputation that stuck and then exploded near the end of the century. Why that happened isn't complicated. For one thing, prostitution is legal, or at least isn't illegal: the business isn't taxed or regulated like, say, casinos or bars, but there is no law against an adult selling his or her body for cash. So you're not going to come down to San José and get busted by an undercover cop. Prostitution is also indigenously rampant and culturally, if quietly, acceptable — 70 percent of those who pay for sex are locals — so you don't feel all that awkward with your arm around a whore.

For another thing, Costa Rica is close, a four-hour flight out of Atlanta. The hard-core-sex destinations — Thailand, Cambodia, the Philippines — require major investments in airfare and flying time, twenty-two hours to Manila on a direct flight, twenty-three to Bangkok. Costa Rica, on the other hand, can be done in a long weekend. It's relatively safe, fairly well-developed, and friendly toward Americans. Plus, with the notable exception of San José, it's a lush little emerald of a nation with plenty of *other* plausible reasons to visit. Tell your wife you're going fishing with some buddies, spend a night at the Holiday Inn, two more in Jacó or another one of the beach towns now overrun with prostitutes, then fly home and brag about all the big ones you caught. Who has to know?

Exactly how many tourists come here every year looking for sex is impossible to determine; "get laid" isn't one of the boxes that can be checked off under "purpose of trip" on the immigration form.

But there are clues. Of the 500,000 or so Americans who visit the country each year, for instance, 25.8 percent are single men. There are also at least eleven companies that offer either complete package tours to San José, including airfare, or lodging, transportation, and women once you land. Solo Adventures bills itself as "a Full Service Travel Agency specializing in pre-designed adult companion packages to all regions of Costa Rica for the single (body or mind) Gent." Bendricks International Men's Club will fly you down, put you up in one of eight luxury resorts for three nights, and supply "companion escorts" for $1,695. "You can enjoy the private company of South American women who can satisfy even the most active imagination in one of the world's great adult travel vacation destinations for men," the Bendricks Web site says. (The company won't say how many men they take down each year. In fact, the guy behind the desk in the Miami office won't say anything at all — he just shakes his head at every question.) But the commercial tours account for just a fraction of the gringos renting women in Costa Rica. (Only the truly inept and incompetent need to hire a middleman anyway.) Aside from the dedicated sex tourists, there are legions of part-timers, guys who come for some other reason and take a side trip, so to speak. The problem is how to separate the dedicated 'mongers from the dabblers? The group from Chicago that flies down to San José every summer, outed last year by the local ABC station and its hidden cameras, would presumably lean toward the dedicated-'monger camp, considering there is absolutely nothing to do in San José other than gamble, drink, and pick up prostitutes. (ABC7's ominous tagline — "the Shameful Obsession" — would suggest as much, too.) The so-called Michigan Boys, on the other hand, might tilt toward dabbler. They hold a legitimate annual fishing tournament, one that in 2004 drew 167 contestants — including a suburban police chief, a school-board president, and a judge — only it was based at a resort that happened to be stocked with prostitutes. "The problem with our trip," one of the organizers told WXYZ-TV in Detroit, which followed the Michigan Boys to Costa Rica, "is that some of the guys go there and party, and they talk too much. And then somebody hears in a bar about [it] — wife or sister-in-law hears — and it's sad because not everybody goes there and does it." Yeah, *that's* the problem — they talk too much. Not surprisingly, though, every other guy that WXYZ asked about the trip denied cavorting with whores. (Warren, Michigan, police chief Danny Clark actually said, "I did not know that they were hookers.")

Or ignore the statistics and junkets. Just look around. Stand at the edge of Parque Morazan and watch the parade of white guys with young brown girls. "This place," says that American expat former cop, "has to be the number one destination in the Western Hemisphere for horny, middle-aged moron-loser-gringos jacked up on Viagra."

Take these American guys in the bar overhanging the lobby at the Holiday Inn — three of them, clean-cut, midthirties. They staggered in on separate flights, which is apparent because they're swapping reports on how crowded each plane was. This is some kind of reunion for them, and they're sitting around, waiting for seven more friends to show up.

Rain is coming down hard outside. "I remember a lot of heavy rain last year, too," one of them says.

"Yeah," the second one says, "and I remember a lot of heavy screaming."

They all bust up at that.

"Seriously, I had no intention of doing anything," the second guy goes on. "I swear to God. But when those two girls grabbed me and said, 'We're drinking tonight,' man, that was it. That was *it*."

A fourth gringo shows up, then a fifth, a sixth. Same pattern every time: flight report, bitch about the rain, recap last year's highlights, always with dramatic emphasis on the last syllable or three.

"I know this massage parlor, anything you want. *An-nee-thing*."

"I had this girl, a hundred thousand colones" — two hundred bucks, give or take — "and I had her for the whole night. *The whole night*."

It goes on like this until the last two guys show up. They've got American girls with them, one a wife, one a girlfriend. Now the boys are talking about . . . rain forests and rafting. And dinner. They're going to the restaurant at the Hotel Del Rey, where the food's pretty good.

One guy looks spooked.

"Nah, don't worry," his buddy tells him. "They don't bother you in the restaurant."

"Yeah," another guy says. "They just stand outside and watch you. And wait."

The academic debate over whether prostitution is a good idea is pretty simple in its extremes. On one side are the abolitionists — some feminist and religious groups and, since 2003, the U.S. government. They believe that selling sex is *always* wrong, inherently demeaning, a fundamental violation of basic human rights. Whether they're philosophically correct is irrelevant to the actual world. The global sex industry, ancient and entrenched, employs/ exploits/enslaves (the verb you choose is a function of your politics and the circumstances of individual prostitutes) tens of millions of women and girls, and generates hundreds of billions of dollars annually. Abolishing it, purging the planet of every escort and bar girl and streetwalker, and prosecuting or shaming every john into submission is no more feasible than eliminating agriculture or the auto industry.

On the other side are libertarians, a tiny minority of prostitutes who prefer to be called "sex workers," and, one would suppose, a good percentage of the men who pay for sex. They believe that consenting adults should be free to do whatever they damn well please, though probably the pragmatists among them will concede that the business should be regulated to ensure everyone's health and safety.

That argument is worse than irrelevant: it's just silly, a utopian notion bordering on idiotic.

Sure, there are a handful of brothels that enforce strict rules on condoms for the men and health checks for the women. But those are a minuscule proportion of the business, the vast majority of which is carried out in dirty hotels and strip clubs, in cars and on street corners, and almost entirely in cash transactions between strangers who prefer anonymity — the very definition of unsafe and unregulated. In poor countries with thriving sex industries, enforcing any semblance of order would be impossible. Even if police corruption and criminal gangs magically vanished, places like Thailand or the Philippines have neither the manpower nor the financial incentive to monitor hundreds of thousands of prostitutes and johns. Even developed countries that attempt some form of regulation and encourage prostitutes to register have had dismal results. In the Netherlands, for instance, fewer than one in ten of an estimated twenty-five thousand prostitutes have chosen to be officially licensed. Believing that will change, that it can change, is naive. Most prostitutes — the ones controlled by pimps or traffickers, the minors, the illegal immigrants — aren't in any position to ask for government help, and the ones who *are* usually don't want an official record of a profession they hope will be temporary. For all the blather about empowering sex workers, few women want prostitution on their resumés.

Moreover, legalizing it in any particular place — in other words, eliminating the risk of arrest and diminishing the immediate social stigma (at least for the men) — almost always increases demand, which in turn requires an increased supply. And since there are never enough local women clamoring to be prostitutes, especially in developed nations, they have to be imported. In the early 1990s, for example, an estimated 75 percent of Germany's prostitutes had been shipped in from South America (a demographic that, since the fall of the Soviet Union, has been largely replaced by women from places like Russia, Romania, and the Ukraine). Common sense, as well as government statistics and a 2005 U.S. State Department report, suggests that at least some of those women were trafficked (that is, lured with the promise of legitimate jobs or simply forced) into the country by outlaw pimps — one of the problems legalization is theoretically meant to solve. What Paraguayan peasant — even if she truly wants to be a whore in Europe — has the money and the connections to get there and go into business for herself?

Or take the Czech Republic, where, for a decade, prostitution has been a misdemeanor offense so widely unenforced that it was de facto legal (and a pro-legalization bill is currently awaiting a vote in parliament). In 2004, the Interior Ministry counted almost nine hundred brothels, two hundred in Prague alone — dramatic growth for an industry that, one expert observes, was "almost nonexistent" in that country a decade ago. On weekends, the Czech border town of Cheb (population thirty-two thousand) is flooded with ten thousand German men who sample the prostitutes from Russia, the Ukraine, Slovakia, Bulgaria, Romania, and Albania — all countries listed by the State Department as sources of trafficked women. And the profits, according to the United Nations Office on Drugs and Crime, are collected by fifteen criminal gangs.

And then there's Costa Rica. For such a beautiful little country that markets itself so aggressively to ecotourists and fishermen, it can't seem to shake its reputation as a sex paradise. San José has long been the hub; Death called it "the very best place in the world to get laid" way back in 2001, after all, and apparently both the Chicago contingent and the Michigan Boys have been chartering down for more than ten years. Yet rather than being contained and controlled in the capital city, prostitution has expanded across the country, growing along with the crowds of tourists that have increased from 435,000 in 1990 to 1,450,000 last year. Prostitutes now shuttle to the ports on both coasts where cruise ships dock, and they're part of the scenery in most of the beach towns.

Fifteen years ago, a *tico* named Jorge used to drive two hours over the mountains with his family to Jacó, a surf town on the Pacific coast and the closest beach to San José. Look at the place now. On a slow night in low season in the Beatle Bar — another joint that's "World Famous," which is apparently code for where a gringo can get a whore — twenty prostitutes are wasting their time on seven white guys and a couple of coeds who don't stay long. When it closes, the girls move down the strip to Monkey Bar. Farther down is Pancho Villa, where the kitchen in the downstairs club is open late, and the entrance to a strip club upstairs is around the corner. Two young guys, pale and preppy, come out with their arms around a couple of tall black women and grab a cab. Then three *chicas* — sixteen, tops — stumble up the street in spike heels. ("You can always tell the prostitutes," Jorge says. "They always look like they just got out of the shower. A really long shower.")

There are no reliable estimates of how many are working in the country — since they're not required to register, they can't be counted, and the trade is highly seasonal — but the consensus among aid groups and Costa Ricans is that there are more than enough and more than before. The conservative guess is that half of those working the gringo crowd are foreigners, women imported from Nicaragua, Cuba, Colombia, the Dominican Republic, and all the other Latin American countries with worse economies and fewer tourists. The U.S. State Department, meanwhile, lists Costa Rica as a source and destination country for trafficked women, as well as a transit point for women trafficked from the Southern Hemisphere and Eastern Europe into the United States and other wealthy nations.

And that's in a place that would prefer the horny gringos stay home.

The barroom discussion about prostitution, on the other hand, isn't a debate at all. It's straight rationalization. It's the expat cop sitting on a stool, waving his glass of gin at all the gringos, channeling their thoughts:

To get a girl like one of those in the States . . .

It's complete bullshit, of course — millions upon millions of working stiffs have beautiful wives and girlfriends, and there's no shortage of rich American assholes with models on their arms — but a particular class of whoremonger will convince himself it's true. That's the point of being in a place such as the Blue Marlin as opposed to paying a crack addict $20 for a blow job — believing that those girls, the pretty, flirty ones in a clean bar, actually *like* you. Sex tourism is built on that very premise: these girls, the *chicas* and the Eastern Europeans and the Southeast Asians, are different from American women, more loving, less judgmental, oblivious to your gut and your hairline and the fact that you're the sort of guy who hires women to have sex with him. Norman Barabash, a nebbishy fellow from Long Island whose company, Big Apple Oriental Tours, guided American men to the bars of Angeles City in the Philippines before the New York attorney general's office shut it down, put it bluntly on a promotional tape:

"Filipinas are not only the most beautiful girls in the world, but also they're among the most passionate," he said. "And best of all, you don't have to date them for five months to find out if they like you enough to give you their passion. Five hours, or five minutes, is more like it. While the ladies back home are working out their hang-ups with their therapists, you'll be having the time of your life right here in mind-blowing, and everything-else-blowing, Angeles City."

Change *Filipina* to *Latina* and the rest of it's interchangeable. Bendricks has its prattle about "women who enjoy exuding an aura of sexual vibrancy." Solo Adventures promises "stunning sensual women providing warm, friendly, and very personal intimate service." The Web pages of freelancers extolling the purportedly genuine sensuality of Latin women run into the thousands.

Ken Franzblau, a consultant for Equality Now (the women's-rights organization that started the campaign to get Big Apple shut down), has been calling tour companies for almost a decade, posing as a potential client, listening to the pitches, even checking references with satisfied customers. It's been a nine-year tape loop playing over the phone. "It's talked about, I guess, like the guys in Ponce de León's expedition talking about the Fountain of Youth," he says. "'You won't believe it. Women throw themselves at you, as much sex as you want. You'll feel like Tom Cruise.' They always say you'll feel like Tom Cruise. Except for the guys who are really old. They'll tell you you'll feel like John Wayne."

The level of self-delusion is stupefying. In April, for instance, a guy who calls himself "Jacó Lover" posted a report on his second trip in two years to the Costa Rican coast, where he got the "total GFE" — girlfriend experience — "for $100, including spending the night." The highlight: "She happily let me eat her very pretty pussy, and if she wasn't having an orgasm, then she was a damned good actress."

Golly, you think?

"There's a part of them that's lying to themselves and creating this fantasy and believing these girls actually like them," says Donna M. Hughes, a professor at the University of Rhode Island who, for sixteen years, has been studying prostitutes and the men who pay them. "They're really just deluding themselves. And I really think that keeping the online diaries is a way of reliving the fantasy. They can edit out any sign that she didn't enjoy this and didn't want to be with this guy."

Which, unless she is as rare among prostitutes as virgins, she didn't. To believe she did is to ignore a basic truth of human nature: no one really *wants* to be a whore. A statistical summary of women in prostitution is a chronicle of human wreckage — economic, physical, and chemical. A 2003 survey of prostitutes in nine countries — Canada, Colombia, Germany, Mexico, South Africa, Thailand, Turkey, the United States, and Zambia — headed up by a clinical psychologist named Melissa Farley revealed women who'd suffered astonishing rates of childhood sexual abuse (from 34 percent in Turkey to 84 percent in Canada and Zambia) or physical abuse (39 percent of Thais to 73 percent of Canadians); current or past homelessness (84 percent in the United States); and current drug problems (75 percent in the United States and 95 percent in Canada). The results of a 1999 UNICEF study of child prostitutes in Costa Rica between the ages of eleven and sixteen — and since most prostitutes start before they turn eighteen, it's relevant — were worse: 80 percent had been sexually abused before their twelfth birthday, 62 percent had been physically abused, and 60 percent smoked crack daily. And the most telling statistic from Farley's survey? Almost every prostitute she talked to wanted out, from 68 percent in Mexico to 92 percent in, of all places, Thailand, the world's premier sex destination.

"I tell you what," says Franzblau. "If these guys knew how many of these girls are thinking about sticking a knife in their back while they're having sex with them, they'd be amazed. Forget amazed. They'd be staying home."

But they don't know, so they keep coming. Who cares what the tourist board says? The hotel clerks, the bartenders, the cabbies — they're all part of the fantasy, all in on the hustle. No one looks at you funny down here if you want to get a girl for the night or just for an hour. No one calls you a loser if you pay to get laid.

There's a *tico* named . . . well, forget his name. He used to be in the business of taking horny gringo dollars, used to manage a club, and he doesn't want to piss off his old boss. Then again, he's not too happy with how this is all turning out for his country. "Remember Bush, the first one, when he said 'the New World Order'?" he says. "In the New World Order, we're the playground."

Grab a cab at the airport, and even if the driver speaks no English he'll say, *"Chicas, sí?"* and he'll know you understand. Tell him you want to go to a club, and he'll drop you off at a strip joint like the one the *tico* used to manage, and he'll collect a thousand colones from the club owner for delivering you. Americans, the *tico* says, are like "Attila, you know, the Hun," but they've got dollars. Pay the cover — ten bucks, including two drinks — and watch the show: strippers, then a live lesbian act, then $2 lap dances, then an amateur act . . . all in an hour and, damn, it's only a Tuesday night. Resist the hard sell for a private dance in the back, two bucks a minute, six minutes minimum. Then quit resisting. Follow her into a bland room with a wastebasket full of tissues and Wet-Naps. "Tip enough," the *tico* says, "and they're all hookers." Want to take her out of the club? One-fifty to the house, one-fifty to her.

Maybe the national economy doesn't need the money, but the club does. The girl does. The cabbie does. The maid changing sheets at the Holiday Inn does. The *tico*'s friend who runs a local tanning salon does. Eliminate prostitution, that friend says, and you eliminate 60 percent of his clientele. No, better to keep it legal, keep it out in the open.

Just don't talk about it too much. For all the bravado, for all the Web chatter, for all the Attila swagger, the gringo whoremongers are exceptionally shy. The guys in the bar don't want to talk. Be a nosy stranger, ask an obvious question — "Whaddya doin' down here?" — and they'll give you a stare that's either blank or surly. The 'mongers who brag so loudly on the Internet don't use their real names. Even the out-of-business *tico* club manager would prefer not to have his name in a magazine no one in Costa Rica will read.

"You know why?" he says. "Because you're touching the darkest part of the human soul. You do this in your own country, you'll have shame.

"Your shame," he says, "brings you here."

On the immigration forms American Airlines passes out on its flights from Miami to San José, in fine blue print just below the usual blocks for your name and passport number and address, there's a curious line in both Spanish and English: "The penalty for sexual abuse towards minors in Costa Rica implies prison. Law #7899."

When you get off the plane, there are posters taped to each of the kiosks where the immigration officers stamp your passport. They show the large, sad face of a teenage girl and, smaller and down in one corner, a pair of white man's hands poking out through what appear to be the bars of a prison cell. "Her soul torn to pieces," the text reads, "and you . . . behind bars." Farther on, next to the door out of customs, there is a life-sized cardboard stand-up of a *tico* — a cabbie, presumably — holding a sign. "Dear tourist," the sign held by the sign says. "In Costa Rica, sex with children under 18 is a serious crime. Should you engage in it, we will drive you to jail. We mean it." Finally, in the cabs that line up outside the terminal, there are versions of the same sign, again with "We mean it" underlined with a red slash.

Welcome to Costa Rica, where it is illegal to rape children. Where it is necessary, in fact, to remind every single tourist entering the country that it is wrong to rape children.

The reason those signs are posted, of course, is that Costa Rica has a reputation as a place where you *can* rape the kids, though it's rarely put that bluntly. Pedophilia? OK, yes, agreed: It's very, very bad, and Costa Rica, like most developing nations, has suffered its share of foreigners preying on its kids. But read the signs again: "under 18" is in bold for a reason, one that is more demurely referred to as having sex with underage prostitutes, the estimated 5,000 to 10,000 teenagers in San José alone who've yet to reach the legal age of consent. Considering that the UNICEF study of young prostitutes found they turned their first trick at the average age of fourteen, it's a huge problem.

In 2002, for example, the FBI, along with the Fort Lauderdale Police Department and the U.S. embassy in San José, set up a bogus travel agency called, unsubtly, Costa Rican Taboo Vacations, which promised, in magazine and Internet ads, to supply tourists with "companions" between the ages of fourteen and twenty-seven. The feds say they were swamped with requests for information, and between December 2003 and August 2004 they arrested eleven people who'd paid deposits or booked trips — with what they believed was a legitimate commercial company — to have sex with kids. Among them: a South Carolina real estate agent and his wife who wanted a pair of sixteen-year-olds; a Hollywood, Florida, cop who also wanted two sixteen-year-olds; and a New Jersey middle-school teacher who paid $1,610 for a package that was to include two twelve-year-olds.

That's one example, the results from one fake company. Now eliminate the middleman, the cash deposits, the hard evidence. Just fly to Costa Rica, get drunk, meet a girl on the street. She'll say she's eighteen. Is she lying? She's got an ID. Is it fake? How can anyone possibly tell? And will the local cops bust the guy who guesses wrong? Do they, in fact, mean it?

Paul Chaves is the man in charge of the Sexual Exploitation Unit in the Ministry of Public Security. He remembers, with something between bitterness and bemusement, when Costa Rica got slammed in the mid-1990s by the foreign media shooting video of underage prostitutes in downtown San José. ABC, NBC, the BBC, even Spanish television. The government ministers would deny on camera that there was a problem, then the reporters would roll the tape, add some line about "trouble in paradise" — devastatingly effective television. "I know how the media works," Chaves says, and several times, because he has two brothers in journalism, which he also says several times.

He also knows that those foreign reporters were right and that his government was wrong — tactically and morally — to say otherwise. So now he's saying the opposite. Confessing it, really, so aggressively and often that he seems almost to be doing penance for the whole country. He's a small, blustery man of thirty-six, quite proud of his accomplishments since he took over the Sexual Exploitation Unit two and a half years ago. (His 120-man department also covers juvenile gangs, auto theft, and, oddly, copyright infringement.) When he started, only six of his men worked the sex beat, he says, sharing one car and never leaving San José. Now he has more than forty officers on the job, covering the entire country. Why, just that day his officers rousted a woman who was pimping girls out of a beauty salon. "Pimps and pedophiles," he says. "Those are my two enemies."

But not prostitutes. He is sympathetic: "Some girls who are doing this are students selling their bodies part-time." He is philosophical: "I don't think it would be worth going after prostitutes. Nonsense. Anyone can sell her body to someone else." He is practical: "To try to police what women do with their bodies, or what men do with their bodies, we would be a police state."

Valid points, all. He would acquit himself well in the academic debate. But what about the real-world debate? What about those sixteen- and seventeen-year-old prostitutes, the ones the TV crews caught on video and the ones who are still in the park by the Holiday Inn? Don't they come with the territory? Isn't that why those signs are cluttering up the airport, making all the legitimate tourists skittish?

"Sometimes," he says, "I have my doubts." Thoughtful pause. "Any man can make a mistake."

So, no, all those airport signs — apparently, they don't mean it.

Chaves hails a cab. It's a long ride to his home on the outskirts of San José. He talks the whole way. About his 120 officers. About how helpful the United States and Britain have been. About his hatred of pimps and pedophiles. About his government finally admitting it has a problem with both.

The cab stops at his house. The chief of the Sexual Exploitation Unit tells the driver, who doesn't speak English, to go on to the Holiday Inn, then says good night. He gets out and closes the door.

The cabbie flips on the dome light, reaches back with his right hand. There's a small pink card between his fingers for a place called Scarlett's Gentlemen's Club.

"Titty bar?"

He knows enough English to get by.

IAN FRAZIER

Out of Ohio

FROM *The New Yorker*

RECENTLY I SAW in a newspaper from Hudson, Ohio, my home town, that they were about to tear down the town's water tower. In principle, I don't care anymore how things I used to love about Hudson change or disappear. Each time a big change happens, though, I feel a moment of resistance before my lack of caring returns. The town's water tower, built in the early 1900s, was its civic reference point, as its several white church steeples were its spiritual ones. The water tower was higher than they, and whenever you were walking in the fields — the town was surrounded by fields — you could scan the horizon for the water tower just above the tree line and know where you were. The cone-shaped top, and the cylindrical tank below it, gave the water tower the aspect of an old-time spaceship, though more squat. Its dull silver color and the prominent rivets in its sheet-metal side added to the antique Buck Rogers look. Or, to switch movies, the tower looked like the Tin Man in *The Wizard of Oz*. Two generations ago, water towers like this one could be found superintending small towns all over the Midwest and West. I'm sure the Tin Man was even based on them.

I lived in Hudson from when I was six until I was eighteen. Sometimes I try, usually without success, to describe how sweet it was to grow up in a small Ohio town forty years ago. As I get into the details, corniness tinges my voice, and a proprietary sentimentality that puts people off. I say the names of my friends from back then — Kent, Jimmy (called Dog), Susie, Bitsy, Kathy, Charlie (called Dunkie), Timmy, Paul — and they sound somehow wrong. They're like the names of characters in nostalgic mid-American movies or

Bruce Springsteen songs, and I start to think of us as that myself, and a blurring sameness sets in, and the whole business defeats me. But then a friend from Hudson calls, or I run into somebody from there, or I hear the rattle of shopping-cart wheels in a supermarket parking lot, and for a second I remember how growing up in Hudson could be completely, even unfairly, sweet.

Most modern people don't belong anyplace as intimately as we belonged to Hudson. Now the town has grown and merged with northern Ohio exurbia, so it's hardly recognizable for what it was. Some of the old sense of belonging, though, remains. A while ago, I went back for a funeral. I took the bus from New York City to Cleveland overnight and then drove down to Hudson in the morning with my brother. We walked into Christ Church, our old church, now unfamiliar because of remodeling, and sat in the back. I saw not many people I knew. Then, over my shoulder, in the aisle, I heard a woman say, "I think I'll just sit here next to Sandy Frazier."

To return home, to have a person call me by name; and to look up and remember her, forty-some years ago, as a junior-high girl in Bermuda shorts at the town's Ice Cream Social, an event sponsored by the League of Women Voters on the town green, where I and my friends chased her and her friends between tables and chairs and across the lawn flicking wadded-up pieces of paper cups at them with long-handled plastic ice-cream spoons, bouncing the missiles satisfyingly off the girls as they laughed and dodged —

I should finish that thought, and that sentence. But the service had begun for Cynthia, a friend to my family and me. She was dead at sixty-seven of Lou Gehrig's disease. Back in the 1960s, someone climbed the water tower and wrote Cynthia's name on it, billboard-large, a declaration of love. It stayed there above the trees for a long time, until the town painted it over. When I was eight or nine, Cynthia made a point of coming up and saying hello to me in the basement of the Congregational church. I was there, I think, because my mother was helping with the scenery for a play. When I was just out of high school, Cynthia heard me telling my friends a story in her living room, and afterward she told me I would be a writer. When I was in my twenties, I came back to town one night from hitchhiking someplace east or west, and I found nobody home at our house, so I went over to Cynthia's, and she put on a bathrobe and came downstairs and heated up a bowl of soup for me and sat with me at the island in the middle of her kitchen as I ate.

In those days I was constantly leaving town. Hudson was made for leaving. The Ohio Turnpike, also called Interstate 80, crossed the town from east to west behind a chain-link fence. The distant sound of traffic on the turnpike was part of the aural background of the town, like the rising and falling of the whistle in the Town Hall every noon. After the turnpike, other interstates came nearby. In Hudson Township, you could go from shady gravel road, to two-lane county asphalt, to far-horizon, four-lane interstate highway in just a few turns of the steering wheel.

When I left the first time to go to college — the original leaving, which set a pattern for later ones — my plane to Boston was on a Sunday morning, and I spent all the preceding day and night going around town, seeing friends, saying goodbye, standing and talking under street lights in hushed, excited tones. Early Sunday, I was lying on the floor of a living room with Kent, Bitsy, and Kathy, listening over and over to the song "Leaving on a Jet Plane." Nobody was saying anything. The girls were quietly crying, not so much about my leaving as about the overwhelmingness of everything: the year was 1969. I cried, and also pretended to cry, myself. From ground level I looked at the nap of the rug and the unswept-up miscellany under the couch. I would never be even a tenth as at home anywhere again.

Four years later, I graduated with a degree in General Studies and no clear plans. Mostly I wanted to go back home. I had had enough of the East, a place I was unable to make much sense of. My college girlfriend, Sarah, whom I was too self-absorbed to appreciate, became fed up with my increasingly wistful home-town reminiscences as graduation day approached. "Don't invite me to your Ohio wedding" was one of her last remarks to me. After I received my diploma, my father came over to me in the courtyard of my dorm as I was talking to friends and hugged me so hard he lifted me off the ground. We loaded the trunk of the family Maverick with my belongings, the textbooks dumped in any which way, and drove straight home on Interstate 90 and the turnpike, arriving before dawn. I stayed awake and had some scrambled eggs my mother made, and then I went into the yard and watched the sunrise through the newly leafed trees. It rains a lot in northeastern Ohio, so the trees are extremely green. All around me, the summer landscape draped like a big hammock. I felt geographically well situated, and defiantly at home.

I didn't bother to take my books out of the trunk of the car — just left them in there, rattling — and a few days later someone ran into my mother from behind on Middleton Road, and they scattered everywhere and got run over. My mother, as of course she would, carefully retrieved them. I still have several of them — for example, *The Power Elite,* by C. Wright Mills, with a black Ohio tire tread running across the cover.

Why did Hudson enchant me? Why was life, there and then, so sweet? I think a million reasons happened to come together, none of which we grasped at the time. We had plenty of leisure. We had cars to drive. Gasoline was still so cheap it was practically free. Our parents, to whom the cars we drove belonged, had leisure, too. In their ease, they were inclined to take long vacations, and indulge us kids. Fathers (and a few mothers) had steady jobs, pensions, health insurance. The economic difficulties that would later take a lot of those away and that I still don't understand had not yet visibly begun. Vietnam was winding down. The draft had just ended, removing a load from all our minds. Et cetera.

In my case, life was good, by comparison, because it had recently been so bad. The previous December, my fifteen-year-old brother, Fritz, had died of leukemia. After that, the last thing my parents wanted to do was to keep my other siblings and me from having any fun we could have. Dad and Mom would be gone a lot of that summer, traveling in India. At our house, I would be in charge.

And then, as a further reason for life's sweetness, there was hot, drowsy, hilly, expansive Ohio itself. Not so many people lived in Ohio then, and its commercial sprawl had narrower limits. Some of the local roads still were dirt, and bisected working farms. Everybody still knew everybody. At Kepner's Bar on Main Street, I might run into a woman in a wild dress and hoop earrings who, it turned out, I'd known since first grade. To the west of town, on the turnpike, the highway went through a cut topped with a scenic (though otherwise unnecessary) bridge supported by a graceful arch that framed a megascreen view of the Cuyahoga River valley and sunlit points beyond. Too big to punish, we could now go where we wanted; a kid I knew got the urge to hitchhike to the East Coast one afternoon and set out in his bare feet, and traveled barefoot the whole journey. I was done with school — finally and thoroughly done. Vague possibilities shimmered in every direction.

Back then it seemed there was a lot more room, especially outdoors. In a town like Hudson every piece of ground did not have to account for itself, in real-estate terms, as it does today. On the edges of town and sometimes beside roads and buildings were plots of weedy, dusty, driven-over earth that no one had given much thought to since Hudson began. At the Academy, where I went to high school, the shadows of trees at sunset stretched three hundred yards across the school's lawns. Often on summer evenings we played Wiffle Ball there. The game was like baseball, only with a plastic ball that didn't go as fast and wobbled in flight, and could be caught barehanded. You didn't need shoes, either, in the lawn's soft grass.

After a game of Wiffle Ball at sunset — after running enormously far across the lawn to catch foul balls, sliding shirtless into base on close plays, reclining itchily in the grass waiting to bat, quitting the game only when it was too dark to see the ball — we would go to the beverage store downtown and stand in the pleasantly frigid walk-in cooler, deciding whether to buy the evening's supply of Stroh's beer by the twelve-pack or the case. And then the evening would continue. At this hour, girls we knew might be sitting on somebody's front porch smoking cigarettes. Twenty minutes of driving around would discover them.

That summer, a woman I'd gone out with when she was a girl happened to be in town. Her family had moved to Wheaton, Illinois, but she had come back to stay with her sister, who lived in an apartment above a store on Main Street. I climbed the outdoor stairs and knocked on the apartment door, and Susie came out, keeping one ear open for her sleeping nephew, whom she was baby-sitting. We were kissing at the bottom of the stairs in the shadows when she considered me for a moment and declared, "You're a real person."

The "you" was emphasized: *"You're* a real person." She meant this not as a compliment but as a statement of fact. I understood what she meant. After growing up in Hudson, where anybody you met you already knew, you found it hard to take people from anyplace else quite seriously. They might be nice, and interesting, and all, but they had a transitory quality. Only people from Hudson you'd known forever could be completely real.

Now I see Hudson as the place where I was spun and spun throughout my childhood in order to have maximum velocity when it finally let me go. My leaving-for-good happened like this:

I hung around that summer until my presence became otiose. Friends' parents started asking me how long I would be in town. My parents, back from India, began to suggest chores, like mowing the lawn. There's a certain nightmare time-warp feeling that can come over you — a sense that you're your present size but sitting in your old desk from elementary school, with your knees sticking up on the sides. The feeling can motivate you to plunge into any uncertainty, just so long as it's present tense. One morning in late August, I packed a suitcase, jumped the turnpike fence, and began to hitchhike west.

First, I went to visit my best friend and former neighbor, Don, in Colchester, Illinois. Colchester is smaller than Hudson, and more intoxicatingly midwestern. The back yards on Don's street were all clothes lines and garden rows of corn, and beyond the corn ran the tracks of a main rail line bound for St. Louis. Don and his friends and I used to smoke dope and sit by the tracks at night waiting for the 11:00 train. At first, it was a little, faraway light, and then suddenly it grew into a blaring, blue-white beam and gigantic noise pounding immediately by. Then in a while the night would be its quiet self again. Just to lie in the back bedroom of Don's house with the curtains billowing inward on the breeze was middle-of-the-country nirvana for me.

From Colchester, I continued on to Chicago, where I got a job on a European-style skin magazine published by *Playboy*. The magazine's editor had written to the *Harvard Lampoon*, which I had worked for in college, and had offered a job to any *Lampoon* person who wanted one. The offices were cavelike, with halls resembling tunnels and fragrant dark-brown cork-board paneling on the walls. In a short while, I learned that writing captions for photos of naked women is a particular talent, one that is surprisingly difficult to fake. I quit the day I was supposed to get a company ID card, which I feared would be a raised bunny head — the *Playboy* logo — stamped on a photo of my face.

Then I lay around my small North Side apartment for a few months on the bare mattress that was its only furniture and read books or looked at the plaster floret on the ceiling. Somewhere I had come across Hemingway's list of the novels he thought it essential for every writer to know and I started in on them. I also spent weeks at a time in uninterrupted, not uncomfortable despair. On Wednesdays, I would go to the newsstand across from the Ambassador East Hotel and buy the latest issue of *The New Yorker*, and then on my mattress I would read every word in it, including the columns of small type in the front. When Pauline Kael reviewed a movie by Sam Peckinpah, I told Susie that Kael had called him "a great and savage artist," and that I wanted people someday to say the same about me. Susie was going to school at the University of Northern Iowa at Cedar Falls. I sometimes took long Greyhound bus rides out to visit her.

My grandmother, a can-do person who enjoyed the challenge of setting wayward relatives on their feet, sent me many letters telling me to come visit her in Florida, and after about the fourth letter I agreed. Before I left Chicago, I gave up my apartment. The landlord was glad to get rid of me. He said that he thought my mattress, surrounded as it was by all the books and magazines I'd been reading, constituted a fire hazard. From Chicago, I rode Greyhound buses for forty-five hours to Key West. On one bus I saw a skinny white guy with combed-high hair try to pick up a black woman sitting next to him, and when she politely moved to another seat he drank a pint or two of whiskey, began to shout at his reflection in the bus window, asked the old woman in front of him if she was wearing a wig, pulled her hair to find out, and eventually left the bus in handcuffs under the escort of the highway patrol, an expression of calm inevitability on his face. Between Georgia and Miami, I listened through the night to a Vietnam veteran with hair longer than Joni Mitchell's talk about a Vietnamese woman he had killed during the war, and about many other topics, his words flowing unstoppably and pathologically until I came almost to hate him. When I finally shot him an angry look, he gave me back a stare of such woefulness and misery that I was ashamed. Out of South Miami I sat next to a psychiatrist who explained to me in psychological terms why the passengers sitting near him objected to his chain-smoking. He was the only seatmate I openly argued with. When my grandmother met me at the Key West bus station, I was furious at her for all I'd been through.

Unlike my parents, Grandmother did not believe in depression. If my mother fell into a gloom, she usually nurtured it into a dark and stationary front that hung over the kitchen for days. As for my father, his strategy when he became depressed was to move from a regular level of depression as much farther down the scale as he could possibly go, getting more and more depressed and thinking up consequent sorrows and disasters of every kind until he reached a near-panic state. Then when he came to himself again, and looked at the actual situation, it seemed not so terrible after all. Grandmother's approach, by contrast, was never to give depression the smallest advantage. Whenever she sensed its approach, she attacked it and routed it and slammed the door.

In Key West, she didn't even allow me to be horizontal for longer than eight hours of sleeping a night. Early in the mornings, she appeared at the front desk of the Southern Cross Hotel, where she had rented me a small room, and she sent the plump and sarcastic German manager to pound on my door with a German-accented witticism. Then she would give me breakfast and hurry me off to the job she had found for me, doing gardening work for a lady even older than she, Minona Seagrove. Minona Seagrove walked very slowly and couldn't really bend down, but she loved to garden, and every day I served as her robot gardening arms, trimming palmetto fronds and planting bulbs while she stood behind me and said what to do. In the evenings, Grandmother made dinner for me and my cousin Libby, who was also visiting. Then sometimes we would play long games of Scrabble with Grandmother, her friend Marjorie Houck, and a very old English lady named Mavis Strange, who consistently won, using words that are in the dictionary but nobody has heard of.

Grandmother's closest friend, Betty Stock, had a daughter named Isabel who worked for *The New Yorker.* Under the name Andy Logan, Isabel wrote the Around City Hall column for the magazine. Just before graduation, I had halfheartedly applied to *The New Yorker* for a staff writing job. Grandmother said if I tried again she would ask Betty to ask Isabel to put in a word with the editor for me. This idea seemed kind of far-fetched, but I said OK: I hadn't brooked Grandmother in anything so far. Grandmother didn't like my hair, so she sent me to her long-time hairdresser and had him cut it. It came out looking bad, though not as bad as I had expected. Grandmother also went through my wardrobe, if it could be called a wardrobe, and singled out a pair of khaki slacks, a shirt, and a blue sweater as acceptable clothing to wear for New York job interviews. I trusted her unquestioningly as an authority on what well-dressed office workers in New York City wore.

After a month or so of this retooling, Grandmother was satisfied, and ready for me to move on. Libby drove me in Grandmother's Ford Fairlane a few miles up the Keys to a good place to hitchhike. In a night-and-day hitchhiking marathon, I made it from the Keys to Morgantown, Kentucky, where my friend Kent was doing volunteer work for the Glenmary Home Missioners. Along the way, I got some wacky Southern rides, including one across South Carolina with a Post Office driver in a small refrigerated truck carrying, he said, "human eyeballs." He was taking them to an eye bank somewhere.

In late afternoon, I arrived at the slant-floored mountain shack Kent had rented, and I was so tired that I immediately lay down and fell asleep on a bed in a side room. It happened that Kent was having a party for the entire community that night. As the guests came in, they piled their coats on top of the bed, on top of me. At the party's height a man and a woman entered the room and closed the door and, not knowing I was there, lay down on the coats and began to talk about the extramarital affair they were having. I emerged from sleep to the sound of their French-movie-type dialogue: "Oh, Roger, I've felt like crying for the last three days!" "Oh, Arliss, [mumble mumble mumble]." Then suddenly the door opened, and from it, like a superloud PA system, the voice of the outraged husband: "Get out of that fuckin' bed, Roger!" The two men adjourned outside for a fistfight while the woman stayed on the coats, sobbing. I began to stir, poking part of my head out from under. The sobbing stopped; silence; then, in complete bafflement, "Who's *he*?"

A few days later, I was back in Hudson. At this slow time of year, none of my friends were around, except Kathy. She had a job at a small, classy store on Main Street that sold women's clothes. I thought that now would be a good opportunity to tell her of the crush I had on her, but as I stood in the store watching her refold sweaters or sat with her on the couch in her family's TV room talking about what our other friends were doing, the moment never came up. Late one night, I went over to her house with an idea of throwing some pebbles at her window, waking her, and telling her how I felt. When I approached through the back yards, the light was still on in her bedroom; as I got closer I saw in the dimness a guy at the edge of her lawn staring so raptly at her window that he never noticed me.

I faded back into the next yard and cut across it and then went to the sidewalk, and as I passed by the front of Kathy's house I saw a cigarette glow on the front steps. She was sitting there, and didn't seem at all surprised to see me. I told her about the guy in her back yard and she smiled. She had a quick smile that went horizontally, like a rubber band stretched between two fingers. The corners of it were so cute they drew your eyes into close-up frame. With undisguisable happiness she said, "That was John."

And so on to New York City. Early one morning before work, Kathy gave me a ride to Exit 13 on the turnpike, just east of town. Local hitchhiking wisdom said that more eastbound trucks got on the highway there. After a friendly hug across the front seat I got out and she drove away. I carried my same suitcase and a cardboard sign on which I'd written "NYC" in large letters with a Magic Marker. I was keyed up. I hadn't asked my parents for money — some of my Minona Seagrove earnings still remained — and I intended not to come back without something to show. I stood, heroic to myself, on the shoulder of the on-ramp in the smell of diesel and the gusts from traffic blowing by. After half an hour or so, a truck pulled over. That moment is always a thrill, when the air brakes hiss and the big machine swerves over and stops just for you. I ran to it, threw my suitcase up through the open door, and climbed the rungs to the cab.

I didn't go very far that day. Many short rides and long waits put me after nightfall at a truck stop in central Pennsylvania. The place had a dormitory floor upstairs and a dozen beds for truckers, and bathrooms with showers. I signed the register in my own name, boldly wrote down that I drove for Carolina Freight, and paid my five dollars for a narrow metal-frame bed. I slept well in a room with a changing group of truckers, each of whom put in his few sleeping hours determinedly and then was gone. In the morning I showered, ate a big breakfast in the restaurant, and, caffeinated and pleased with the day so far, stood by the parking-lot exit with my sign.

The truck that pulled over for me there looked so unpromising that I hesitated before getting in. The tractor was gas-powered, not diesel, with a rusty white cab and a small trailer — the kind of rig, smaller than an eighteen-wheeler, that hauls carnival rides. Its driver appeared equally off-brand. He had strands of black hair around his too-white face and he lacked a few teeth. After saying hello, he told me that he had just taken a lot of methamphetamines. I asked if he was feeling them yet, and he whipped off his sunglasses and said, "Look at my eyes!" Bedspring spirals of energy seemed to be radiating from his black irises. He was beating on the steering wheel with his palms, fiddling with the all-static radio, and moving from one conversational topic to another randomly.

It is perhaps unfair to say that drivers of carnival trucks are horny guys; free-floating lust howls down every highway in the world, sweeping all kinds of people along. This particular speed-popping driver, however, closely fit the horny-guy profile. As his conversation caromed around, it kept returning to, and finally settled on, the subject of a whorehouse he said was not far up the road. He talked about how much he liked it, and what he did there, and the girls who worked in it, and the old man who owned it, and how popular he, the driver, was there.

Soon the driver was going to suggest that he and I make a visit to this whorehouse. I could tell; clearly his drift tended no other way. As he went on, I considered how I would respond. Sanity said, obviously, no. Under no circumstances go to a whorehouse with this guy. Say thanks but no thanks, and jump out as soon as possible. I was ready to be sane and do that. But then I thought . . . I wasn't bound for New York just to demur and make my apologies. Begging off of anything at this point didn't feel right. New York City was the big time, and I wanted to be big time when I got there. When the moment came to jump, I intended to jump. Right then the guy turned to me with a wicked and challenging glint to his sunglasses. Almost before the words left his mouth I thanked him politely and said that yes, going to this whorehouse sounded like an excellent idea.

For a while after that, the guy fell silent. I flattered myself that maybe I'd taken him by surprise. He turned the truck off the highway and proceeded along a two-lane country road. I had no idea what I would do when we got to the whorehouse. The thought of going to it scared me dizzy. I figured I would come up with a plan when I had to. Ahead I saw a tall, narrow, three-story house, its bare windows sealed inside with blinds. A small neon beer sign lit a side door. "There she is!" the driver said, perking up. No cars were in the gravel parking lot as he coasted in, downshifting. He leaned across the dash and pulled over by the side door to examine it closely, giving a few light taps on the horn. No reply or sign of life. More taps on the horn. A few minutes passed. Then, reluctantly, he concluded that no one was about, and he headed back to the highway.

Oh, the intense and private joy of the uncalled bluff! Until now, I had experienced it only in games. This felt a hundred times greater than any game. Keeping my face nonchalant I exulted inwardly, and made a resolve that in my new life in New York City I would bluff whenever the occasion arose. At that moment on the road in the middle of Pennsylvania, I quit living in Hudson and began to live in the world.

The guy let me off someplace in eastern Pennsylvania. By then, the pills he had taken had evidently set him back down, and he looked different, kind of shriveled and mumbly, behind the wheel. I was relieved to be shut of him and out of his spooky cab, and I shouted with the pleasure of being alone as soon as his truck was out of sight. The next ride I got was with a guy about my age from San Isidro, Costa Rica. He must've been part Indian, because he had straight black hair like a Sioux's and an Aztec nose. He was littler than a Sioux, though, and olive-skinned. He drove a big-engine car, the kind they had back then that looked like slabs, and its rear seat was full of cardboard boxes of his stuff. He had lived in Chicago and was moving to New York City, he said. I told him I was, too. With a companion we knew better each of us might have been cooler and more restrained, but as he maneuvered the big car through Jersey traffic we cheered at the first glimpse of the city skyline faintly gray on the horizon.

I hadn't seen a lot of cities then, and I didn't know that New

York, to a traveler coming from the west, affords the best first-time, big-city view in the U.S.A. The guy from Costa Rica and I cruised across the long and splendid drum roll of open-sky swamp up to the Hudson River. Then we swerved down the elevated highway toward the Lincoln Tunnel, and the city suddenly and manifestly filled the windshield and side windows, rising from the Hudson as if lifted by eyelids when you opened your eyes. No skyline I know of is its equal; across the windows it ran, left to right, like a long and precise and detailed and emphatic sentence ending with the double exclamation points of the World Trade Center towers.

It was a mild day in early March, just before rush hour. Lights had come on in some of the buildings, and dusk was beginning to gather in the spaces between them. We went through the Lincoln Tunnel and popped up on the city floor, with buildings and vehicles impending all around. Our windows were open; the city smelled like coffee, bus exhaust, and fingernail polish. The Costa Rican was going to stay with relatives in Queens, a place as exotic to me then as Costa Rica. I was going to Greenwich Village to meet my friend David, who had told me he could find me a place to stay. I got out at Thirty-fourth and Seventh, the southwest corner. When I pass by that corner occasionally today, I still think of it as the place where I landed. The Costa Rican and I wished each other good luck, without pretending to exchange phone numbers (we didn't have them, anyway) or saying we'd keep in touch. We were now each a little part of the other's past, and in New York the past was gone.

TAD FRIEND

The Parachute Artist

FROM *The New Yorker*

ON THE EVENING AFTER the rainiest summer day in Melbourne's history, Tony Wheeler's dinner guests, who were British, wanted to discuss the weather. Wheeler gradually redirected the conversation to the Falkland Islands. He had recently written a new Lonely Planet guide to the Falklands, and also one to East Timor, exactly the sort of backpacker destinations that he and his wife, Maureen, had in mind when they established Lonely Planet, in 1973, as the scruffy but valiant enemy of the cruise ship and the droning tour guide. The Wheelers' guests, who were touring Australia, were Roger Twiney, a flatmate of Tony's in England in the early seventies, and Roger's wife, Susanne. As both couples sat in the Wheelers' living room, watching the sun set across the Yarra River, Tony spoke of the Falklands' king and rockhopper penguins; of tracing Ernest Shackleton's footsteps on South Georgia Island; and of the peculiarities of the local "squidocracy," those grown rich from fishing the cephalopod mollusk.

"But isn't it cold, windy, inhospitable?" Roger asked.

"No, no!" Tony said. "It's just like Yorkshire."

"*I'm* from Yorkshire," Susanne said, with a don't-tell-me-about-Yorkshire tone.

"Well, the Falklands actually get less snow than your home region!" Tony replied, seeming confident that she would be as delighted by this arresting fact as he was. Susanne fell silent.

A slight, graying man of fifty-eight, Tony Wheeler is at least two people. Tony No. 1, who goes to the office every day in subfusc clothing and carries a passport from his native Britain, is so self-contained that he appears, as a colleague puts it, "almost socially retarded." When he gave me a tour of Lonely Planet's head office, in Melbourne, not one of the three hundred eager twenty- and thirty-somethings who work there greeted him as he passed. "I met Tony in our Oakland office a few years ago and I expected him to be this huge presence, this Tony Robbins of travel," Debra Miller, a Lonely Planet author, says. "But he's sort of the Woody Allen of travel."

Like one of those dehydrated sponges which inflate to astonishing size when dropped into their proper element, Wheeler becomes a vastly different and more voluble person when he's on a trip (or recalling or anticipating a trip). This is Tony No. 2, who carries a passport from his adopted Australia. Tony No. 2 and Maureen and I were leaving the next day for the Sultanate of Oman. They were then going on to Ethiopia, and later this year Wheeler planned to visit Macau, Shanghai, Singapore, Finland, the Baltic States, Poland, Italy, Switzerland, Germany, Iceland, and Japan, and to sweep from Cape Town to Casablanca by air safari.

Tony No. 2 relishes being the face of Lonely Planet and of independent travel, regularly rising before dawn — and ignoring Maureen's tart remarks — to appear on Australia's *Today* show, a program that he acknowledges is "pretty awful." He is a valued guest because, having explored 117 countries, he can speak knowledgeably on almost any topic, from the issues faced by rickshaw drivers in Calcutta to such larger mysteries as why Egypt lacks a major industry. Like Benjamin Franklin and the Norway rat, he is a citizen of the world.

His company's reach is equally broad. Lonely Planet now markets some 650 titles, from *Aboriginal Australia* to *Zion and Bryce Canyon National Parks,* in 118 countries. With annual sales of more than six million guidebooks — about a quarter of all the English-language guidebooks sold — it is the world's largest publisher of travel guides.

"Lonely Planet is the bible in places like India," Mark Ellingham, the founder of Rough Guides, the cheeky British series, says. "If they recommend the Resthouse Bangalore, then half the guesthouses there rename themselves Resthouse Bangalore." The series' authority is such that the team accompanying Jay Garner, the first American administrator of occupied Iraq, used *Lonely Planet Iraq* to draw up a list of historical sites that should not be bombed or looted. The writers Marianne Wiggins, Jilly Cooper, and Pico Iyer have used Lonely Planet guides to immerse themselves in the feel of a far-off locale for novels set in, respectively, Cameroon, Colombia, and Iran. And, in perhaps the greatest tribute, the Vietnamese have begun to manufacture ersatz Lonely Planet guides to complement their line of fake Rolexes.

At the same time, however, a number of the company's authors worry that Lonely Planet itself has begun to manufacture ersatz Lonely Planet guides. As the company has expanded to cover Europe and America, markets already jammed with travel guides, it has been updating many of its guidebooks every two years, which requires that it use more and more contributors for each book — twenty-seven for the forthcoming edition of the United States guide alone. The books' iconoclastic tone has been muted to cater to richer, fussier sorts of travelers, many of whom, like the Wheelers themselves, fly business class. And Lonely Planet's original flagship, its "shoestring" series for backpackers, today makes up only 3 percent of the company's sales.

"Our Hawaii book used to be written for people who were picking their own guava and sneaking into the resort pool, and we were getting killed by the competition," a Lonely Planet author named Sara Benson told me. "So we relaunched it for a more typical two-week American mid-market vacation. That sold, but it didn't feel very Lonely Planet." Every Lonely Planet series was relaunched last year in a slicker format that jettisoned much of the discussion of local history and economics; the books now commence, as most guides do, with snappy "Highlights" and "Itineraries." "We're trying to insinuate ourselves into Tony Wheeler's world," Mike Spring, the publisher of the hotels-and-fine-dining-focused Frommer's Travel Guides, says, "and he's trying to insinuate himself into ours."

Around the time of the relaunch, the Wheelers relinquished day-to-day control of the company, but they still own 70 percent of it. Tony keeps looking for new places to cover, and he and Maureen continue to reject offers to license the company's name. John Singleton, an Australian advertising magnate whose limited partnership owns the rest of Lonely Planet, says, "Tony and Maureen would rather be broke than be prostitutes, and God bless 'em."

Yet over the years, Wheeler seems to suspect, something essential was lost. "Those vivid colors of the early books," he said to me, "once they get blended with so many other authors and editors and concerns about what the customer wants, they inevitably become gray and bland. It's entropy, isn't it?"

At dinner with the Twineys, as Tony was uncorking a fourth bottle of wine, Maureen Wheeler mentioned her chronic insomnia. An ardent woman with a deeply amused laugh, she grew up in Belfast and moved to London in 1970, at the age of twenty. Within a week, she had met Tony on a park bench when he noticed her copy of Tolstoy's *Childhood, Boyhood, and Youth.* Before too long, they were off to Afghanistan in a decrepit 1964 Austin minivan. "I keep waking up from the same dream," she said now. "My father, who actually died when I was twelve, is still alive, but I'm a spinster, with no prospects."

"I just had a dream where I was being chased through a shopping center, and I was in a dark room with all these doors, and they were all shut but one," Tony said. "I was trying to get out that door, and it kept shrinking — and then about fifty women came through the door and prevented me from getting out."

"It's funny," Maureen said. "Because you of all the people I know are the one person who does exactly what he wants at all times." Her voice was taking on an Irish lilt, as it does when she gets worked up. "You're never thwarted. You go off and do what you like and leave everyone else to clean up the mess."

"Oh, *now*," Tony said. "It's funny. I never have sexy dreams, or frightening dreams, just dreams of annoyance and frustration."

"Dreams are surreal," Maureen said. "They reveal something important by twisting and heightening it."

"Surreal just means 'not real,'" Tony said crossly. "Dreams are dumb."

In the late 1980s, I traveled in Asia for a year, and the Lonely Planet guides were my lifeline. I ate and slept where they told me to, on Khao San Road in Bangkok and Anjuna Beach in Goa; I oriented myself by their scrupulous if naively drawn maps; and on long bus rides I immersed myself in the Indonesia book's explanation of the Ramayana story. The guides didn't tell me to wear drawstring pants and Tintin T-shirts or to crash my moped — I picked that up on my own — but they did teach me, as they taught a whole generation, how to move through the world alone and with confidence.

I learned to stuff my gear into one knapsack; never to ask a local where I should eat but, rather, where *he* ate; never to judge a country by its capital city; never to stay near a mosque (the muezzin wakes you); how to haggle; and, crucially, when I later went to Mongolia, to shout "*Nokhoi khor!*" — "Hold the dog!" — before entering a yurt. When you spend months with a guidebook that speaks to you in an intimate, conversational tone, it becomes a bosom companion.

Through studying "The Lonely Planet Story" at the back of the books and talking with other travelers, I versed myself in the creation myth: how, after meandering across Asia's Hippie Trail for nine months and fetching up in Sydney with only twenty-seven cents, the Wheelers self-published *Across Asia on the Cheap*, in 1973. The ninety-four-page pamphlet, which Tony had written at their kitchen table, sold eighty-five hundred copies in Australian bookstores. With its buccaneering opinions on the textures of daily life — "The inertial effect of religion is nowhere more clearly seen than with India's sacred cows, they spread disease, clutter already overcrowded towns, consume scarce food (and waste paper) and provide nothing" — the book hearkened back to the confident sweep of the great European guides of a century before. Guidebooks had emerged in the early 1800s as a resource for Byronic travelers in search of picturesque views, but the best of them illuminated an entire way of life. *Baedeker's London and Its Environs 1900* told readers, for instance, that the city's public baths were "chiefly for the working class who may obtain a cold bath for one penny."

After spending another year in Asia, in 1975, Tony and Maureen holed up in a fleabag hotel in Singapore for three months while he wrote *South-East Asia on a Shoestring*. Tony's former profession — in England, he had been an engineer at Chrysler — clearly influenced the books' format: they read like engineering reports, with topics such as "History," "Climate," and "Fauna & Flora" to contend with before you got to the actual sights. This eat-your-vegetables earnestness made reading the books feel like taking up a vocation.

"Lonely Planet created a floating fourth world of people who traveled full time," Pico Iyer says. "The guides encouraged a counter-Victorian way of life, in that they exactly reversed the old imperial assumptions. Now the other cultures are seen as the wise place, and we are taught to defer to them." A passage from my old *Lonely Planet Thailand* is illustrative:

Recently, when staying in Phuket for an extended period (Kata-Karon-Naiharn area), I talked with a few Thai bungalow/restaurant proprietors who said that nudity on the beaches was what bothered them most about foreign travelers. These Thais took nudity as a sign of disrespect on the part of the travelers for the locals, rather than as a libertarian symbol or modern custom. I was even asked to make signs that they could post forbidding or discouraging nudity — I declined, forgoing a free bungalow for my stay.

Note the pointed assertion of independence — and the seemingly casual aside that it was an "extended" stay. There was a self-righteousness about the tone, of course, but I liked that Lonely Planet, unlike the other major guidebooks, didn't accept advertisements, and that it donated 5 percent of its profits to charity. (After the tsunami in December, the company gave nearly four hundred thousand dollars toward relief efforts.)

I did occasionally wonder just how independent I was learning to be. When Lonely Planet set me down on an island like Ko Samui, then relatively unspoiled but already speckled with bungalows, I realized that I was seeing a parallel Thailand that bore little relation to the "real" thing. Serving up cultural comfort food is a traditional feature — or failing — of guides. Cairo is "no more than a winter suburb of London," an 1898 Cook's Tours pamphlet assured tourists. Richard Bangs, the cofounder of Mountain Travel Sobek, the adventure travel company, says that Lonely Planet travelers "like to think they're out there on the edge, but they're all reading the bible and moving in big flocks."

Yet Tony Wheeler's most important advice — reprinted in the guides until last year's relaunch — was "Just go!" Don't book hotels, don't worry unduly about shots and itineraries or even buying a guidebook — just go. This was an existential call to arms that amounted to a politics and even a morality: more than one Lonely Planet author told me that had George W. Bush ever really traveled abroad, the United States would not have invaded Iraq. The most serious political wrangle the company has got into is over publishing its Myanmar book despite international sanctions against that country and the stand taken by the country's Nobel Peace Prize–winning dissident, Aung San Suu Kyi, who has urged travelers to boycott the junta. Lonely Planet's *Myanmar (Burma)* guide pays deference to her argument, and lists the ways that you can minimize supporting the government, but concludes that travel "is the type of communication that in the long term can change lives and unseat undemocratic governments."

Movements like Lonely Planet need their martyrs, and in the eighties I heard stories in guesthouses across Asia that Tony Wheeler had recently died in spectacular fashion. There were hundreds of variations of the tale, but all had Wheeler running out of luck at the end of the trail somewhere: in a train, bus, or motorcycle accident; from malaria; at a bullfight; at the hands of the mujahideen. Not for nothing was the South-East Asia guide, with its distinctive yolk-colored cover, known as the "yellow bible." Even today, there are animated discussions on Lonely Planet's online forum, "The Thorn Tree," about whether Wheeler is the Jesus of travel or the Moses, "since the LP was not written, it was revealed."

High in the western Hajar mountains in northern Oman, our four-wheel-drive Honda lurched down a dirt pass. The one-lane road plunged among the crags toward the goal far below: Wadi Bani Awf, an arroyo filled with date palms, a rare vein of green in an arid land. The brakes were squeaking and giving off a worrisome odor, and my right thigh quivered from jabbing the nonexistent passenger-side brake pedal whenever Tony bent to peer at the odometer, checking the trip distances listed in the Lonely Planet guide. He wasn't planning to write about Oman — the Wheelers were here simply out of curiosity — but he checks every fact, everywhere. As the Lonely Planet author Ryan Ver Berkmoes puts it, "Tony is a trainspotter to the world."

"This is rather nice, isn't it?" Tony said. "Not a bad road at all." From the back seat, Maureen gave a small sigh.

Glimpsing a sign for the mountain village of Bilad Sayt, Tony stopped just past the turnoff. "Let's go see it, shall we?" he said. He began a three-point turn, backing toward the cliff. "Oh, dear," Maureen said. "Oh, dear, oh, dear, oh, drat!" The car kept backing. "Stop!"

He stopped, six inches from the edge, and, after a moment, we all laughed. "I'm fine and so are you," Tony said. And the village proved to be a wonder — a cluster of mud-brick houses clinging like a wasp's nest to a cliff, circled by falcons. We might have taken the turnoff not to Bilad Sayt but to the seventeenth century.

Traveling with the Wheelers is like that — you take every side road and see much more than you expect, much more convivially, and at much higher speed. It began at the Dubai airport: Tony and Maureen, who travel very light, charged up the stairs to get to the front of the line at immigration, leaving me feeling sheepish for taking the escalator like everyone else. As we waited at the Hertz counter, Tony studied the road map that he had brought along and announced, "Saudi Arabia and the United Arab Emirates are the two countries with the highest rate of road accidents." Then he was largely silent as we drove south, ignoring even the first camels.

The Lonely Planet guide had been rather vague about the procedure for crossing into Oman here, near Hatta, and on arriving at the Oman border we were told that we needed first to officially leave the Emirates — there had been an unmarked checkpoint at the Hatta Fort Hotel, a few miles back.

"We're in legal limbo," Tony said, as we headed north. "Here we are coming back to the U.A.E., and we're going to have to explain why we haven't left yet."

"We're going to have to explain this better in the book," Maureen said.

"When you're leaving JFK Airport," Tony continued, "they don't ask you to go to the Hilton to get your passport stamped. So *this is interesting.*"

Finding this Tony — Tony No. 2 — was like tuning in a distant radio station late at night: nothing, nothing, and then a sudden flare of chatter. This occurred whenever he saw something strange: a pedestrian underpass in the middle of nowhere, an oddly translated sign — "Sale of Ice Cubes" — or the goat souk in Nizwa, where potential buyers give the billy goats' testicles a considering squeeze.

For more than a week, we moved through Oman's northern, more populous half in a long, clockwise oval. The days would begin with a 7:30 A.M. breakfast at which Tony buried himself in his map and Lonely Planet's *Oman and the United Arab Emirates* and regional Arabian Peninsula guides, plotting the stops en route to that night's hotel, which would usually be the best available. (The Wheelers' room at the Chedi, in the capital, Muscat, cost some four hundred dollars a night.) He would toggle between the books, frowning: the Oman book provided far better cultural context but was woefully out of date. (No new edition was being readied, because the guide had sold only thirty-two thousand copies since it was published, in 2000.) And then, abruptly, we were off. Tony drove, and Maureen chatted or sang "Landslide" or "Diamonds on the Soles of Her Shoes" in a pleasing contralto, and we were in and out of the car all day long until nightfall. A few minutes into any museum or souk, you'd see Tony's eyes turn glassy, and he'd twitch his map-of-Africa cap and say, "On, on."

When Wheeler was ten, he asked for a globe and a filing cabinet for Christmas, and he is still a mixture of impulsive and compulsive — ideal qualities for a guidebook writer. He told me, "To research a big guidebook, you need some people who live in the country, but you also need some parachute artists, someone who can drop into a place and quickly assimilate, who can write about anywhere. I'm a parachute artist."

We began to orient ourselves around the country's ruler, Sultan Qaboos bin Said, whose portrait — which shows a bearded, gravely smiling man with warm brown eyes — is as omnipresent as his public-works projects. Every museum in Muscat devoted extravagant space to Qaboos's achievements (though none mentioned, as the Lonely Planet guides did, that he had kicked out the previous sultan, his father, in a bloodless coup in 1970, or that Qaboos's father had been so resistant to Western innovation that he had banned even eyeglasses). A phrase from the English-language Oman *Daily Observer* became one of our refrains: "The Sultan is always thinking of the benefit of his people."

Well aware that the country's petroleum reserves are dwindling, Sultan Qaboos has encouraged "Omanization," in which guest workers will be replaced by Omanis — and yet almost every hotel and restaurant we went to was staffed by Indians. And so "Omanization" became another, mildly sardonic refrain, as recurrent as Maureen's remark whenever we left a restaurant recommended by Lonely Planet: "Take it out of the book."

"The Omanis don't have a café culture, so we never see them," Maureen remarked one morning.

"Part of it is they've got too much money and they don't have to work," Tony said. Later that day, a police car pulsed its siren at us so that three black sedans could sweep by. "Mercedes, of course," Tony said. "You spend too long in places like Tanzania, where all

the rich assholes and government officials drive around in their
Mercedeses, and you begin to hate that car."

"It's not Mercedes' fault," Maureen said.

"Yes, it is!" Tony said. "They stand for that sort of thing. As a result, I will never own a Mercedes." (The Wheelers own an Audi, a
Mini, and a Lotus.)

The day we went to Bilad Sayt, we made our way down the pass afterward and had a late lunch. Then the question was how to get
back around the mountains to our hotel in Nizwa. The main road
lay to the southeast, but, looking at the map, Tony suggested a
more direct route to the northwest. "It's sealed roads, all the way,"
he said, asserting a faith in the map, and the Sultan's pavers, which
proved unfounded eight miles in, when the road became dirt and
began to labor up into the mountains. We came to one fork, then
another, then a third and a fourth, all unmarked on the map and
all lacking signs. The map suggested that we should be aiming at
the village of Rumaylah, but the map was ridiculous. "Every road
has to lead somewhere," Tony said, sneaking a peek at his global-
positioning device and turning toward the setting sun.

"You won't ask for directions," Maureen said.

"No real man does," Tony said. An hour later, we were going ten
miles per hour on a road that had narrowed to a sinister goat track,
in a canyon that bore no trace of human passage.

"All this is is a lack of information," Tony said. "We should have
asked the restaurant owner the best way."

Maureen snorted. "And then you would have said 'Tssh!' and we
would have still come this bloody road." They both laughed.

After a few more flying U-turns — the signature Wheeler driving
move — we finally emerged from the mountains at dusk, three
hours later, twenty-five miles north of where we expected to be.
Rumaylah remained a rumor, somewhere behind us. As we turned
south for Nizwa, Maureen saw a fort to the west, and, rather in the
manner of a mother trying to distract a child from an approaching
ice-cream truck, began a flow of chatter about the mountains to
the east.

"Should we take a quick look at the fort?" Tony asked. "A drive-by
fort?" We had already been to half a dozen of the country's five
hundred forts, all somewhat of a piece: the pillowed room for
the *wali*, or governor; the dungeons; the machicolations for pour-

ing hot date syrup on invaders. Hearing nothing from the back seat, he continued, "I think there's probably a book on the forts of Oman."

"*We're* not going to publish it," Maureen said.

"No, I meant there probably is one out there."

"Thank God."

The young Tony Wheeler once drew painstaking maps of his walks around the neighborhood. It was, perhaps, a way of trying to hold on to an ever-shifting landscape. Wheeler's father was an airport manager for British Overseas Airways Corporation, the precursor to British Airways, and the family kept moving: Pakistan, the Bahamas, Canada, America, England. "Being always the outsider, never spending two whole years in the same school, it does fuck you up," Wheeler told me.

"Tony has a story for every occasion, but he's not very good with personal questions," the photographer Richard I'Anson, who has often traveled with Wheeler, says. "We were in Delhi together in 1997 when he got the news that his father had died. You would possibly expect that he'd talk with his friend about that, but I knew not to ask him about it then, and I wouldn't ask him now."

Wheeler says, "I don't think I was particularly close to either of my parents; there was an English coolness there — though I did love going to the airport with my father. But what the hell — I'm sure Maureen and I fucked up our kids, too." The Wheelers have two children — Tashi, now twenty-four, and Kieran, twenty-two — and they brought them along nearly everywhere; hostels were their nursery schools. "My memories are all messed up from when I was younger," Tashi Wheeler told me, cheerfully. "Sometimes I remember a place as Peru, and it was Jakarta. We were always traveling, traveling."

In retrospect, the growth of Lonely Planet from such rootless soil is both unlikely and entirely apt. The Wheelers came along when the world had begun to tire of the strictly-for-tourists approach of Fodor's and Frommer's and Fielding's, which was packed with alarming puns (the Hotel Piccadilly in London "puts shoppers right in the limey-light"); to tire of the naiveté propounded in books such as *How to Travel Without Being Rich* (1959), which declared, "Mexico is the best place in the world for economical travelers who like to bring back things to astonish their friends . . . woven straw geegaws, works of art in tin and heaven knows what else."

"In the seventies and eighties, there hadn't been any new guides out for decades," Mark Ellingham, who founded the competing Rough Guides in 1981, says. Then airlines deregulated, making cheap tickets widely available, just as Vietnam and China and, later, Eastern Europe were opening up. "We filled a need, but we were young and ignorant and amateurish."

It was only after Lonely Planet's India guide unexpectedly sold a hundred thousand copies, in 1980, that the Wheelers realized that their scrappy startup was a real business. But the enterprise remained disarmingly ad hoc; for a time, the *Africa on a Shoestring* book said, of the Comoros Islands, "We haven't heard of anyone going there for a long time so we have no details to offer. If you do go, please drop us a line."

"Tony and Maureen would pluck these people out of a bar, or somewhere, and have complete confidence in them," Michelle de Kretser, a former Lonely Planet publisher who is now a novelist, says. "In 1992, they handed me this plum job, running the new Paris office, which I was totally unqualified for. I said, 'How do I do that?' And they said, 'You know, just go and do it, whatever — you know.'" For years, whenever problems arose, Tony would respond rather as the Red Queen did to Alice, saying, "Let's just run faster!" And for years it all worked.

The Wheelers long maintained an implicit nonaggression pact with other countercultural handbooks. But, as Tony Wheeler tells it, in 1984 he noticed that the Moon Travel Handbook's renowned Indonesia guide was seriously out of date, so he commissioned a book on that country. After Penguin bought a majority stake in Rough Guides, in 1996, Wheeler noticed that Rough Guides were undercutting Lonely Planet's prices. "So we thought, how can we hit back?" he told me, with a steely grin. "We targeted their twelve or so top-selling guides and produced competitive titles for every one. They stopped being so aggressive on pricing."

"Penguin is one of the most ruthless media organizations in the world — it'd be happy to squash us like a bug," Mark Carnegie, an investment banker who sits on Lonely Planet's board, says. ("We completely compete with Lonely Planet, but we're not squashing people," Andrew Welham, who supervises the Rough Guides and the DK Eyewitness series for Penguin, observes.) "But Tony is the Rupert Murdoch of the alternative travel space," Carnegie added. "He knows when and how to squash back."

One afternoon in Tiwi, a pretty town on the coast road to Sur, the Wheelers and I had a very good Indian-food lunch. As we strolled out to the car, a small boy in a blue soccer jersey smiled and asked for "*baisa, baisa*" — money. He was the first beggar we'd met.

"No *baisa*," Maureen said in a friendly way. She showed a real interest in children, and always replied to them. This boy waited till we got in the car and then flipped her the bird. She flipped it back: "Sit and spin, kid!"

"I don't know if you should do that, Maur," Tony said calmly, as he drove off. "If you know what that gesture means, that means Western women know what it means, and that reinforces the idea that they're loose and easy."

"If I weren't in the car, I'd slap the little bastard," Maureen said. "Would he do that to an Arabic woman? Would he do that to his own mother?"

Thirty years ago, Wheeler took a different view of cross-cultural sexual politics. He wrote, in *Across Asia on the Cheap*, that in Muslim countries women are going to "get their little asses grabbed," so "if you can lay hands on one of the bastards, take advantage of it and rough him up a little." In the early days, Lonely Planet advocated what might be called a playground model of behavior: here's the score on Lebanese grass and Balinese mushrooms, here's where to buy carpets in Iran before child-labor laws drive up the price, here's how to sell blood in Kuwait to pay for the rugs. You should avoid unwashed fruit, and you should wear a short-hair wig to fool the uptight cats in Singapore immigration, but, in general, the world is yours.

As the guidebooks grew up, the museum model took hold: foreign cultures are fragile, and should be observed as if through glass; a practice you abhor may simply be a custom you don't understand. In the 1988 edition of the guide to Papua New Guinea, a notoriously lawless place, Wheeler himself wrote, "It is very easy to apply inappropriate Western criteria, and what appears to be uncontrolled anarchy is often nothing of the sort. . . . A case that appears to be straightforward assault may well be a community-sanctioned punishment. Looting a store may be in lieu of the traditional division of a big man's estate."

The first edition of Lonely Planet's Japan guide, in 1981, had lengthy treatments of swinging with Japanese couples, live sex shows, and *toruko,* establishments where men could get soaped up to full satisfaction. Over the years, this section was pruned and then eliminated. "When we were selling five thousand Japanese guidebooks a year, who cared what we said?" Maureen told me. "At fifty thousand, you have a different responsibility."

Though sales kept rising, by the late nineties Lonely Planet had begun to falter. The company's rapid expansion — in 2000 it published eight new series, including *Watching Wildlife* and *City Maps* — was accompanied by constant cash-flow crises. Sixty percent of the guides weren't getting to the printer on time. "Everyone was lovely, but no one had a clue," Maureen said, during one stretch of driving. "When Tony was away in 1998 — he was traveling a lot, because he didn't want to deal with it — I told the managers they had to go. And I said to Tony, 'If you let them talk you out of it, I am leaving you.'" Tony kept his eyes on the road. Later, Maureen told me, "Without Tony, Lonely Planet wouldn't exist; without me, it wouldn't have held together."

The morning after the planes hit the World Trade Center, in 2001, the company called an emergency meeting, knowing that travel was about to plummet. A hundred people (19 percent of the workforce) were later laid off, and author salaries were reduced by up to 30 percent. The company was further buffeted by SARS, the terrorist bombing in Bali, the Iraq war, and the threat of avian flu, and it lost money for two and a half years running.

The relaunch, a response to all those changing conditions, subordinated editorializing to giving travelers a well-stuffed factual cushion that they could place between themselves and danger or discomfort. Call it the information model. Tony Wheeler explains, "I would expect someone writing for us about Spain to delve into bullfights, and either to say it's a cruel and primitive spectacle or to say that it's just as great as Hemingway said — and, either way, here are the hours the bullring is open, and do bring sunscreen."

At the same time, "Just go" was replaced, as a corporate ethos, by the words "attitude and authority," which one hears in the Melbourne office every fifteen seconds or so. Equally common are references to the new "consumer segmentation model," which sorts travelers into such categories as "global nomads" and "mature adventurers." And the company that had prided itself on not taking advertisements is about to start a hotel-booking service on its Web site. "When Tony washed up on the deserted shores of Bali thirty years ago, it was great to 'just go,'" John Ryan, Lonely Planet's digital-project manager, says. "If you just went to Bali now, you might not have a place to stay. We're thinking about every phase of the travel cycle — dream, plan, book, go, come back — and trying to fill each one with Lonely Planet content." Like Apple and Starbucks and Ben & Jerry's, all of which began as plucky alternatives, Lonely Planet has become a mainstream brand.

Last year, the company grossed $72 million, with a before-tax profit margin of 17 percent. But the Wheelers' withdrawal during this tumultuous period has left many authors feeling marooned. Sixteen Lonely Planet veterans have established a private e-mail network to trade yearning recollections of the old days of unfettered travel and unedited prose, of princely royalties and heavy drinking and broken marriages. "Now authors are data collectors for editors," the author Joe Cummings told me. The veterans gripe that the editors don't even return their e-mails, a state of affairs they call "black hole syndrome."

For their part, the Wheelers speak of "mad-author syndrome." But they are equally skeptical of the company's new marketing surveys and slogans: clearly, Maureen is attitude and Tony is authority. One night over dinner at a Melbourne restaurant, Maureen said, "I used to feel that Lonely Planet was very *real* — we'd steam stamps off letters and reuse them, and everyone who worked there became our friends. And then we hired all these people —"

"These lawyers and accountants," Tony said. "I hate paying them. I walk through our parking garage and see a Mercedes — a Mercedes!"

"Anyway," Maureen said, "the point is, we're learning how to be people who just *inspire* — but Lonely Planet doesn't feel real to me anymore."

One measure of how the company has changed is that when the new head of trade publishing, Roz Hopkins, took the job, in 2002, she quickly, if regretfully, cancelled Wheeler's forthcoming book about his travels in rice-growing countries. "That sort of book had been quite a dismal failure," she told me, referring to other idiosyncratic Wheeler efforts featuring Richard I'Anson photographs. "They don't articulate the message of the brand." So Wheeler wound up underwriting *Rice Trails* with nearly forty thousand dollars of his own money — effectively using Lonely Planet as a vanity press.

The Wheelers often hear complaints that they have helped to ruin certain destinations — that, as Richard Bangs, of Mountain Travel Sobek, affectionately puts it, "Tony can turn an out-of-the-way secret place like Lombok into something that's loved to death." They respond that change is inevitable, that guidebooks don't inspire travel so much as channel it, and that it's better to have educated travelers than clucks on tour buses. But the way Tony Wheeler rushes about suggests that he feels with particular keenness the age-old traveler's anxiety about getting there before it all goes. (As early as the 1870s, John Muir denounced the tourists who were ruining Yosemite as "scum.") Wheeler's fears were realized at one of Oman's signature seasonal riverbeds, Wadi Bani Khalid. As we approached the wadi, deep in the mountains, the road became a rugged dirt track and Wheeler brightened; arduousness, for him, promises happiness. Then we rounded a bend and joined a new road swarming with construction workers. He sank back as if he'd been punched: "It's appalling!"

"The Sultan is always thinking of the benefit of his people," Maureen murmured.

After we parked, five local boys shepherded us up to the rock pools, chattering away in the universal pidgin of the tourism encounter: "Where you from? What your name? First time come Oman?" The pools were a refreshing aquamarine, but they were also clotted with trash. The boys asked us to come for a Bedouin meal, and, when we declined, one boy suggested, "Give me money — one *rial.*" Taking our refusal slightly sulkily, they turned back toward the parking lot.

"They'll be proper little guides soon," Maureen said. She considered the concrete picnic areas and the beginnings of what looked like a snack stand — a grader was noisily leveling the earth nearby — and said, "You have to destroy everything in order to appreciate what you have. They'll learn that people are paying more to get away from all this."

We were soon back on the road, heading north. "You grow up,

and then you grow old," Maureen said suddenly. "The first part is all right . . ."

The modern version of straw geegaws is cultural capital in the form of stories and photographs. "Tony and Maureen are in the travel-information insurance business," Mark Carnegie says. "If the educated consumer is spending ten thousand dollars on a vacation, and someone says to him, 'For an extra thirty dollars, I will give you a sunrise that will make you cry' — well, he's going to take out that insurance."

Even Lonely Planet, however, hasn't figured out a way to market its epiphanies other than by using the impoverished language of travel writing. And so "palm-fringed beaches" and "lush rain forests" and other "sleepy backwaters" are invariably counterpoised against "teeming cities" with their "bustling souks." Every region has a "colorful history" and a "rich cultural tapestry." And every place on earth is a "land of contrasts." As the Arabian Peninsula guide observes, "Bedouin tribesmen park 4WDs alongside goat hair tents; veiled women chat on mobile phones while awaiting laser hair removal," and so on.

Peering through the windshield as another unnamed village ghosted by — mud-brick houses, men in white slouched in the shade — Maureen said, "We're outsiders, we don't speak the language, we only glean what we can through what we read. I can *see* their lives, but I'd love to be in their heads for a few hours — what's it like to *be* their lives?"

Entranced by every sort of strangeness, Tony often wondered aloud: What are these "pee caps" that hotel bars forbid you to wear? Why are there so many "Gents Tailors" in the town of Sohar? But he never stopped, preferring to note the street misnamed on Lonely Planet's Sohar map, and the absence of the promised *biryani* joints. He wants to discover by observation or exploration, but not to have to ask, a form of cheating. When I was younger, I might have inquired more myself — there was a time when every new thing, even durian slushies, seemed worth investigating. But now, I realized, I had been perfectly content to follow Wheeler's lead, and so I was leaving Oman with a thoroughly researched yet tentative impression of a country of forts, wadis, and a pleasant capital, Muscat.

I asked Wheeler what he thought Lonely Planet should do about Oman. He suggested that a small, high-priced book that focused on the forts, the wadis, and Muscat might work — but in truth he seemed to be already looking ahead to his next destination, Ethiopia, and then to all the trips beyond. "In the early days," he said, "doing the third or fourth edition of *South-East Asia on a Shoestring,* I remember feeling like we were trapped: We set this up to travel, and all we're doing is going to Singapore and Bangkok over and over, updating."

"Now that the company is launched, Tony can really travel," Maureen said.

Tony thought that over, its possible meanings, and replied, "In many ways, I don't think we've traveled a lot, because we've had the business distracting us. It got in the way."

Late one afternoon, we hiked up Wadi Shab, a steep canyon. The first hour was an easy hike, and then it became a scramble over shaley outcroppings and around acacia thorns. Finally, as the canyon filled with shadows, we arrived at a crisp blue pool where a few local teenagers were splashing about and diving into the adjacent underground caves. The last rays of sun lit the spot: a perfect reward after a long drive and a healthy walk. But Tony shifted with frustration as Maureen and I sat on a boulder and turned our faces to the sun. He had noticed three tourists in bathing suits above us on the faint indications of a trail. "I'll just go on for twenty more minutes," Tony said. We got up and walked with him a ways, and then Maureen took up a perch against the canyon wall. "I'm not going on," she said. "I'll stay here." I was thinking about nightfall, and finding the path down, and the two-hour drive along the sea cliffs to the hotel.

"Well, I'm just going on for a bit," he said. Having, across the years, thrown off most of his burdens, Tony No. 1 now adjusted the one piece of baggage that remained — his backpack, which was ringed with sweat — and strode on as Tony No. 2. Or was it the reverse? In a few moments, he was around the corner.

"The trick with Tony is, if I'd been in that comfortable place by the pool he would have gone on and on," Maureen said. "But, knowing I'm in this uncomfortable place, he'll feel guilty and come back sooner. He has to go around that bend, though — it's his obsession. He has to go farther than the tourists. And, if there's someone else around that bend, he'll keep going until he's past them, until he's the farthest out."

PICO IYER

Our Lady of Lawson

FROM the *New York Times Magazine*

TO LIVE IN JAPAN without eating Japanese food seems an advanced kind of heresy. My sushi-loving friends in California regard me as a lost cause; my housemates in Japan simply shrug and see this as ultimate confirmation — me dragging at some lasagna in a plastic box while they gobble down dried fish — that I belong to an alien species. I grew up in England, I tell them, on boarding-school food, no less; I like Japan at some level deeper than the visible (or edible). They look away and try not to scream.

Yet the habit that has won me complete excommunication on both sides of the world is my readiness to eat (twice a day) from Lawson, my tiny local convenience store in Nara, the old Japanese capital. A convenience store speaks to many of us of all that is questionable in modern Japan: a soulless, synthetic, one-size-fits-all lifestyle that the efficiency-loving country has perfected to the nth degree. It marks, most would say, the end of family, tradition, and community as well as the advent of a homogenized future that has many people running for "slow food."

The convenience store is a model of Japan in miniature: the triumph of function over fuss and of ease over embarrassment. Just as you can buy whiskey, eggs, pornography, and even (it is said) women's underwear in vending machines, so you can all but live in convenience stores. I pay my phone bills and send my packages through the local branch of the national Lawson chain (named after the defunct American Lawson); I buy my bus cards there and tickets for Neil Young concerts. I make the convenience store my de facto office, lingering by the photocopier for hours on end and then faxing an article, say, to New York. Yet the first law of Japan, even in Lawson, is that nothing is what it seems, and that you can find all the cultures of the world here, made Japanese and strange. Here, in the four thin aisles of my local store, are the McVitie's digestives of my youth — turned into bite-sized afterthoughts. Here are Milky Bar chocolates, converted into bullet-sized pellets. Here are Mentos in shades of lime and grape, cans of "Strawberry Milk Tea" and the Smarties I used to collect as a boy, refashioned as "Marble Chocolate." Were Marcel Proust to come to Lawson, he would find his madeleines daily but made smaller, sweeter, and mnemonically new.

It's common to hear that Japan has created a promiscuous anthology of the world's best styles. And the convenience store is the center of this. Tubs of Earl Grey ice cream, sticks of mangosteen chewing gum, green-tea-flavored KitKat bars: they're all here in abundance (though, in fashion-victimized Japan, no sooner have I developed a fondness for KissMint chewing gum "for Etiquette" than it has been supplanted by ice creams in the shape of watermelon slices). And even the smallest chocolate bar comes with an English-language inscription that, in the Japanese way, makes no sense whatsoever, yet confers on everything the perfume of an enigmatic fairy tale: "A lovely and tiny twig," says my box of Koeda chocolates, "is a heroine's treasured chocolate born in the forest."

In modern Japan, the convenience store is taken to be the spiritual home of the boys in hip-hop shorts and the girls with shocking yellow hair and artificial tans, who try with their every move — eating in the street, squatting on the sidewalk — to show that they take their cues from 50 Cent and not Mrs. Suzuki. The door of my local Lawson has badges to denote police surveillance, and where the great twentieth-century novelist Junichiro Tanizaki praised shadows (nuance, ambiguity, the lure of the half-seen) as the essence of the Japan he loved, Lawson speaks for a new fluorescent, posthuman — even anti-Japanese — future. And yet, in the twelve years I've lived on and off in my mock-California suburb, the one person who has come to embody for me all the care for detail and solicitude I love in Japan is, in fact, the lady at the cash register in Lawson. Small, short-haired, and perpetually harried, Hirata-*san* races to the back of the store to fetch coupons for me that will give me ten cents off my "Moisture Dessert." She bows to the local gangster who leaves his Bentley running and comes in the store with his high-heeled moll to claim some litchi-flavored strangeness. When occasionally I don't show up for six or seven hours, she sends, through my housemates, a bag of French fries to revive me.

The Japanese are so good at keeping up appearances that few signs are ever evident of the series of recent recessions. But over the years, I have seen poor Mrs. Hirata's husband (the store's manager) open his doors around the clock and take the graveyard shift himself. The place started to stock tequila-sunrise cocktails in a can, and little bottles of wine. Soon even the Hiratas' two high-school-age sons were being pressed into service (unpaid, I'm sure).

It's no easier to understand Japan in Western terms than it is to eat noodles with a knife and fork. Yet it has been evident to me for some time that the crush of the anonymous world lies out in the temple-filled streets; the heart of the familiarity, the communal sense of neighborhood, the simple kindness that brought me to Japan, lies in the convenience store.

Early last year, writing an article on paradise, I surmised that my modest neighborhood could be improved only by the addition of a cinema, but given the laws of human longing and limitation, such an arrival would probably mean the end of my favorite convenience store. Be careful of what you write. Days before my article came out, a sign appeared on my local Lawson, announcing it was going out of business. Almost everyone in the neighborhood was shaken, but no one knew what to do. (How to express your gratitude to a convenience store?) We'd watched the owners' sons grow up while their parents served up bags of chicken nuggets in three spicy flavors.

I went home, found a set of elegant bowls I'd bought in case of a sudden need for a wedding present and returned to the store. They were being transferred to a far-off shop in the countryside, Mrs. Hirata said; she feared for her kids. She was even afraid of going out there herself. Then I handed over the box, and she realized why I had come. She began to waver for a moment, then turned away from me and put a calzone in the microwave. A true Japanese to the end, she wanted to protect me from her tears.

MARK JENKINS

A Short Walk in the Wakhan Corridor

FROM *Outside*

THE OLD WAKHI HORSEMAN sucks deeply on his pipe, the opium glowing scarlet in the darkness, and blows smoke in my face. We're lying side by side on pounded wool mats in a cavelike hut in far northeastern Afghanistan. The stone walls and stick ceiling drip with black tar from decades of burning yak dung. A goat is butting its horns against the crooked door. Outside, the sheep are shuffling nervously inside the stone corral, waiting for a wolf to take one of them.

The fire is almost out and everyone is asleep — pressed together for warmth like the animals — except the horseman and me. His wind-shot eyes are shut. He inhales, his craggy face relaxing, then exhales, the psychoactive smoke swirling around my head.

Another long day done. Our team of eight — three Americans, our Pakistani guide, and four Wakhi horsemen — is walking the Wakhan Corridor, Afghanistan's ancient, forgotten passageway to China. We are more than halfway through, en route to Tajikistan. Marco Polo passed this way 734 years ago. It was medieval then, and it still is.

It was late afternoon today when we climbed out of the dark canyons up onto the treeless, thirteen-thousand-foot steppe. Two vultures, with their pterodactyl-like six-foot wingspans, were circling above a yak carcass. Our day's destination, a place called Langar, turned out to be this solitary hut out on the vast brown plain. A gaunt woman in a maroon shawl invited us into the smoke-choked shelter and gave us salt tea in a chipped china cup. Her name was Khan Bibi. She was thirty-five, but she was weather-beaten and missing teeth and looked twice her age. She began making flatbread, wetting handfuls of flour with water from a pail. She sent her youngest child, a four-year-old girl whose nose was running with green snot, out to collect disks of fuel. With blackened hands the woman slapped the slabs of dough against the horseshoe curve of the clay hearth. As they finished baking and fell off into the fire, she reached into the flames and passed them to us.

We all went back outside when we heard a chorus of baaing. Khan Bibi's husband, Mohammad Kosum, forty-five, and their seven-year-old son, both in black Russian fur caps with earflaps, were bringing the sheep and goats into the corral. Together this family of four began lifting lambs and kids from a cellar, placing them with their correct mothers, allowing them to suckle, then dropping them back down into the two-foot-deep hole where their combined body warmth would keep them alive. With eight hundred animals to move, the process lasted till dark.

Khan Bibi returned to the hearth and squatted there for the next three hours, making us rice and more flatbread and more salt tea. There was no electricity, no lamp, no candle. Dim orange firelight and a shaft of blue moonlight cut down through the whirling smoke from a square hole in the roof. The tiny girl fetched water from a snowmelt creek that runs through the reeking carcasses of yaks that died during the snowy spring. When we were all fed, Khan Bibi curled up on the shelf above the fire with her two children and pulled a yak-hair blanket over the three of them.

Now, hours later, the old horseman is next to me, blowing smoke in my face. He's on his fourth or fifth bowl. I can't keep track anymore. I'm floating on secondhand smoke, back to my first day in Afghanistan.

I'm running up Aliabad, a mountain in the middle of Kabul. Tilting dirt streets with runnels carved down the middle by sewage. I pass two faceless women, heads trapped inside helmets of blue mesh. In the rocks above the flat roofs, I pass a shepherd girl shooing sheep along the mountainside. I reach the top and begin to run along the ridge top in pink light. Up and down through trenches, stepping on piles of rusty four-inch-long bullet casings, skirting a blown-apart artillery gun, leaping an ordnance dump.

Below me, Kabul is brown. Everything in Afghanistan is brown. Smog obscures the city, but there's not much to see anyway: mudbrick houses and miles of ruins. Supposedly in the seventies there were paved, tree-lined streets and outdoor cafés and a university and women with faces who wore flowered skirts. Today it is apoca-lyptic — the destroyed capital of a country that has been at war, with invaders and itself, for twenty-five years. Make that twenty-five centuries.

I'm running along thinking about baby-faced, flak-jacketed American soldiers in their armored convoys when I glance at the ground and stop dead in my tracks.

I'm surrounded by rocks painted blood red. I know what this means — it's the first thing you learn upon arriving in Afghanistan: land mines. My eyes shoot side to side, searching for the rocks painted half red, half white. Cleared paths through minefields are lined with such bicolored rocks, the white side indicating safety.

But there is no path. I hold myself motionless. Try to breathe calmly, look over your shoulder. I am twenty feet into the mine-field. Very carefully, step backward. I place one foot precisely in its own footprint. Do this with the other foot. Delicately, imagining myself as weightless as the ghost I could become, I retrace my steps.

Beside me, the horseman is still smoking. A few days ago, on the road outside Kabul, I met a man whose eleven-year-old son, Gulmarjan, was killed by a land mine while tending a flock of goats. Now, in a hazy, smoky dream, I see Gulmarjan running through red rocks, chasing a goat. Suddenly he's up in the air, his face stricken, blood splattering the brown sky and the brown earth and his feet still in his boots but not attached to his knees. My friend Greg's voice floats back to me, saying, "Three million land mines in a country of twenty-five million — that's at least one for each family . . . The Russians made ones that looked like little butterflies. Curious children still pick them up . . ."

The horseman is asleep, his face smashed against the wool mat, the pipe still glowing. Gathering up my sleeping bag, I escape the hut. The air is ice sharp, the sky buckshot with stars, the walls of the encircling mountains black, the snow along their crests as lumines-cent as a crown. I walk out into the pale-blue steppe and find a spot among the slumbering yaks.

I slide into this distant night in no man's land. Lie back, look up, breathe. Safe and sound in this eternally unsafe, unsound country.

In 2000, Greg Mortenson and I hatched the idea of traversing the length of the Wakhan Corridor, the thin, vestigial arm of northeastern Afghanistan that extends eastward to the border of China, separating Tajikistan from Pakistan. As founder and director of the Bozeman, Montana–based Central Asia Institute (CAI), a nongovernmental organization that has built more than fifty schools in the tribal borderlands of Pakistan and Afghanistan, Greg had plenty of experience navigating the region's dicey political landscape.

We were planning to go in the fall of 2001. Then, on September 9, Ahmed Shah Massoud, commander of Afghanistan's anti-Taliban Northern Alliance, was assassinated by Al Qaeda suicide bombers. Two days later, 9/11. A month later, American cruise missiles were detonating on Taliban positions. Within half a year, the war in Afghanistan was putatively over, but it wasn't. It's never over in Afghanistan.

Afghanistan is a palimpsest of conquest. The Persians ruled the region in the sixth century B.C., then came Alexander the Great two hundred years later. The White Huns in the fourth century A.D., Islamic armies in the seventh, Genghis Khan and the Mongols in the thirteenth. It wasn't until the eighteenth century that a united Afghan empire emerged, then came the British, then, in 1979, the Russians. And now the Americans and their allies.

In October 2004, Afghanistan elected President Hamid Karzai, but his control barely extends beyond Kabul. As it has been for centuries, the Afghan countryside is ruled by tribal and regional leaders. It's a complex power network fraught with shifting allegiances. In the eighties, Afghan mujahideen ("freedom fighters") were armed and funded by the CIA to resist the Russians. After the Soviet occupation ended, in 1989, Afghanistan plunged into a state of internecine fighting: warlords — regional leaders backed by independent militias — clashed, and the country fractured into a patchwork of fiefdoms. In 1996, the Taliban, a generation of Afghan Islamic fundamentalists that had grown frustrated with civil war, seized control of Kabul. They subsequently gave safe haven to Osama bin Laden and his Al Qaeda fighters. Today, despite the presence of thirty-three thousand NATO and coalition troops, Afghanistan remains a violent, dangerous mess.

If any region of the country stands apart, it's the remote, sparsely populated Wakhan Corridor, which has been spared much of the recent bloodletting. Carved by the Wakhan and Panj rivers, the two-hundred-mile-long valley, much of it above ten thousand feet, separates the Pamir mountains to the north from the Hindu Kush to the south. For centuries, it has been a natural conduit between Central Asia and China, and one of the most forbidding sections of the Silk Road, the four-thousand-mile trade route linking Europe to the Far East.

The borders of the Wakhan were set in an 1895 treaty between Russia and Britain, which had been wrestling over the control of Central Asia for nearly a century. In what was dubbed the "Great Game" (a term coined by British Army spy Arthur Conolly of the 6th Bengal Native Light Cavalry), both countries had sent intrepid spies into the region, not a few of whom had been caught and be-headed. (Conolly was killed in Bokhara in 1842.) Eventually Brit-ain and Russia agreed to use the entire country as a buffer zone, with the Wakhan extension ensuring that the borders of the Rus-sian empire would never touch the borders of the British Raj.

Only a handful of Westerners are known to have traveled through the Wakhan Corridor since Marco Polo did it, in 1271. There had been sporadic European expeditions throughout the second half of the nineteenth century and the beginning of the twentieth. In 1949, when Mao Zedong completed the Communist takeover of China, the borders were permanently closed, sealing off the two-thousand-year-old caravan route and turning the corridor into a cul-de-sac. When the Soviets invaded Afghanistan in December 1979, they occupied the Wakhan and plowed a tank track half-way into the corridor. Today, the Wakhan has reverted to what it's been for much of its history: a primitive pastoral hinterland, home to about seven thousand Wakhi and Kirghiz people, scat-tered throughout some forty small villages and camps. Opium smug-glers sometimes use the Wakhan, traveling at night.

In 2004, American writers John Mock and Kimberley O'Neil crossed much of the Wakhan, exiting south into Pakistan. As far as Greg and I could find out, for decades no one had traversed the en-tire length of the Wakhan, following the old Silk Road from its en-trance at the big northward bend of the Panj River all the way across to Tajikistan. We had no idea if it could even be done.

By the time our schedules matched up, four years later, Greg was so busy running the CAI that he no longer had time to attempt the Wakhan traverse. But he was still passionate about the journey, and delighted to help make it happen. In his former life he'd been a climber and adventurer — it was the path that had led him to aid work. Coming off K2 in 1993, weak and exhausted, he'd been taken in by villagers in Pakistan. Because of their kindness, Greg had promised to return the following year and build a school. Which he did. Three years later, he founded the CAI.

Greg believed that the only way to truly understand Afghanistan, with all its contradiction and complexity, was total immersion. Excited about the trek, he found a partner for me: Doug Chabot, director of the Gallatin National Forest Avalanche Center, in Montana, and a long-time Exum mountaineering guide. In an e-mail, Greg described Doug as "a tough, hardworking, easygoing, non-ego guy." Since we planned to attempt at least one virgin peak in the Wakhan, Chabot's avalanche experience "would be good life insurance." Our plan was to cross the Wakhan from west to east, using a four-wheel-drive van as far as we could, then going by foot or horseback.

The first time we all assembled was in Greg's dingy room in the Kabul Peace Guest House, a small hotel in central Kabul, in late April 2005: Greg, forty-seven, comfortably attired in a dirt-brown *shalwar kameez*; Doug, forty-one, tan, trim, with big green eyes and an inimitable laugh; and Teru Kuwayama, thirty-five, a New York–based photographer who had previously shot in Pakistan and Iraq.

We'd be relying on Greg's contacts with regional leaders to secure safe passage through the Wakhan, but the real uncertainty was getting out of Afghanistan. Although we had visas for Tajikistan (and China, just in case), none of us knew anything about the borders at the end of the Wakhan. We could be stopped by Tajik guards and sent back, forced to retrace our journey in reverse. Or we could be arrested.

The corner of the Wakhan where Tajikistan, China, Afghanistan, and Pakistan meet is sensitive territory. On the China side, the Uighur, a Muslim Turkic population of eight million, are clamoring for independence. In Kashmir, Pakistan and India have yet to resolve their decades-old dispute over borders and ethnic governance. To the north, the former Soviet republic of Tajikistan is run by an unstable, authoritarian government, and the country is an integral part of the global opium pipeline. (As much as half of all opium produced in Afghanistan is exported via Tajikistan.) Islamic fundamentalist guerrillas have been known to infiltrate the region; if we encountered them — or were mistaken for guerrillas ourselves — it could get ugly.

Greg said he'd try to meet us within ten days in Sarhadd, in the middle of the Wakhan. He introduced us to fifty-year-old Sarfraz Khan, his right-hand man.

"Sarfraz will be going with you," he said.

A tall, dark, mustached man stood up and extended a crippled hand toward me. "I am very pleased to meet you," he said.

Over the years, Greg had told me stories about Sarfraz. Born and based in the Chapurson Valley, in northern Pakistan, he had served as a commando in Pakistan's elite mountain force; while stationed in Kashmir, he was wounded twice by Indian troops. One bullet passed through his palm and paralyzed his right hand. He spoke English, Urdu, Farsi, Wakhi, Burushashki, and Pashto. He'd spent years traveling the Wakhan as a yak trader. In a land where everything was impossible, Sarfraz would be our indispensable, indefatigable fixer.

We spent several days in Kabul before heading north, shopping for supplies and exchanging dollars for bricks of Afghan banknotes at the Shari Nau market, and bicycling out to the now abandoned blue-domed Ministry of Vice and Virtue, whose Taliban enforcers had patrolled the city, whipping women for infractions as minor as revealing their ankles.

While the Afghan government has ratified treaties to improve women's rights, the country still has a long way to go to meet the standards it has set. A few days after we arrived in Kabul, the BBC and other international news sources reported that a twenty-nine-year-old woman named Amina had been buried up to her chest and stoned to death near Faizabad, the capital of northern Afghanistan's Badakhshan province, for alleged infidelity. According to the reports, seventy people from the community, including her husband and father, participated in the murder. In early May, two hundred women gathered in Kabul to call on the post-Taliban government and Islamic leaders to oppose acts of violence against women, a first step on a very long, dangerous journey.

One day we visited the village of Lalander, south of Kabul, for a tribal meeting at a CAI school. It was a brand-new whitewashed, plumb-walled building amid helter-skelter mud homes. CAI schools are joint projects: the costs of construction and paying teachers are split between the CAI and the village. (Most of Greg's work is financed by private donations; the CAI receives no U.S. government funding.) With few exceptions, its schools are coed.

At the Lalander school, boys and girls were lined up in their Friday best to present Greg with wreaths of paper flowers. After the welcoming ceremony, he spoke at the *jirga* — the council of elders — which met inside the village mosque. Forty stone-faced, bearded men sat cross-legged on worn Afghan rugs. Greg asked for Allah's blessing, thanked the greatness and wisdom of Allah, asked Allah to guide the judgment of the *jirga*. Lalander, he said, would be recognized as the most powerful village in all of Afghanistan, because of its courage to build a school that both boys and girls could attend.

Later, Greg told me that some of the men at the *jirga* were Taliban. "My dream is to build a school in every village from Kabul to Kandahar right to Deh Rawood, the village of Mullah Mohammed Omar, fugitive leader of the Taliban."

As we were driving out of Lalander, Greg saw a man standing on a hillside near a pile of rocks and stopped our van. We walked over to talk to him. He was Gulmarjan's father; in June 2004, the boy had been blown to pieces by a land mine just a hundred yards from the half-completed school. According to the International Committee of the Red Cross, leftover land mines and ordnance killed or wounded some 847 people in Afghanistan in 2004; despite determined de-mining efforts, the carnage continues.

The man told us how excited Gulmarjan had been about going to school with his younger sister. As he spoke, he raised his arms in the air, as if expecting his son, alive and whole, to drop back into them.

It took us three days to drive to Faizabad, home to the northernmost American military base. En route we passed dozens of stripped Russian tanks, most of which had been repurposed as bridges, retaining walls, storage units, and playground equipment. Even art installations: in a field by the side of the road we saw a row of three half-buried tanks sticking out of the ground like an Afghan version of Cadillac Ranch.

In Kunduz, a jovial Afghan teacher helped me order charcoal-grilled sheep shish kebab from a street vendor, and we struck up a conversation. "It took the Russians only a few weeks to take Afghanistan — just like you Americans," he said. "And I believe the regret began immediately."

We spent a night in Faizabad, then drove a few hours east to Baharak, the last town in which we could buy provisions. Doug, using his avalanche forecaster's waterproof pad and clear script, was our quartermaster. A veteran of extended climbing expeditions to Pakistan, he knew exactly what we needed. He'd announce the acquired item, then mark it off his list.

"Ten kilos rice: check. Ten kilos potatoes: check. Two kilos salt: check. Aluminum pot: check. Plastic pail: check. Fifty feet nylon cord: check."

In Baharak we stayed with Sardhar Khan, a powerful leader in the Badakhshan province. We'd been told we needed his blessing to pass through his territory and into the Wakhan.

Khan, forty-eight, is a small ethnic Tajik with a creased chestnut face who calls himself a former warlord. One of the most feared and respected commanders in Afghanistan, he spent fifteen years bivouacking in the mountains with his militia — ten years fighting the Russians, five years fighting the Taliban — but the man I met was polite and soft-spoken. He personally laid out the silverware for a picnic in his tiny apricot orchard and told us about the school he'd built with Greg last year. It was the CAI's largest — a fortresslike structure with stone walls four feet thick and a wood-burning stove in each of the eight classrooms. More than 250 kids would be attending the school this fall.

With his wars over for now, Khan was writing poems. Greg sent me a sample of his verse after our trip:

> You may wonder why I sit here on this rock, by the river,
>   doing nothing.
> There is so much work to be done for my people.
> We have little food, we have few jobs, our fields are in shambles,
>   and still land mines everywhere.
> I am here to hear the quiet, the water, and singing trees. This is the
>   sound of peace in the presence of my Allah Almighty.
> After 30 years as a mujahideen, I have grown old from fighting.
>   I resent the sound of destruction. I am tired of war.

The next day, our fourth day out of Kabul, we reached the village of Eshkashem, at the mouth of the Wakhan Corridor. Here we met another strongman, Wohid Khan, a tall, taciturn, handsome Tajik in his early forties. As commander of the Afghan-Tajik Border Security Forces, he oversees two hundred Afghan troops in their patrol of a 330-mile stretch of the Afghan-Tajik border, including the entire northern boundary of the Wakhan. Khan granted us permission to traverse the corridor, one end to the other, but he couldn't guarantee our safety once we crossed into Tajikistan. The most he could do was provide us with a handwritten note that vouched for our honorable intentions.

On either side of a flat, brown valley, enormous white mountains — the Hindu Kush to the south, the Tajikistan Pamirs to the north — rose like a mirror image. The huge teeth of these peaks, with a tongue of dirt down the middle, reminded me of a wolf's mouth. The valley disappeared into the distance, a throat of land that reached toward the steppes of western China.

The rough road that the Russian invaders had cut, following the camel path of the Silk Road, was all but gone — covered by rockslides or swept away by floods and avalanches. Our four-wheel-drive Toyota van crept alongside slopes where we were sure we'd roll, crossed fulvous streams so high we were almost carried away. When we sank axle-deep in mud and got stuck, it took hours of digging with ice axes to extract the van.

Many of the peaks on both sides of the valley were unclimbed. Doug kept shouting for the driver to stop so we could crawl over our duffel bags, spill out the side door, and take pictures.

Back in the early seventies, stories of expeditions to the Wakhan's twenty-thousand-foot summits generated enormous excitement. The Brits, Germans, Austrians, Spaniards, Italians, Japanese — they'd all come here to climb. In 1971, Italian alpinists led by Carlo Alberto Pinelli explored the eastern Wakhan's Big Pamir range and climbed three of its highest mountains, Koh–i–Marco Polo (20,256 feet), Koh-i-Pamir (20,670 feet), and Koh-i-Hilal (20,607 feet). On the very western edge of the Wakhan, in the Hindu Kush, 24,580-foot Noshaq was a popular peak.

But the 1979 Russian invasion essentially put an end to Wakhan mountaineering for more than two decades. In 2003, Pinelli returned and managed to galvanize a successful expedition to Noshaq, but not a soul had summited in the heart of the Wakhan for a generation. Doug and I were itching for an ascent.

That first night in the Wakhan we slept in a *khun*, a traditional

Wakhi home with a layered, square-patterned wood ceiling and red
Afghan rugs spread over an elevated platform. The Wakhi, a tough-
knuckled, wiry tribe, have ancient Iranian roots and have lived in
the Wakhan for at least a thousand years. They speak Wakhi, an old
Persian dialect, and adhere to the Ismaeli sect of Islam. Subsistence
farmers, they use yaks to till the sandy soil and plant potatoes,
wheat, barley, and lentils. The growing season is extremely short,
the winters hideously harsh. One out of three Wakhi infants dies
before the age of one, and women still commonly die in childbirth.

The extended family that took us in that night — grandparents,
parents, kids, aunts, uncles — were old friends of Sarfraz, but it
wouldn't have mattered; throughout the trip, wherever we stopped,
we were warmly welcomed with food and a bed. An Afghan's wealth
and generosity are measured by the kindness he shows strangers.
Sarfraz's friends fed us ibex and brown rice, which we ate with our
hands from a common plate. Several months earlier, the village
school had been destroyed by an avalanche. Sarfraz spent the evening working on a plan to build a new CAI school.

The next day we continued up-valley, often walking ahead of
the grinding, bottom-scraping van — our stubborn, modern-day
camel. We were passing into the Wakhan's Big Pamirs, but the
valley was so deep and the mountains to either side so high, we
couldn't see any peaks beyond those along the front range. We
were searching for what appeared on the map to be a cleft in the
left-hand wall. We needn't have worried. It was obvious the moment we saw it — a V-shaped fissure with a three-hundred-foot waterfall crashing onto boulders.

We stopped in a yak meadow near the falls, at ten thousand feet.
Sarfraz was taking the van back to Faizabad to pick up Greg and
bring him out to meet us. This was base camp. We dragged out our
backpacks and duffel bags, and then Sarfraz was gone. We had one
week to climb the mountain.

As often happens in very remote, sparsely populated places, a man
showed up out of nowhere: a Wakhi named Sher Ali, rough as a
rock, with his own alpenstock. He helped clear away the yak pies
and set up our tents, then stood off at a distance, staring.

"You guys know how to cook?" Teru asked, chewing on a chunk
of jerky.

Doug and I looked at each other and laughed.

"Right," said Teru. Thenceforth, Teru the photographer was also Teru the base-camp cook. He was good — dicing onions, experimenting with spices — and each meal was better than anything us two dirtbags could have cooked up with a full kitchen.

That day Doug and I reconned above the waterfall, following a steep-walled drainage up to the snow line. Beyond was a spiky wilderness of white. We couldn't see Koh-i-Bardar — "Mountain of the Entrance," in Wakhi, and the peak we hoped to climb — but we knew it was back there somewhere.

That evening, Doug and I decided to attempt our sight-unseen peak in a single, unsupported push, while Teru waited at camp with Sher Ali.

We busted out early the following morning with so much energy we could barely keep up with our legs. We had the same pace and made swift progress. By noon, we were crossing brilliant snowfields, passing beneath Teton-like granite spires. By 12:15 we were marooned.

In the space of fifteen minutes, the temperature had warmed just enough for the four-inch crust to soften to the point that it wouldn't support body weight. It was like breaking through ice. Suddenly we were both wallowing chest-deep, fracturing off chunks of crust as we tried to crawl back onto the surface.

"Time to camp," said Doug.

"Here? Now?"

"You wanna swim to the mountain?"

We tromped out a platform and spent the rest of the afternoon eating and napping and sunbathing. Up at 4:00 the next morning, we reached our sixteen-thousand-foot assault camp on the Purwakshan Glacier by 10:00. We dropped our packs and did a fast recon up to the base of Koh-i-Bardar to find our line: a steep couloir to a knife-edge ridge to the summit. We were back by midday and had our tent up before we once again became castaways in an ocean of snow. We couldn't take one step off our tent platform without drowning.

"We'll have to climb it entirely at night," said Doug. We were inside the oven of our tiny two-man tent, baking to death.

Already Doug was one of the best partners I'd ever had. He was fast, funny, could sleep anywhere, in his clothes, farted like a horse, never whined, and, most important, simply loved the mountains. He was the epitome of parsimony — carrying the right, light gear and absolutely nothing extra, except Peet's French-roast coffee, of course.

We watched snow squalls come and go, trying to scare us, took sleeping pills at 6:00 P.M., got up at 11:00, and were crunching up the glacier before midnight. Headlamps burning, we blazed over the glacier in crampons, found the right couloir, front-pointed straight up, catwalked along the knife edge, both fell into crevasses on the summit glacier, and swapped leads postholing right to the 19,941-foot summit of Koh-i-Bardar.

It was 6:45, forty-eight hours since we'd left base camp. Standing atop the summit block, we saw the whole world spread below us — jagged, pale pink, chaste. There hadn't been another first ascent in the Wakhan since 1977.

After Sarfraz and Greg met us at base camp, we drove farther into the corridor. Greg had another school meeting to attend in Sarhadd, a Wakhi village fifteen miles down the road.

At the welcoming ceremony, all the children lined up, looking like brilliant, unidentifiable flowers in their rags and robes of reds and maroons. The little girls wore strings of lapis lazuli, and the little boys blue Chinese Wellies. Once again Greg gave a speech to the assembled elders, but this time, for this crowd, it was different: more emphasis on the economic benefits of education, less on Allah. How one of these children right here, once they learned their three R's, could go to a trade school in Kabul and return home to fix the village tractor.

That night, when we were all in our sleeping bags — Teru already asleep, Doug busy noting the day's weather in his journal with hand-drawn symbols, Sarfraz somewhere outside negotiating our horses for the morning — Greg and I, insomniacs both, sat with our backs against the stone wall and talked about his vision for Afghanistan.

"The U.S. fired eighty-eight Tomahawk cruise missiles into Afghanistan in 2001," he said. "I could build forty schools for the cost of one of them. The Taliban are still here. They're just waiting for us to leave. You can kill a warrior, but unless you educate his children, they will become prime recruits."

Greg pulled his scarf up around his face, looking just like an Afghan in the candlelight. He would not be coming with us deeper into the valley. There are about 550 Wakhi families in the western Wakhan, and he and Sarfraz had identified twenty-one villages that needed schools. "Educating girls, in particular, is critical," he continued. "If you can educate a girl to the fifth-grade level, three things happen: infant mortality goes down, birthrates go down, and the quality of life for the whole village, from health to happiness, goes up. Something else also happens. Before a young man goes on jihad, holy war, he must first ask for his mother's permission. Educated mothers say no."

I asked him how the villages paid for their half of building and supporting a school.

"Often they provide labor in lieu of money," Greg replied, "but most of the money in many Afghan villages outside the Wakhan comes from growing poppies."

"Opium."

"Opium," said Greg. "It can't be eliminated. These villages are desperately poor. They're utterly dependent on this income. Eliminating opium farming will only cause more poverty and more hopelessness, which will cause more killing and more wars."

I let it rest.

In 2004, Afghanistan produced 4,200 tons of opium, 87 percent of the world's total supply. The revenue from the illegal trade was estimated at $2.8 billion, roughly two-thirds the amount Afghanistan receives in foreign aid. In 2005, the United States allocated about $774 million to the effort to eradicate poppy farming in Afghanistan. Is there a better way? The Senlis Council, an international drug-policy think tank, recently proposed a radical alternative: legalize opium for medicinal purposes.

India is already licensed by the International Narcotics Control Board, an independent watchdog group that monitors the trade of illicit and medicinal drugs, to grow opium and produce generic pain medication for developing nations. Afghanistan could do the same. The cost of creating such a program has been estimated at only $600 million. Ideally, the farmers would get cash, the drug lords would get cut out, the developing world would get more pain-relief medicine, and the major demand for the global traffic in heroin could be drastically reduced.

It's a compelling strategy — accepting the reality on the ground rather than fighting it — and it's exactly how Greg operates. He doesn't get caught up in moral abstractions; he focuses on what works, no matter how tortured or contradictory.

Sarhadd, roughly halfway up the Wakhan Corridor, is at the end of the road. From here, all travel would be by foot or horseback. We had eighty miles in front of us to reach Tajikistan.

On a cold, windy morning, Sarfraz, Doug, Teru, and I left Sarhadd with four packhorses and four Wakhi wranglers. For two days we hiked along the bottoms of immense canyons, in the shadows, jumping boulders, fording side streams, imagining Marco Polo doing the same thing. We climbed two small passes to escape the canyons and reach the upper Wakhan settlement of Langar and Khan Bibi's grim stone hut.

From Langar we walked to Bazai Gonbad, a Kirghiz burial ground consisting of a dozen domed, chalk-white mausoleums. Beyond Bazai Gonbad, the Wakhan widens dramatically. The valley is too high for farming — twelve thousand feet — hence the eastern Wakhan is inhabited primarily by Kirghiz nomads. In general the Kirghiz are wealthier and healthier than the Wakhi, although ever since the borders were closed in 1949, there has been a symbiotic relationship between the two peoples. The Wakhi need animals and the Kirghiz need grain, so they barter.

The Kirghiz are cowboys, and Sarfraz, a great rider himself, managed to get us saddle horses. Teru, the New Yorker, was the most natural cowboy among the Americans, followed by Doug, who is originally from New Jersey. I grew up in Wyoming working on ranches and can't ride a horse to save my life.

The upper Wakhan is one of the last refuges for at least three endangered species — the snow leopard, the Himalayan wolf, and the Marco Polo sheep. All are still hunted by the Kirghiz. (We saw wolf-skin coats for sale on Chicken Street in Kabul and were told the pelts came from northeastern Afghanistan.) In a heavy-snow winter, the Kirghiz hunt snow leopards and wolves that prey on their sheep, and sometimes even on children; they hunt the sheep for food. But change is coming: biologist George Schaller, vice president of science and exploration at the New York–based Wildlife Conservation Society, has been inventorying Marco Polo sheep in the area since the 1970s — most recently visiting in 2004 and 2005 — and he's campaigning to make the entire region a protected international park.

One evening we stopped in a Kirghiz camp called Uchkali, "Place of the Ibex," where there were nine families living in nine yurts and an untold number of goats and sheep and yaks. Kirghiz lives are interwoven with the lives of their animals, and they subsist almost entirely on red meat, milk, and yogurt. Although they speak a Turkic dialect, their ancient ancestors may have been Mongols. After welcoming cups of tea, the old chief, a man named Yeerali, set before us a battered cardboard box. Inside the box was a gas-powered generator.

Yeerali had bought the generator the previous autumn, along with several gallons of gas and a box of electrical supplies, and brought them here by horse in hopes of having lights during the long, snow-buried winter. Of course the generator broke soon afterward and the camp spent another winter in darkness.

We were Americans, were we not? Visitors from the land of machines. Certainly we would fix the generator.

After having been given so much by the people of the Wakhan, it was our chance to give something back. Besides, we were on the spot. Doug and I took up the challenge.

First we carefully examined the little beast, talking back and forth in a professional tone, making a good show of our diagnosis. Then we got out our multitools and went to town. We fiddled with the gas mixture and the throttle spring and the adjustment screws and the choke lever and the spark-plug gap.

The machine was no more complicated than a lawn mower, but the gaze of the entire camp was on us. After we'd done all we could possibly think of and then some, I yanked on the pull cord.

Nothing. The Kirghiz's disappointment was palpable.

We fiddled some more, I pulled the cord: a cough. Their eyes lit up. More adjustments, I pulled the cord, and the little engine that could roared to life.

Doug and I were instant heroes. Yeerali ordered two men to kill the biggest sheep of the herd, which they did forthwith, cutting its throat and skinning it right there in front of us. While the various parts of the sheep were being cooked, Doug and Sarfraz and I dug into the box of electrical supplies and proceeded to electrify the camp, stringing wire and lights to the nearest yurts as if they were Christmas trees.

When the platter of food arrived, we sat down beneath the abundant light of a single dangling bulb.

Now, there's something special about Wakhan sheep, a Central Asian breed called turki qoey: they have two distinct camel humps of fat on their behinds. Like whale blubber to the Inuit, sheep-ass fat is a delicacy to the Kirghiz.

Two large lumps of steaming ass sat in the middle of the platter, surrounded by the boiled head and testicles.

Doug and I glanced at each other and, without hesitation, sprung open our belay knives, cut off large slices of greasy butt fat, and plopped them into our mouths.

"Not bad," said Doug. Then he cracked open the sheep's head and took a bite of the hot, soft cheek, and I ate one of the big, slippery testicles.

We traveled by horseback for two more days across the upper Wakhan, stopping in Kirghiz nomad camps along the way. We spent our last night in the Wakhan in Urtobill, a community of four extended families. Together they'd pooled their resources and bought Chinese solar panels, a car battery, a TV, and a video player. That evening we sat with them inside a Kirghiz *utok*, or community house, and watched their only video: a grainy 1975 documentary called *The Kirghiz of Afghanistan.*

The next day, we galloped up to the Tajikistan border, which was marked by a tangled, partly downed barbed-wire fence. Nobody was there. Just more open brown country.

It was the end of the road for Sarfraz. We dismounted and took pictures. Sarfraz had become a friend, and we were going to miss him — just how much, we had no idea. We hugged and shook hands, and then Doug and Teru and I walked into Tajikistan.

We followed a washed-out tank track due east along the barbed-wire fence, passing two tall, abandoned guard towers. After ten miles we still hadn't seen a soul. Up on the hill to our left were another guard tower, some tanks buried in tank pits, and some buildings, but the place appeared deserted, so we kept going.

A quarter-mile past the outpost, we heard a pop and a zing. "That's a shot," said Doug. He was brilliant.

We heard another round and spun on our heels to see an officer with an AK-47 running down the hill toward us. We put our hands in the air. In seconds the officer was upon us, screaming in Russian and waving his rifle in our faces. "Dokumenty! Dokumenty!"

He was the spitting image of a young Robert De Niro in *The Godfather: Part II*, and seemingly just as volatile and unpredictable. I could see his finger trembling on the trigger.

We slowly handed him our passports, along with the note from Wohid Khan.

"Wohid Khan, Wohid Khan," we said in high, choirboy voices. The name seemed to register.

He marched us to the base. All the buildings were abandoned but one. We were taken inside, past a small kitchen, into an even smaller office, the door closed behind us. A metal desk, a shelf with Russian military books, a couch. We sat on the couch while Vito Corleone laid his AK-47 on the table and allowed us to see that he was also packing a sidearm. He looked like the kind of guy who was waiting for us to do something stupid so he could blow us away right there.

Eventually he got up, opened the door, and motioned for us to step out. We were taken to a little kitchen and served tea and cookies. In the next room we could hear Vito calling his superiors. Two hours later another officer arrived.

"Welcome in Tajikistan," he said happily, then shook our hands. He looked like a bearded Antonio Banderas.

We thought he actually spoke English, but he didn't, so the interviews took a long time. Vito and Tony had some kind of comic-book interrogation manual that they used to extract information from us.

Were we Al Qaeda? Were we Taliban? Were we CIA? Were we drug smugglers?

We answered no to all of the above.

What were we, then?

Tourists.

Tourists. Tourists who walked all the way across the Wakhan?

Yes.

We showed them our route on the map.

That is not possible, they said. No one has ever crossed this border.

We know. That's why we're here.

Vito and Tony were dismayed. They decided to go through the contents of our backpacks, one item at a time. Toothbrush, dirty underwear, unwashed bowl. They made a complete inventory, but it was obviously a letdown. No guns, no drugs, no secret documents. Had we been real spies or at least drug smugglers, Vito and Tony would have been promoted and could have gotten out of this shithole outpost. On the other hand, since we really were three stupid American tourists, they could chill out.

That night our interrogators gave us their own bunks while they slept on the hard floor of the office.

I was so thrilled I couldn't fall asleep.

"We did it, guys," I whispered. "We crossed the Wakhan!"

"And now we're under arrest," said Teru.

"I would call it temporarily detained," said Doug.

It took us five days to work our way through the red tape. We were transferred north through Tajikistan — in beat-up cars that ran out of gas, and on foot — one military base to the next, one interrogation to the next. We were put up in rooms, heated by small piles of burning sagebrush, with Soviet pinup girls on the walls. We were served platters of Marco Polo meat and treated like visiting dignitaries, then informed we were going to prison. We played volleyball with bored boy-soldiers, then were told we were dangerous spies.

Back in Afghanistan, word of U.S. interrogators at Guantánamo torturing Muslim captives and flushing the Koran down the toilet had ignited anti-American riots throughout the country. Backing out of the Wakhan, Greg had been caught up in the conflagration and was laying low in a hotel in Faizabad. Still, he managed to get a sat-phone call to the U.S. embassy in Kabul, informing them of three errant Americans.

We were released into the custody of U.S. embassy officials, who drove us to the Tajikistan capital of Dushanbe. The moment the doors closed on the bulletproof embassy Land Cruisers, we were home. Outside it was Tajikistan; inside it was America. We drove to a fancy hotel listening to Van Morrison, eating Pringles, and drinking Coke.

HEIDI JULAVITS

Naked Ambition

FROM *T: Travel, New York Times Style Magazine*

"WHY BE GIVEN A BODY," Katherine Mansfield asked, "if you have to keep it shut up in a case like a rare, rare fiddle?" My rare fiddle was first exhibited to a mixed audience in Marin County, California, circa 1991, on a nude beach north of the Golden Gate Bridge where leering men failed miserably to impersonate sunbathers. If you didn't mind being addressed while your breasts were scrutinized, it was a fantastic place to go. I also discovered, on the city side of the bridge, the Osento Bath House for Women, which, with its multiculti sister vibe, offered a serene, almost utilitarian clothing-optional experience. But I, the budding naturist, craved something in between the total pervfest and the total perv refuge, a place where a sensual yet risk-free *frisson* stirred the waters, as when naked men and women, strangers all, share a single, often slimy-bottomed wooden hot tub.

So, my college boyfriend suggested we spend a weekend at Wilbur Hot Springs, a two-and-a-half-hour drive northeast of San Francisco. Wilbur straddles a dirt road in the middle of an 1,800-acre nature preserve. On one side of the road leans Wilbur's turn-of-the-century hotel, cockeyed and rambling, with bunk rooms, a communal kitchen, and some private bedrooms; on the opposite side is the "bathhouse," a roof on stilts with fancifully curling eaves that shade a series of long, resistance-pool-shaped tubs. It was there that I learned my first lesson in nude coexistence: your naked body is not the most potentially embarrassing thing about you. If I felt any self-consciousness or anxiety, it was on behalf of my boyfriend's naked body, which exposed more about me than mine did.

Which was not that much of a problem among the earthy yet aloof Wilbur clientele. At Wilbur, nudity is permitted in certain places but not in others, the result being that you feel utterly comfortable while sitting elbow to elbow in water that smells like rotten eggs (in fact, a pleasant smell), but weird and tense when forced to chop vegetables at the kitchen island with strangers whose genitals, now hidden beneath drawstring pants, are vividly familiar to you. After dinner, prepared stiffly and judgmentally by each couple or group of friends, we sat in the common area, flipping through magazines or playing cards. One twosome, a man and a woman of practiced peacenik pretension, dramatized a telling scene from their relationship. The man played a bamboo flute while his wire-thin partner perched at his feet, nibbling a rice cake and gazing up at him with desperate adoration as he ethereally ignored her.

I was smitten. Not with being naked with strangers per se, nor with being naked in nature — because California, unlike New York City, where I now live, is teeming with quasi-secret hot springs. I was interested in the places where a domestic routine is imposed upon a hippie-leaning community that I, without my clothing, could invisibly infiltrate. Far more revelatory than people's sexual organs are their kitchen habits, their reading habits, their romantic relationships in action. After many awkward dinner preps in communal kitchens with strangers whom I'd seen naked, I've realized that the awkwardness has nothing to do with the genital factor. Cooking next to a stranger requires far more intimacy than exposing your body; it's an extension of the shame you occasionally feel while scrutinizing strangers' groceries, their habits and predilections bobbling along the conveyor belt.

The most enjoyable, and friendly, place for human observation that I've found is Orr Hot Springs, thirteen miles west of Ukiah, California, in the shaded crotch of the oak-and-eucalyptus-sided hills — so enjoyable that I try to go back at least once a year. The Orr décor is funky 1970s Whole Earth Catalog: dark, dank wood and homemade stained-glass windows, along with the lingering odors of wet wool and menthol. There's a communal kitchen featuring kindly suggestive notes on water conservation; a library that has everything from decade-old *Vanity Fairs* to *The Natural Healing and Nutrition Manual, 1991*; and an English garden tended by an actual Englishwoman. The main hot tub is capable of holding up to six strangers comfortably, more if the foreign flab boundary isn't a concern. About flab and other bodily unruliness: the obsessively hair- and flab-free do not frequent the likes of Orr. Coed hairiness is OK, as is sag, as is flab, even the kind that bobs gently on the waves created by the languid, in-utero movements of your tubmates. Everyone's comfort with their bodies, however flawed, means that you don't stare as much. Casual eye contact (and eye-body contact) is encouraged, if only because you quickly realize that refusing to register a person achieves the same alienating, even rude, effect as ogling; there is, thus, a certain enjoyable freedom at Orr, to be accepted for who you are: an unexceptionally naked stranger.

Until, of course, you start chatting with your tubmates. Then it becomes clear that, like an American traveling through Cuba, you are engaged in a less-than-ordinary pursuit inspiring both a sense of camaraderie and a vague tingle of competitiveness. I've often been asked, "Is this your first time at Orr?" No, I reply, not without relief (my shaved armpits are enough of an outsider stigma). Then the talk turns to other hot springs. (Orr devotees complain that Harbin Hot Springs, near Calistoga, California, is too big, and the New Age vibe is oppressive; Wilbur is more low-key but too small.) Soon you begin exchanging harmless personal details: where you live, what you do. Because the world is an inevitably teensy place, connections with your clothed life begin to accrue. During my last visit, I found myself talking to a couple in their late twenties who were visiting from Portland, Maine, which is my hometown and where I was scheduled to give a reading from my novel in two weeks. "You should come!" I urged. As I departed the tub, unselfconsciously flashing my lobster-red bum, I realized that this could create a distressing social situation.

For the most part, however, I've managed to keep a low profile; eavesdropping is more enlightening and requires less pretending. *(Of course I know about the homeopathic remedy for acid reflux!)* I've listened as a woman asked whether another woman had her Bragg Liquid Aminos on hand or, barring that, tamari sauce. I've watched an irretrievably lonely woman — her loneliness on hold because of Orr's sense of community, as well as the sense that happiness is just a soak away — pad around the garden in her robe, herbal tea in one hand, a book about spiritual self-discovery in the other. I've overheard impassioned people seated around the low Japanese tables — these lifestyle-only inheritors of the 60s radical left — engage in wide-eyed conversations about the threat of genetically engineered food, about fluoride in the water, about vaccines. Where clothes and even gravity are an occasional superfluity, these microscopic menaces take on a dire importance, whereas war, politics, and global warming do not weigh as heavily. Here, you fool yourself into believing that you can control an enclosed universe: your own insides.

A native East Coaster, I find this focused self-regard on the mysterious interior fun for a two-day vacation, the hippie equivalent of Civil War role-play, but I always leave before my relaxation is counteracted by inbred skepticism. In *Ways of Seeing*, the critic John Berger wrote, "To be naked is to be without disguise." My forays into clothing-optional hot springs have been as much about slipping convincingly into a culture that isn't mine and partaking of the pursuit of inner physical purity as though I weren't a stranger to its ways. For this, there is no better disguise than the naked body.

YIYUN LI

Passing Through

FROM the *New York Times Magazine*

AFTER THE TIANANMEN SQUARE massacre in 1989, the Chinese Ministry of Education began sending future students of Beijing University, a hotbed of pro-democratic protest, into the military for a year. So in 1991, at the age of eighteen, instead of beginning studies, I entered the army. There, along with 1,500 other students, I spent hours in formation training and even more time being lectured on the inevitable demise of capitalism and the victory of Communism.

The next spring, the army sent us on a march through Mount Dabie to get to know our "revolutionary heritage"; the mountain area served, between the 1920s and 1930s, as a base for the Communist Party. Hard as the marching was, with no bath for weeks and blisters on our feet, the mountain air and spring fields made the trip into a kind of sightseeing adventure. That was why we entered a village one particular evening smiling and holding our hands up to the sky.

We were the only girls' company, and we marched behind a battalion of boys; the road across the village was shrouded by dust. A water buffalo, used to the tramping, grazed undisturbed. A villager saw us and called out, "Girl-soldiers this time." The villagers appeared in every door, bowls of rice in their hands, pointing at us with their chopsticks. "Girl-soldiers," young children echoed, running along beside us. We smiled, waved, and kept walking. An old woman was pounding dried peppers in a huge stone mortar. The breeze spread the fine powders, and many of us sneezed; the villagers laughed.

Outside the village, we were ordered to take a break. The dust settled, and hundreds of green-uniformed figures sat single file by the winding road. The scene was soon disrupted by the village children, all holding out their hands, begging for candies and refusing to leave when they got their share. Even the most charitable soldiers among us started to shoo away the children like flies. When yet another girl stood in front of me, I said, "How many do you have to have before you go home?"

"Can I just have a candy wrapper?" she asked. I looked at the girl, too small for her passed-down blouse. "Do you collect candy wrappers?" I said. She nodded and showed me a dog-eared book. Between the pages were mostly cheap wrappers, red and green with plain characters, *tang guo* (candy) printed on them diagonally.

"How old are you?" I asked. "Eight," she said. "Are you in school?" She shrugged. Not many girls in the mountains would receive much education. They worked hard for their parents until they were old enough to work for their husbands. Today, I suppose, if girls from this region manage to leave their villages, they might try to participate in the Chinese economic boom by becoming laborers in a factory.

I handed her a candy. She unfolded the wrapper and returned the chocolate to me. I watched her flatten it between her palms. It had snowy mountains and blue sky in the background, with a small white flower blooming in the center.

At her age, I collected candy wrappers, too, and I understood the joy of having a prize wrapper in your collection. I had one that was given to me by a Westerner in the late 1970s, when foreign faces were still rare in Beijing. It was made of cellophane with transparent gold and silver stripes, and if you looked through it, you would see a gilded world, much fancier than our everyday, dull life.

By the time I turned ten, I was working at the goal set by my parents: to excel in schoolwork so that one day I could go to the United States. I attended a high school in Beijing that admitted only the students with the best scores in the entrance exam. Financed by UNESCO, it had an indoor swimming pool, color TVs, and a science building.

I did not change my life because of a candy wrapper, but it was the seed of a dream that came true: I left China for an American graduate school in 1996 and have lived here since.

The girl studied the wrapper before putting it in her book. I wondered if it would nourish thoughts about other worlds. But I did not tell her about my collection. I did not tell her that the candy had come all the way from Switzerland. I could not explain that the flower on the wrapper was edelweiss or that it was featured in a song in the American movie *The Sound of Music* — I had watched it many times at my school so that we could perform the songs when Western delegates visited.

Even at eighteen, despite my forced reeducation in the army, I knew I was luckier than she was, a passer-by on this mountain and bound for a better destination. I knew that she would never see a blooming edelweiss anywhere but on a wrapper.

P. J. O'ROURKE

The Mother Load

FROM *The Atlantic Monthly*

SOMETIMES IT SEEMS that the aim of modernity is to flush the romance out of life. The library, with its Daedalian labyrinth, mysterious hush, and faintly ominous aroma of knowledge, has been replaced by the computer's cheap glow, pesky chirp, and data spillage. Who born since 1960 has any notion of the Near East's exotic charms? Whence the Rubáiyat? Whither Scheherezade? The Thief of Baghdad is jailed, eating Doritos in his underwear. As for romance itself . . . "Had we but world enough, and pills, / For erectile dysfunction's ills." And nothing is more modern than air travel.

As stimulating adventure, flying nowadays ranks somewhere between appearing in traffic court and going to Blockbuster with the DVD of *Shrek 2* that my toddler inserted in the toaster. Thus the maiden flight, on April 27, 2005, of the Airbus A380, the world's largest airliner, did not spark the world's imagination. Or it did — with mental images of a boarding process like going from Manhattan to the Hamptons on a summer Friday, except by foot with carryon baggage. This to get a seat more uncomfortable than an aluminum beach chair.

What a poor, dull response to a miracle of engineering. The A380 is a Lourdes apparition at the departure ramp. Consider just two of its marvels: its takeoff weight is 1.235 million pounds. And it takes off. The A380 is the heaviest airplane ever flown — 171 tons heavier than the previous record holder, the somewhat less miraculously engineered Soviet Antonov An-124.

The A380 can fly as fast as a Boeing 747–400, and farther, and the twin passenger decks running the full length of its fuselage give it half again more cabin space.

However, the only expressions of awe over the A380's specifications that I've heard have been awful predictions of the crowding inside. These tend to be somewhat exaggerated. "Oh, my God — Southwest to Tampa with a thousand people!" said a member of my immediate family who often shepherds kids to Grandma's on budget carriers while their dad has to take an earlier flight "for business reasons."

Airbus maintains that with its recommended seating configuration, the A380 will hold 555 passengers, versus about 412 in a 747–400. The U.S. House of Representatives, the Senate, the president, the vice president, the Cabinet, two swing-voting Supreme Court justices, and Karl Rove can all fly together in an A380. (Maybe *that* statistic will create some popular excitement, if they fly far enough away.) But the London *Sunday Times* has reported that Emirates, an airline with forty-five of the new planes on order, "would pack as many as 649 passengers into the A380." The president of Emirates, Tim Clark, told the *Times,* "Personally, I'd have liked to put 720 seats in." And the chairman of Virgin Atlantic Airways, Sir Richard Branson, has bragged that each Virgin A380 will have a beauty parlor, a gym, double beds, and a casino — three out of four of which sound worse than 719 seatmates.

I consulted an old friend, Peter Flynn, who is the sales director for Airbus North America. He assured me that the A380 is an incredible airplane. It didn't sound like mere professional assurance. Peter was a navy helicopter pilot during the Vietnam War and remembers when flying was really a stimulating adventure.

Two months to the day after the A380 first became airborne, Peter and I were at Airbus headquarters, in Toulouse, France, in the A380 systems-testing facility. The building is as blank-walled as the Kaaba and much larger. We stood on a glassed-in balcony three stories above the main floor looking at something called the Iron Bird. This is a full-scale installation of all the mechanical, electrical, and hydraulic connections within an A380 and of all the moving parts to which they are joined except the engines. The Iron Bird was very busy trying out the levers, gears, cylinders, struts, and things-I-don't-know-the-names-of that work the landing gear, rudder, elevators, ailerons, and things-I-don't-know-the-names-of either.

We think of a passenger plane as a pod, a capsule wafting through the atmosphere containing mainly us and, if we're lucky, our luggage. Jet power plants are simply automatic typhoons, effortlessly blowing hot air. And while we fervently hope the jets continue to do that, it doesn't occur to us that an airliner has a greater confusion of innards than anything we dissected in science lab, even if we went to veterinary school. I wonder what the ancient Romans would have divined from such entrails. Certainly not aviation. The Iron Bird couldn't have looked less avian. Nor — airplanes being made of aluminum and carbon-fiber composites and such — was much ferrous metal involved. The iron in the Iron Bird was in the steel ramps and ladders branching over and through it so that engineers could go to and fro.

Our corporate tour guide, the cheerful and patient Debra Batson, the manager for "scientific media," pointed out one of the Iron Bird's most important components. This looked to me like a tangle of extension cords from an overambitious attempt at outdoor Christmas lighting. Airbus was the first producer of commercial aircraft to make its planes all fly-by-wire. That is, there are no rods or cables — nothing that can be pushed or yanked — between the flyer and the flown. Everything is accomplished by computer command. And I trust that the nose wheel pays more attention to its e-mail than I do to mine.

Debra pointed out another of the most important components, which looked like a tangle of garden hoses from an attempt to put out the fire caused by the outdoor Christmas lighting. This was the hydraulic system that operates the A380's control surfaces. In the A380, the pressure in the hydraulic system has been increased from the usual three thousand pounds per square inch to 5,000 psi, making the system smaller, lighter, and as powerful as the kick to the back of my passenger seat from the child sitting behind me. The hydraulics also handle the braking on the A380's twenty-wheel main landing gear. A 302-page promotional Airbus publication titled *A New Dimension in Air Travel* informed me that "the brake is capable of stopping 45 double-decker buses traveling at 200 mph, simultaneously, in under 25 seconds." It is an ambition of mine to learn enough math to figure out comparisons like that and write them myself. But I'm afraid I'd get carried away with digressions about what kind of engine you'd have to put in a double-decker bus to make it go that fast, where you'd drive it, how you'd find forty-four people to drive the other buses, and what would happen to the bus riders.

I *did* get carried away thinking about the miracle of engineering. It is not vouchsafed even to the pope to see the very mechanism by which miracles are performed. Would the pope be as confused by his kind of miracle as I was by the Iron Bird? Would this affect the doctrine of papal infallibility?

"Above my pay grade," Peter said. He and Debra and I went to the other side of the building to look at the cockpit simulators. These were arrayed along a wall and curtained off like private viewing booths for the kind of movie you aren't supposed to see. We peeked inside one. That kind of movie wasn't playing on the simulator's windscreen. A speeding runway came toward us, followed by dropping land, and enveloping haze, and more vertigo than we would have felt if the floor had moved. It hadn't. "Unfortunately," Peter said, "the rock-and-roll simulator was booked up today. You can crash that one. And it makes really embarrassing noises."

The simulator we were in was computer-linked to the Iron Bird. Two pilots in sports clothes sat at the controls while people with clipboards stood behind them taking notes. The pilots didn't seem to do much. Mostly they tapped on computer keyboards or fiddled with a trackball mouse. This was what was causing the frenetic activity in the Iron Bird — a teenager's immersion in Grand Theft Auto leading to an actual car's being stolen somewhere.

I sat in the pilot seat of another simulator. Peter took the copilot position. There wasn't even a jump seat for Debra. "This whole big damn thing," I said, "is flown by . . . you and me?"

"Yep," Peter said, "and it doesn't need me."

I, however, couldn't find any controls except rudder pedals to pump. I hope these weren't computer-linked to anything and that I didn't initiate wild yaw that knocked any Iron Bird engineers off their ramps and ladders. In front of me, instead of a yoke, was a foldout desktop. Perhaps these days the most important function of a pilot is to fill out Homeland Security forms with information on suspicious passengers.

"Look over to your left," Peter said.

"But it's like the joystick on an Atari game," I said.

"Yep," Peter said.

"Could you fly one of these?" I asked. "I mean, and land it?"

"Yep," Peter said. "The computers do all the work."

And there were a lot of computers — eight LCD screens. They showed . . . well, they showed lots of things.

"I've never played Atari," I said.

Debra explained that the A380 has essentially the same computer hardware and, indeed, essentially the same cockpit as all other Airbus aircraft, from the 107-seat A318 on up.

"So you just build a plane," I said, "and the cockpit plugs in like a memory stick."

"I don't think we put it that way in the promotional literature," Debra said.

The promotional literature cites the advantages of "Flight Operational Commonality." Airbus estimates that pilots of its A340 series aircraft, which carry 300 to 380 passengers, can be certified to fly the A380 with just a week or two of additional training, thanks to the adaptive flexibility of computer technology.

I've never liked computers as much as I like the stuff that *I* call hardware. Computers seem a little too adaptively flexible, like the strange natives, odd societies, and head cases we study in the social sciences. There's more opposable thumb in the digital world than I care for; it's awfully close to human.

"Does spam ever pop up on the cockpit computer screens?" I asked. "Or unwanted Jude Law babysitter sex videos?"

"No," said Debra.

Debra took us to the A380 interior mockup, to see how the human beings that we'll be awfully close to will be seated on the A380. Toulouse, of course, is where Lautrec was from — he of perfect proportions for modern airline seating. But I didn't mention it. Debra did mention that Airbus has no final responsibility for what airlines do with the A380's interior, let alone for the behavior of the passengers. But Airbus tries to keep air steerage from being foisted on the public. And the designers of the A380 interior mockup tried to wrest the graciously spacious from the ghastly vast.

Clever partitioning eliminated the tube-of-doom look and gave the rows of seats theaterlike proportions. In theaters, after all, people regularly sit more tightly confined in harder chairs for worse experiences than an airline flight. At least that was my experience with *Rent*. In the forward cabin wide steps rose to the upper deck, and in the tail a spiral staircase descended. For some reason a spiral staircase always adds zest to a setting. Perhaps it speaks to the DNA helix in us all.

Airbus wasn't trying to kid anyone with this mockup. No bowling alleys, squash courts, or lap pools were to be seen. Instead there was a small duty-free shop, a couple of miniature barrooms where you could stand with your foot on the rail, a nook with built-in davenports, and other places in which you could stretch, be free and easy, and not feel like you were trapped in a Broadway extravaganza and would catch hell from your wife and the eighteen people between you and the aisle if you bolted.

The first-class section, of course, was supplied with those investment bankers' La-Z-Boys — Laissez-Faire-Boys, if you will — that can turn themselves into club chairs, chaise longues, or featherbeds and are equipped with buttons to press to get practically anything you want other than Jude Law's babysitter. Business class had something similar, with maybe one fewer caviar spoon and champagne bucket per customer.

But most of us travel as plain old "gate freight." The A380's size is what seems to worry people, yet the size is also the selling point — offering potential comfort as well as potential low fares. The A380, although it contains 50 percent more room than a 747, is supposed to contain only 35 percent more seats. The A380's upper passenger deck is almost as wide as the main deck of a 747, and the lower one is nineteen inches wider. Airbus says proudly — a bit too proudly — that 1.3 inches in seat width is gained in economy class. This is modest progress. The 747 was introduced thirty-five years ago. I've gained 1.3 inches in seat width since the last time I bought pants.

A better measure of comfort than width is what's termed pitch. This is the distance between my expanding posterior and the aching back of the person in front of me. Airbus wants seats to have a minimum pitch of thirty-four inches and urges airlines to choose the thinnest seatback designs. But room is lost to that Satan's looking glass, the in-seat video screen.

A thirty-two-inch pitch, or even less, is common in the airline industry. I am five feet nine. Sitting in a living-room chair, I can measure twenty-six inches from my wallet to the disappearance of my trouser creases. Subtract another four inches for the TV-thickened seat in front of me, and stuffing a copy of *The Truth About Hillary* into my seatback pocket means arthroscopic surgery.

In the economy section of the A380 mockup, Airbus designers compensated for this dark truth with relentlessly cheerful carpet and upholstery in subtropical-fruit colors. I think they overdid it. One shade of citron pleaded to be called "Lemony Snicket." The mockup also had a mood-lighting system that projected upon the cabin ceiling a beautiful morning, noon, or nighttime sky, according to the hour of the day. This would be perfectly unnecessary if the fool in the window seat would quit watching *Wedding Crashers,* open his shade, and look outside.

I looked outside myself, and a real A380 was standing on a taxiway. The Airbus corporate complex sprawls like an American Sunbelt development, but with the Toulouse airport at the center of it instead of a golf course. The A380 was a three-wood and a five-iron away. It didn't look so large. Then I noticed next to the A380 a wide-body A340, the largest Airbus plane until now. The A340 was diminutive in its ordinary hugeness.

Even so, the A380 was more impressive for its presence than for its bulk. The wingspan is 261 feet eight inches — fifty-three feet longer than an A340-600's. There is a reassuring double amount of surface to the A380's wing. This wing is so thick where it meets the fuselage that you could park a car inside. The A380 cockpit, instead of being perched on the catbird seat like a 747's, is placed low in the fuselage, where the pilots can mind their business with the ground. It gives the plane a high-foreheaded, thoughtful look.

The A380 in fact has not two but three decks — the lowest devoted to luggage, freight, and crew rest facilities for long-range flights. The decks are contained in an oval cross section with a smooth ship-hull curve. The wings sweep back at thirty-three degrees, almost in the shape of a jib, and the stabilizer fin is as wide and tall and rakishly set as a Cunard funnel. The A380 seemed nautical — more liner than airliner. No one ever quailed at the prospect of the *Queen Mary 2*'s carrying 720 passengers.

"Five hundred and fifty-five," Debra corrected.

The A380 — the only one flying at that time — taxied away and then turned and rolled in our direction. Now it did look like an airplane, carrying itself with dignity and tending a bit to embonpoint. It had none of the fashionable emaciation of the old 707, with its gaunt runway-model (as it were) looks. Nor did it have the DC-10's scary put-the-engines-anywhere accessorizing style. Rather, the A380 had *ton*. (And tonnage.)

"Can I get on a test ride?" I asked.

"No," Debra said.

"Why?"

"Insurance," Peter said.

"Insurance" is not usually a romantic word, but think of death and all the other romantic things there are to be insured against. Maybe aviation hasn't lost its glamour.

The A380 rose decisively, and before I thought it would. A 747 needs a third of a mile more to take off. The A380 flew over our heads with a Brobdingnagian whisper. It makes half a 747's noise. And then the A380 flew away, into a haze very similar to the haze projected on the windscreen of the A380 cockpit simulator. Let the haze stand for predictions about the future of travel. Will it ever be fun again?

Anyway, building an A380 seemed like fun. Debra and Peter and I went to the production line. Surprise at the scale of the A380 was quieted by surprise at the scale of the place where three more of them were being built. I did not know there was so much indoors. The factory, Debra said, can be seen from space.

Actually, the A380 is built all over Europe. This was the final-assembly plant. The plane arrives in seven pieces sounding like some provincial soup recipe: three slices of fuselage, two wings, a fin, and a tail. The parts come to Toulouse by way of ocean freighters, canal barges, road convoys, and Airbus's whale-shaped and more than whale-sized Beluga transport plane. (Measured by cargo volume, the Beluga is even larger than the A380.) I particularly liked picturing whole wings and great cabin sections strapped to humble barges, bringing a bit of industrial reality (and swamped decks) to people taking those French canal-boat tours and trying to pretend that travel is fun.

The constituent parts of an A380 are placed in a single enormous jig — a Jell-O mold with the miniature marshmallows, fruit slices, and nutmeats aligned by means of laser technology to degrees of precision that take a lot of zeros behind a variety of decimal points to express.

Engineering miracles have always required genius, but the miraculousness has gotten to a point where comparable genius is needed to explain it. Fortunately, a genius showed us around the factory. This was Charles Champion, an Airbus executive vice president and the head of the A380 program since the project was launched, nearly five years ago. Champion has since been promoted to chief operating officer of Airbus. But he is first an engineer. And he all but glowed with enjoyment at the A380's engineering.

For example, the A380's wings are clad in an esoteric alloy. What an ordinary mechanical engineer would call "unobtainium."

The wing panels are up to 108 feet long and nine feet wide, and in places they are only an eighth of an inch thick. They need to hold a "double curved aerodynamic shape." The way to achieve this is with a twenty-four-hour application of varying temperatures and loads to create "stress relaxation" and "permanent deformation." The process is called "creep age forming," and opportunities for Michael Jackson wisecracks aside, I have no idea what I'm talking about.

But Charles Champion did. And he made everything, if not exactly clear, clearly exciting.

Peter was looking around as if he were on a machinery Mount Olympus, watching the powers of the firmament come together, this Leda mating (aided by laser technology) with that swan. Peter is a romantic about machines. When he was a helicopter pilot, machines saved his life any number of times. Of course, it was machines that put his life in jeopardy. But that's romance.

Charles Champion told us how the first A380 built wasn't flown but was towed to a static test platform, where its wings and fuselage were twisted and bent and loaded with weights until the plane was destroyed.

"That must have been horrible," I said, "to see that happen to your first A380."

"Engineers love to break things," Champion said.

And French industrial workers love to make them. At least they seemed to at Airbus. The assembly plant had a calm, cheerful, collegial air. Everything was tidy and well lit. Only the most muffled noises of manufacture could be heard. If Charles Dickens had visited Airbus, he might have given up on the frenzied life of writ-

ing and lecturing that eventually killed him and reconsidered the
blacking factory.

It had been a day of reconsideration for me, too. I was reconsidering my free-trade principles. The governments of France,
Germany, Britain, and other European Union countries have "invested" in the A380. Boeing calls this a subsidy and has gone off in
a snit to the World Trade Organization — as if Boeing didn't sell
Air Force One to the U.S. government for a pretty penny. Should I be
upset that taxes on Europeans will help pay for American airfares?

I was also reconsidering my free-market ideals. Charles Champion said that among the difficulties of the A380 program were
the political considerations of which factories were to make what
where. The result, it seems to me, is that the most expensive parts,
such as the wings and the cockpit, are manufactured in the most
expensive places, such as England and France. A Chinese electron-
ics company might as well outsource production to Manhattan and
Beverly Hills. But do we really want Guatemalan child laborers sew-
ing the treads to the tires on our landing gear?

And I was reconsidering the French. They were welcoming at
Airbus and everywhere else in Toulouse. They didn't make fun of
Peter when he spoke their language or me when I spoke mine.
Food was *magnifique*. Manners were *charmant*.

At a *magnifique* lunch given in the Airbus executive dining room
by the elegant Barbara Kracht, the vice president of media relations, manners remained *charmant* even when I asked her, "What's
with the *bus*?"

"You could have called the company," I said, "'Airphaeton,' 'Air-
limousine,' even 'Airyacht.'" She responded politely, saying that
when Airbus was founded, in 1970, it was still difficult to get people
to think of flying as an affordable means of transportation.

We've gotten over that little hurdle. One thing I wasn't reconsidering was air travel. I had a flight home the next day and was trying
not to think about it — with some success, considering I was standing next to a vehicle designed to provide the most air travel in history.

We were on a platform beside a nearly completed A380. The
wingtip was just above our heads. "Go ahead," Charles Champion
said to me. "Grab it." I reached up and tentatively curled my fingers
over the metal. "Now pull down," he said.

The A380 wing is one of the mightiest structures ever created —
9,100 square feet of ribs, spars, and skin able to thrust itself out
147 feet into nothingness and give lift to its half of 1.235 million
pounds. I pulled, and this great formation bowed to my eye level,
supple as a living thing.

With the whole wing flexing at my light grasp, all the poetic,
fanciful wonder of living in 2005 came back to me. I'd outdone
Keats and Shelley in matters of the sublime. It touched them. I
touched it.

I was full of quixotic fervor. I would fly on an A380 straight to
hell. And unless airport amenities, immigration clearance, baggage delivery, customs inspection, and the courtesy of security personnel improve dramatically before the A380 goes into service, I
will.

MICHAEL PATERNITI

XXXXL

FROM *GQ*

ONE DAY while loitering at my desk, I happened upon a newswire story about a giant. The story was of the variety that appears from time to time, offering a brief snapshot of the oldest/smallest/fattest person on earth, a genre in which I take a keen interest. But there was something else about this one. The giant was reported to be thirty-three years old, residing in a small village with no plumbing in a very poor region of the Ukraine. He lived with his mother and sister, who happened to be tiny. How he'd gotten so huge wasn't entirely known, because the giant wasn't interested in seeing doctors anymore. Something inside of him had been broken or left open, like a faucet, pulsing out hormones as if his body presumed that it still belonged to that of a proliferating pubescent boy. This apparently was the result of an operation he'd had as a child. Under the knife that saved him from a blood clot in his brain, his pituitary gland had been nicked. Now he was over eight feet tall — and still growing.

In the article, the giant was pictured sitting at his small dining-room table, reaching up to change a light bulb at a height that a normal-sized person couldn't have reached standing. Another picture captured the giant in an unguarded moment, staring in astonishment at his hand, as if he'd just picked an exotic, oversized starfish from a coral reef. Near the end of the article, he said something that killed me. He said that his happiest hours were spent in his garden because only the apples and beets don't care what size you are.

Beyond my admittedly voyeuristic interest in the facts of the giant's life — his huge hands, his constant search for clothes that fit, the way he traveled by horse and cart — that one comment brought with it the intimation of something heartbreaking and holy. It began a story: *Once upon a time, there was a giant who kept growing* . . . And yet this was a real life. And what kind of life was it when you had to find solace among fruits and vegetables? Maybe he was an angel. Turned out of heaven, or thrown down to save the world. What other explanation could there be?

In the days and weeks after I'd read the article, the giant came back to me as I stood in the kitchen making dinner (did he use an oversized spatula?) and while bathing my kids (how did he bathe if he couldn't fit in a shower or tub?). He returned to me in the lulls, while I was brushing my teeth or driving among a trance of red tail-lights. Maybe I cracked an egg when he did, and maybe I didn't and just believed I had.

Fall arrived. The leaves changed. I didn't forget about the giant; no, he'd only become more insistent. He was out there, and stuck inside of me, too. Why? It made no sense, really. It was almost irresponsible. I had two great kids and a pregnant wife whom I loved, but a part of me — my old self or soul or me-ness — had been subsumed by fatherhood. I'd let it happen, of course, but then there were still moments when I found myself going a bit haywire. Having children was its own kind of proliferation. You suddenly found yourself at the center of something that was growing wildly around you. Extra hands and feet and voices getting louder, a world of sippy cups, dirty diapers, and sleepless nights stretching from here to 2020. I felt as if I were lost in a kid world, unable to form an adult sentence. Except this one:

It was time to see the giant.

I broke the idea gently to my wife, Sara, expecting the worst.

"OK," she said calmly. In her mind, maybe she was already imagining the days she was going to cash out in return, the eighty-miles-per-hour drive with a friend to the nearest hotel that offered room service and in-house salt glows, what the Romans called quid pro quo and others call "me-time." I know that most guys spend theirs on rounds of golf or buddy weekends at a casino, but that's never quite worked for me.

So I packed a bag, said my goodbyes to the children — it never hurts any less — and made a beeline for the airport. There, I strode straight up to the Northwest Airlines counter like a black-market-arms dealer and bought a ticket to Kiev. It may rank as one of the most pleasing, impulsive things I've ever done. Maybe I was already imagining a fable in which some essential truth is revealed. Or maybe I was just hoping to escape, for a moment, what I was growing into and return to who I'd been. Either way, hadn't I earned a little me-time with a Ukrainian giant?

There was only one road leading to the giant — a ribbon of battered, unlined pavement wide enough for exactly two and a half cars. Landing in Kiev, I was able to pick up a translator and a driver, whose beat-up black Audi smelled like the inside of a gas tank. Before leaving the city, we stopped and bought a cake. Somehow cake seemed like the right sort of gift for a giant, lest he confuse his hunger, as giants sometimes did in fairy tales, for a normal person like me.

We drove west toward Poland and Slovakia, through all the small villages inhabited by all the small and average-sized human beings of the country. The people here — the babushkas and the hunched old men — looked as if they might have been out meandering on this same road three hundred years ago. Ancient and ruddy-faced, they wore old wool hats and sat on the hard benches of their carts, driving their horses, hauling their beets to market, payloads of what looked to be purple hearts.

We followed the Teterev River, winding westward through flatlands, and knew we were close when we came upon a town called Chudnive, or "Miracle." The giant allegedly lived nearby, in Podoliantsi, a tiny backwater of four hundred people, which sat on a vein of blue granite. We drifted off the highway near a rail yard, came over the tracks, which were lit by a string of indigo lights that seemed to stretch all the way to Minsk, then skirted the edge of an endless field, finally turning right on a dirt road.

There was no WELCOME TO PODOLIANTSI sign, just a bunch of hens running loose and the smell of wood smoke. It was dusk, without much light left in the sky, though the sun had come down under the gloom and momentarily lit the land crosswise, throwing long, spindly shadows, catching a nearby cloud, making it glow orange over the village until the last beams of light tipped higher into space as the sun fell beneath the horizon line, like a spotlight suddenly diverted. That's when panic rose in my throat, a stifled upchuck.

What in the name of bullcrap was I doing here?

We asked directions to the giant's house from a woman at a well, drawing water, and without a word she blushed and pointed ahead to another little dirt lane. We turned and stopped before a stone one-story with a blue-painted gate. Apple trees loomed everywhere over the house. When we got out of the car, my eyes were slow to adjust to the shadows. There was mostly silence, some wind blowing quietly out across the fields rustling some faraway trees, until a hinge squeaked loudly, which caused the air to exhale from my lungs and my heart to skim seven or eight beats. I could feel a thudding reverberation emanating up into my body from the earth. Suddenly, a voice passed through the dark: it had its own special reverberation, too.

"*Dobryi den*," the giant said from behind the gate, among the trees. He didn't boom it out in some Fee-fi-fo-fum, he said it almost delicately, politely, so as not to startle anyone. He was behind the trees, and among them. Slowly, I could make out the low, interleaving branches and then some higher branches, with silver apples trembling there, on a level with the gutter of his stone house. And just above them, breaching, came the giant's head. It was enormous, and he ducked down to come to our level.

"*Dobryi den*," he said again. Good day. As if he'd been waiting. He was smiling as he undid the gate, teeth like mahjong tiles. He was tall. The top of my head reached only to his elbows. And he was wide. On his own, he was a walking family of four, maybe five. My hand instinctively shot out, and he hesitated, then took it. Hand in hand, mine vanished in his like a small goldfish. He seemed to measure its weight a moment, considered its smallness, then squeezed. Yes, ouch — without realizing it, trying to be gentle — very hard! His palm was too wide to clasp fingers around. Meanwhile, he was crushing certain fine bones I didn't realize I had. But I was doing what you do when you meet a real giant in a strange, faraway land: I was smiling like hell, nervously gesturing toward the cake in my other hand.

"*Dobryi den*," I said. And these two small words were a spell cast over everything. Holding my hand, he ceased to be a giant at all. Rather, in his world now, I became the dwarf.

His name was Leonid Stadnik. He had a thicket of chestnut-colored hair cut neatly over the ears and hazel eyes that squinted ever so slightly. His feet were shod in black leather shoes, size twenty-six, so large that later, when I tried to lift one, I needed two hands. When he walked, he did so heavily, with knocked knees and a precipitous forward lean, his legs trying to keep pace with the momentum of his upper body. He led me into the house, ducking and squeezing through doorways as he went, doorways through which I passed with an easy foot of clearance. His head brushed the ceiling that I couldn't reach without leaping.

We entered a cluttered foyer into the kitchen, where there was a small refrigerator, a wood stove, and various religious icons on the wall, including Saint Mary and, as he put it, "Saint Jesus." Leonid took me into a little living room off the kitchen. Spanning almost its entire length stood a bed — not a normal bed but one that was at least ten feet long, extra wide, covered with a green blanket of synthetic fur and, up near the pillows, three stuffed bunnies. There were heavy rugs hung from the wall, cheaply made Orientals, and several Soviet-era wardrobes along the near wall, spilling over with unruly swatches of fabric: exceptionally long shirtsleeves or stray pant legs, the world's largest gray suit, a bright sweater with enough wool to make a half-dozen sweaters. It brought to mind parachutes and gift-wrapping the Reichstag.

He offered me a chair and sat on the bed, reclining with his back against the wall. In the light, he was good-looking and boyish. He was perfectly proportional to himself, if no one else. If his growth surge had been the result of a surgeon's errant knife, he didn't technically suffer from gigantism, which is almost always caused by tumors on the pituitary gland. And he didn't *look* like other giants, with their heavy foreheads, prognathic jaws, abundant body hair, joints and limbs gnarled and misshapen. Also, unlike other giants about whom I'd read, his skin wasn't coarse or oily, and he was not odoriferous in the least. I don't know that he smelled at all, because the only detectable scent was that of the house, the land, the air here — of the Ukraine — a strong, earthy, manure-laced, rotting-apple odor that suffused everything. It was the smell of agriculture, of human beings living partially submerged in the earth, in the mud and muck from which they originally came, and it wasn't at all unpleasant.

In the days leading up to my visit, I'd done some research. Being big — the kind of big that happened in the one foot of stratosphere above the seven-foot-six Yao Mings of the world and was the province of only an elite group of giants — was both physically and psychologically traumatic. Problems ranged from crippling arthritis to lost vision, severe headaches to sleep apnea, tumors to impotence. Many giants simply could not be supported by their enlarged hearts. To find one alive past fifty was a rarity; forty was an accomplishment. And many ended up living alone, on the margins of society, their only claim to fame being their height. There were Web sites devoted to tracking these people the way stocks are tracked: Hussain Bisad, a man from Somalia, was reported to be seven feet nine inches tall. Ring Kuot, a fifteen-year-old Sudanese boy, was rumored to be eight feet three. And until Leonid's emergence at eight feet four inches last spring, people generally assumed that Radhouane Charbib of Tunisia, at seven feet nine, was the tallest documented man in the world. Which was fine with Leonid, because he didn't want the title. To have it meant that it was only a matter of time before his body betrayed him. It meant an early death. It might be next year, it might be ten years from now, but the clocks in the house were echoing.

We began with the easy stuff. Leonid talked about his favorite foods, which included a dish of rice and ground meat wrapped in cabbage leaves called *holubtsi*. "I like sweet things, too — cakes and candies," he said. "I adore ice cream, like a child. Pancakes with jam. But I'm not demanding. We grow all that we use: potatoes, cucumbers, carrots, tomatoes, pumpkins, apples, pears, grapes, plums, cherries . . ."

The list continued, and he cut himself short, saying it would take another fifteen minutes to name everything they cultivated in their fields and garden and then differentiate between the categories of apples and cherries, the ten kinds of grapes and squashes. "You know, when I was in Germany, I could not understand why they live so well," he said. He'd traveled to Germany last spring, and not only was it the epic event of his life, but it remained a constant point of reference. "They have very bad land," he continued, "and we have great land. We have natural resources and the Germans don't, but they have a better life."

That first night, he talked while I marveled, as one marvels in the presence of seemingly impossible creations, whether they be exalted paintings or unusual horses. He sat hugging himself, in a red-plaid shirt and heavy brown slacks. When he raised a finger to make a point, it was dramatic, huge, as if he were waving a nightstick. He had a twitch in his left eye and a way of dreamily staring into space as he spoke that suggested he saw something there or was merely trying to see something through the opacity of his life.

Every once in a while, Leonid's sister, Larisa, appeared. She was elfin, under five feet tall, and looked more like a boy than a woman in her early forties. Her only nod to femininity was a *hustina*, the traditional Ukrainian scarf that she wore over her head. At one point, she ferried plates of brown bread, fish, tomatoes, teacups, vodka glasses, cheese, and cold uncooked pig fat called *salo* to the table, as well as an unlabeled bottle of vodka. She didn't try to communicate with us, just nodded once and disappeared again. By this time it was very dark — and cold — and Leonid said she was going out to bring in the cows, who'd been grazing somewhere at the edge of the village.

From another room came the sound of a television and the intermittent voice of Leonid's mama, Halyna. She was even shorter than Larisa, wrapped in crocheted blankets in the classic rounded, robust shape of a sixtysomething babushka, her leg heavily bandaged. The family had suffered a shock in July when, while lugging a large milk jug up the front step, she had stumbled and fallen, the jug crushing one of her legs. "Mama tried to save the milk," said Leonid.

Not owning a car — not having the money to buy one and not being able to fit in anything smaller than a microbus — Leonid and his sister had driven their horse and cart miles to visit their mother in the hospital. This is how he'd been traveling for over a decade, and how people had been traveling here since before the birth of Christ. It was an investment the family made after Leonid couldn't bear the traumas of riding the bus — where he became a target of derision — and after his weight had destroyed several bikes. "My sister stayed near the horse, and I went to see Mama in the hospital," he said. "Then we shifted, and I stayed with the horse and my sister visited Mama. That's the problem with a horse and cart: someone always has to stay with the horse."

After her release, Leonid's mama had returned home to her bed where she'd been for months ever since. But if there was any doubt, she was still very much in charge, barking orders, overhearing snippets of conversation, and shouting spirited rejoinders.

"Yes, Mama," Leonid called back.

"I know, Mama," he said.

"OK, Mama."

We drank, all of us except Leonid, who claimed never to have had a drop of alcohol in his life. The vodka was very good, home-made from potatoes. I asked him how he could avoid drinking when their family made vodka this good. "It's a matter of principle. It's not that I don't drink. I do drink. Water, juice — cherry juice especially — but I don't drink alcohol. I have a motto: 'Try to do without the things that you can.' Look at me. I've been broken by my height. Probably I would become a drunk if I started drinking."

He wasn't looking at anyone when he said it but gazed out the dark window again — at something, or nothing. If people throw off vibrations, if certain people move molecules because of their words or actions or presence, Leonid sat in the room like a herd of buffaloes about to thunder. "In my life, I've done my best to become a normal person," he said, "to reach something. But because of my unusual body, I will never have a family or wealth or a future. I'm telling you, I've done my best. Everything that depended on me, I've done."

He was silent again, but his whole disposition had suddenly changed, as if he'd been thrown down on dungeon stones. "There's a saying here in the Ukraine," he said. "'God punishes the ones he loves most.'"

I returned early the next morning. Leonid didn't seem to mind my presence or my questions, he just took me on as his little-man apprentice. He had risen sometime after five, as he always did, and started by milking the cows. It was as dark outside as when I'd left him the night before — the air wrapped close around the morning bodies in cloaks of purple and black — and it was just as cold.

He put on his shoes at the door and walked across the flat granite patio of the inner yard, past two chained dogs rolling in their own feces, through the muddy passage between the small barn and the granary and the outhouse, past towering piles of stacked wood, and entered a room where LaSonya and Bunny, the cows, stood munching hay. Following him and imagining him simply as a form moving through the predawn, one could say he was, physically speaking, a true behemoth. His back was several tectonic plates; his head was more rectangular than round — his nose was a straight, emphatic line; his chin, a mesa — but he didn't give the impression of being sharp-edged, willful, or stressed by these geometries. He was just 150 percent as big as the world in which he lived and had figured long ago that the only way to live in it at all was to remain absolutely calm — and to make himself as small and invisible as possible. Here, at home, was the only place where he was still Leonid, the boy.

He towered over those cows as they chewed cud, and though he professed that they could be unmanageable, they grew still in his presence. The evening before, he'd said that one of his loves, one of his gifts, was the way he communed with animals, the way they fell under his sway. This was evident with the cat, called Striped One, who constantly sought him out, like a persistent lover, to have his ears scratched. But when it came to the cows and horses, the animals seemed to sense that, in this one case, they were in the company of a much larger being. So they became followers.

When milking, he used only his forefinger and thumb, because that's all that fit down there, squeezing out the teats, streams of white liquid clinking in a metal bucket. He sat on a stool, which left him lowly placed, and because of his size, he had to reach down so far to the udder that he rested his head on top of the cows' haunches. I kept having an image of him, after he'd finished, hoisting the cow up over his shoulder just because he could.

Having once worked at the local collective as a vet, Leonid knew his way around a farm. He loved digging, the feel of the earth in his hands. But unlike others in the village, he was fairly well-educated, having attended a local institute, graduating with honors. And yet his height defined everything. At fifteen, he was closing in on seven feet, growing several inches a year. By the time he went to college, he was a full-fledged giant. He needed new clothes every four to six months, and finding them was nearly impossible. After he'd outgrown store-bought clothes, he turned to a local dressmaker. "Sometimes she was successful, and sometimes she was not," he said. His eyesight became poor, and his legs began to fail. He slipped on the ice and broke his leg. He got frostbite commuting the seven kilometers to work and finally quit his job. By then, he'd long ago let go of his friends; he'd become afraid of crowds, afraid of anyone who might point a finger and laugh.

"I don't like to look at myself from the outside," he said. "I don't like the way I walk. I don't like the way I move. When I became tall, I felt shy and separated from my friends. A friend is a person with whom you can share your happiness and unhappiness. My best and most loyal friend is my mother."

When he spoke in his deep baritone, the trivial things he said felt metaphoric: "Lilies that don't work are more beautiful than any other flower in the world. But this is controversial." Or: "I wouldn't say I like to fish, but I like to look at people who like to fish." Or: "Everything depends on pigs and how fast they grow."

After milking, he took the buckets and emptied them into large jugs and then went out to meet the milkman. It was nearly ten before he made himself some rice and ground beef and rested for a while, reading the Bible.

"Here you're so busy," said Leonid, seated on his bed again. "You work until you see the moon in the sky, and that means it's evening. When I was in Germany, there were days when we didn't have to do anything; we had no special plans. So we could not wait for the end of the day, because there was nothing we had to do and nothing to do. Here every day seems very short."

Ah, Germany. He explained how a Ukrainian expat named Volodymyr, now living in Germany, had read an article and contacted him. It turned out that the two were distant relatives, and Volodymyr invited Leonid to visit Germany, all expenses paid. He had a special bus to pick him up and then drove him all the way through the western Ukraine and Poland to southern Germany, a two-day trip. At each stop along the way, the giant of Podoliantsi emerged from the bus as a great spectacle, to the awe of people who wanted his picture, his autograph, a few words. "You're a movie star," said Volodymyr. This was somehow different from the reaction he sometimes faced at home in the Ukraine. In this case, the awe wasn't mean or intrusive; it was "cultured," as Leonid said. In one town where there was a festival that included carnival performers, he walked into a restaurant and sat down, drinking apple juice with Volodymyr. People assumed he was part of the carnival, too, and couldn't help staring.

If they were looking at him, Leonid was looking back. He shared their sense of awe, even if the source of his were the amazing little things he saw around him. "There were so many bikes in the street," he said. "And the roads! Compared to ours, there is no comparison. I had a small table in my bus where I could put my glass with tea, and in the Ukraine there was great movement and in Poland a slight movement, and when we were driving in Germany there was no movement at all!"

He wanted me to know, however, that German roads and prosperity did not make Germany a better place. "When we went to Germany, we crossed the border, and even looking around, we could see that it's another country," he said in professorial tones. "Germany is a specific country. It is a strict country. Even the color of their buildings is usually gray, brown, some pale colors." He paused seriously, marshaling the full force of his memory. Surely few from Podoliantsi had ever been to Germany, and it was clear that some relatives, and maybe some of his mother's friends, had sat rapt through these recollections before, wondering what secrets he had brought back from abroad.

"The ornaments on the wall were different," he said.

At the end of each day with Leonid, I went back to Kiev, where, for me, the ornaments on the wall were different — as were my strange, empty hotel on Vozdvyzhenska Street and the late-night drunks lurching through the shadows. I thought about Leonid and how he seemed trapped inside of something growing out of control. Not just his body but the effect his body had on the world around him. Shy and sensitive, his only defense had been to withdraw. In so many ways, he was still a child who'd missed so much of life: first love, friends, marriage, children of his own. He no longer had a profession, just a business card with a picture, one made up for him by Japanese businessmen who had come to visit, of Leonid towering over a seven-story building.

He was a full-time giant now, waiting. But for what?

I called home and spoke to my wife. I could hear the kids in the background. By being here, I hadn't escaped them at all; in that hotel room, they seemed everywhere. And yet, by not being able to touch them — wrestling around with my son, Leo, or getting power hugs from my daughter, May — I felt more lost. They were growing, changing, proliferating, and I wasn't there. I was here, halfway around the world, trying to find some glimmer of what I thought I'd lost.

Over the days, the routine with Leonid was similar: I usually brought food and gifts. I gave Leonid's mother a scented candle and she responded happily, tickled, saying, "I've smelled one of

these before and will look forward to smelling it again!" Then she
barked to Larisa. "Matches!"

We spent many hours in the room with the big bed off the
kitchen, chatting with Leonid, who sometimes brought a plate of
walnuts to the table, crushing three or four at a time in his hand,
then picking bits of meat from the serving tray of his palm. It was
hard to say enough about his hands, to describe their power and
enormousness. He was proud of them, the one thing he was un-
afraid to show the world. He also knew that if he ever hit someone
with them, "that person would be dead," as he succinctly put it.

Larisa came and went, harried, rosy cheeked. She regarded us
openly, without expression, like an animal. A squirrel, to be exact.
Sometimes she became impatient with Leonid's loafing and stood
for an extra moment glaring at him — even muttering single words
like "carrots" or "cows" to signify the task at hand — while he spoke
on, oblivious, staring out the window into space. "I don't always
have the will to pursue my goals," he said. "I force myself to finish
very dull work. But my sister, she is persistent. She never gives up. I
can give up, but she can't."

So that was her role, the sister of the giant of Podoliantsi. To
work twice as hard while caring for her mother and brother. And
that would be the role for the rest of her life, as both of them became more and more infirm. And Leonid's role, for us at least, was
to reflect on his life, to offer it like some gilded manuscript, one
with missing pages, of the things he'd actually missed in life and
the things that were too painful to recall. He wouldn't discuss his
operation at all, for instance, even when I pressed for details. "All
you ask about is trifles and some negative moments in my life," he
said, almost angrily. "Ask me about something gay and something
happy, though I have few moments like that."

About his height, he said it was something he couldn't comprehend when he was young. He said everything seemed normal after
the operation until one day, in ninth grade, the class was measured
and the two-meter tape was too short for him. After that, he became acutely aware of people laughing out loud when there wasn't
a block of empty seats on the bus and, unable to stand on his legs,
Leonid would squat, as if over a hole in the ground. "One in a million would have survived what I survived on that bus," he said.

But somehow he did. He kept surviving.

And if God was punishing him, God had also kept him alive.

Leonid had nearly died five times. In the first year of his life, he slipped into a coma and couldn't breathe. His parents bid their last goodbyes and made preparations for his burial — and he came back. When he was twelve, the Lord was more emphatic, letting loose the blood clot in his brain. Leonid couldn't move his hands or legs. To alleviate the paralysis, a risky procedure was performed inside the brain. Before he was put under, he remembered being wheeled through a ward of paralyzed children and then his parents saying goodbye once more. But whatever saved him that day doomed him to be a giant forever.

Realizing his fate over time, suffering the unbearable loneliness of giants, he twice tried suicide by hanging. ("My angels were awake," he said of those two attempts. "They did not want me to die. And my skeleton would not be broken.") And then, in his cart a few years ago, being pulled by his horse Tulip, he hit a rut. The cart toppled, and all 480 pounds of him were suddenly in the air, then beneath the heavy cart. What would have killed anyone else, what would have cleanly snapped a spine or neck, did not kill him. He came up from under the cart and went chasing his horse.

God had kept him alive. That's what he believed, so that's what the truth was. And he believed he'd been kept alive for a purpose.

"Do you talk to God and ask him?" I said.

"I ask him, but He doesn't hear me," Leonid said. "The Bible says that those who cry in this world will then be happy in heaven. I'm not sure it will be like this, but I want to believe it. But secretly, I think those that suffer here will suffer in heaven, too."

"But why did God choose you for this?" I asked.

"I'm too tired to think about it," he said, finding the last bit of meat from the walnuts. "I used to think about it all the time, and now I don't want to think about it anymore. My future is only black."

Almost on cue, Larisa appeared again, muttering the word "apples." Her appearance was perfectly timed. This time Leonid smiled broadly and said, "Come," waving his hand for me to follow. "We'll go pick some." He forced himself to his feet and ducked through the first doorway, listing through the cramped house without so much as disturbing a spoon. He grabbed his coat and cap, squeezed through two more doorways, then went out into the day, which was still full of light.

*

Leonid was a prankster — and a giggler. He had a sweet giggle, very boyish and innocent. At one point, seated on his bed, he reached into his pocket, as if suddenly remembering something important, and produced a mobile phone, which he seemed to check for missed messages. With his pointer finger, he somehow plinked out a number. To give him his privacy, the translator and I began chatting, until her phone engaged, too, and she formally excused herself to take the call. She answered, "*Dobryi den*" and then Leonid answered back from three feet away, in his booming baritone, "*DOBRYI DEN!*"

Watching the translator's surprise, his eyes became slits, his cheeks rose, and there was an enormous uplift at the corners of his mouth. His face, which was wind-chapped from so many hours in the garden, became its own planet. His ears, the shape and size of a hefty split Idaho potato, wiggled; his prodigious chin raised to reveal a patch of whiskers he'd missed while shaving; his two eyes were ponds of hazel water, suddenly lit by a downpour of sun. All the features of his face were complementary and, taken together, offered no clue that he was a giant. It's only when they were set against the rest of humanity that he became, in every way, more exaggerated . . . and, well, gigantic.

And yet his happiness was such a feathery, redemptive force. He had the same smile in one of the only pictures that still existed from when he was a boy — a picture that hung in a frame over his mama's bed, of a towheaded three-year-old with almond-shaped eyes. It had been taken on a special outing at the Kiev Zoo, one of the few times the family had been out of their village together, on a proper trip. It was sepia-toned, as if taken a century ago.

Looking up at that little-boy face in the picture and then looking at Leonid's now was like watching the arc of an entire life being drawn between two points. More than anything, the primary experience of Leonid's life had been his growing, though his primary desire had been to go back to that moment when he was simply a child again.

"I was a little guy, and now I'm a big one," Leonid said when he showed me the photograph, his mama sitting nearby, still bundled in blankets.

"He was so nice when he was small," she said, with a touch of longing. "At least he has a suit for his funeral."

So it came down to this: on the day his life was saved by doctors operating on his brain, Leonid lost the ability to determine his own fate. On that day, he became chosen, as he pointed out — but he also became powerless. No wonder he was so dedicated to the Bible, reciting certain parables to whoever would listen. Long ago, he had thrown his life over to God, with his Old Testament temper, because nothing could explain what was happening to him. God was his hands and his feet and his mahjong teeth.

Maybe because of my size, mere mortal that I was, I had choices. And my god wasn't his god. In fact, I wasn't sure about who my god was. Maybe he was a feeling I got sometimes, a feeling that there *could* be a god. Or a glimmer I occasionally saw in the trees.

God was in the apple trees and red oaks or a bend in the river that we'd come upon yesterday where leaves fell into the current and were borne to the Black Sea in gold trails. God was the cows chewing cud and Tulip the horse pulling the cart and the dogs rolling in their own shit. God was the vein of blue granite running beneath the ground here and the milk in the jugs that pinned Leonid's mama, crushing her leg.

God was that moment when Leonid went out to pick apples and I followed. He used a little stool, and I took a crude metal ladder and leaned it against the house. We levitated way up in the top boughs of the trees, and the apples thudded as they were dropped in the buckets. We were up in the trees, Leonid and I, and he began singing, in his own tongue, gently twisting fruit from each branch. His voice, that sweet song, sounded as if it came from some deep underground river.

The town of Miracle lay beyond him. Across the fields, a train sounded. God was the trees and the apples and the glowing clouds overhead. We were part of the same body, the earth as it was, as it had been created by some cosmic force. When I think of this, I still get that feeling, up there in that tree, that feeling of belonging to something sizeless.

I get that feeling of being up in the trees with Leonid, and everything that really matters, everything worth it, is up there with us, too: my children, his mama. All of our giants and dwarves. The apples are sources of warmth on that cold day, as if heated from within. To touch them was divine.

My time with Leonid was coming to an end. I'd gotten fleas — or something — from my hotel bed and was itching like a possessed maniac. When I'd filled the tub to wash, cold, smelly green water had eagerly obliged. Anyway, Halloween was approaching, and I would be returning to my kids, returning to watch them grow. And I was returning to one day set them free of this giant body, our family: to eventually put them on a bus somewhere so that they might come back and tell us of the ornaments they saw out there. I realized that once I left Leonid, I was really returning for good, that my next probable meeting with the giant would come some random afternoon at my desk, when I'd stumble across a newspaper item about his death, the tallest man in the world finally subsumed by his size.

Here were the basic facts: he would die having grown to eight and a half, nine, nine and a half feet, perhaps as the tallest man that ever lived, a title he'd never wanted. He would die a virgin, without ever having had a lover. Without having close friends, for that matter. He would die without children, having made it to Germany once, but no farther. It would have been many years since he'd been able to run or swim. He might or might not have a suit to fit him when he was put in his casket and lowered by the village men, at least a dozen of them, into the earth of Podoliantsi.

Until then, he clung to his otherworld, half made of dream and half made of manure. "I have no bad thoughts about the end," he said. He ate ice cream, sucked down a dozen raw eggs at a time, chewed cold pig fat, sang, and slept with three stuffed bunnies. He fell into bitter moods, cursed his God, then contritely read his Bible. He received his pilgrims and told them the tale of his life, hugging himself, gazing out the window, while Larisa came and went, muttering words like "beets" and "melon." He wasn't an angel or a beast after all, just a man, forming his beliefs from the body he'd been given. He said goodbye among the apple trees, where he'd first said hello, crushing my hand again, turning the colors of the leaves as we drove away.

But I remember him most vividly in a moment just before leaving. I went for a little walk to see the cows. When I returned, I came upon him standing in the shadow of the apple trees, leaning against his gate, looking out from his stone house at the landscape, the red oaks on fire now, villagers using their wooden plows to turn the fields, the sun coming down just opposite him in the melancholic end of day. He had no idea I was there. He just breathed it all in. There was a presence behind his eyes — not just his enormous brain and eardrums, but *him,* his himness or soul or whatever. It was a moment where he just *was.* Contented.

He stood against the fence, and a neighbor child drifted by. The neighbors had cherubic boys and girls, blond and fresh and smiling, like he once was. Maybe, in another life, one of them would have been his own, light enough to hold up in one hand. But now, hidden in the shadows beneath the apple tree, invisible, Leonid gently said, "*Dobryi den,*" which sent the boy skyward. He hadn't seen the giant there at all, and that was before factoring in that the voice belonged to an actual *giant* who happened to be his neighbor.

"*Dobryi den,*" the boy said in a startled whisper. He looked up into the branches, gazed upon Leonid's face there, and stumbled. Then he put his head down and hurried on.

It took two days to get home. In the lounge at the airport in Munich, still itching madly, I realized that something smelled. Did anyone bathe in Germany? Yes, they did. It was me: I smelled like Podoliantsi, and I could tell people were thinking twice about sitting near me. I got up and found a terminal shower that I could use and stood in warm, clear water for nearly a half hour, washing it all away.

On the flight to Boston, I looked down on the world for all signs of life on land and sea, but from that height many of the fine details of the earth, including large houses and tankers, were simply erased. After landing at Logan, I waited in line, passed through customs, and again waited for my luggage to appear from behind rubber ribbons, trusting it would. The minute it did, I ran like a madman for the bus. I was so shot through with adrenaline, I was floating.

Soon the bus cloverleafed onto the highway. Two hours north now, to home, fitting neatly in my seat. When I saw this familiar land outside the window — fall here, too, flat land with its own forest flaring — and when I saw my wife, her stomach rounded against her sweater, and my daughter in funny pigtails there at the station, waiting, and I could finally touch them again, and when I lifted and held my little boy, Leo, in my arms again and felt my heart beating hard enough to know that I wanted to live a very long time, I took his hand up against mine, just to check, just to see what had occurred in my absence.

His hand lay in mine, and I felt its weight: the little bones and the smooth, scarless skin so soft it didn't seem real. Mine dwarfed his, but still I held his hand up and inspected his fingers for a moment. He thought I was being funny, and he laughed, a little-boy giggle. His breath smelled like cookies. Yes, his fingers were bigger, and I was not frightened. Maybe the betrayals lay out before us somewhere in our murky future. Maybe we were all growing until someday nothing would work for us anymore. But I was not frightened. I was filled with joy.

It read 4:00 on the wall — on the east coast of the United States of America — and at that very moment, somewhere, the giant was sleeping on his oversized bed. His huge shoes lay empty near the doorway, his pants thrown over the chair. His enormous suit hung in the closet, waiting.

Soon he would rise to milk the cows, feed the pigs, pick the rest of the apples. In the dirt lane before his house, carts would come and go, bearing payloads of huge purple hearts. And there he would be, the giant, alone up in the apple tree, gently picking fruit, humming the notes again.

At the bus station, my children began singing.

TONY PERROTTET

The Joy of Steam

FROM *WorldHum.com*

> Sex, wine, and the baths may ruin our bodies, but they make life worth living.
> — *Ancient Roman gravestone*

ARRIVING IN THE SULTANAHMET district of Istanbul, built atop the ruins of the Greek city of Byzantium and the Roman capital of Constantinople, I already felt like I'd traveled halfway back in time to the ancient world. Then, in tea houses all over the city, I found dog-eared leaflets advertising the pleasures of Cagaloglu Hamam, the city's oldest bathhouse:

HAVE YOU EVER BEEN IN A TURKISH BATH? IF YOU HAVEN'T, YOU'VE MISSED ONE OF LIFE'S GREAT EXPERIENCES AND NEVER BEEN CLEAN!

The sales pitch added that Kaiser Wilhelm of Germany, the composer Franz Liszt, Florence Nightingale and Cameron Diaz had all enjoyed steam baths here. No less than 138 films had been shot within the hamam's walls, and innumerable newspaper stories written:

THE PRESS HAS MUCH PRAISED THIS BATHING HABIT!

How could I resist? For anyone interested in how antiquity has survived to the modern day, a visit to a Turkish bath is essential: the Islamic hamam is possibly the most striking link we have to a key social practice of the Greco-Roman world — especially for a traveler.

Two thousand years ago, if you were visiting any city in the Roman Empire, you would be woken by the melodious bass of a copper gong resounding through the streets at dawn, announcing the opening of the thermae, or heated public baths — a sound, Cicero rhapsodized, that was sweeter than the voices of all the philosophers in Athens. These ancient baths were far more than mere palaces of cleanliness: they were the Western world's first true entertainment complexes, combining the facilities of modern gyms, massage parlors, restaurants, community centers, and tourist information offices. They were the ideal place to meet locals or get hot travel tips: in those palatial halls, citizens of all classes lolled by the pools, met their friends, played ball games, relaxed, flirted, drank wine, and even had elegant candlelit dinners. And like nightclubs or gyms today, a city's baths were unofficially graded: some were chic, others déclassé; some were expensive, others cost only a copper; some were magnificently designed, as large as cathedrals, decorated with enormous mosaics of Neptune and his dolphins.

In short, a visit to the baths was the ideal way to enter the social life of a strange city.

Modern Turkey offers a unique connection to this ancient tradition. Two thousand years ago it was the Roman province of Asia Minor, and it's the only place in the Mediterranean where the historical line back to the thermae is unbroken. In Western Europe, the habit of public bathing did not survive the collapse of the Roman Empire. During the Middle Ages, good Christians became ashamed of their bodies, and showed their repugnance of earthly matters by refusing to wash, remaining smelly, squalid and flea-bitten until the late nineteenth century. But in the Eastern half of the Empire, soon known as Byzantium, the great Roman baths stayed open, and were even more popular after the Ottoman Empire conquered Turkey in the fifteenth century A.D. Islam adhered to the ancient obsession with personal cleanliness, as well as the Greco-Roman tradition of bathing in public. Of course, there were some big changes, too: total nudity was forbidden under Islam; men wore loincloths, and women were provided with separate baths. But the connection is still powerful. In modern Turkey, many bathhouses even still stand on the original classical sites. In fact, the very name "Turkish bath" was given by British visitors to Constantinople in the sixteenth century, who saw the ancient Roman thermae still in operation and incorrectly assumed they were an Ottoman invention.

Today, there are over sixty baths still officially registered in Istanbul. Sadly, these last hamams are under siege, as Turks in the big city increasingly prefer Western-style bathing in the privacy of their homes. Young Turks find steam rooms decidedly outré — several warned me that they were dens of disease and foot rot, frequented only by country bumpkins, geriatrics, and male prostitutes. And yet the venerable institution staggers on.

Visiting Istanbul was obviously my big chance to experience this ancient travelers' tradition. Still, I found myself delaying: the embarrassing fact was, I'd never had a massage, let alone visited an actual bathhouse back home in New York. But by the time I'd picked up my tenth leaflet singing the praises of Cagaloglu Hamam, I finally decided to give this famous washing experience a shot. After all, it was reputed to be the most palatial bathhouse extant in all Turkey, and has been in continuous operation at least since 1741. An English photographer I was traveling with reluctantly agreed to join me. I wasn't sure if Nik was a wise companion: even more than most of us self-conscious Westerners, he viewed public bath houses as deeply seedy places and held an unshakable conviction, apparently gleaned from *Lawrence of Arabia* and *Midnight Express*, that Turks were polymorphously perverse.

But we grabbed our towels and headed off valiantly into the night, on a modest expedition into the damp underbelly of antiquity.

Admittedly, my first vision of Cagaloglu's exterior did give me pause. In a noisy side street, a sunken entrance displayed a frayed sign in four languages, along with a string of bleached photographs showing a parade of rather louche-looking semicelebrities who had sweated it up here in the 1960s.

"Are we feeling confident in our masculinity?" Nik mused.

Inside, the once-palatial entryway looked grimier than 260 years of continuous use could possibly account for. The courtyard of marble and mahogany must once have been an uplifting sight; now, its latticework was dark and dimly lit. The elegant fountain was dry, and half a dozen cockroaches lay belly up in one corner, alongside an empty Evian bottle.

An old man at the desk woke from a deep slumber and blinked at us in surprise.

"Are you open tonight?" I asked.

He shuffled some papers. "Why not?" He raised a hand, and an attendant in a bright orange loincloth slouched like a tubercular genie from the shadows.

Ahmed the masseur was thin and wiry, with sunken eyes, and decidedly yellow around the gills; he appeared to be coated from head to foot in nicotine. He stood solicitously by as we made the financial arrangements. I passed on the obscure "Sultan Service" and agreed to the standard "bath and massage." Nik cautiously paid up for bath only.

"Ahmed's not really my type," he helpfully explained.

At the sight of the change rooms, dank little vinyl-covered cubicles, Nik was all for turning back, but I had a sense of duty. This was my direct link to the Romans — although it occurred to me, and not for the last time, that a lot can change in two thousand years.

Back in the fourth century A.D., when Constantinople was the Empire's jewel, the atmosphere at its bathhouses was not unlike a crowded Mediterranean beach in summer today. The noise was infernal. All around, merrymakers were exercising, splashing water and playing handball; food vendors bellowed from their podiums; and professional hair-pluckers induced shrieks of pain in their clients that rose well above the general din. Petty thieves worked the crowd, rifling through belongings while the owners swam or slept, while the wealthy trawled the steam rooms handing out banquet invitations to potential sexual partners.

It's not surprising that the Christians were horrified by pagan behavior at these places: bathing, sex, and food were the Holy Trinity of the Roman good life, and the coed thermae encouraged all three. Romans learned to parade naked in the heated pools — those who hid themselves were ridiculed. The poet Martial was affronted when one young woman refused to share a bath with him; he assumed she was trying to hide some dreadful physical defect. Even worse, from the Christian point of view, were the male-only baths, since homosexuality was openly accepted in Roman society, at least between teenage boys and their adult "mentors."

Erotic foreplay continued all the way from the steam rooms to the baths' bars and restaurants, where flushed lovers — or wealthy women and their Adonis-like young slaves — could eye one another over a jug of chilled wine and figs. Private rooms were provided for consummation, decorated with lewd frescoes. Special magical spells were devised to incite romance at the baths. (Some were a little bizarre: "To attract a lover at the thermae: First, rub a tick from a dead dog on your genitals . . ." Another spell needed to be written in the blood of a donkey on a papyrus sheet, which should then be glued onto the ceiling of the vapor room — "you will marvel at the results," the author promised.) As one graffito in a Herculaneum bath crowed: "We, Appelles the Mouse and his brother Dexter, lovingly fucked two women twice."

Soon Nik and I were ushered from the fetid changing booths to the first steam room, where a wall of hot, stale air hit like the exhalations of a demonic laundry.

I had to admit that the domed vault of Cagaloglu was impressively cathedral-like — there were even Corinthian columns harking back to the Roman style — and shafts of white light glowed through thick swirling mist, descending from holes in the domed ceiling and ricocheting off the polished marble interior. But a sullen lethargy pervaded the air. About a dozen sallow customers in loincloths lolled about in the shadows, groaning ominously, as if they were drunk. A couple of guys looked as if they hadn't left this room for years.

I lay for a while on a hot stone block, before Ahmed the masseur emerged again from the mist like a zombie in the Louisiana bayous. Without fanfare, he got to work for the skin-scraping, wielding an abrasive mitten — the modern descendant of the ancient strigil, a curved metal instrument that removed dirt, sand, sweat, and exfoliated skin, all mixed up in the olive oil that was used throughout antiquity as a soap; this nauseating mixture would then be flicked by the ancient masseurs onto a nearby wall. Ahmed kept swiping languidly, as if he was brushing a longhaired dachshund, while the scent of tobacco mingled with the perfume of foot odor wafting from the floor. Abruptly, he paused and brought his head next to my ear.

"You want — special service?" Ahmed breathed.

"No!" I jumped. "Why? What is it?"

"Shampoo massage," he confided, pointing to a running fountain. I could get a real massage — but I had to pay top dollar.

"Going for a little rough trade?" Nik asked from the nearby mat, after I'd agreed.

Ahmed looked at him archly. "You would like special massage also?"

"Not me," Nik put up his hands defensively. "I'm strictly self-service."

We have a modest insight into how a Roman traveler might have behaved at this stage of a bathhouse visit, thanks to the fragmentary survival of a bilingual Greek-Latin phrase book. Like any modern Berlitz guide, its vocabulary list is complemented by a colloquia, or "dialogue scene." The Roman speaker arrives with a sizeable party of friends and imperiously chooses a slave attendant: *Follow us. Yes, you. Look after our clothes carefully, and find us a place.*

Let me have a word to the perfumier. Hello, Julius. Give me incense and myrrh for twenty people. No, no, best quality.

Now, boy, undo my shoes. Take my clothes. Oil me.

All right, let's go in.

A few minutes into my modern "special massage," I could have done with a language phrase book myself. Specifically, what was the Turkish for: My spleen is about to burst.

As my unaccustomed flesh was torn and chopped by Ahmed's tobacco-cured fingers, I tried to distract myself, yet again, with the knowledge that I was part of a tradition dating back to Cicero and Caesar. But I had to admit that only the most superficial elements of the Roman bath habit had really survived.

The formal structure of a visit may be the same — the ancients went from steam rooms to washing rooms to massage rooms — but the fact is, for the Romans, these had really only been excuses for a visit to the thermae. It was the peripheral circus — the people-watching, the chance meetings, the dinner invitations, the ball games, the snacks, the gossip, the pick-up artists, the vendors and beauticians — that made the baths so addictive in antiquity. Today, thanks to the inroads of Western bathing habits in Istanbul, convincing many Turks to shower at home, there has been a quantum leap from that original social purpose.

In one last forlorn echo of Roman times, Cagaloglu did maintain a restaurant in its shadowy foyer for a postmassage treat — although all it apparently stocked was moist pistachios instead of fresh fish, venison, blood sausage, and pig's trotters.

When I staggered out of the steam room, Nik was the only one there, quietly chugging down a warm beer. He motioned to a bench. "Take a seat — if it's not too painful, that is."

As I was recovering, a trio of pale Danish visitors wandered in, looking around with some confusion, and then were ushered into the changing rooms. Most things may have changed in the baths since Roman times, I thought, but at least the travelers were still hopeful: it was only tourists to Istanbul, really, who were keeping Cagaloglu's doors open.

You could call it the last vestige of ancient tradition — which was something, I supposed.

ROLF POTTS

Tantric Sex for Dilettantes

FROM *PerceptiveTravel.com*

I. The Girl

YOU SPOT THE GIRL on your first afternoon in Rishikesh. She is
long-limbed and graceful, and she walks carefully along the path,
as if not to disturb the dirt beneath her bare feet. She wears loose
cotton pants, and tiny bells in her hair. She is smiling. Her stomach
is browned and taut; the tiny hairs on her arms are bleached from
the sun. When she spots a cow in her path, she stops to stroke its
neck and whisper into its ear. You watch, and you wish you were
that cow.

You think to yourself: *If I have come here to learn Tantric sex, I want
that woman to be my partner.*

II. The Holy Place

Rishikesh straddles the Ganges just below the point where the sacred river comes roaring out from the mountains. The water here
is clean and cold: in the morning, Hindu pilgrims tip offerings of
fresh milk from the riverside ghats; in the afternoon, helmeted
tourists — Indian and foreign alike — bump through the current
in rubber white-water rafts. Monkeys chatter in the trees along the
shore.

As in other holy places in India, the dreadlocked *sadhus* near the
river do a steady side-business posing for tourist photographs. Middle-aged Indian men stroll the alleys, offering you marijuana in the
same chirpy, unconcerned voice one might use in offering snack

pellets to a pet gerbil. Kids here tug on your sleeve and ask you for ballpoint pens.

You did not initially come here to learn Tantric sex. Rather, you stopped here en route to the Himalayas, on the recommendation of a yoga-obsessed friend. You are not much into yoga, but one charm of travel is that it frees you to be a dilettante. Just as you tried scuba diving in Thailand and windsurfing in Galilee, you intend to try yoga in Rishikesh and decide later if you really want to make it an active part of your life.

Advertisements for yogis are pasted everywhere in Rishikesh, and you sometimes stop to read them. Your favorite comes from a certain Swami Vivekananda. "I mix the rational understanding of the West with the mystical approach of the East," his flyer states. "I will not bother you with religious nonsense, weird rituals, dogmas, or superstitions."

The true selling point, however, is printed at the bottom. It says: "Sundays: A step-by-step approach to the oral secret tradition of the Tantric schools of India and Tibet."

You don't know a lot about Tantra, but you're pretty sure it's a technique that allows you to have sex for hours and hours at a stretch.

You elect to remain in Rishikesh until Sunday and pay Swami Vivekananda's ashram a visit.

III. *The Rooftop Restaurant*

You've been staying in a two-dollar hotel in the heart of Rishikesh. Your room is small and bare, but you like its ascetic vibe. Sometimes you hear elementary Vedic chants coming up through the pipes in the bathroom. Other times, the pipes emit snoring noises, or the tinny whine of your downstairs neighbor complaining about his diarrhea. The showers run cold, but a boy at the front desk will bring you a bucket of hot water at no extra cost.

There is a restaurant on the roof, and it serves Italian food. The lasagna is subpar, but the view of the Ganges attracts a steady stream of diners, who gather to discuss yoga, Hindu philosophy, and where to find the street vendor who sells the bran muffins. Pink-faced rhesus monkeys infest the surrounding buildings, and sometimes they leap across to steal leftover garlic bread, or fight one another over bowls of tea sugar. The waiters chase them away, but they always come back.

Though you have yet to see The Girl on the roof of your hotel, you do meet various other travelers. They say things like, "Yeah, yoga till Friday, then I go rafting"; or: "I'm just getting my yin and yang in order, getting a little exercise; it can't hurt." Some of the more earnest seekers explain to you how the seven chakras correspond to the seven planets, or how it's hard to travel in Cuba if you're a vegetarian.

Scott, a young guy from New Zealand, has also noticed The Girl. He tells you he thinks she's from Latvia, and that she is probably gaining positive karmic energy from your infatuation. "Mae West was actually one of the first Westerners to be aware of karmic energy, back in the 1930s," Scott tells you. "She took all that lustful male energy that was directed at her, and she cultivated it like a garden. It made her into a stronger person." The more you consider this, the more you enjoy the idea that — even if you have not yet mustered the courage to speak to The Girl — you are at least making her into a stronger person.

In the early evenings, you leave the rooftop and go for hikes in the forest outside Rishikesh. The black-faced lemurs that live in the trees there are gentle and graceful and shy. Unlike the rhesus monkeys that haunt the hotel rooftop, they do not squabble, bare their teeth at you, or try to get at your food. If you stand silent among the trees, they will walk out on their branches and stare down at you with calm curiosity.

IV. *The Tantra Class*

When Sunday arrives, you go to Swami Vivekananda's ashram, where you are met with two initial disappointments. First, you find out that men and women are required to take the class separately. Second, you discover that the swami is not from India, but Romania. He is tall, bulky, and bespectacled, and he quotes Hindu scripture with vague Count Dracula inflections, pausing occasionally to brush a shock of brown hair from his eyes.

Swami Vivekananda quiets the class and explains that it is difficult to get beyond a certain point of spiritual awareness unless you learn to redirect your sexual energy. "Tantric practitioners seek to reverse the Pavlovian connection between orgasm and ejaculation," he says. "Ejaculation is in-built for species reproduction, but it interferes with the true spiritual nature of orgasm."

This declaration yields a flurry of questions. Does a Tantric orgasm feel like a regular orgasm? "It does not." Does a Tantric orgasm still originate in the genitals? "Not exactly. It is not even purely physical; it is a spiritual orgasm." Is a spiritual orgasm really better than a physical orgasm? "Yes," the swami says, losing patience. "And a man who has tasted honey doesn't want to eat shit anymore."

Continuing in this culinary vein, Swami Vivekananda suggests that developing a Tantric awareness of sex is akin to cultivating a refined taste for food — turning it into a spiritual act instead of a mere pleasure-survival reflex. The kissing, biting, and massaging encouraged by the *Kama Sutra*, he explains, is not mere sexual foreplay, but part of a recipe for deeper spiritual awareness.

"Sexuality is not of the body, but of the mind," the swami concludes, "and it is through the mind that we wage war with the ingrained reflexes of the body. Tantric masters learn to keep their physical instincts behind the point of no return, and this yields sexual and spiritual rewards."

Again, the class buzzes with questions. How exactly do you stay behind the point of no return? "Self-discipline is not a part-time job; it must be strengthened over time." But how? "By pulling your sexual energy into your mind and your chakras." But how do you actually do that while you're having sex? "You learn new ways to overcome your instincts; it's like training an animal by using a carrot." So is the carrot, like, counting backward from a thousand or something? "No! Tantra is about mindfulness, not distraction."

Eventually, Swami Vivekananda becomes exasperated with ejaculation questions. "Look," he says, "there are some pelvic muscles that can help control ejaculation, and the best way to strengthen them is to urinate in short, start-stop bursts instead of one continuous stream. But please. Let us stick to spiritual matters."

As he says this, a palpable sense of relief fills the room. The swami continues to explain the mystical essence of Tantric discipline, but nobody thinks to ask any more questions.

v. *The Girl, Part II*

The following day, as if by holy miracle, The Girl shows up on the roof of your hotel. When her tea arrives, she stretches her long arms up above her head, and you watch the graceful curve of her torso, the flat ripple of her stomach. She opens her shoulder bag, takes out a bran muffin, and places it on her table.

You watch this, gathering up your nerve, and you think: *Tantra is about mindfulness.*

Before you can approach her, however, a rhesus monkey hops down from a nearby roof and climbs onto her table. The Girl's smile brightens. Whispering something you cannot hear, she slides a hand forward and begins to stroke the yellow-brown fur on the monkey's leg. You watch, and you wish you were that monkey.

Then, suddenly, the little pink-faced creature rears back and swats the teacup off the table. As The Girl flinches, the monkey grabs her muffin and leaps up onto an adjacent roof.

For a moment, everything on the rooftop is still. The Girl stares down at the streaks of tea on her shirt. The monkey clutches the muffin and stares down at The Girl. Conversations stop, and everyone at the restaurant silently waits to see what will happen next.

You fully expect The Girl to whisper up at the monkey — to coax it down, cradle it into her arms, and walk off peacefully to share the muffin on the shores of the holy Ganges. Instead, her face reddens, and she snatches a tin of tea sugar. Curling her thin, lovely lips, she screams, "COCK-SUCKING FUCKING MONKEY!"

The sugar tin whangs off the roof and explodes into a grainy white cloud. The monkey blinks coquettishly at The Girl, and begins to nibble at the bran muffin. The Girl seizes a white plastic dining chair, and — in what you now recognize as a California drawl — bellows: "COME HERE, YOU STUPID LITTLE FUCKER!"

Before The Girl can hurl the chair, an Indian waiter rushes over and places his hands on her shoulders. In what appears to be a weary and well-practiced routine, he tells her to please calm down — that everything will be OK, that the monkey did not mean her any harm, and that he will be happy to clean up the mess and fetch her another tea.

Roughly shaking off the waiter's touch, The Girl drops the chair and bursts into tears. She snatches her bag and runs out of the restaurant. Everyone on the roof smirks and turns back to their tea or lasagna.

You flag the waiter, pay your bill, and head for the forest.

VI. *The Holy Place, Part II*

As you walk through the trees, you keep quiet and look for lemurs.

You're coming to realize that travel anywhere is often a matter of exploring half-understood desires. Sometimes, those desires lead you in new and wonderful directions; other times, you wind up trying to understand just what it was you desired in the first place. And, as often as not, you find yourself playing the role of charlatan as you explore the hazy frontier between where you are, who you are, and who it is you might want to be.

Before long, you sense motion in the trees, and drop to a crouch. After a minute or so, a lemur walks out onto a branch, gray-furred and dignified, his tail curved up over his head for balance. As he stares down at you, you realize how privileged you are to be in Rishikesh.

Later, when you return to your hotel room, you hear a strange, intermittent gurgling noise coming up from the bathroom pipes. For a moment, you can't place it; then, you smile at the sheer optimism of the sound.

It's your downstairs neighbor. He is urinating in short, start-stop bursts.

Rediscovering Libya

FROM *National Geographic Adventure*

"YOU COME, MADAME," the man says to me. He wants to show me something — something "special." And maybe it's the sincere look in his eyes, the supplication, the knowing, but I follow this complete stranger across Tripoli's Green Square and through the stone gate of the ancient medina, or historic Arab quarter. It's my first night in Libya; I arrived only three hours ago in a country that's still a mystery of culture shock and conjecture. So many people told me not to come here. Terrorist cells, they warned. Don't forget the Lockerbie bombing. And of course Muammar Qaddafi, global pariah, former patron of every rogue cause the world over. The U.S. State Department advises extreme caution.

It all gives me the shivers, like entering a house that's supposedly haunted. I keep looking over my shoulder. Can people tell I'm American? Such paranoia.

Few are out tonight. It's the eve of Eid al-Fitr, the three-day Muslim holiday that marks the end of the month-long fast of Ramadan. The storekeepers look at me curiously as I pass, and I touch my hair before their glances; most Libyan women wear headscarfs and long coats to hide the shape of their bodies. Libyan men wear whatever they please — Western clothes, usually, though some prefer the traditional djellaba: baggy pants and a shirt reaching to the knees. An old woman passes, wrapped head-to-toe in a white garment, a burnoose, held tightly over her face, a single eye peering out at me through the folds. Otherwise, the medina is mostly deserted, the small stores like lighted vestibules in the dark and cavernous depths of the Old City.

The man urges me down a dim passageway, but I pause at the edge of the shadows. Where are we going? I demand in French. What do you want to show me?

"Something special," he insists, beckoning.

We enter the heart of the medina. Built over the ancient Phoenician town of Oea, its carved columns are still visible at the corners of buildings. Modernity has all but vanished here, and I trespass in a time when donkey carts shuddered by and slaves were driven down the narrow streets.

"Come, come," the man urges.

We go deeper into the labyrinth. Great stone arches cross overhead, cutting shadows across the dank walkways. The scent of incense wafts down the corridors, our footsteps loud and impudent in the silence. The man stops. He enters a clothing store and sends away the young boy tending it. Stepping behind the front counter, he raises his eyebrows at me in conspiratorial confidence.

"Come," he whispers.

I do, stepping forward gingerly.

He looks out at the front of the store. At the aisles around him. No one. He slowly pulls out something small, balled in his fist. Eyes wide and intent on me, he shakes it out.

"Yes, Madame?" he asks. "You want to buy?"

I lean down to see what it is: a lace bra with matching thong panties.

It's hard to know what's real in Libya. I finger the Qaddafi T-shirts in a gift shop at the Roman ruins of Leptis Magna, outside of Tripoli. Qaddafi poses on them like a rock star, face hardened and puckered, eyes gazing majestically toward the clouds. He hangs in every building, in every city intersection, large and wide and belligerent over the streets. There aren't billboards in Libya — there is Qaddafi.

His country used to be one of the poorest in Africa until, in 1959, Esso (now Exxon) discovered massive oil deposits beneath the sands — the largest petroleum reserves on the African continent. A decade later, Qaddafi, then a twenty-seven-year-old idealist, seized control of the wealthy nation from its monarchy in a near-bloodless coup. In a country larger than Alaska with a population smaller than Connecticut's, he began testing his "Third Universal

Theory," a self-created political philosophy that meshes, among other things, nineteenth-century French anarchist thought, socialism, and the two-thousand-year-old dictates of the Koran. But to Qaddafi's credit, most Libyans will tell you, everyday life dramatically improved; great modern cities rose from the dust of the Sahara, making Libya a kind of latter-day utopia.

The store clerk asks my nationality, and I tell him the truth: American. I've been telling some people that I'm Canadian — seems safer, easier in a country that has an "American Aggression" postage stamp series. But the man smiles enthusiastically. "American?" he repeats, as if to make sure he's heard right. I nod. "Ah! You are welcome to Libya!"

I wish I could believe him. Not very long ago, Americans weren't welcome here. In 1981, with Qaddafi openly supporting revolutionary and Islamic extremist causes, then-President Ronald Reagan declared Libya a state sponsor of terrorism and severed all diplomatic ties. Qaddafi went on to use his vast oil revenue to develop chemical and biological weapons. And then, in 1988, the bombing of Pan Am flight 103 over Lockerbie, Scotland, cemented Libya's rogue status. It would take Qaddafi's delivery of two Lockerbie suspects to the United Nations in 1999, followed by his 2003 renouncement of weapons of mass destruction programs to put him on the course of reconciliation with the West. U.S. travel restrictions were finally removed in 2004, nearly five years after the European Union lifted theirs — which explains why, of the hundreds of nationalities listed in the Leptis Magna guest book, I come across only two Americans.

The last time Libya was so closed to the West was back in the early 1800s, when most Europeans entered the country as slaves captured by the notorious pirates of North Africa's Barbary Coast. This didn't stop Scotsman Hugh Clapperton, who, in 1824, became the first Westerner to fully explore inner Libya and reach the interior of Africa by crossing the Sahara. I have come to Libya, in part, to follow his trail, to see how he accomplished such a difficult feat. Clapperton is a hero of mine, one of those old-time explorers who was always sick with one serious illness or another (dysentery, malaria) in a time when drinking mercury or bleeding was one's only medical recourse. Still, he plodded through the triple-digit heat of the bandit-ridden Sahara. His journals — the fullest, most unbiased account of early Libya — were lost for nearly two centuries. They were finally unearthed in a South African archive and published for the first time in 2000.

I carry Clapperton's journals with me now as I head out to the ruins, a couple of "tourist policemen" eyeing me. Groups of more than two foreigners aren't allowed to travel in Libya without the accompaniment of such government-assigned watchdogs. But as I'm traveling with only one other person, photographer Bobby Model, I escape most of this scrutiny. The lack of public transportation to many of the popular sites means that visitors like us may do better joining an adventure tour.

Leptis Magna was once the largest Roman city in Africa. I'm not the sort who usually gets into Roman ruins, can only handle about a day of them, but here the city is so well-preserved that it allows you to dream. There are the marble-covered pools of the Hadriatic Baths, great Corinthian columns rising thirty feet. There's the nearly intact coliseum, three stories high, where you can crawl through lion chutes and explore the gladiators' quarters. They don't make cities like this anymore, every architectural detail attended to, no plan too lavish, no material too dear. Bearded gods gaze down from friezes. Maidens and warriors lounge among the carved porticos. Even the communal toilets remain nearly unscathed, the marble seats shiny from thousands of ancient buttocks.

Libya is a land overflowing with antiquities. Beyond its extensive Roman and Greek ruins are some of the best ancient rock paintings and carvings in the world. Testament to when the Sahara was once verdant and life-supporting, many of Libya's southern mountain ranges are dotted with petroglyphs, magical scenes created twelve thousand years ago: men hunting rhinoceroses and riding horse-drawn chariots.

It reminds me that so many empires have come and gone in Libya. The Garamantes, the Phoenicians, the Greeks. The Romans, Byzantines, and Arabs. And more recently, the Turks, Italians, and British. For a few decades after World War II, even the Americans operated an air base on Libyan soil. I walk along a beach littered with building stones from Leptis. Waves caress the giant chunks of marble, slowly reducing them to the smooth white pebbles beneath my feet. There's too much of Leptis to save. It was too great, too vast. That it could end — I shudder at the thought. Theories abound about the cause of its demise. A great earthquake. A flood. The fall of the Romans and the later invasions of the Arabs. Slowly, perhaps imperceptibly, the sands took over. Will that be, I wonder, the fate of Qaddafi's utopia?

Driving anywhere in Libya takes days. We cruise through the western desert, headed south, away from the mere 2 percent of arable land along the coast. The country appears as an empty wasteland of gravel plains and sand. Rarely does a bush break the monotony of sky and earth. Rarer still are trees. Or animals. Looking at the dusty emptiness, it's easy to understand why the majority of Libya's population clings to the coast.

In the distance appears a flash of whitewashed buildings and a flourish of date palms: Ghadamis. The ancient town sits among verdant oasis fields, once a major stop on the old caravan route from Timbuktu. Inhabited by the Berbers, Ghadamis fell victim to Qaddafi's modernization plan, the inhabitants forced out en masse in the 1980s into modern apartments in nearby New Town.

Some people, however, wouldn't leave this charmed place without a fight, which is not surprising. Ghadamis is less a town than a gigantic labyrinth of narrow passageways that cut around and beneath adobe homes. Living here is like living in a subterranean world, the sun and its heat cut off by the rise of centuries-old buildings, each built into the next and accessed by an interlocking tunnel system. Now deserted, the town has an eerie quality of being just unearthed. I explore the dark, empty passageways with my flashlight, coming upon dead ends and mysterious chambers built from Roman columns. I squeeze through an open palm-wood door, climbing dusty stairs to the highest floor. Part of the ceiling has fallen in, and incongruous sunlight gleams on white walls painted with cryptic red Berber designs.

Once on the roof, I gaze out on a scene straight out of *Arabian Nights*: countless whitewashed terraces spreading toward the setting sun and the distant hills of Algeria. Nearby, palm gardens resound with bird song and the burbling of aquifer water. The call to prayer wails from the squat mud minarets of a nearby adobe mosque, and I can only take it all in silently, reverentially, like a devotee.

Two days later I finally cross paths with Clapperton in the town of Marzuq. He made frequent visits to the *bey*, or ruler, of Fezzan, who lived in a castle in town — an impressive stone structure that still stands, rising over a deserted courtyard that once held a booming slave market. Between the seventh and nineteenth centuries, half of the estimated nine million to fourteen million black Africans that crossed the Sahara to Arab coastal markets passed through Libya. Most would have entered Marzuq, where slaves were sold to middlemen or "fattened up" for further travel to Tripoli, Egypt, and beyond.

Slaves weren't the only ones to cross this desert. In the early twentieth century, explorers passed through this area in search of one of the world's last great mysteries: the Lost Oasis of Zerzura. First mentioned in a fifteenth-century Arab text, *The Book of Hidden Pearls*, Zerzura was described as a "white city" in the midst of the Sahara, full of "great riches." Still, by the twentieth century, no one had found it. If it existed at all, explorers surmised, it must be located in the middle of the nearly impenetrable sands of eastern Libya. Technology finally caught up with the search in 1933, with Hungarian Laszlo Almasy (the real-life English Patient) flying his biplane over three unknown wadis (dry river beds) hidden among cliffs. Further exploration on foot revealed no sign of gold or ruins, but Almasy was convinced that these were the Zerzura oasis. His discovery all but closed the books on the legend, though some scientists and explorers still believe it has yet to be found.

As do I. I conduct my own search for information about Zerzura among the supposed caretakers of the secret: the fierce, nomadic Teda people, Saharan aborigines whom some experts believe to have inhabited Zerzura. Clapperton described them in his journal as "thieves to a man [who] steal from all." The reputation still stands. The presence of armed Teda outlaws prevents me from traveling through various regions of the Fezzan in search of Zerzura.

It isn't easy finding this elusive people. They number only about a thousand in Libya, and I hear about a small scattering of them on the outskirts of the desert oasis of Zawilah. As our Land Cruiser approaches the unusual clusters of conical thatch huts, I feel my apprehension rise, recalling explorers' terrifying accounts of confrontations with the Teda. But when I exit the vehicle, their chief, Sidi Loso Mohamed, greets me cordially and welcomes me to his

village. I ask some of the older men of the tribe if they know anything about the location of Zerzura. Their eyes dart over my face.
They smile quickly, cryptically. No. They know nothing. Almasy allegedly tricked an old Teda camel herder into revealing the names
and locations of the Zerzura wadis, but these men will tell me nothing.

I give up the search for now and we head east to the village of
Tmassah, where the road — and civilization — ends. We have a
second vehicle, a truck: a safety precaution for deep Saharan travel.
Our entourage now includes two drivers, Omar No. 1 and Omar
No. 2, a cook named Mohamed, and our guide Magdy, making us
six in total. We're in search of a spectacular desert anomaly that
rises from the center of the Sahara: an extinct volcano called Waw
an Namus, "Volcano of the Mosquitoes." Finding it will require several days of off-road driving through one of the driest deserts on
earth.

We enter the roadless Sahara, crossing a flat, sandy plain. Omar
No. 2 hits the gas, but no matter how fast we move, no matter which
direction we look, the view remains exactly the same: flawless blue
sky stretching over amber-colored sand. The Land Cruiser's odometer reaches sixty, seventy, eighty miles an hour. Nothing changes.
We shoot through an empty, vast landscape that makes a mockery
of speed, which seems to have no beginning or end.

Our Land Cruiser slows down as we descend onto a gravelly plain
that runs between two mountain ranges. It's hot: my thermometer
reaches the high eighties and keeps climbing. Our vehicles roar
and lurch over the rocky terrain, the hours passing in the dust and
the heat. As the sun sets, we stop to set up camp below a high white
dune, and I lay my sleeping bag under the stars. Sleep in the Sahara
and you can see every star in the graceful curve of Orion's bow, the
great sweep of the Milky Way at his back. A small desert rat climbs
over me and stops only inches from my face, looking at me before
slipping off into the night.

The desert has its own soul. And it isn't insignificance that I feel
in the face of this, but the aching candor of being alive. These great
dunes around me — carved and shaped by the wind, baked by the
sun — were once stone. And if mountains can dissolve, then what
of me — so much more fragile, so much softer, so quick to bleed
and easy to destroy. Maybe it's heady reflection, but I think it, lying

in the sand and gazing at this world: the marvel that I am here. Such an ecstasy of wonder and gratitude. I am here, I am here!

The volcano, Waw an Namus, reminds me why I travel: to see what cannot be imagined, to be taken into my dreams. It rises from the gravel plains of central Libya, a large black mountain several thousand feet high, twenty miles round. We drive to the top. Though the volcano was officially discovered by an Italian explorer in 1931, the nomadic tribes of the Sahara have known about it for centuries; according to local legend, they sent offenders here to be exiled.

But what a place to spend the last days of one's life, looking down into the crater, from the lip of the enormous volcano, at a turquoise lake surrounded by palm trees. Seeing any water at all in this desert — let alone a large lake and a verdant spread of grasses — is more than I could've asked for. It's surreal. Unbelievable.

We get back on Clapperton's trail, following him to the far southwestern corner of the Fezzan. This region, known for its mountains, the Jibal Akakus, attracts more tourists than any other area in Libya. With giant stone arches, narrow mesas, and otherworldly rock formations, the Akakus are a geologist's paradise, offering, indisputably, some of the most unique desert vistas in the world. Bobby, an accomplished climber enamored of the small sandstone spires, has been practicing his bouldering skills while I wander among the rocks, listening to the desert's silence.

But just as Clapperton went on to the old Sahara caravan stop of Ghat, so do we, arriving just after noon in a dusty, idyllic town of around sixteen thousand people. Once a major point on the trading route from Timbuktu, Ghat was — and still is — controlled by Tuareg tribesmen. This hearty nomadic people can be found all over the Sahara, though in Libya most have settled down in towns.

We rendezvous with the Tuareg man who is supposed to guide us for the next few days. But after Magdy explains our plans, he says, "To hell with you," and walks off. This becomes the usual reaction whenever we approach any Tuareg, and all because I want to visit the "Devil's Hill," Kaff Jinoon. It's a curious series of eroded sandstone peaks jutting from the dunes north of Ghat. Unique not only for its two obelisklike spires, or horns, it's also believed to be Grand Central Station for genies — spirits — from thousands of miles around. And not just any spirits, but those most wicked and base. The spirits of torturers and murderers. The spirits of those wrongly slain. Lost and sickened souls, attracted to the vortex that is Kaff Jinoon.

Clapperton and his companion Dr. Walter Oudney camped near the mountain, to the terror and vexation of their Tuareg guides who believed that small, red-bearded devils lived on it and caused mischief to all who passed. Wrote Clapperton, "[My guide] Hatita said he would not go up it for all the dollars in the world." And it's the same story now in Ghat; no Tuareg is willing to travel with us to the mountain, no matter how much we'll pay. They all have their own stories. There were the French tourists a few years back. They drove out to the mountain, thinking it'd be a good joke to climb it, but as soon as they got out of their car they were attacked by wasps. Libyan authorities found the group wandering along the road, unable to get in their vehicle, their faces covered with stings. And this, I'm told, was minor. Much worse has occurred. Like the Libyan soldier at a checkpoint near the mountain who saw something so awful, so terrifying, that he went into shock and couldn't walk for a year.

Jinoon and its vicinity has been considered a stomping ground for evil genies for centuries. Intrepid Arab traveler Ibn Battuta first wrote about this desert in the fourteenth century, describing it as a place "haunted by demons; if the [traveler] be alone, they make sport of him and disorder his mind, so that he loses his way and perishes." Western explorers journeying in the Fezzan regarded such tales with derision, determined to see the mountain and to try to climb it. In 1822, Dr. Oudney made the first recorded attempt, reaching the mountain's 4,500-foot saddle and returning without incident. Later explorers were less successful. British adventurer John Richardson attempted the climb in 1853, getting lost on the descent and wandering in the desert, near death, for two days. Robust German explorer Heinrich Barth had an almost identical experience in 1857. I am determined to see the place. I want to climb the mountain. We decide to go there unguided.

Magdy tells me that Omar No. 2 pulled him aside to ask if I'm crazy. Don't I know it's lunacy to climb Jinoon? But Magdy shrugged. If I want to risk my life climbing a mountain haunted by demons, so be it. Bobby is the least chagrined of the group. He recently lost one of his closest friends in a car accident. So screw the evil genies. Hell, maybe something good will happen to him if he climbs the mountain.

We strap on our backpacks and head up the nearest slope. The ground is covered with rocks and boulders that prevent easy walking. Still, gratefully: no wasps. We ascend a ridge on the far western end of the saddle — some distance from the mesa, but seeming to provide the smoothest way up. In a short time, we reach the top. Golden dunes spread out like serpent trails across the valley below. Beyond them, the black rise of the Marzuq massif glitters in the heat waves.

This has been the easy part. We hike along the top of the saddle, the route barely three feet across with sheer drops on either side. When we reach the mesa, it doesn't look good: a great wall of stone rises forty feet before us. After scouting around, we find a fissure of loose sandstone. It's our only way up and, thankfully, Bobby goes first. I watch him climb slowly, meticulously, pieces of rock breaking off beneath his feet. Footholds and handholds are few, but he welcomes the challenge. I don't, following reluctantly. Nearly to the top, the rock I'm standing on loosens and snaps off, shattering on the boulders below. I cling desperately to the cliff, searching for a new place to put my feet, finding only an unreliable ledge. Shaking from adrenaline, I keep climbing, finally reaching the flat top of the mesa where I realize a climber's greatest anxiety: getting back down.

But it was worth it. Before us is one of the two spires — a giant rectangular block of sandstone rising over 120 feet, with flat sides and sharp ninety-degree angles, its proportions so near perfect that it almost resembles an obelisk. I search it for signs of ancient writing. Nothing. There's no sign of humanity whatsoever on this small mesa — no cairns, no climber detritus, no markers. Others must have made it up here, though I can't be sure.

Down below, a tiny dot of white in a sea of sand, sits the Land Cruiser, waiting for us. Bobby and I enjoy the view for a while, but I'm anxious to get back down, to get off this mountain. Genies may not have attacked me, but I do feel as if I've pushed my luck.

We descend the same way we came up, looking for our own little cairns to show us the route down the rock faces. Before long, I'm on the slope below the saddle, heading in the direction of the vehicle. It occurs to me that Libya, itself, is like Jinoon. The den of the evil genies. The bastion of all my fears. Terrorist cells. Qaddafi. A country full of bogeymen lurking in every crevasse.

When Magdy and the others see me and Bobby safely returned, they smile and let out a cheer. So much for all our fears.

We stop at a tourist camp along the highway outside of the town of Awbari and indulge in our first shower in nearly two weeks. Gloriously clean, we head off to Gebraoun Lake. One of the largest salt lakes in the Sahara, it's a great place to sunbathe and swim. I change into a pair of shorts and a tank top — risqué, to the Omars — and jump into the lake, watching Bobby clamber up a one-thousand-foot-high dune. Gebraoun is the only place in Libya where you can sand ski. He reaches the top, puts on the skis he's rented, and a moment later he's shooting downhill, kicking up clouds of sand.

I'm still hoping to find Clapperton among these eroding sand and rock plains of the Fezzan, to pick up his exact trail. I arrange to hire camels and Tuareg guides so that Bobby, Magdy, and I can re-create one of his most treacherous desert journeys — his route deep into the Awbari Sand Sea to a remote oasis called Trona. We meet our guides, Salaka and Mohamed, at the town of Takartibah. They have five camels with them, choosing two as pack animals to carry our gear and supplies, the unlucky pair growling in wrath with every tug of the girth. The ultimate desert machines, camels can drink nearly twenty-five gallons at one fill — more than twice what it takes to top off the tank of my Toyota back home — lasting them, in the cooler winter season, several weeks without a refill.

The Tuaregs decide to place me on the largest of their camels, an enormous beige creature called Watani, meaning "The Patriot." They tug at its nose reins and hiss the animal down to a bony-kneed squat, and I use the curve of its neck as a launch pad, leaping into the saddle. Camels themselves are more a novelty than a necessity in Libya these days, with the previously nomadic peoples buying cars and settling down in Qaddafi's modern towns. Which might explain why, as we head across the desert, we become the tourist attraction, flocks of Land Cruisers making a beeline toward us. These frequent visits by outfitted tours scare the camels and halt our pace, guffawing French and Italians lining up to get their pictures taken beside our Tuareg guides. But soon, thankfully, we head north into deeper desert, the Land Cruiser trails vanishing from the sands. We travel through a gradually rising valley, encircled by high beige dunes, our barefoot Tuareg guides leading their camels. It becomes only us and the sun now, which burns my skin even as a cool breeze gives me constant gooseflesh.

At sunset, we stop among the dunes to camp, the peace of the desert like a blanket over us, calming thoughts, settling moods.

Then we get the news. Someone forgot to pack our drinking water.

"Un-freaking-believable," I say to no one in particular. What would Clapperton think?

Magdy searches through our baggage strewn about the desert. All at once, he makes a discovery: the dishwater! He's found a jug of it.

"And it's safe to drink that?" I ask, incredulous.

"No problem," he says.

But early the next morning, my bowels do a double take. I might actually have a bowling ball caught in my intestines. Our Tuareg guides seem unfazed, getting up after dawn, eating a slow breakfast, and taking all of three hours to load the camels and break camp. We leave at the pitiably late hour of 10:00 A.M., whereas Clapperton and his guides left each day at around 5:00 A.M. — typical for caravans. "[We] travel from before sunrise to sunset without halting," Clapperton wrote, "having only two meals a day — one before we start and the other after we halt at night." We, on the other hand, end our second day well before sunset, stopping near the small salt lake of Umm al-Maa.

I hold a powwow with everyone, Magdy translating, and ask our two Tuareg guides if we can't try to do things the way Clapperton did. No being easy on us foreigners. No late breakfasts or early dinners. I want to experience real-deal camel travel, from dawn to dusk.

Reluctantly, they agree. As I go off to take a swim in Umm al-Maa, I'm beginning to fear what I've asked for.

The next morning, everyone is up early and mobilizing, breaking camp and packing animals. And we have a new guest, a Tuareg named Yahya, whom Magdy brought in to guide the two Tuaregs who are supposed to be guiding us. Wearing a traditional Tuareg face wrap and a not-so-traditional fluorescent yellow jacket, Yahya proves to be the real deal — he doesn't tolerate loitering, frequent stopping, bathroom breaks, or anything that can result in a slowing or stopping of our pace. He takes hold of the reins of one of the camels and begins walking, never looking back. If we want to get to Trona tonight, he insists, we will need to get moving, and stay moving, for the entire day. Expect at least eleven hours of travel.

Our less-than-the-real-deal Tuareg guides yell out, begging him to wait for us, but he's having none of it. We all scamper to get organized and mounted on our camels.

Meanwhile, Yahya is a tiny figure in the distant heat waves, his fluorescent yellow jacket like a beacon in the great sea of sand. Our group rushes to catch up with Yahya. We leave behind a wide valley, heading into high dunes. It's fortunate for us that he knows where he's going, because none of the rest of us does.

As the sun begins to set, we follow a narrow wadi due east. Finally, there are bushes and signs of life, a large-eared fox trotting behind a dune. Yahya has been walking at a near-jog, barefoot, for over nine hours now, stopping only when the rest of us decided to have lunch. And he hasn't once drunk water or taken a toilet break. Me, I try to walk along with him, leading my camel, but the coarse desert sand soon scours the soles of my feet and covers them with blisters. The tradeoff is riding, but the saddle chafes my inner thighs and butt until they feel raw. How, I wonder, can anyone travel like this for more than a few days? I imagine the weeks Clapperton must have suffered until he became habituated to the saddle. I wonder if there's anyone left in this world who compares to the explorers of old.

I want to get to Trona — and soon. Already, the sun has set. Our group climbs up the steepest dunes we've yet encountered and, at the top of the highest, we look off into the dusky distance. Down below is an enchanting site: an island of green that can only be Trona. Nestled in the nook of sand hills that rise several hundred feet, the uninhabited oasis, with its quaint blue lake and forests of date palms, looks all the more wonderful after nearly twelve hours of hard travel. The camels raise their heads and sniff the air. Yahya begins to sing. Everyone — human and beast — suddenly picks up speed, rushing down the dune and trotting anxiously to the sanctu-

ary of green. "We arrived in Wadi Trona," Clapperton wrote, "and
. . . Ali brought us some water — which we drank with a greater relish than if it had been the sweetest wine."

In Trona, there's still freshwater, a cool oasis pool, and all the
dates I can eat. But, more important, there is rest.

Though I'm back in Tripoli, I am still at Trona in my mind, sitting
in the silent emptiness of the Sahara with the stars above whispering their infinity. Walking with Magdy along the noisy streets of
Libya's capital, I come upon a *zawia*, a Sufi mosque, which is having
its evening service. Sufism is considered heretical by many Muslims
for its belief that one can merge with God — a belief that has
forced this mystical tradition underground in many Muslim countries. In Libya, however, it enjoys a place of tolerance in society.

Chanting filters into the dusk and I ask Magdy if I can witness
their ceremony. We enter the *zawia*'s long courtyard, and the sheikh
comes out — the equivalent of a priest. Magdy explains my interest, and Sheikh Hamza tells me that I can watch the ceremony
through a window, but it's the best he can do: females are not allowed inside. I take my place where instructed, looking through
metal bars into the prayer hall.

The ceremony, or *dhikr,* begins. Men form two large circles, some
of them glancing at me through the window with suspicious, ques-
tioning eyes. A man begins playing a guitar, singing the poetry of
Muslim saints, and the group starts beating on little drums. All of
this is unique to Sufism, Magdy explains; it's how initiates meet
God and enter into union with Him. The two circles begin swaying
and bobbing, slowly at first and then more frenetically. The music
increases in volume. "All-ah, All-ah," the men chant, louder and
louder, their entreaties turning into shouts.

After close to a half hour of this, the music reaches its peak, becomes a great cacophony of sound that stops with such abruptness
that the ensuing silence seems almost profane. Everyone looks
around, unsure momentarily of where they are or why. And now
something strange is happening throughout the room — bodies
contort, limbs freeze into strange positions; men drop to their
knees, quaking and sobbing. Those who can move help the ones
who cannot, massaging bodies back into movement and holding
anyone who cries. One man points helplessly to his throat, as if

something were stuck inside. Water is brought and poured for him, which he swallows in a rush.

The ceremony over, an assistant passes around little shot glasses full of coffee with slices of bread. I don't expect him to remember about me, but he comes over to the window, smiling, offering me a glass. As the men file out, I stay back, away from the courtyard, but no one seems to mind my female presence now. When I see the man who'd been clutching his throat, I call out to ask him how he is.

"*Kway-yis,* "he says. Good. His eyes are bright and dancing. "Where are you from?"

It is my last night in Libya, and yet the question still gives me a touch of fear. "America," I say.

He looks unfazed. "Have you seen a Sufi ceremony before?" he asks.

I tell him no.

"You are welcome," he says.

GEORGE SAUNDERS

The New Mecca

FROM *GQ*

Put That Stately Pleasure Palace There
Between Those Other Two

IF YOU ARE LIKE I was three weeks ago, before I went to Dubai,
you may not know exactly where Dubai is. Near Venezuela? No,
sorry, that is incorrect. Somewhere north of Pakistan, an idyllic
mountain kingdom ruled by gentle goatherds? Well, no.

Dubai, actually, is in the United Arab Emirates, on the Arabian
Peninsula, one hundred miles across the Gulf from Iran, about six
hundred miles from Basra, 1,100 from Kabul.

You might also not know, as I did not know, what Dubai is all
about or why someone would want to send you there. You might
wonder: Is it dangerous? Will I be beheaded? Will I need a translator? Will my translator be beheaded? Just before we're beheaded,
will my translator try to get out of it by blaming everything on me?

No, no, not to worry. Dubai, turns out, is quite possibly the safest
great city in the world. It is also the newest great city in the world.
In the 1950s, before oil was discovered there, Dubai was just a cluster of mud huts and Bedouin tents along Dubai Creek: the entire
city has basically been built in the last fifty years. And actually, the
cool parts — the parts that have won Dubai its reputation as "the
Vegas of the Middle East" or "the Venice of the Middle East" or "the
Disney World of the Middle East, if Disney World were the size of
San Francisco and out in a desert" — have been built in the last ten
years. And the supercool parts — the parts that, when someone
tells you about them, your attention drifts because these morons

have to be lying (no one dreams this big or has that much available capital) — those parts are all going to be built in the next five years.

By 2010, if all goes according to plan, Dubai will have: the world's tallest skyscraper (2,300 feet); largest mall; biggest theme park; longest indoor ski run; most luxurious underwater hotel (accessible by submarine train); a huge (two-thousand-acre, sixty-thousand-resident) development called International City, divided into nation-neighborhoods (England, China, France, Greece, etc.) within which all homes will be required to reflect the national architectural style; not to mention four artificially constructed island mega-archipelagoes(three shaped like giant palm trees, the fourth like a map of the world) built using a specially designed boat that dredges up tons of ocean-bottom sand each day and sprays it into place.

Before I saw Dubai for myself, I assumed this was bluster: brag about ten upcoming projects, finally build one — smaller than you'd bragged — hope everyone forgets about the other nine.

But no.

I've been to Dubai, and I believe.

If America was looking for a pluralistic, tax-free, laissez-faire, diverse, inclusive, tolerant, no-holds-barred, daringly capitalist country to serve as a shining City on the Hill for the entire Middle East, we should have left Iraq alone and sponsored a National Peaceful Tourist Excursion to Dubai and spent our ninety quadrillion Iraq War dollars there.

Maybe.

In Which I Fall in Love with a Fake Town

From the air, Dubai looked something like Dallas circa 1985: a vast expanse of one- or two-story white boxes, punctuated by clusters of freakish skyscrapers. (An Indian kid shouted, "Dad, looks like a microchip!") Driving in from the airport, you're struck by the usual first-night-in-new-country exotica ("There's a *Harley-Davidson* dealership — right in the *Middle East!*"), and the skyscraper clusters were, okay, odd looking (like four or five architects had staged a weird-off, with unlimited funds) — but all in all, it was, you know, a city. And I wondered what all the fuss was about.

Then I got to my hotel.

The Madinat Jumeirah is, near as I can figure, a superresort consisting of three, or possibly six, luxury sub-hotels and two, or maybe three, clusters of luxury villas, spread out over about forty acres, or for all I know it was twelve sub-hotels and nine luxury-villa clusters — I really couldn't tell, so seamless and extravagant and confusing was all the luxury. The Madinat is themed to resemble an ancient Arabian village. But to say the Madinat is themed doesn't begin to express the intensity and opulence and areal extent of the theming. The site is crisscrossed by 2.3 miles of fake creeks, trolled night and day by dozens of fake Arabian water taxis *(abras)* piloted by what I can only describe as fake Arabs because, though dressed like old-timey Arabs, they are actually young, smiling, sweethearted guys from Nepal or Kenya or the Philippines, who speak terrific English as they pilot the soundless electrical *abras* through this lush, created Arabia, looking for someone to take back to the lobby, or to the largest outdoor pool in the Middle East, or over to Trader Vic's, which is also themed and looks something like a mysterious ancient Casbah inexplicably filled with beautiful contemporary people.

And so, though my first response to elaborate Theming is often irony (Who *did* this? And *why?* Look at that *modern exit sign* over that *eighteenth-century bedstead.* Haw!), what I found during my stay at the Madinat is that irony is actually my first response to tepid, lame Theming. In the belly of radical Theming, my first response was to want to stay forever, bring my family over, set up shop in my hut-evoking villa, and never go home again.

Because the truth is, it's beautiful. The air is perfumed, you hear fountains, the tinkling of bells, distant chanted prayers, and when the (real) Arabian moon comes up, yellow and attenuated, over a (fake) Arabian wind tower, you feel you are a resident of some ancient city — or rather, some ancient city if you had dreamed the ancient city, and the ancient city had been purged of all disease, death, and corruption, and you were a Founder/Elder of that city, much beloved by your Citizens, the Staff.

Wandering around one night, a little lost, I came to the realization that verisimilitude and pleasure are not causally related. How is this "fake"? This is real flowing water, the date and palm trees are real, the smell of incense and rose water is real. The staggering effect of the immense scale of one particular crosswalk — which joins two hotels together and is, if you can imagine this, a four-story ornate crosswalk that looks like it should have ten thousand cheering Imperial Troops clustered under it and an enigmatic young Princess waving from one of its arabesquey windows — that effect is *real*. You feel it in your gut and your legs. It makes you feel happy and heroic and a little breathless, in love anew with the world and its possibilities. You have somehow entered the landscape of a dream, the Platonic realization of the idea of Ancient Village — but there are real smells here, and when, a little dazzled, you mutter to yourself ("This is like a freaking dream, I love it, I, wow . . ."), you don't wake up, but instead a smiling Filipino kid comes up and asks if you'd like a drink.

On the flight over, I watched an interview with an employee of Jumeirah International, the company that manages the Madinat. Even though he saw it going up himself, he said, he feels it is an ancient place every time he enters and finds it hard to believe that, three years ago, it was all just sand.

A Word About the Help

UAE nationals comprise about 20 percent of the city's population. Until three years ago, only nationals were allowed to own property in Dubai, and they still own essentially all of it. Visually identifiable by their dress — the men wear the traditional white dishdashas; the women, long black gowns and abayas — these nationals occupy the top rung of a rigid social hierarchy: imagine Hollywood, if everyone who'd been wildly successful in the movie business had to wear a distinctive costume.

A rung down from the Emiratis are some 200,000 expats (mostly Brits but also other Europeans, Russians, Lebanese, Indians) who comprise a kind of managerial class: the marketing people, the hotel managers, the human-resource gurus, the accountants, the lawyers, etc. But the vast majority of Dubai's expat population — roughly two thirds of it — comes from poorer countries all around the world, mainly South Asia or Africa. They built Dubai, they run it with their labor but can't afford to own homes or raise their families here. They take their dirhams home and cash them in for local currency, in this way increasing their wealth by as much as tenfold.

They live here for two years, five years, fifteen years; take home-leaves as often as every three months or as infrequently as never.

And even within this class there are stratifications. The hotel workers I met at the Madinat, for example, having been hand-picked by Jumeirah scouts from the finest hotels in their native countries, are a class, or two, or three, above the scores of South Asian laborers who do the heavy construction work, who live in labor camps on the outskirts of town where they sleep ten to a room, and whose social life, according to one British expat I met, consists of "a thrilling evening once a month of sitting in a circle popping their bulbs out so some bloody Russian chickie can race around hand-jobbing them all in a mob."

You see these construction guys all over town: somewhat darker-complexioned, wearing blue jumpsuits, averting their eyes when you try to say hello, squatting outside a work site at three in the morning because Dubai construction crews work twenty-four hours a day, seven days a week.

There is much to be done.

The Wild Wadi Epiphany

A short, complimentary golf-cart ride down the beach from the Madinat is Wild Wadi, a sprawling, themed water park whose theme is: a wadi is flooding! Once an hour, the sound of thunder/cracking trees/rushing waves blares through the facilitywide PA, and a waterfall begins dropping a thousand gallons of water a minute into an empty pond, which then violently overflows down the pedestrian walkways, past the gift shop.

Waiting in line, I'm part of a sort of United Nations of partial nudity: me, a couple of sunburned German women, three angry-looking Arab teens, kind of like the Marx Brothers if the Marx Brothers were Arabs in bathing suits with cigarettes behind their ears, who, I notice, are muttering to one another while glowering. Then I see what they're muttering/glowering about: several (like, fifteen) members of the United States Navy, on shore leave. You can tell they're Navy because they're huge and tattooed and innocently happy and keep bellowing things like, "Dude, fuck that, I am all *about* dancing!" while punching each other lovingly in the tattoos and shooting what I recognize as Rural Smiles of Shyness and Apprehension at all the people staring at them because they're so freaking loud.

Then the Navy Guys notice the Glowering Muttering Arabs, and it gets weirdly tense there in line. Luckily, it's my turn to awkwardly blop into a tube, and off I go.

This ride involves a series of tremendous water jets that blast you, on your tube, to the top of Wild Wadi, where, your recently purchased swim trunks having been driven up your rear by the jets, you pause, looking out over the entire city — the miles of stone-white villas, the Burj Al Arab (sail-shaped, iconic, the world's only seven-star hotel) out in the green-blue bay — just before you fly down so fast that you momentarily fear the next morning's head-line will read MIDDLE-AGED AMERICAN DIES IN FREAK WA-TER SLIDE MISHAP; BATHING SUIT FOUND FAR UP ASS.

Afterward, I reconvene with my former line mates in a sort of faux river bend. Becalmed, traffic-jammed, we bob around in our tubes, trying to keep off one another via impotent little hand flips, bare feet accidentally touching ("Ha, wope, sorry, heh. . ."), legs splayed, belly-up in the blinding 112-degree Arabian sun, self-conscious and expectant, as in: "Are we, like, stuck here? Will we go soon? I hope I'm not the one who drifts under that dang *waterfall* over there!"

No one is glowering or muttering now. We're sated, enjoying that little dopey buzz of quasi accomplishment you feel after a surprisingly intense theme-park ride. One of the Arab kids, the one with the Chico hair, passes a drenched cigarette to me, to pass to his friend, and then a lighter, and suddenly everybody's smiling — me, the Arab Marxes, the sunburned German girls, the U.S. Navy.

A disclaimer: it may be that, when you're forty-six and pearl white and wearing a new bathing suit at a theme park on your first full day in Arabia, you're especially prone to Big Naive Philosophical Realizations.

Be that as it may, in my tube at Wild Wadi, I have a mini epiphany: given enough time, I realize, statistically, despite what it may look like at any given moment, we *will* all be brothers. All differences will be bred out. There will be no pure Arab, no pure Jew, no pure American-American. The old dividers — nation, race, religion — will be overpowered by crossbreeding and by our mass media, our world Culture o' Enjoyment.

Look what just happened here: hatred and tension were defused by Sudden Fun.

Still bobbing around (three days before the resort bombings in Cairo, two weeks after the London bombings), I think-mumble a little prayer for the great homogenizing effect of pop culture: Same us out, Lord MTV! Even if, in the process, we are left a little dumber, please proceed. Let us, brothers and sisters, leave the intolerant, the ideologues, the religious Islamist Bolsheviks, our own solvers-of-problems-with-troops behind, fully clothed, on the banks of Wild Wadi. We, the New People, desire Fun and the Good Things of Life, and through Fun, we will be saved.

Then the logjam breaks, and we surge forward, down a mini-waterfall.

Without exception, regardless of nationality, each of us makes the same sound as we disappear: a thrilled little self-forgetting Whoop.

We Buy, Therefore We Am

After two full days of blissfully farting around inside the Madinat, I reluctantly venture forth out of the resort bubble, downtown, into the actual city, to the Deira souk. This is the real Middle East, the dark *Indiana Jones*-ish Middle East I'd preimagined: an exotic, cramped, hot, chaotic, labyrinthine, canopied street bazaar, crowded with room-sized, even closet-sized stalls, selling everything there is in the world to buy, and more than a few things you can't imagine anyone ever wanting to buy, or even accept for free.

Here is the stall of Plastic Flowers That Light Up; the stall of Tall Thin Blond Dolls in Miniskirts with Improbably Huge Eyes; the stall of Toy Semiautomatic Weapons; the stall of Every Spice Known to Man (SAFFRON BUKHOR, BAHRAT, MEDICAL HERBS, NATURAL VIAGRA); the stall of Coffee-Grinding Machines in Parts on the Floor; the stall of Hindi Prayer Cards; the stall of Spangled Kashmiri Slippers; of Air Rifles; Halloween Masks; Oversized Bright-Colored Toy Ships and Trucks; a stall whose walls and ceiling are completely covered with hundreds of cooking pots. There is a Pashtun-dominated section, a hidden Hindi temple, a section that suddenly goes Chinese, entire streets where nothing is sold but bolts of cloth. There's a mind-blowing gold section — two or three

hundred gold shops on one street, with mysterious doors leading
to four-story minimalls holding still more gold shops, each overflowing with the yellow high-end gold that, in storybooks and Disney movies, comes pouring out of pirate chests.

As I walk through, a kind of amazed mantra starts running
through my head: *There is no end to the making and selling of things
there is no end to the making and selling of things there is no end . . .*

Man, it occurs to me, is a joyful, buying-and-selling piece of work.
I have been wrong, dead wrong, when I've decried consumerism.
Consumerism is what we are. It is, in a sense, a holy impulse. A human being is someone who joyfully goes in pursuit of things, brings
them home, then immediately starts planning how to get more.

A human being is someone who wishes to improve his lot.

Speaking of Improving One's Lot: The Great Dubai Quandary

Dubai raises the questions raised by any apparent Utopia: What's
the downside? At whose expense has this nirvana been built, on
whose backs are these pearly gates being raised?

Dubai is, in essence, capitalism on steroids: a small, insanely
wealthy group of capital-controlling Haves supported by a huge
group of overworked and underpaid Have-Nots, with, in Dubai's
case, the gap between Haves and Have-Nots so wide as to indicate
different species.

But any attempt to reduce this to some sort of sci-fi Masters and
'Droids scenario gets complicated. Relative to their brethren back
home (working for next to nothing or not working at all), Dubai's
South Asian workers have it great; likewise, relative to their brethren working in nearby Saudi Arabia. An American I met, who has
spent the last fifteen years working in the Saudi oil industry, told
me about seeing new South Indian workers getting off the plane in
Riyadh, in their pathetic new clothes, clutching cardboard suitcases. On arrival, as in a scene out of *The Grapes of Wrath,* they are
informed (for the first time) that they will have to pay for their
flight over, their lodging, their food (which must be bought from
the company), and, in advance, their flight home. In this way, they
essentially work the first two years for free.

Dubai is not, in structure, much different: the workers surrender
their passports to their employer; there are no labor unions, no or-

ganizing, no protests. And yet in Dubai, the workers tell you again and again how happy they are to be here. Even the poorest, most overworked laborer considers himself lucky — he is making more, much more, than he would be back home. In Saudi, the windfall profits from skyrocketing oil prices have shot directly upstairs, to the five thousand or so members of the royal family, and from there to investments (new jets, real estate in London). In Dubai, the leaders have plowed the profits back into the national dream of the New Dubai — reliant not on oil revenue (the Dubai oil will be gone by 2010) but on global tourism. Whatever complaints you hear about the Emirati ruling class — they buy $250,000 falcons, squash all dissent, tolerate the financial presence of questionable organizations (Al Qaeda, various national Mafias) — they seem to be universally respected, even loved, because, unlike the Saudi rulers, they are perceived to put the interests of the people first.

On the other hand, relative to Western standards, Dubai is so antilabor as to seem medieval. In the local paper, I read about the following case: a group of foreign workers in Dubai quit their jobs in protest over millions of dirhams in unpaid wages. Since by law they weren't allowed to work for another company, these men couldn't afford plane tickets back home and were thus stuck in a kind of Kafka loop. After two years, the government finally stepped in and helped send the men home. This story indicates both the potential brutality of the system — so skewed toward the employer — and its flexibility relative to the Saudi system, its general right-heartedness, I think you could say, or at least its awareness of, and concern with, Western opinion: the situation was allowed to be reported and, once reported, was corrected.

Complicated.

Because you see these low-level foreign workers working two or three jobs, twelve, fourteen, sixteen hours a day, longing for home (a waiter shows me exactly how he likes to hold his two-year-old, or did like to hold her, last time he was home, eight months ago), and think: Couldn't you Haves cut loose with just a little more?

But ask the workers, in your intrusive Western way, about their Possible Feelings of Oppression, and they model a level of stoic noble determination that makes the Ayn Rand in you think, Good, good for you, sir, best of luck in your professional endeavors!

Only later, back in your room, having waded in through a lobby full of high rollers — beautifully dressed European/Lebanese/Russian expats, conferring Emiratis, all smoking, chatting, the expats occasionally making a scene, berating a waitress — thinking of some cab driver in the thirteenth hour of his fourteen-hour shift, worrying about his distant grandchild; thinking of some lonely young Kathmandu husband, sleeping fitfully in his sweltering rented room — do you get a sudden urge to move to Dubai and start a chapter of the Wobblies.

On the other hand:

A Kenyan security guard who works fourteen-hour days at Wild Wadi, euphoric about his new earning power, says to me: "I expect, in your writing, you will try to find the dark side of Dubai? Some positive, some negative? Isn't that the Western way? But I must say: I have found Dubai to be nearly perfect."

Complicated.

The University of the Back of the Cab

A partial list of wise things cab drivers said to me in Dubai:

1) "If you good Muslim, you go straight, no talking talking, bomb blast! No. You go to mosque, to talk. You go straight!"
2) "This, all you see? So new! All new within! Within one year! Within within within! That building there? New within three year! All built within! Before, no! Only sand."
3) "You won't see any Dubai Arab man driving cab. Big boss only."
4) Re the Taliban: "If you put a man into a room with no way out, he will fight his way out. But if you leave him one way out, he will take it."
5) "The Cyclone Club? Please to not go there. It is a disco known for too many fuck-girls."

One night my driver is an elderly Iranian, a fan of George W. Bush who hates the Iranian government. He tells me the story of his spiritual life. When young, he says, he was a donkey: a donkey of Islam. Then a professor said to him: You are so religious, so sure of yourself, and yet you know absolutely nothing. And this professor gave him books to read, from his personal library. "I read one, then more, more," he says, nearly moving himself to tears with the memory. After two years, the driver had a revelation: all religious knowledge comes from the hand of man. God does not talk to us directly. One can trust only one's own mind, one's own intelligence. He has five kids, four grandkids, still works fourteen-hour days at sixty-five years old. But he stays in Dubai because in Iran, there are two classes: The Religious and The Not. And The Religious get all the privileges, all the money, all the best jobs. And if you, part of The Not Religious, say something against them, he says, they take you against a wall and . . .

He turns to me, shoots himself in the head with his finger.

As I get out, he says: "We are not different, all men are . . ." and struggles to remember the word.

"Brothers?" I say.

"No," he says.

"Unified?" I say.

"No," he says.

"Part of the same, uh . . . transcendent . . ."

"No," he says. He can't remember the word. He is old, very old, he says, sorry, sorry.

We say goodbye, promising to pray for our respective governments, and for each other.

Cleaning Among the Mayhem

Dubai is a city of people who come from elsewhere and are going back there soon. To start a good conversation — with a fellow tourist, with the help, with just about anybody — simply ask: "Where are you from?" Everyone wants to tell you. If white, they are usually from England, South Africa, Ukraine. If not, they are from Sri Lanka, the Philippines, Kenya, Nepal, India.

One hotel seems to hire only Nepalese. One bar has only Ukrainians. You discover a pocket of Sri Lankan golf-cart drivers, all anxious to talk about the tsunami.

One day, inexplicably, everyone you meet, wherever you go, is from the Philippines.

"Where are you from?" you say all day, and all day people brightly answer: "Philippines!"

That night, at a club called Boudoir, I meet L, an employee of Ford in Dubai, a manic, funny, Stanley Tucci–looking guy from Detroit, who welcomes me into his party, gets me free champagne, mourns the circa-1990 state of inner-city Detroit: feral dogs roaming the streets, trees growing out of the upper stories of skyscrapers where "you know, formerly, commerce was being done, the real 1960s automobile fucking world-class commerce, man!" The night kind of explodes. This, I think, this is the repressive Arabian Peninsula? Apparently, anything is permitted, as long as it stays within the space within which it is permitted. Here is a Palestinian who lives in Los Angeles and whose T-shirt says LAPD — WHERE EVERYBODY IS KING. A couple of blond Russian girls dance on a rail, among balloons. On the dance floor, two other blonds dance alone. A guy comes up behind one and starts passionately grinding her. This goes on a while. Then he stops, introduces himself, she shakes his hand, he goes back to grinding her. His friend comes up, starts grinding her friend. I don't get it. Prostitutes? Some new youthful social code? I am possibly too old to be in here? The dance floor is packed, the whole place *becomes* the dance floor, the rails are now packed with dancers, a Lebanese kid petulantly shouts that if this was *fucking Beirut,* the girls would be *stripped off* by now, then gives me a snotty look and stomps off, as if it's my fault the girls are still dressed. I drop my wallet, look down, and see the tiniest little woman imaginable, with whiskbroom, struggling against the surge of the crowd like some kind of cursed Cleaning Fairy, trying to find a small swath of floor to sweep while being bashed by this teeming mass of gyrating International Hipsters. She's tiny — I mean *tiny,* like three feet tall, her head barely reaching all the gyrating waists — with thick glasses and bowl-cut hair.

Dear little person! It seems impossible she's trying to sweep the dance floor at a time like this; she seems uncommonly, heroically dedicated, like some kind of OCD janitor on the *Titanic.*

"Where are you from?" I shout.

"Philippines!" she shouts, and goes back to her sweeping.

My Arrival in Heaven

The Burj Al Arab is the only seven-star hotel in the world, even though the ratings system only goes up to five. The most expensive Burj suite goes for $12,000 a night. The atrium is 590 feet from floor to ceiling, the largest in the world. As you enter, the staff rushes over with cold towels, rose water for the hands, dates, incense. The smell, the scale, the level of loving, fascinated attention you are receiving, makes you realize you have never really been in the lap of true luxury before. All the luxury you have previously had — in New York, L.A. — was stale, Burj-imitative crap! Your entire concept of *being inside a building* is being altered in real time. The lobby of the Burj is neither inside nor out. The roof is so far away as to seem like sky. The underbellies of the floors above you grade through countless shades of color from deep blue to, finally, up so high you can barely see it: pale green. Your Guest Services liaison, a humble, pretty Ukrainian, tells you that every gold-colored surface you see during your stay is actual twenty-four-karat gold. Even those four-story columns? Even so, she says. Even the thick fourth-story arcs the size of buses that span the columns? All gold, sir, is correct.

I am so thrilled to be checking in! What a life! Where a kid from Chicago gets to fly halfway around the world and stay at the world's only seven-star hotel, and *GQ* pays for it!

But there was a difficulty.

Help, Help, Heaven Is Making Me Nervous

Because, for complicated reasons, *GQ* couldn't pay from afar, and because my wife and I share a common hobby of maxing out all credit cards in sight, I had rather naively embarked on a trip halfway around the world without an operative credit card: the contemporary version of setting sail with no water in the casks. So I found myself in the odd position of having to pay the off-season rate of $1,500 a night, in cash. And because, turns out, to my chagrin, my ATM has a daily withdrawal limit (surprise, dumb ass!), I found myself there in my two-floor suite (every Burj room is a two-story suite), wearing the new clothes I had bought back in Syracuse for the express purpose of "Arriving at the Burj," trying to explain, like some yokel hustler at a Motel 6 in Topeka, that I'd be happy to pay half in cash now, half on checkout, if that would be, ah, acceptable, would that be, you know, cool?

My God, if you could have bottled the tension there in my suite at the Burj! The absolute electricity of disappointment shooting back and forth between the lovely Ukrainian and my kindly Personal Butler, the pity, really . . .

Sorry, uh, sorry for the, you know, trouble . . . I say.

No, sir, the lovely Ukrainian says. We are sorry to make any difficulties for you.

Ha, I thought, God bless you, now *this* is service, this is freaking Seven-Star Service!

But over the next few hours, my bliss diminished. I was approached by the Lebanese Floor Butler, by several Mysterious Callers from Guest Services, all of whom, politely but edgily, informed me that it would be much appreciated if the balance of the payment could be made by me pronto. I kept explaining my situation (that darn bank!), they kept accepting my explanation, and then someone else would call, or come by, once again encouraging me to pay the remaining cash, if I didn't mind terribly, right away, as was proper.

So although the Burj is a wonder — a Themed evocation of a reality that has never existed, unless in somebody's hashish dream — a kind of externalized fantasy of Affluence, if that fantasy were being had in real time by a very rich Hedonistic Giant with unlimited access to some kind of Exaggeration Drug, a Giant fond of bright, mismatched colors, rounded, huge, inexplicable structures, dancing fountains, and two-story-tall wall-lining aquariums — I couldn't enjoy any of it. Not the electronic curtains that reveal infinite ocean; not the free-high-speed-Internet-accessing big-screen TV; not the Burj-shaped box of complimentary gourmet dates; not the shower with its six different Rube Goldbergian nozzles arranged so that one can wash certain body parts without having to demean oneself via bending or squatting; not the complimentary $300 bottle of wine; not the sweeping Liberace stairs or the remote-control front-door opener; not the distant view of The Palm, Jumeirah, and/or the tiny inconsequential boats far below, full of little people who couldn't afford to stay in the Burj even in their wildest dreams, the schmucks (although by the time of my third Admonitory Phone Call, I was feeling envious of them and their little completely-paid-for boats, out there wearing shorts, shorts with, possibly, some cash in the pockets) — couldn't enjoy any of it, because I was too cowed to leave my room. I resisted the urge to crawl under the bed. I experienced a sudden fear that a group of Disapproving Guest Services People would appear at my remote-controlled door and physically escort me down to the lobby ATM (an ATM about which I expect

I'll be having anxiety nightmares the rest of my life), which would once again prominently display the words PROVIDER DECLINES TRANSACTION. It's true what the Buddhists say: Mind can convert Heaven into Hell. This was happening to me. A headline in one of the nine complimentary newspapers read, actually read: AMERICAN JAILED FOR NONPAYMENT OF HOTEL BILL.

Perhaps someone had put acid in the complimentary Evian?

Mon Petit Pathetic Rebellion

On one of my many unsuccessful missions to the ATM, I met an Indian couple from the U.K. who had saved up their money for this Dubai trip and were staying downtown, near the souk. They had paid $50 to come in and have a look around the Burj (although who they paid wasn't clear — the Burj says it discontinued its policy of charging for this privilege), and were regretting having paid this money while simultaneously trying to justify it. Although we must remember, said the husband to the wife, this is, after all, a once-in-a-lifetime experience! Yes, yes, of course, she said, I don't regret it for a minute! But there is a look, a certain look, about the eyes, that means: Oh God, I am gut-sick with worry about money. And these intelligent, articulate people had that look. (As, I suspect, did I.) There wasn't, she said sadly, that much to see, really, was there? And one felt rather watched, didn't one, by the help? Was there a limit on how long they could stay? They had already toured the lobby twice, been out to the ocean-overlooking pool, and were sort of lingering, trying to get their fifty bucks' worth.

At this point, I was, I admit it, like anyone at someone else's financial mercy, a little angry at the Burj, which suddenly seemed like a rose water–smelling museum run for, and by, wealthy oppressors-of-the-people, shills for the new global economy, membership in which requires the presence of A Wad, and your ability to get to it/prove it exists.

Would you like to see my suite? I asked the couple.

Will there be a problem with the, ah . . .

Butler? I said. Personal butler?

With the personal butler? he said.

Well, I am a guest, after all, I said. And you are, after all, my old friends from college in the States. Right? Could we say that?

We said that. I snuck them up to my room, past the Personal Butler, and gave them my complimentary box of dates and the $300
bottle of wine. Fight the power! Then we all stood around, feeling
that odd sense of shame/solidarity that people of limited means
feel when their limitedness has somehow been underscored.

Later that night, a little drunk in a scurvy bar in another hotel
(described by L, my friend from Detroit, as the place where "Arabs
with a thing for brown sugar" go to procure "the most exquisite African girls on the planet" but that was actually full of African girls
who, like all girls whose job it is to fuck anyone who asks them night
after night, were weary and joyless and seemed on the brink of
tears), I scrawled in my notebook: PAUCITY (ATM) = RAGE.

Then I imagined a whole world of people toiling in the shadow
of approaching ruin, exhausting their strength and grace, while
above them a whole other world of people puttered around, enjoying the good things of life, staying at the Burj just because they
could.

And I left my ATM woes out of it and just wrote: PAUCITY =
RAGE.

Luckily, It Didn't Come to Jail

Turns out, the ATM definition of *daily* is: After midnight in the
United States. In the morning, as I marched the 2,500 dirhams I
owed proudly upstairs, the cloud lifted. A citizen of the affluent
world again, I went openly to have coffee in the miraculous lobby,
where my waiter and I talked of many things — of previous guests
(Bill Clinton, 50 Cent — a "loud-laughing man, having many ener-
getic friends") and a current guest, supermodel Naomi Campbell.

Then I left the Burj, no hard feelings, and went somewhere even
better, and more expensive.

Heaven for Real, Plus in This Case It Was Paid for in Advance

The Al Maha resort is located inside a stunningly beautiful/bleak,
rugged desert nature preserve an hour outside of Dubai. My Personal Butler was possibly the nicest man I've ever met, who proudly
admitted it was he who designed the linens, as well as the special

Kleenex dispensers. He had been at Al Maha since the beginning. He loved it here. This place was his life's work.

Each villa had its own private pool.

After check-in, we're given a Jeep tour of the desert by a friendly and intensely knowledgeable South African guide, of that distinct subspecies of large, handsome guys who love nature. I learn things. The oryx at Al Maha have adapted to the water-sprinkler system in the following way: at dusk, rather than going down to the spring, they sit at the base of the trees, waiting for the system to engage. I see a bush called Spine of Christ; it was from one of these, some believe, that Christ's crown of thorns was made. I see camel bones, three types of gazelle. We pass a concrete hut the size of a one-car garage, in a spot so isolated and desolate you expect some Beckett characters to be sitting there. Who lives inside? A guy hired by the camel farmer, our guide says. He stays there day and night for months at a time. Who is he? Probably a Pakistani; often, these camel-feeding outposts are manned by former child camel jockeys, sold by their families to sheiks when the kids were four or five years old.

For lunch, we have a killer buffet, with a chef's special of veal medallions.

I go back to my villa for a swim. Birds come down to drink from my private pool. As you lower yourself into the pool, water laps forward and out, into a holding rim, then down into the Lawrencian desert. You see a plane of blue water, then a plane of tan desert. Yellow bees — completely yellow, as if spray-painted — flit around on the surface of the water.

At dusk, we ride camels out to the desert. A truck meets us with champagne and strawberries. We sit on a dune, sipping champagne, watching the sunset. Dorkily, I am the only single. Luckily, I am befriended by B and K, a beautiful, affluent Dubai-Indian couple right out of Hemingway. She is pretty and loopy: Angelina Jolie meets Lucille Ball. He is elegant, reserved, kind-eyed, always admiring her from a little ways off, then rushing over to get her something she needs. They are here for their one-and-a-half-year anniversary. Theirs was a big traditional Indian wedding, held in a tent in the desert, attended by four hundred guests, who were transported in buses. In a traditional Indian wedding, the groom is supposed to enter on a white horse. White horses being in short supply in Dubai, her grandfather, a scion of old Dubai, called in a favor from a sheik, who flew in, from India, a beautiful white stallion. Her father then surprised the newlyweds with a thirty-minute fireworks show.

Fireworks, wow, I say, thinking of my wedding and our big surprise, which was, someone had strung a crapload of Bud cans to the bumper of our rented Taurus.

She is her father's most precious possession, he says.

Does her father like you? I say.

He has no choice, he says.

Back at my room, out of my private pool, comes the crazed Arabian moon, which has never, in my experience, looked more like a Ball of Rock in Space.

My cup runneth over. All irony vanishes. I am so happy to be alive. I am convinced of the essential goodness of the universe. I wish everyone I've ever loved could be here with me, in my private pool.

I wish *everyone* could be here with me, in my private pool: the blue-suited South Indians back in town, the camel farmer in his little stone box, the scared sad Moldavian girls clutching their ostensibly sexy little purses at hotel bars — I wish they could all, before they die, have one night at Al Maha.

But they can't.

Because that's not the way the world works.

"Dubai Is What It Is Because All the Countries Around It Are So Fucked Up"

In the middle of a harsh, repressive, backward, religiously excessive, physically terrifying region, sits Dubai. Among its Gulf neighbors: Iraq and Iran, war-torn and fanatic-ruled, respectively. Surrounding it, Saudi Arabia, where stealing will get your hand cut off, a repressive terrorist breeding ground where women's faces can't be seen in public, a country, my oil-industry friend says, on the brink of serious trouble.

The most worrisome thing in Saudi, he says, is the rural lower class. The urban middle class is doing all right, relatively affluent and satisfied. But look at a map of Saudi, he says: all that apparently empty space is not really empty. There are people there who are not middle class and not happy. I say the Middle East seems something like Russia circa 1900 — it's about trying to stave off revolution in a place where great wealth has been withheld from the masses by a greedy ruling class.

That's one way of saying it, he says.

Then he tells me how you get a date if you are a teenage girl in Saudi Arabia:

Go to the mall, wearing your required abaya. When a group of young guys walks by, if you see one you like, quickly find a secluded corner of the mall, take out your cell phone, lift your veil, snap a picture of your face. Write your cell number on a piece of paper. When the boys walk by, drop the scrap at the feet of the one you like. When he calls, send him your photo. If he likes the photo, he will call again. Arrange a secret meeting.

The world must be peopled.

The Truth Is, I Can't Decide What's True, Honestly

One night, at dinner with some People Who Know, I blurt out a question that's been bothering me: Why doesn't Al Qaeda bomb Dubai, since Dubai represents/tolerates decadent Western materialism, etc., and they could do it so easily? The Man Who Knows says, I'll tell you why: Dubai is like Switzerland during World War II — a place needed by everyone. The Swiss held Nazi money, Italian Fascist money. And in Dubai, according to this Person, Al Qaeda has millions of dollars in independent, Dubai-based banks, which don't always adhere to the international banking regulations that would require a bank to document the source of the income. A Woman Who Knows says she's seen it: a guy walks into a bank with a shitload of money, and they just take it, credit it, end of story. In this way, the People Who Know say, Dubai serves various illicit organizations from around the world: the Italian Mafia, the Spanish Mafia, etc., etc. Is this known about and blessed from the top down? Yes, it is. Al Qaeda needs Dubai, and Dubai tolerates Al Qaeda, making the periodic token arrest to keep the United States happy.

Later, the People Who Know are contradicted, in an elevator, by another Man Who Knows, a suave Luxembourgian who sells financial-services products to Dubai banks. Dubai has greatly improved its banking procedures since 9/11. Why would a terrorist group want to bank here? he asks. Think about it logically: Would they not be better served in a country sympathetic to them? Iran, Syria, Lebanon?

Good point, I say, thanking God in my heart that I am not a real Investigative Journalist.

In Which Snow Is Made by a Kenyan

Arabian Ice City is part of a larger, months-long festival called Dubai Summer Surprises, which takes place at a dozen venues around town and includes Funny Magic Mirrors, Snow Magician Show, Magic Academy Workshop, Magic Bubble Show, Balloon Man Show, and Ice Cave Workshop, not to mention Ice Fun Character Show.

But Arabian Ice City is the jewel.

Because at Arabian Ice City, Arab kids see snow for the first time.

Arabian Ice City consists, physically, of: wall-length murals of stylized Swiss landscapes; two cardboard igloos labeled GENTS' MOSQUE AND LADIES' MOSQUE respectively (actual mosques, with shoes piled up inside the mock-ice doorways, through which people keep disappearing to pray); a huge ice cliff that, on closer inspection, is a huge Styrofoam cliff, being sculpted frantically to look more like ice by twenty Filipinos with steak knives; and a tremendous central cardboard castle, inside of which, it is rumored, will be the Snow.

This is a local event, attended almost exclusively by Emiratis, sponsored by the local utility company; an opportunity, a representative tells me, to teach children about water and power conservation via educational activities and "some encouraging gifts." Has he been to America? He makes a kind of scoffing sound, as in: Right, pal, I'm going to America.

"America does not like Arabs," he says. "They think we are . . . I will not even say the word."

"Terrorists," I say.

He shuts his eyes in offended agreement.

Then he has to go. There is continued concern about the safety of the Arabian Ice City. Yesterday, at the opening, they expected one hundred people in the first hour, and instead got three thousand. Soon the ice was melting; the children, who knew nothing of the hazards of Snow, were slipping, getting hurt, and they'd had to shut the whole thing down, to much disappointment.

Waiting in the rapidly growing line, I detect a sense of mounting communal worry, fierce concern. This is, after all, for the children. Men rush in and out of the Ice Palace, bearing pillows, shov-
els, clipboards. Several Characters arrive and are ushered inside: a
red crescent with legs; what looks like a drop of toothpaste, or,
more honestly, sperm, with horizontal blue stripes; the crankiest-
looking goose imaginable, with a face like a velociraptor and a
strangely solicitous Sri Lankan handler, who keeps affectionately
swatting the goose-raptor's tail and whispering things to it and
steering it away from the crowd so they can have a private talk. The
handler seems, actually, a little in love with the goose. As the goose
approaches, a doorman announces, robustly, "Give a way for the
goose!" The goose and goose tender rush past, the tender swatting
in lusty wonderment at the goose's thick tail, as if amazed that he is
so privileged to be allowed to freely swat at such a thick, realistic
tail.

The door opens, and in we go.

Inside is a rectangle about the size of a tennis court, green bor-
dered, like one of the ice rinks Sears used to sell. Inside is basically
a shitload of crushed ice and one Kenyan with a shovel, madly
crushing. And it does look like snow, kind of, or at least ice; it looks,
actually, like a Syracuse parking lot after a freezing night.

Then the Arab kids pour in: sweet, proud, scared, tentative, trying to be brave. Each is offered a coat, from a big pile of identical
coats, black with a red racing stripe. Some stand outside the snow
rink, watching. Some walk stiff-legged across it, beaming. For others the approach is: bend down, touch with one finger. One affects
nonchalance: snow is nothing to him. But then he quickly stoops,
palms the snow, yanks his hand back, grins to himself. Another boy
makes a clunky snowball, hands it politely to the crescent-with-legs,
who politely takes it, holds it a while, discreetly drops it. The goose
paces angrily around the room, as if trying to escape the handler,
who is still swatting flirtatiously at its tail while constantly whispering asides up at its beak.

And the kids keep coming. On their faces: looks of bliss, the kind
of look a person gets when he realizes he is in the midst of doing
something rare, that might never be repeated, and is therefore of
great value. They are seeing something from a world far away,
where they will probably never go.

Women in abayas video. Families pose shyly, rearranging themselves to get more Snow in the frame. Mothers and fathers stand beaming at their kids, who are beaming at the Snow.

This is sweet, I scribble in my notebook.

And it is. My eyes well up with tears.

In the same way that reading the Bible, listening to radio preachers, would not clue the neophyte into the very active kindness of a true Christian home, reading the Koran, hearing about "moderate Islam," tells us nothing about the astonishing core warmth and familial sense of these Arab families.

I think: If everybody in America could see this, our foreign policy would change.

For my part, in the future, when I hear "Arab" or "Arab street" or those who "harbor, shelter, and sponsor" the terrorists, I am going to think of the Arabian Ice City, and that goose, moving among the cold-humbled kids, and the hundreds of videotapes now scattered around Arab homes in Dubai, showing beloved children reaching down to touch Snow.

What Is Jed Clampett Doing in Gitmo?

Having a Coke after Arabian Ice City, trying to get my crying situation sorted out, it occurred to me that the American sense of sophistication/irony — our cleverness, our glibness, our rapid-fire delivery, our rejection of gentility, our denial of tradition, our blunt realism — which can be a form of greatness when it manifests in a Gershwin, an Ellington, a Jackson Pollock — also causes us to (wrongly) assume a corresponding level of sophistication/irony/worldliness in the people of other nations.

Example One: I once spent some time with the mujahideen in Peshawar, Pakistan — the men who were at that time fighting the Russians and formed the core of the Taliban — big, scowling, bearded men who'd just walked across the Khyber Pass for a few weeks of rest. And the biggest, fiercest one of all asked me, in complete sincerity, to please convey a message to President Reagan, from him, and was kind of flabbergasted that I didn't know the president and couldn't just call him up for a chat, man-to-man.

Example Two: On the flight over to Dubai, the flight attendant announces that if we'd like to make a contribution to the Emirates Airline Foundation children's fund, we should do so in the provided envelope. The sickly Arab man next to me, whose teeth are rotten and who has, with some embarrassment, confessed to "a leg problem," responds by gently stuffing the envelope full of the sugar cookies he was about to eat. Then he pats the envelope, smiles to himself, folds his hands in his lap, goes off to sleep.

What one might be tempted to call *simplicity* could be more accurately called a *limited sphere of experience*. We round up "a suspected Taliban member" in Afghanistan and, assuming that Taliban means the same thing to him as it does to us (a mob of intransigent inconvertible Terrorists), whisk this sinister Taliban member — who grew up in, and has never once left, what is essentially the Appalachia of Afghanistan; who possibly joined the Taliban in response to the lawlessness of the post-Russian warlord state, in the name of bringing some order and morality to his life or in a misguided sense of religious fervor — off to Guantánamo, where he's treated as if he personally planned 9/11. Then this provincial, quite possibly not-guilty, certainly rube-like guy, whose view of the world is more limited than we can even imagine, is denied counsel and a possible release date, and subjected to all of the hardships and deprivations our modern military prison system can muster. How must this look to him? How must *we* look to him?

My experience has been that the poor, simple people of the world admire us, are enamored of our boldness, are hopeful that the insanely positive values we espouse can be actualized in the world. They are, in other words, rooting for us. Which means that when we disappoint them — when we come in too big, kill innocents, when our powers of discernment are diminished by our frenzied, self-protective, fearful post-9/11 energy — we have the potential to disappoint them, bitterly, and drive them away.

Look, Dream, but Stay Out There

My fourth and final hotel, the Emirates Towers, is grand and imperial, surrounded by gardens, palm trees, and an elaborate fountain/moat assembly that would look right at home on an outlying *Star Wars* planet.

One Thai prostitute I spoke with in a bar said she'd stayed at the Emirates Towers four or five times but didn't like it much. Why not? I wondered. Too business-oriented? Kind of formal, a bit stuffy? "Because every time, they come up in the night and t'row me out," she said.

Returning to the hotel at dusk, I find dozens of the low-level South Indian workers, on their weekly half-day off, making their way toward the Towers, like peasants to the gates of the castle, dressed in their finest clothes (cowboy-type shirts buttoned to the throat), holding clunky circa-1980s cameras.

What are they doing here? I ask. What's going on?

We are on holiday, one says.

What are their jobs? When can they go home? What will they do tonight? Go out and meet girls? Do they have girlfriends back home, wives?

Maybe someday, one guy says, smiling a smile of anticipatory domestic ecstasy, and what he means is: Sir, if you please, how can I marry when I have nothing? This is why I'm here: so someday I can have a family.

Are you going in there? I ask, meaning the hotel.

An awkward silence follows. In there? Them?

No, sir, one says. We are just wishing to take photos of ourselves in this beautiful place.

They go off. I watch them merrily photographing themselves in front of the futuristic fountain, in the groves of lush trees, photos they'll send home to Hyderabad, Bangalore. Entering the hotel is out of the question. They know the rules.

I decide to go in but can't locate the pedestrian entrance. The idea, I come to understand, after fifteen minutes of high-attentiveness searching, is to discourage foot traffic. Anybody who belongs in there will drive in and valet park.

Finally I locate the entrance: an unmarked, concealed, marble staircase with wide, stately steps fifty feet across. Going up, I pass a lone Indian guy hand-squeegeeing the thirty-three (I count them) steps.

How long will this take you? I ask. All afternoon?

I think so, he says sweetly.

Part of me wants to offer to help. But that would be, of course, ridiculous, melodramatic. He washes these stairs every day. It's not my job to hand-wash stairs. It's his job to hand-wash stairs. My job is to observe him hand-washing the stairs, then go inside the air-conditioned lobby and order a cold beer and take notes about his stair-washing so I can go home and write about it, making more for writing about it than he'll make in many, many years of doing it.

And of course, somewhere in India is a guy who'd kill to do some stair-washing in Dubai. He hasn't worked in three years, any chance of marriage is rapidly fading. Does this stair washer have any inclination to return to India, surrender his job to this other guy, give up his hard-won lifestyle to help this fellow human being? Who knows? If he's like me, he probably does. But in the end, his answer, like mine, is: that would be ridiculous, melodramatic. It's not my job to give up my job, which I worked so hard these many years to get.

Am I not me? Is he not him?

He keeps washing. I jog up the stairs to the hotel. Two smiling Nepalese throw open the huge doors, greeting me warmly, and I go inside.

Goodbye, Dubai, I'll Love You Forever

Emirates Airlines features unlimited free movies, music, and video games, as well as Downward-Looking and Forward-Looking live closed-circuit TV. I toggle back and forth between the Downward-Looking Camera (there are the Zagros Mountains, along the Iraq-Iran border) and *Meet the Fockers*. The mountains are green, rugged. The little dog is flushed down the toilet and comes out blue.

It's a big world, and I really like it.

In all things, we are the victims of The Misconception From Afar. There is the idea of a city, and the city itself, too great to be held in the mind. And it is in this gap (between the conceptual and the real) that aggression begins. No place works any different than any other place, really, beyond mere details. The universal human laws — need, love for the beloved, fear, hunger, periodic exaltation, the kindness that rises up naturally in the absence of hunger/fear/pain — are constant, predictable, reliable, universal, and are merely ornamented with the details of local culture. What a powerful thing to know: that one's own desires are mappable onto strangers; that what one finds in oneself will most certainly be found in The Other.

Just before I doze off, I counsel myself grandiosely: fuck concepts. Don't be afraid to be confused. Try to remain permanently confused. Anything is possible. Stay open, forever, so open it hurts, and then open up some more, until the day you die, world without end, amen.

DAVID SEDARIS

Turbulence

from *The New Yorker*

ON THE FLIGHT TO RALEIGH, I sneezed, and the cough drop
I'd been sucking on shot from my mouth, ricocheted off my folded
tray table, and landed, as I remember it, in the lap of the woman
beside me, who was asleep and had her arms folded across her
chest. I'm surprised that the force didn't wake her — that's how
hard it hit — but all she did was flutter her eyelids and let out a tiny
sigh, the kind you might hear from a baby.

Under normal circumstances, I'd have had three choices, the
first being to do nothing. The woman would wake up in her own
time, and notice what looked like a shiny new button sewn to the
crotch of her jeans. This was a small plane, with one seat per row on
Aisle A, and two seats per row on Aisle B. We were on B, so should
she go searching for answers I would be the first person on her list.
"Is this yours?" she'd ask, and I'd look dumbly into her lap.

"Is what mine?"

Option No. 2 was to reach over and pluck it from her pants, and
No. 3 was to wake her up and turn the tables, saying, "I'm sorry, but
I think you have something that belongs to me." Then she'd hand
the lozenge back and maybe even apologize, confused into thinking that she'd somehow stolen it.

These circumstances, however, were not normal, as before she'd
fallen asleep the woman and I had had a fight. I'd known her for
only an hour, yet I felt her hatred just as strongly as I felt the stream
of cold air blowing into my face — this after she'd repositioned the
nozzle above her head, a final fuck-you before settling down for
her nap.

The odd thing was that she hadn't looked like trouble. I'd stood behind her while boarding and she was just this woman — forty at most — wearing a T-shirt and cutoff jeans. Her hair was brown and fell to her shoulders, and as we waited she gathered it into a ponytail and fastened it with an elastic band. There was a man beside her, who was around the same age and was also wearing shorts, though his were hemmed. He was skimming through a golf magazine, and I guessed correctly that the two of them were embarking on a vacation. While on the gangway, the woman mentioned a rental car and wondered if the beach cottage was far from a grocery store. She was clearly looking forward to her trip, and I found myself hoping that, whichever beach they were going to, the grocery store wouldn't be too far away. It was just one of those things that go through your mind. *Best of luck,* I thought.

Once on board, I realized that the woman and I would be sitting next to one another, which was fine. I took my place on the aisle, and within a minute she excused herself and walked a few rows up to talk to the man with the golf magazine. He was at the front of the cabin, in a single bulkhead seat, and I recall feeling sorry for him, because I hate the bulkhead. Tall people covet it, but I prefer as little leg room as possible. When I'm on a plane or in a movie theater, I like to slouch down as low as I can and rest my knees on the seat back in front of me. In the bulkhead, there is no seat in front of you, just a wall a good three feet away, and I never know what to do with my legs. Another drawback is that you have to stow all of your belongings in the overhead compartment, and these are usually full by the time I board. All in all, I'd rather hang from one of the wheels than have to sit up front.

When they announced our departure, the woman returned to her seat, and hovered a half foot off the cushion, so she could continue her conversation with the man she'd been talking to earlier. I wasn't paying attention to what they were saying, but I believe I heard him refer to her as Becky, a wholesome name that matched her contagious, almost childlike enthusiasm.

The plane took off and everything was as it should be until the woman touched my arm and pointed to the man she'd been talking to earlier. "Hey," she said, "see that guy up there?" Then she called out his name — Eric, I think — and the man turned and waved. "That's my husband, see, and I'm wondering if you could maybe swap seats so that me and him could sit together."

"Well, actually —" I said, and before I could finish her face hardened, and she interrupted me, saying, "What? You have a *problem* with that?"

"Well," I said, "ordinarily I'd be happy to move, but he's in the bulkhead, and I just hate that seat."

"He's in the *what?*"

"The bulkhead," I explained. "That's what you call that front row."

"Listen," she said, "I'm not asking you to switch because it's a bad seat. I'm asking you to switch because we're married." She pointed to her wedding ring, and when I leaned in closer to get a better look at it she drew back her hand, saying, "Oh, never mind. Just forget it."

It was as if she had slammed a door in my face, and quite unfairly, it seemed to me. I should have left well enough alone, but instead I tried to reason with her. "It's only a ninety-minute flight," I said, suggesting that in the great scheme of things it wasn't that long to be separated from your husband. "I mean, what, is he going to prison the moment we land in Raleigh?"

"No, he's not going to *prison,*" she said, and on the last word she lifted her voice, mocking me.

"Look," I told her, "if he was a child I'd do it." And she cut me off saying, "Whatever." Then she rolled her eyes and glared out the window.

The woman had decided that I was a hard-ass, one of those guys who refuse under any circumstances to do anyone a favor. But it's not true. I just prefer that the favor be my idea, that it leaves me feeling kind rather than bullied and uncomfortable. *So, no. Let her sulk,* I decided.

Eric had stopped waving, and signaled for me to get Becky's attention. "My wife," he mouthed. "Get my wife."

There was no way out, and so I tapped the woman on the shoulder.

"Don't touch me," she said, as if I had thrown a punch.

"Your husband wants you."

"Well, that doesn't give you the right to *touch* me." Becky unbuckled her seat belt, raised herself off the cushion, and spoke to Eric in a loud stage whisper: "I asked him to swap seats, but he won't do it."

He cocked his head, sign language for "How come?" and she

said, much louder than she needed to, "'Cause he's an *asshole,*
that's why."

An elderly woman across the aisle turned to look at me, and I
pulled a *Times* crossword puzzle from the bag beneath my seat.
That always makes you look reasonable, especially on a Saturday,
when the words are long and the clues are exceptionally tough.
The problem is that you have to concentrate, and all I could think
of was this woman.

Seventeen across. A fifteen-letter word for enlightenment. "I am
not an asshole," I wrote, and it fit.

Five down. Six-letter Indian tribe. "You are."

Look at the smart man, breezing through the puzzle, I imagined
everyone thinking. He must be a genius. That's why he wouldn't
swap seats for that poor married woman. He knows something we
don't.

It's pathetic how much significance I attach to the *Times* puzzle,
which is easy on Monday and gets progressively harder as the week
advances. I'll spend fourteen hours finishing the Friday, and then
I'll wave it in someone's face and demand that they acknowledge
my superior intelligence. I think it means that I'm smarter than the
next guy, but all it really means is that I don't have a life.

As I turned to my puzzle, Becky reached for a paperback novel,
the kind with an embossed cover. I strained to see what the title
was, and she jerked it closer to the window. Strange how that happens, how you can feel someone's eyes on your book or magazine
as surely as you can feel a touch. It only works for the written word,
though. I stared at her feet for a good five minutes, and she never
jerked those away. After our fight, she'd removed her sneakers, and
I saw that her toenails were painted white, and that each one was
perfectly sculpted.

Eighteen across: "Not impressed."

Eleven down: "Whore."

I wasn't even looking at the clues anymore.

When the drink cart came, we fought through the flight attendant.

"What can I offer you folks?" she asked, and Becky threw down
her book saying, "We're not together." It killed her that we
might be mistaken for a couple, or even friends. "I'm traveling with

my husband," she continued. "He's sitting up there. In *the bulk-head.*"

You learned that word from me, I thought.

"Well, can I offer —"

"I'll have a Coke," Becky said. "Not much ice."

I was thirsty, too, but more than a drink I wanted the flight attendant to like me. And who would you prefer, the finicky baby who cuts you off and gets all specific about her ice cubes, or the thoughtful, nondemanding gentleman who smiles up from his difficult Saturday puzzle saying, "Nothing for me, thank you"?

Were the plane to lose altitude and the only way to stay aloft was to push one person out the emergency exit, I now felt certain that the flight attendant would select Becky rather than me. I pictured her clinging to the door frame, her hair blown so hard it was starting to fall out. "But my husband —" she'd cry. Then I would step forward saying, "Hey, I've been to Raleigh before. Take me instead." Becky would see that I am not the asshole she mistook me for, and in that instant she would lose her grip and be sucked into space.

Two down: "Take that!"

It's always so satisfying when you can twist someone's hatred into guilt — make them realize that they were wrong, too quick to judge, too unwilling to look beyond their own petty concerns. The problem is that it works both ways. I'd taken this woman as the type who arrives late at a movie, then asks me to move behind the tallest person in the theater so that she and her husband can sit together. Everyone has to suffer just because she's sleeping with someone. But what if I was wrong? I pictured her in a dimly lit room, trembling before a portfolio of glowing x-rays. "I give you two weeks at the most," the doctor says. "Why don't you get your toenails done, buy yourself a nice pair of cutoffs, and spend some quality time with your husband. I hear the beaches of North Carolina are pretty nice this time of year."

I looked at her then, and thought, *No.* If she'd had so much as a stomachache, she would have mentioned it. Or would she? I kept telling myself that I was within my rights, but I knew it wasn't working when I turned back to my puzzle and started listing the various reasons I was not an asshole.

Forty across: "I give money to p —"

Forty-six down: "— ublic radio."

While groping for reason No. 2, I noticed that Becky was not making a list of her own. She was the one who had called me a name, who had gone out of her way to stir up trouble, but it didn't seem to bother her in the least. After finishing her Coke, she folded up the tray table, summoned the flight attendant to take her empty can, and settled back for a nap. It was shortly afterward that I put the throat lozenge in my mouth, and shortly after that that I sneezed, and it shot like a bullet onto the crotch of her shorts.

Nine across: "Fuck!"

Thirteen down: "Now what?"

It was then that another option occurred to me. *You know,* I thought. *Maybe I will swap places with her husband.* But I'd waited too long, and now he was asleep as well. My only way out was to nudge this woman awake and make the same offer I sometimes make to Hugh. We'll be arguing, and I'll stop in mid-sentence and ask if we can just start over. "I'll go outside and when I come back in we'll just pretend this never happened, OK?"

If the fight is huge, he'll wait until I'm in the hall, then bolt the door behind me, but if it's minor he'll go along, and I'll reenter the apartment saying, "What are you doing home?" Or "Gee, it smells good in here. What's cooking?" — an easy question, as he's always got something on the stove.

For a while, it feels goofy, but eventually the self-consciousness wears off, and we ease into the roles of two decent people, trapped in a rather dull play. "Is there anything I can do to help?"

"You can set the table if you want."

"All-righty then."

I don't know how many times I've set the table in the middle of the afternoon, long before we sit down to eat. But the play would be all the duller without action, and I don't want to do anything really hard, like paint a room. I'm just so grateful that he goes along with it. Other people's lives can be full of screaming and flying plates, but I prefer that my own remains as civil as possible, even if it means faking it every once in a while.

I'd gladly have started over with Becky, but something told me she wouldn't go for it. Even asleep, she broadcast her hostility, each gentle snore sounding like an accusation. *Ass-hole. Ass-ho-ole.* The landing announcement failed to wake her, and when the flight attendant asked her to fasten her seat belt she did it in a drowse, without looking. The lozenge disappeared beneath the buckle, and this bought me an extra ten minutes, time spent gathering my things, so that I could make for the door the moment we arrived at our gate. I just didn't count on the man in front of me being a little bit quicker and holding me up as he wrestled his duffel bag from the overhead bin. Had it not been for him, I might have been gone by the time Becky unfastened her seat belt, but as it was I was only four rows away, standing, as it turned out, right beside the bulkhead.

The name she called me was nothing I hadn't heard before, and nothing that I won't hear again, probably. Eight letters, and the clue might read, "Above the shoulders, he's nothing but crap." Of course, they don't put words like that in the *Times* crossword puzzle. If they did, anyone could finish it.

SALLY SHIVNAN

Airborne

FROM *The Georgia Review*

> . . . flight's greatest gift is to let us look around.
> — William Langewiesche, *Inside the Sky*

I'M FLYING, with windows for wings. Under my nose — literally
— are things I would not know any other way, for example, that the
predominant color of city lights at night is gold.

There are also facts that other folks might figure out some other
way, but that have come to me only by pressing my nose to the
Plexiglas. For instance, how the design of most golf courses is fan-
folded, and how it is possible for people to drive right past huge
quarries and never see them. How the circular pivot-irrigation fields
of Oklahoma are racked together like billiard balls for hundreds of
square miles, yellow ones, orange ones, lavender, rusty gold, every
shade of green. How horseshoe bends in rivers become, in time,
lonely oxbow lakes. How trees follow even dry watercourses. How
roads don't take you to all the places that are.

Some of this is window-seat trivia, of limited interest. I am after
the big picture, or at least, *a* big picture. What I've figured out so
far is this: that from high above, the topography bursts through everything man-made, overwhelms it, and that, from up there, those
landforms are astonishingly beautiful. There are people who disagree — the late geographer John Brinkerhoff Jackson, the writer
and pilot William Langewiesche, and the photographer Emmet
Gowin, who feel the view from the sky reveals, primarily, not the
earth's brilliant geology but the tracks and designs of humans upon
it. All of these men, though, I would note, have done their observing at small-plane altitudes, flying much lower than I do.

In Gowin's photographs, eerie, wondrous landscapes wear the scars of our scribing and digging, from nuclear test craters and bomb disposal sites to silver mine tailings and abandoned desert trailer parks, though even in these dark pictures there are lovely shapes — the loops and spirals of off-road vehicle tracks on salt flats, the perfect roundness of a giant pivot-irrigation field made delicate by a dusting of snow. Georgia O'Keeffe had a different vision from the air, which I feel closer to — after a round-the-world airplane tour in 1959, she painted pictures of what she'd seen out the window; *Sky Above Clouds IV* is an endless flat sea of little white pancakes stretching far away to a faintly pink horizon, an image of unbelievable serenity. But, of course, she was flying at a higher altitude than those others, and she did not look down, but out, at the clouds.*

Too low or too high, and the view I crave is altered — pictures taken from the space shuttle sweep in too much, at too great a distance; geological features are lost, land masses start to look like maps. Satellite images of the Grand Canyon, as historian Stephen Pyne puts it, "[reduce] its immense complexity to the status of a mudcrack." (Planes are prohibited from flying directly over the canyon, but they tell me on some routes it can be seen from not too far away.) Astronauts always talk in bland platitudes about the beauty of the earth from orbit. I have no doubt they are overcome by the view and find it hard to describe their feelings, but I also think they're vague because what they're seeing is vague, losing definition.

Mine is an ordinary airline passenger's view, from an ordinary, cramped, tweedy-upholstered seat by a little oval window, call it 38F or 11A. Cruising altitude is what I've got — what so many of us have got, herded aboard and packed in like the human cargo we are, on our way to meetings and vacations and Thanksgivings and weddings. I am sympathetic to those who prefer aisle seats, who have other things they want to do — read, sleep, watch the movie. Sometimes my eyes almost hurt. I squeeze them tight, like some lit-

---

* An exception to the low-flying critics is Antoine de Saint-Exupéry, who flew small planes but was enraptured by everything he saw. He flew, however, in the 1920s and 1930s in places that were little disturbed by human progress — the Pyrenees, the Sahara. "How empty of life is this planet of ours!" he says in *Wind, Sand, and Stars*. "What a deal of the earth's surface is given over to rock and sand!"

tle kid, but then they pop open again. I pray for clouds, the thick kind that are nothing to look at.

I am not unsociable. Flying offers natural opportunities for chit-chat with the neighbors. On a recent trip I sat beside a paralegal from Brooklyn and, in the aisle seat, a seventeen-year-old reading a book of funny facts. The paralegal was sipping at his plastic cup of white Zinfandel, the seventeen-year-old was giggling over his book, and I was looking out the window. We'd already done the *who are you* and *what are you* and *why are you going* so I felt comfortable saying, "Hold up, I have an announcement."

The paralegal set down his wine. The giggler lowered his book to his lap. They'd seen nothing but the back of my head for the last ten minutes, but now my face was turned on them like the sun. They shrank back from the light, their kidneys pressed against the armrests. "The country underneath us," I told them, "has turned flat!"

No reaction.

"It's official," I added. "The country is officially flat now."

"That's cool," said the paralegal.

"Yeah," said the teenager.

"It'll stay flat," I said, "till we reach the Rockies." They nodded; they understood. "There's this river down there — the land's kind of rolling and hilly on one side, flat as a pancake on the other." I knew flat as a pancake was a cliché, but at that moment it conveyed absolute flatness better than anything else I could think of. I turned back to look, but the river was gone. I saw squares of green and brown, and roads that crossed at right angles and ran straight forever.

I love to just stare at these things that pass beneath me, but there's more to it — the big picture that I want to understand is, partly, about the variety of human impulses embedded down there that can be discerned from high above. In this way, my interests are not so different from those of people like Langewiesche and Gowin. Some impulses are specific to certain places, for instance, the way Manhattan, from the air, is so clearly a human eruption *straight up* (although even Manhattan, viewed from the right altitude, is defined not by its population density but by the chunk of rock between two rivers that it stands on; it is an island with a city on it, not a city on an island).

Some of our impulses are more widespread, more general, like the tendency to settle at the edges of exposed places, not in the middle, and along rivers wherever they are found, and to congregate in clumps large and small — there's something comforting about these patterns of habitation, viewed from the air. Nothing looks warmer to me than flying into a city, out of the dark interior places, at night — the lights, red and white against the blackness, each a point of life.

Other revealing human tendencies include the ranch-driveway phenomenon, out in the flattest, emptiest parts of Texas and Oklahoma. This is the tendency of those long drives back to the ranch house not to run straight, like all the roads in those parts, but instead go straight only at first and then swerve, or dogleg, or even carve out a big S curve. As if their owners were overcome by a need to break with that landscape, to soften it before they could bear to drive across it. Every driveway a little different from the neighbors' driveways (neighbors separated by miles, driveways each maybe a mile — or more? — long), the owners' way of asserting their creativity, their uniqueness, in this harsh land that would make anyone feel small. I cannot help but project myself there, on the ground, driving on some road, looking across the empty land to the dust plume sent up by a pickup truck flying down one of those S curves. No straight-line plume, but a shape-shifting thing, appearing to pinch or stall where the truck turns in my direction, then stretching again, opening up, as it turns another way.

The big picture I'm after is also heavily geological. In the United States, the whole story down there is wet-to-dry (east to west) or dry-to-wet (west to east), with the westward direction, flying into the dry, edging out the other for dramatic impact. It starts in the tightly wound Northeast, where the woods and farms are crammed together and the fields are crazy shapes like Aztec animals, then slips over the woolly Appalachians and on to the Midwest, where the world turns flat and the perfect squares of the grid appear, the grid that laid out America's settlement west in the days of the Homestead Act. Everything is green, and the towns are small and many, and relatively close together — it looks neighborly and productive down there. And then the change, continuing west — its gradual nature is its great fascination: the green slowly dulls, the squares get larger, the clouds disappear. The rivers, revealed by the dense, dark lines of the trees that follow them, go winding across the flat land, like tortuous varicose veins. The squares take on new colors, dun, mauve, and pinkish hues, and bits of bright irrigated green. Those varicose watercourses begin to eat into the land, shallow precursors of canyons. The grid gets ever larger, whole blocks of it missing; soon the blocks are big enough whole towns fit within a block with room to spare. The irrigation circles appear, visually breaking the grid, and then they cease, and the land is creased and parched, the remains of the grid just ghost-lines now, broken everywhere by the twisting, deep arroyos. There are cattle down there — the occasional salt lick or water tank is visible from the faint starburst around it, the rays of the star formed by the tracks of the cows. The creases become canyons, and they widen, and widen more, until they are not canyons but great flat expanses, and the highlands that are left between them are mesas.*

All of this is only the beginning: the Rockies lie just west, and then the true deserts on the other side of them. About the Rockies, all I can say is how amazingly cool it is to fly right over a knife-edge ridge, like a photographer on an Imax movie. From the air, much of what you see is the zone above the tree line — different from how the mountains look if you're down in them, looking up at the evergreens and aspen. Bare rock and scree are predominant, their dull color hard to describe — like the gray of a newborn's eyes before the pigment appears. In winter, of course, there is much more snow, but in summer it is dotted along the rock, in its hollows and turns, as if dabbed by a Q-Tip. I see countless places where I know no human has ever stood. It is beautiful where the sun hits the rock: golden.

Southern Utah lets me pretend I am a space explorer, orbiting an alien planet. Bizarre, colorful, pink and rose and cream wild-ass canyon lands. Depending where the plane is headed, I might get the strange, gray Mojave, which in places loses its scale utterly at thirty thousand feet — could be a pile of mud at my feet, half washed away from a thunderstorm — or the wondrous basin and range of Nevada, where long straight ridge and bare wide plain,

---

* Flying the other way, west to east, the land gradually smooths, becomes less incised. The mesas that stand above the desert floor get broader, then turn into a single flat table that has canyons cutting into it; the visual effect is of the land turned inside out. The dim lines of the grid appear, where people have tried to map out squares, ranging and irregular: wishful-thinking squares. I have to remind myself, flying west to east, that the people moved the other way — the squares didn't appear and define gradually, rather, they disappeared, slowly, as they became harder to maintain, as the land got drier and drier.

and long straight ridge and bare wide plain, on and on, dozens of them, pass under me. It's the emptiest country I've ever seen, more vacant somehow than Utah or the Mojave, because of that repetition, I suppose. Because of those wide flat basins, and the loneliness of those long, meandering ridge lines, which have names on maps but don't from up here. The country is colorless, not really gray, not really beige.

It's an illusion, of course, the perfection of the land seen from that altitude, as Gowin's photographs remind me. Way up there, I can't see the missile silos he sees, and I can't see broken glass in vacant lots, or people panhandling, or billboards, or giant flags over car dealerships. Rural poverty is completely invisible, since I can see settlement only where it is clustered. What I think of the world is entirely altitude dependent — again, I need to be not too high, not too low, but in between, like Goldilocks, situated just right, just so, between heaven and earth. Admittedly, my view from up there is a distortion, even though it's the real thing I'm looking at, not pictures of it. But I could make a case that if the view from the air is distorted, maybe the view from the ground is, too, and the truth lies somewhere between the air and the earth. That each should concede something to the other. And maybe I see what I *want* to see. But it's still what I see. Why do I feel a little defensive here, for thinking the earth is beautiful? It *is* beautiful — look at it. Perhaps the weight of sadness in the world is too much, and we can never consider beauty completely apart from it.

Oddly, I have less sense of the land when my feet are on the ground — my line of sight is so limited — but from the air all I see is rock, water, rock, trees, rock. And if I am lucky enough to fly all the way to the edge, I see ocean, extending out of sight forever, a reminder there is more world out there to see, simply a matter of getting on the right airplane.

Here's something I wonder about, when I go flying around: Why do I feel a need to link what I see out the window to a map in my mind? Why is it important to me to wonder, are we still over Wyoming? In my worst moments, I have silently shrieked *would somebody lay a map over this thing!* Some airlines have television monitors above the aisles that periodically flash maps of where the plane is, a fun feature until the in-flight movie puts an end to all that and I am hurled out over the middle of the country, uprooted, hapless, soon lost.

On any flight, there are parts where I feel situated, and parts where I have to let it go. Even if I had maps, I don't know that I would use them; they are too unlike the terrain they depict — the roads out the airplane window, for example, are dwarfed by what's around them, nothing like the bold red and blue lines that dominate paper. The shapes of the states, the boundaries between them, so deeply engrained in the picture files of our brains, simply do not exist on the ground, but the acceptance of that, over the course of an airplane flight, comes gradually. It begins with resistance, as the plane leaves the ground, particularly if I'm starting from the familiar territory of home. At first, I delight at the landmarks I know and am pleased at how much sense a lot of it makes, but sooner or later I get lost (frustrated because I don't know "where I am" — over Tennessee or Kentucky, someplace like that? Would that be the *Ohio* River?). I am forced to give up trying to identify everything and simply shift to thinking, *that's a river, that's a road up a mountain,* and at that moment I tremble on the threshold of an alien country, where I will see how things are laid out, what nature and man have done, but I won't know what anything is. The most interesting point is when I'm right on the edge between those two zones, the half grasped and the unknown, and I'm wavering, feeling myself slip into a new way of seeing.

Resistance gives way to acceptance and finally elation as I realize these landscapes exist and are what they are *without* being called anything, something like the Garden of Eden before Adam started hanging name tags on the animals, and that the land is a *whole,* that there is nothing about it that exists in parcels, nothing that can be divided from anything else, even though the transitions, in places, can be abrupt — the lifting of the Sierra Nevada, for example, out of California's Central Valley. The slow movement of the view out the window underscores this seamlessness (at cruising altitude, a feature on the ground takes about two and a half minutes to transit the window). This pace is slow enough to let me study and ponder, while always offering new stuff to look at, continually displacing what I've caught in the frame.*

---

* Treating the window as a clock face and sitting, say, on the port side of the plane, two and a half minutes is the time it takes something to travel from 3:00 to 9:00; a feature noted at 4:00 and followed to its disappearance at 8:00 takes about a minute and forty seconds, because it is closer. Changing one's position, of course — shifting forward to prolong the look back — can buy more time.

Once, I saw a strange line of futuristic white towers atop the long, crenellated edge of a mesa east of Albuquerque. At first I thought, microwave antennas? But there were too many, arranged too purposefully, and they were far below but they were so *white*. They were windmills. I stared at them, and the cliff edge on which they stood, for a full two and a half minutes. I knew we had just passed Albuquerque only because the pilot came on and told us. I was grateful, it helped me situate the sight, but I hadn't seen Albuquerque, it must have been on the other side of the plane, and it made me think how every flight is tracing its own unique trajectory, dividing the planet into port and starboard and giving me just a sampling of the earth below, reminding me that even though the view out my window looks wide, I am seeing very little.

It is hard, in the end, to escape the tyranny of place names and maps. On a flight back from Phoenix once with my sister, we used one of the airline's cocktail napkins, which featured a map of the United States with the airline's routes all over it, to locate ourselves as we looked out the window. We suffered incapacitating attacks of giggles (giddy and fatigued from travel) imagining the pilot navigating with the same paper napkin.

But the desire to understand where you are is natural enough, and it is thrilling to recognize exotic physical features from the air. Flying over Yosemite — *there's Half Dome!* — and out of the disorienting wilds of the Mojave, the *Salton Sea*, unmistakable. Once I saw a red rock place in the desert that had to be Sedona. And flying over what was clearly the Mississippi, recognizing Memphis on its east bank *(yes, that must be Memphis)*, seeing in fact the I-40 bridge over the river, which connects Memphis, and everything that is Tennessee and everything that is the east, to the endless flats of Arkansas and all that lies beyond, a bridge I had in fact crossed once on my way west — I felt pulled out of my window seat, pulled down there with superhero zoom-lens eyes, all the way down to that bridge, where I remembered so vividly the sign halfway across: a sign for the interstate that should have had a red and blue shield with "I-40" on it above a separate rectangle saying "west" but which was missing the shield part, so the bridge out of Memphis, across the Mississippi, had hanging on it only that single word, *west*.

It's a private showing, the in-flight movie out my window, but I see other people looking, too, sometimes. It's possible to peer forward down that crack between the seats and the wall, maybe three or four rows, until a shoulder, an arm, a head leaning into that space blocks the view. There I can see (though he doesn't see me) a guy absorbed in studying the world below, though his face, turned as it is to the window, is hidden. Maybe somebody three rows back from me has watched me, too — no way to know. The window seat of a commercial jet is one of the most private spaces in the public places we inhabit. The high seat backs separate you from the other passengers, the white noise of the engines blurs the sound around you. No one can see the expression on your face as you gaze, dreamy, then suddenly start at some new vision: a field of sand dunes, a pocket of them in the rain shadow of some mountain, a strange sandy-pink color, all rippled like cake icing.

I often get to airports early, not because of security, or worry about delays or ticket lines. I arrive early so I can be in Group A, if I'm flying on a certain discount airline that does not believe in assigned seats, but instead labels their passengers As and Bs and Cs. When I look down and see that giant A in big black print on my boarding pass I am at peace, because I know I'll get a window seat — no one can prevent my getting one. And yea, though I walk down the aisle with a B on my pass sometimes, I fear not, for chances are if I'm near the front of the B group and willing to walk to the back of the plane, I can still get a window.

I have a recurring fantasy of boarding a plane and usurping someone's window seat, kicking him or her out of there, explaining I'm sorry, I *have* to have this seat, because I'm writing an essay about things you see out the window — I need to work here. I've got work to do. And I could keep using this, doing this to people, long after the writing was done, why not? Who would know?

I used to think I practiced this window-seat obsession in honor of my ancestors who never saw, who never dreamed of seeing — who never dreamed of what they'd see if they could see — the topside of a cloud. (Don't get me started on clouds: clouds like the soft batting that quilters use to stuff their quilts; clouds that are thin and gauzy like wet tissue that's pulling apart; popcorn clouds, floaty little things, casting shadows like splats of purple paint on the fields below; clouds that carry their sail aloft like clipper ships, their color, in that clear, thin air something a paint company would call "Painful White.") But now I think I do it to honor, not their unimagined chance to see the tops of clouds, but their unimagined view of the earth, of the land. Until a few decades ago, nobody flew. My grandmother never flew; it never occurred to her. The Wright Brothers took off just over one hundred years ago, and all the generations before, who never conceived of paved roads, let alone airplanes, had no idea of looking down from above to see what farms and towns and mountains looked like from up there. Now it's so commonplace that many people prefer aisle seats; we feel we are *made* to go up in planes, that we are parked in the air, in a dead space between origin and destination, so different from a trip in a car or on a train which lets you feel the passing through.

When I fly, I don't often think of the people on the ground, but if I try I can imagine the ghosts of the ones who never flew, down there, looking up at the sky. And I think of those ranchers, the ones with the driveways that carve great curves across the dust — I think of them, far below, looking up to note the progress of my jet plane over their world. Ian Frazier, in *Great Plains,* describes their view: "In New Mexico and west Texas, the hard white sky is screwed onto the earth like a lid . . ." What a rush, to be a part of that sky! Although maybe, to them, my plane mars their sky. Once again, perceptions can be altitude dependent.

Beauty, as they say, is in the beholder's eye. And this thought gets me thinking again about where beauty fits in. I think of Emmet Gowin's photographs — the role of art is to agitate. It is meant to take us to edges we don't normally look over. Art's function is also to let us see things we already see but in new ways. This can include showing us beauty we did not realize — I think, here, of O'Keeffe's clouds.

For my part, I am privileged to be a collector of airborne miracles. Here's the last one I'll share: flying out of Fort Lauderdale at night, swinging out over the Atlantic and then slowly banking around over the land to head north, the view of Florida's east coast below, twinkling, glittering in the dark, with the great black ocean beyond. But then, continuing to fly inland and suddenly seeing the glitter line stop, nothing but darkness beneath us. Wait, I thought, this can't be right, this can't be the Gulf of Mexico. What we'd just flown over was too narrow to be the whole width of the Florida peninsula. And we had no reason to fly out over the Gulf — we were supposed to be headed north. But there it was, black empty void beneath us. I told myself *think!* and then I got it: Everglades. Dark in there.

We flew into overcast — nothing quite like that, flying at night in clouds. It was dark out the window but the flashing lights on the wings lit up the cloud in pulses. Between each flash, I was left with my own reflection in the window, a double reflection because of the inner and outer panes. I could see solidly only where the two overlapped, and where they didn't overlap the images were blurred, transparent, so I could see through myself, through my wrists, my fingers. It was all very dim, I couldn't see my own face at all; the jewelry on my hands and wrists picked up the little light there was. After spending so much time looking out the window, extending outward, over crystal-sharp vast expanses, I was being drawn back in, I was losing clarity, I was thrown back on myself. It was curious and quiet and close; it was a strange trip.

What a contrast with the big blue sky: how when the plane makes a turn, and the wings dip, and the side I'm sitting on gets canted up toward the sky, and I see that powerful cerulean blue fill the screen of my window. I used to feel it was taking my view away from me; now I accept it as my cue to look up, into that great blue space, to be reminded that the earth is not just a landscape below, but a planet hanging in the heavens.

GARY SHTEYNGART

A St. Petersburg Christmas

FROM *Travel + Leisure*

SOME COUNTRIES live off collective memory — rough-hewn stone monuments, mournful anthems, goats ritually slaughtered in honor of some lunar god — but here in Russia the national pastime is forgetting. After being in St. Petersburg for less than four hours I can no longer remember many things: my reason for being here, the Russian word for "taxi" (it's *taxi*), the name of my hotel, my *own* first name and patronymic. There are little snippets of consciousness floating in a sea of black. At one point I am sitting on a glacial bench with a friend breathing in thimbles of cold night air; now I am falling down in the marble vestibule of a familiar metro station, my galoshes making comical half circles above my head; and finally I am parked amid the Art Nouveau curlicues of the Grand Hotel Europe's Lobby Bar with a lit Cohiba in one hand, a glass of Fonseca port in the other, and several bewildered young women across the table listening to me pontificate.

And then it's all coming back to me. I'm here in St. Petersburg, Russia, to witness the holiday season to end all holiday seasons. According to a new law passed by the country's insane parliament, Russian workers now enjoy a ten-day respite (from January 1 to January 10) from whatever employment they may still have. This extended winter break, centered around the Russian Orthodox Christmas — which, according to the Julian calendar, falls on January 7 — was greeted with alarm by conscientious citizens. Some Petersburgers feared an unprecedented booze binge, others a crime spree that would rekindle the city's reputation as an Al Capone–era Chicago. In actuality, after all was said and drunk, the city's criminals mostly stayed home with their loved ones, while the number of residents hospitalized for alcohol poisoning increased a meager 10 to 15 percent. My trip to Petersburg was an attempt to partake in this mad winter carnival without somehow joining the merry band in the hospital. On my first night, I nearly did.

It all started with a perverse case of jet lag and a chest cold that would outwit the Western world's most powerful antibiotics. When my friend K. picked me up at the airport, I was performing the unique trick of somehow coughing and sneezing and hiccupping at the same time. "We need to get you well," K. said, and I knew exactly what he meant. The Russian cure for any ailment ranging from stomach ulcers to delusions of grandeur is 150 grams of vodka (about three shots). But for a cold this serious K. prescribed two bottles of *gorilka*, a Ukrainian firewater blended with honey and pepper.

K. and I have a tradition — the first thing we do when I get to town is head to the Mountain Eagle (Gorny Oryol) restaurant. The Eagle used to sit humbly by the Petersburg zoo; it was an ad hoc outpost of plastic chairs and wooden tables that served the best Georgian cuisine and the most delicate mutton kebabs in the city. But all that humility, wood, and plastic are now gone, replaced by an overlit gaudy palace fit for a minor Romanov. In its size and style, the new Mountain Eagle's entry hallway recalls an abandoned train station at midnight, and the rest of the place is a kind of architectural guide to New Russian taste — columns, pediments, fountains, fortress towers, massive unexplained outcroppings of stone and marble. The once eclectic clientele has been replaced by midlevel *biznesmeni* conspicuous by their shaved heads and fatalistic expressions. "We are in the land of Zurab Tsereteli!" I sneeze at my friend, referring to the sculptor who in the past decade has disfigured the Moscow skyline with a 310-foot statue of Peter the Great that looks like a baroque Russian Godzilla. I am faced with two possibilities: either the tasteful, stoic city of my birth is gone, or I have accidentally landed in Moscow.

And then the bottles of Ukrainian *gorilka* are brought out. We toast our friendship, our families, Ukraine's recent Orange Revolution and the hope that a similar one will someday sweep Putin out of power in Russia. The Ukrainian alcohol has a bright and chewy taste, the honey and pepper coating one's tongue with thick sheets of sugar and spice. We chase the *gorilka* with a plate of pickled peppers, cabbage, and garlic, and follow that up with *khachapuri*, a Georgian flat bread filled with soft ricotta-like cheese. Soon, with the first bottle of *gorilka* safely inside me, the jet lag, the unvanquished flu, and the alcohol combine to rob me of what little sense I had cleared through customs. I fall victim to what I call Dostoyevsky Disease: the need to be overbearingly kind to some person in lesser circumstances, which in poverty-stricken Russia presents a fairly wide tableau. So when the homely young waitress brings the bill I hand her an unheard-of tip: $20.

"What, are you crazy?" K. says.

The waitress blushes, her little red nose twinkling. "Thank you!" she cries. "Thank you, young man! This will be my New Year's present!"

"O-ho, life is short, life is short!" I happily intone. "We must be good to one another, dear one!" And after those words are uttered we cut to the episode I have already described: my tenure on the ice-crusted bench, my stumble down the metro, my lost evening of Cohibas and port and pontification at the Grand Hotel Europe Lobby Bar. Throughout the ensuing night, covered with an immense winter comforter, I am atremble with happy fraternal thoughts and sunk deep into my own forgetting. A fairly typical start to most Russian visits.

St. Petersburg is the most beautiful city in the world. If you don't believe me, you should wake up in Room 403 of the Grand Hotel Europe and look out your window. Directly ahead you'll find the vast snowed-in lemon wedge of the Neoclassical Mikhailovsky Palace, designed by the ubiquitous court architect Carlo Rossi to resemble a Russian country house (it's the size of a city block). To the left, the flamboyant gold and tutti-frutti domes of Church of the Savior on the Blood. Built as a nationalist rebuke to this elegant and slavishly European city, the church will bring to mind the famous onion domes of St. Basil's in Moscow (no wonder Petersburg's Europhile architectural snobs wanted to dynamite it). To the right, the golden spire of the Engineers' Castle, a quirky apricot fortresslike chateau, erected on the orders of the rightly paranoid Czar Paul, who was strangled with his own sash a mere forty days after moving in. And, finally, in the distance across the Neva

River, the festively lit Soviet-era television tower, its construction supervised by a brigade of sturdy female comrades. There you have it — architectural hubris, nationalist reaction, regicide by sash, beautiful Socialist women conquering new heights — all out one window, all hemmed in by the bright winter snow, all of it looking hallucinatory, imposing, and anything but real.

No matter how much *gorilka* one puts away the previous night, in the wintertime it is important to wake up, drink some coffee, and get your galoshes on by 8:30 in the morning, while the sun is still rising. I eat a delectable hard-boiled egg laid by a scruffy post-Soviet chicken that has never met a Western hormone, and head for the Griboedov Canal. I find a spot on the bank next to the pedestrian Lion's Bridge, marveling at the four winged lions, their delicate foreheads dusted with snow, their mouths cleverly issuing the suspension cables that keep the whole structure intact. Later, I stroll down the massive Nevsky Prospekt — a combination of New York's Fifth Avenue, Chicago's Michigan Avenue, and L.A.'s Sunset Strip. I haven't been to the city in two years, and the changes shock me. The 24/7 pop culture parade that is now Russian television — one makeover show might as well be titled *Western Eye for the Slavic Guy* — has clearly had an effect. In the new Moscow-styled St. Petersburg the words *espresso* and *double latte* are as commonly heard as *default* and *bankruptcy*. In the city center, sushi and sashimi saturation is complete. Young people are looking less and less like refugees from a Slayer concert and are learning to wear Columbia mountain fleece jackets with abandon. Trying to keep out of a sudden rainstorm, I duck into the new Grand Palace mall at 44 Nevsky Prospekt. There is enough marble here to redo the Parthenon, but the actual patrons are scarce. Petersburg was recently ranked the tenth most expensive city in the world (New York was twelfth, by comparison; Tokyo topped the list), a paradox given the fact that the average citizen earns only a few thousand dollars a year, while fewer than half of Petersburg's men will survive until the retirement age of sixty. Sadly none of my Petersburg friends can afford one of the $8,000 Paula shot glasses at the fabulous but empty Moser glassware store on the mall's second floor, nor will they be raiding the nearby Escada, Bally, or Kenzo outlets anytime soon.

I cross the Neva River, gleaming patches of ice clogging its vast curving artery, to the city's fashionable Petrogradskaya side. After devoting a glance to the azure tiles and twin fluted minarets of the St. Petersburg mosque — reminiscent of the fabled mosques of the Silk Road city of Samarkand — I walk down Kronverk Prospekt to the mansion of the scandalous prima ballerina Matilda Kshesinskaya, lover of the ill-fated Nicholas II, the last czar of Russia. Imperial lovemaking aside, the Kshesinskaya mansion played a pivotal role in the history of the revolution: the Bolsheviks set up a base camp here, and Lenin took to haranguing agitated workers from its balcony. Inside, fittingly enough, one can find the Museum of Russian Political History, a collection of artifacts tracing Russia's miserable experiments with monarchism, Communism, capitalism, and any other ism to come along. There is a copy of the famous Soviet poster showing a gaggle of happy blond children thanking Comrade Stalin "for our happy childhoods." To get the gist of those "happy childhoods," I walk to another part of the museum where, resting eternally under glass, one can find a simple homemade doll in a black dress sewn by a female labor camp inmate for her young niece.

Luckily, Russians are adept at turning their political misfortunes into rich, sibilant laughter. A kitschy new restaurant called Lenin's Mating Call (*Zov Ilicha* in Russian) brings the whole Soviet era into perspective by interspersing Communist party speeches with Western pornography on a series of flat-screen televisions. If you're a budding grad student looking for a poststructuralist dissertation, look no further. My friend and I toast the portrait of a young red-goateed Lenin in a biker jacket hoisting a beer our way, then we make short work of the appetizers. Lenin's Mating Call may be a theme restaurant, but the food, surprisingly, is excellent. The *zakuski*, which are essentially vodka chasers, include a delicate salmon in vodka, slippery marinated black mushrooms, and a comforting plate of homey boiled potatoes in a thick mayo sauce. For our entrée we have the bear-meat *pelmeni* (Russian ravioli) — soft, buttery, and rich, imbued with a vague hint of winters comfortably spent in a lair. Our Komsomol uniform–clad young waitress smiles at us with all thirty-two of her beautiful teeth, a hammer-and-sickle armband snapped tight over one of her creamy thighs, while a woman's voice over the intercom breathlessly describes the revolutionary things she wants to do to a young pioneer boy. Brimming with vodka (and sundry desires), I head for the bathroom, where an LCD screen has been set up over the urinal. I never thought I would relieve myself while watching Andropov pinning medals on some Kazakh shepherd intercut with footage of buff California porn stars pinning each other to the mattress. I guess you could call this closure.

Kitsch and minimalism are locked in a daily struggle throughout St. Petersburg, and at the Triton restaurant, on the banks of the Fontanka River, kitsch is winning. It's a seafood restaurant, you see, but just in case you missed the point, there's a porpoise hanging from the ceiling, a waterfall dripping above your bouillabaisse, and actual aquariums set into the walls, floors, and even the toilet's water tank. Upon entering the joint I see a fat rich kid, about five years old, in a Dolce & Gabbana outfit sullenly gawking at the prized osetra sturgeon scurrying underfoot. I'm not sure who his parents are, but the restaurant is filled with several "proactive" Russian men in gray sports jackets and black turtlenecks, as well as the nine-foot-tall women in yellow leather pants who love them. Passing through, I catch snatches of conversation from two fellows at another table:

"What do we do about Sergei?"

"It's a delicate question."

Indeed. Meanwhile, as Sergei's future is settled, the outrageously priced food takes both good turns and bad. The tartare of salmon and tuna is pleasantly rife with spring onion and sea salt. The grilled Scottish salmon in cream sauce — the most simple dish around — is succulent, but the lobster is so tough it should be taken out back and roughed up a little. Possibly so should Sergei.

After the daylong gorging process is complete, it is time to turn to the spiritual. Tonight is Christmas Eve, according to the Russian Orthodox tradition. The date is not the only thing that differentiates Orthodox Christmas from our own. Unlike the dollar-denominated shop-a-thon back home, Christmas here is still a low-key affair, an austere meal of honey-soaked wheat kasha being one of the highlights. For the midnight Mass, I head to the city's main functioning church, the Kazan Cathedral, an elegant early-nineteeth-century rip-off of St. Peter's in Rome. Approaching the church past the snow-covered empty streets, I am mesmerized by the yellow-lit cupola and the sound of the bells slowly rising in pitch and purpose. Inside, the proceedings are suffused with a lavender glow, flickering amber candles, and overpowering incense. I see women in woolen scarves, their thick purple glasses hiding the kernels of blue eyes. On the previous day I visited the church to get permission for a British photographer to take pictures of the midnight Mass. I spoke to an angelic-looking young priest with a small flaxen mustache who gladly gave us permission. On the night of the Mass, the mustached priest is conducting the services, and we are confronted by an elderly church worker, his face as red as a beet, a single tooth in his crooked mouth. We tell him that a priest has blessed our request to photograph the service, but the old fellow's not buying it. "This is our holiday, our *Orthodox* holiday," he says, staring down my Jewish nose. "We don't need *your* people here."

"Merry Christmas," the British photographer says to him.

My Christmas does get merrier the next day when my friend K.'s girlfriend, Yanna, invites us to a holiday dinner in a small apartment in the southern suburbs. Yanna's family is from Yakutia (also called Sakha), a Russian republic that occupies most of the northeastern part of the Asian continent and is home to the Pole of Cold, the absolute coldest point in the Northern Hemisphere. As freezing as their land may be, the Yakuts receive us with a warmth, openness, and hospitality I find genuinely touching. Yanna's mother is a shamaness, and after I walk through the door she whips me with a white horse's tail to drive out evil spirits. After my whipping, we are treated to an incredible meal of pony rib meat practically falling off the bone, salty iced fish, and a smooth horse-blood sausage that takes me as close as I've ever come to experiencing the essence of an animal. By the end of the evening, thanks to either the horse-tail whipping or the medicinal bear intestine still sticking to the inside of my cheek, I emerge from the Yakuts' cozy lair with my flu finally vanquished.

My health restored, K. and I decide to finish off Christmas day with a trip to the Colorado Father strip club on the far side of Vasilevsky Island. Most of Petersburg's nightlife can be characterized by Susan Sontag's dictum on popular culture: "So bad it's good." And by that measure the Colorado Father (*Koloradsky Otets*) is very good. It's hard to tell why the club's owners decided that the great state of Colorado somehow represented their brand of melancholy vice, but the walls are indeed covered with huge murals of

mesas, cowboys, cacti, and (fairly or unfairly as far as the female
population of Colorado is concerned) women with gigantic asses.
Before heading into the Amsterdam room, where the actual stripping takes place, we give the disco a shot. Here girls of roughly student age release their Slavic pheromones to the music of 50 Cent,
their flea-market miniskirts held together by bobby pins and sheer
will. In the Amsterdam room, desperation and testosterone tickle
the nose in equal measure. After several vodka shots chased with
beer, I settle into another Dostoyevskian moment — feeding the G-
string of some poor damaged blond a series of one-hundred-ruble
notes whilst mumbling something about life and beauty and re-
demption. On Wednesdays, I'm told, the members of a male strippers' collective called the Colorado Stallions shake it up Western-
style. Luckily, it's Friday.

Later I meet my friend C. at the new and hip Dacha club near
Nevsky Prospekt. Picture the most crowded joint in Williamsburg,
Brooklyn, and multiply the body density by ten. I know it's the
weekend, but people are having way too much fun: overheated
twentysomethings crashing into one another's beer mugs, wide-col-
lared hipsters raucously losing their cool as their girlfriends manage to look like Pat Benatar without even trying. Otherwise all the
signs of a tenuously progressive atmosphere are here: Kraftwerk on
the sound system, NO MORE PUTIN! graffiti in the bathroom, sarcastic foosball loudly played in the back room. The décor, I must
note, is complemented by the fine Belarusian wallpaper in a jaunty
peacock motif; say what you will about Dacha, but you can't find
that in Williamsburg. Over the roar of the local multitudes, my
friend C., a long-entrenched expatriate, tells me that the new Petersburg is becoming way too rich for his blood. "Why don't you
leave?" I ask him. Yes, of course, he wants to leave, but then his
flash new Russian girlfriend in the woolen hat is just so damn cute.
I swill my beer and nod along. He's not going anywhere.

On my last day in Petersburg, I have a solitary, nonalcoholic lunch
at a restaurant simply called Moscow (*Moskva*). I nibble on the perfect veal kidneys in port wine while looking out the window at the
perfect panorama of the icy Neva River. Waiters in perfectly dis-
tressed jeans and T-shirts dash around tossing plates of $20 foie
gras to the perfectly coiffed new elite. Who wouldn't be happy?

And yet somehow, this is not how I want to end my visit. So I take the metro down to Moskovskaya Ploshchad, the enormous Stalin-era square where I spent the best part of my childhood.

A model of Soviet "gigantomania," the square is centered around a statue of Lenin with his coat sexily unfurling in the wind (some locals have dubbed him the Latin Lenin). The architecture is held up by an endless array of heavy Stalinist columns, one building's façade featuring workers, peasants, and soldiers marching eternally toward the bright Socialist future. If the year was 1979 and you were a child playing hide-and-seek with your father in the square's cluster of pine trees, there was the glorious feeling that you were a part of something bigger than your winter-red nose and fur-trimmed galoshes would indicate. More recently, the square's dramatic impact has been somewhat lessened by the Citibank branch down the street, the slot machines around the corner, the produce stand hawking bright oranges, ethereal red peppers, and glossy pears. At night, the square is at its most festive and imposing, with the columns lit up, the pine trees illuminated purple, blue, and green. If you close your eyes and stand still you can almost hear the whirring of bank machines, the revving of a Ford engine at a nearby car dealership.

My favorite building in Petersburg is just a few blocks from here. The raspberry-and-white candy box of the Chesme Church is an outrageous example of the neo-Gothic in Russia, made all the more precious by its location between the worst hotel in the world and a particularly gray Soviet block. The eye reels at the church's dazzling conceit, its mad collection of seemingly sugarcoated spires and crenellations, its utter edibility. Here is a building more pastry than edifice. Once, drawn by its candy-cane domes, I committed the ultimate sacrilege by getting my toy flying helicopter stuck in one of them. Today there are no children out on the streets, only beat-up-looking workers trudging toward a shaky tomorrow. Their faces wear an overcast gruffness that I remember all too well. Their strange new experiment with winter sloth is coming to an end. It is January 10, and in a few hours the holiday season will at last be over.

CHRISTOPHER SOLOMON

Let's Ski Korea

FROM *Ski*

ON THE FIFTH DAY of skiing in the Land of Almost Right — after hearing the Voice of God, watching malevolent puppets exert Confucian order on the lift line, even after an assault by a computerized toilet — I finally experience something that truly shakes me. The twitching leg does it. It's evening. Tall night-skiing towers line Muju's icy slopes, and in their weird lunar glow a not inconsiderable crowd swarms and bumps like moths beneath a porch light in August. Except the boy. The boy, he's a blur moving fast toward the bottom of the ski hill. He makes no attempt to turn. He doesn't scream. Remarkably, he makes no sound at all as he hits a restraining fence at twenty miles an hour. He hits so hard that momentum bends his body under the fence and sends him skittering thirty feet beyond. He's unconscious and immobile when I reach him. Except for his leg. His left leg is twitching spasmodically.

It seems a very long time before the boy opens his eyes. He sits up, swats at the snow on his pants, stands unevenly, and starts to gather his goggles and poles. Back in the lift line, Pom is waiting for me. Pom, a twenty-three-year-old university student and part-time ski patroller at Daemyung Vivaldi Park Ski World, is my guide and translator as I visit three of South Korea's top resorts. After the crash, Pom told a bystander to call the patrol. There, apparently, his interest in the matter ended.

For me, on the other hand, it's the worst crash I've seen in twenty years of skiing and my heart is pounding like Tito Puente on Benzedrine. I need to talk to someone. I need, as we say in America, to "process" this. That leg. Jesus. Didn't he notice that leg? Jesus. Pom looks . . . well, he looks rather bored at the moment.

"Did you see that?" I say. It comes out like a yelp. Pom's slack expression is the face of hard-won stoicism. Maybe it's the patroller in him. Or maybe it's the fact that he sleeps every night beside a border of two million land mines. When he does speak, his voice is a shrug.

"Not very unusual," he says.

Let us imagine for a moment that you are a skier in search of epic turns and big adventure. You board a 737 that climbs into the pinking western sky. You sit smugly with your tomato juice and your complimentary *Economist* as your airplane arcs over the world-class slopes of Vail and Keystone and the Wasatch legends of Alta and Snowbird before descending into LAX. There, you board a fatter plane and head out over the blue Pacific. Eleven hours later you arrive in South Korea, your mind cobwebby with jet lag. Still, you are excited. Now before you is the chance to plunder the slopes of a land that is 70 percent mountains yet remains terra incognita to Western skiers.

If you did this, you could say that you are an open-minded world traveler. You could say that you have an unslakable thirst for the undiscovered steep-and-deep — that you're a Magellan among powderhounds.

You'd be what the Koreans call *pah-bo*. Loosely translated, it means you are a damned fool.

If, however, you come for the sheer phenomenon that is skiing in South Korea — if you come to glimpse how it's done in this land that quite possibly holds the future of skiing — well, now you're on to something.

By some accounts, South Korea is home to the fastest-growing skiing scene in the world. Visits to the country's ski areas have ballooned nearly 75 percent over the past decade. This winter a thirteenth resort opened, and at least seven more are planned. Next year, car manufacturer Hyundai hopes to start building a ski area in North Korea, which would open the DMZ to tourists from the south. Korean détente, it seems, may yet arrive — on a pair of Völkl Supersports. Along with China, which now has more than two hundred ski areas, South Korea is where tomorrow's skiers are being grown.

Their embrace of the sport is all the more remarkable for the fact that the skiing in South Korea is — let us speak plainly, shall we? — breathtakingly awful. At least by the standards of the American West. Most of Canada. Europe. And pretty much anywhere else north of the horse latitudes where man has strung a rope tow, with the possible exception of the Midwest and Pennsylvania.

But this is beside the point. The more I learned about South Koreans' love for the sport that I, too, love, the more I wanted to see them enjoying it. What a wellspring of passion these people must have, that skiing's fragile flower can blossom in such rocky soil! What hardships a people must have endured to forge the heartiness needed to ski here! What heartiness that few soft-bottomed Americans could ever muster!

Before I leave, an expat American skier who lives in Seoul offers me some insight. Much in South Korea feels a nudge off-center, she says. This is a country in which yellow traffic lights precede greens as well as reds, with predictably dangerous results, she says. I think of my book about Korea, which speaks of a country where things are done both energetically and half-assedly, where the people "often appear incompetent, and yet they achieve." Across the crackling phone line, the expat skier says she has a phrase for this Korea. The Land of Almost Right, she calls it.

The way to the mountain is lined with fish. This is not a Zen koan. There are actually fields and fields of fish beside the road that leads to Korea's oldest ski slope, YongPyong.

"*Hwang-tae,*" says Pom, as we pull over the van.

"What?"

Pom produces an inscrutable device that looks like a pocket calculator and punches keys. "'Alaskan pollock,'" he reads. The fish, he says, are carted here from the docks to cure in the brutal winds that right now are blowing down from Siberia. "Specialty of the region," he says. The fish? I wonder. The wind? Outside, a million pairs of shriveling eyes stare up at the quilted sky. The air smells of snowflakes and low tide on a hot day. This combination strikes me as unpropitious. We pull back onto the road to YongPyong.

Americans like to think of skiing as a Thoreauvian escape. We like to push off on a quiet run beside still woods, to hear the swoosh of new snow beneath our skis, to feel the cold biting our face as we reconnect with nature.

At YongPyong, nature has been augmented by a ten-foot-tall television screen in the middle of the ski slope upon which, at this moment, a Korean model is rubbing foundation into her porcelain skin. Next to her is a slope lined with billboards of the size seen along interstate highways. Night skiing is big in South Korea, and the towers are ablaze with lights.

Pom and I head up for a few runs. I see that the giant television and the billboards and the truck that's playing cartoons — all these are nothing next to the noise. Speakers on the lift towers blare tinny Korean hip-hop. Ski patrollers blow traffic whistles. Every Korean owns a high-tech cell phone that makes American telephony look like so many tin cans and string, and each uses it ceaselessly. The slope is an aviary of electronic chirps and squeaks and barks and bleats. The noise is complete, it is enveloping, and the Koreans wear it as comfortably as a sweater.

Occasionally the thrum of hip-hop ceases and the Voice of God booms across the slopes. "What is she saying?" I ask Pom (for the Voice of God, in case you ever wondered, is female).

Pom cocks his head. "'Choose your slope as your ability.'"

Saturday morning, 9:00. Forty-six tour buses fill the parking lot. Every few minutes another bus arrives from Seoul. A few of the skiers inexplicably wear white surgical masks, as if there were something lurid and miasmic in the tart mountain air.

A food stall outside the mammoth base lodge sells curried hot dogs; another pours red ginseng lattes; a third hawks skewers soaking in hot broth beneath an English sign that reads "Fish Guts." English has cachet here. Vending machines sell cans of Let's Be Coffee and Pocari Sweat, which I never do plunk down a thousand won for because I never receive a satisfactory translation for *Pocari*.

The rental shop is busy. The lodge is busy. The line for the gondola is already crammed. Whoever dubbed South Korea "The Land of the Morning Calm" has obviously never skied here. I am reminded of the many cautions I have received about skiing in South Korea. "Total mayhem," one American ski consultant who worked here chuckled unhelpfully, "but they love it." The most recent warning came the previous evening, from another American, in the hotel lounge. "They ski," he said, "like they drive." This wouldn't be a bad thing if we were in, say, Sweden, and everyone were driving sensible Volvos, sensibly, on sensibly maintained roads. But South Korea has one of the highest traffic mortality rates in the world. Though things have improved from a decade ago, somehow this is not comforting.

And then there is what I have come to think of as the *juche* problem. Koreans have a deeply rooted belief in *juche*, or self-reliance. In other words, an amateur can tackle anything if he puts his mind to it. This goes some way toward explaining why there are lines everywhere this morning except at the Daegwalleong Ski School desk. Still, it is sunny and bright as we board the chairlift, and the attendant bows and smiles, which is nice.

I can think of many ways to describe what I experience next. Most of these include the words "pinball" and "blunt-force trauma." I learn that the quaint Western concept of skier density limits does not translate in a country where fifty million people live in a crawlspace the size of Pennsylvania. I watch Seoul-raised Pom glide through the crowds like water around rocks.

A few South Korean skiers are very talented. Pom is one of them. The rest are terrible. No, not terrible. Terrible and swift. The conditions don't help. The wind blows hard, drawing a bony finger down your spine but bringing little snowfall. Snow guns keep skiing alive. The resulting slopes are bulletproof, unforgiving, New Hampshirean. I see a hundred near-misses to bring a mother grief. I see men hit children. *Juche*, again. Yet no one gets angry, or apologizes. Another American expat says it's the best skiing he's seen in years.

Everywhere I see it — on billboards, the trail map, signs — I find myself drawn to the lavish Korean script called *han'geul*. To the Westerner, *han'geul* is a thing of chaos and beauty, with its dashes and swoops, its circles and beams and stone-stacks of ellipses, all sheltered by peak-roofed carats. The longer I stare, the more intriguing a secret each line becomes. What transcendental insights might be clapped up in each squiggle and tent!

One day in the summit lodge I stare at one particular sign so long that it infects me. I track down Pom. I bring him to the room. I show him. I ask him, a little excited, what it says, and wait for the beam of light.

"'Don't throw your cigarettes in the urinal'," reads Pom. Then he goes into a stall for a smoke.

That afternoon we head to YongPyong's crest, to a trail that's been bulldozed into the ridge to create a scenic top-to-bottom run. The scenic run is rather narrow and lined by a severe chain-link fence to keep skiers from dropping off the edge. The pinched run does not discourage snowboarders from sitting down in the middle and pulling out their cell phones. Others talk while skiing. Occasionally, men pull over and have a smoke and talk on their phones. Where some gather, more gather. It's like watching a blood clot forming. On the way downhill I see a ski patroller, a lonesome anticoagulant, standing over a snowboarder, blowing his whistle in the wind.

At 4:30, the lifts close and a pack of snowcats rolls out to Zamboni the ice. I watch a girl wearing her helmet backward return her rental skis. A few families head to the private karaoke rooms. By 6:00, when the night lights have chased off the twilight, a crowd lines up again as if it were a powder day. On the highway to the next ski resort, I watch a BMW try to pass a speeding ambulance.

At Vivaldi Park Ski World, each of the thirteen ski runs is named for a type of music. There is a yellow (intermediate) run called Jazz and a black run called Rock. Ballads, the bunny hill, is so littered with bodies it could be Flanders Field. At the bottom of Hip-Hop is a small patch of practice moguls that have been painstakingly carved by hand. Vivaldi's modest size hasn't dissuaded the giant Korean developer that owns it from building an underground mall and four Trumpesque condominium towers across the street — the latest of them painted shell pink.

In the lift line an attendant stands on a raised wooden platform, a sort of traffic cop with a beauty-pageant sash over her parka and a furry puppet on each hand. She is waggling the puppets in a way that seems vaguely menacing.

"Why does she shake her hands like that?"

"Good service," says Pom, elliptically. Pom is a part-time patroller at Vivaldi. He points out — a little smugly, I think — that at YongPyong there was not much hand-waggling, which, I gather, doesn't say much for YongPyong.

"What does her sash say?"

"'Don't drink alcohol.'"

I wouldn't mind some gut-warming *soju* about now. If possible, it's even colder here than at YongPyong, and colder still once night falls. We stop for a cup of fish broth at a slopeside stand. The air is filled with the whanging guitars of Korean power ballads. I can hear the futile patrol whistles being blown at prostrate skiers on the bunny hill, persistent and ignored, like the mating call of some hardy but senseless winter bird.

On one of our evening chairlift rides, I decide I need to meet more Koreans. They're a famously gregarious people once you get to know them, I have read. A little standoffish to strangers, I have also read. All right, actually rather rude to strangers at times. But surely they'll want to chat with a gregarious American.

When we board the chairlift with two guys in their thirties, I see my opening. I nudge Pom. "Ask them, 'Hi, how are you doing? How's your skiing?'"

"Ah, no," says Pom.

"Why not?"

Pom says nothing.

I'm a little annoyed with Pom. "What would they say?"

"'Are you crazy? Are you mad? Do you want to fight with me?'" replies Pom.

He lights up a cigarette. We ride for a while in silence.

After sundown, Vivaldi's underground arcade fills with kids. They milk long games out of each five-hundred-won coin. Except for one. None of them, I notice, is very good at the skiing video game.

The next morning, we rise early to watch Pom's ski patrol colleagues get ready to open the slopes. Two dozen young men stand at attention in their red jackets and black pants.

"Now we sing," the head patroller barks in Korean. They plant their poles and waggle their arms up and back. They sing a child's song from a cartoon. They sing a song old folks would know.

"*Motjin* patrol!" says the leader. "Great patrol!"

"*Motjin* patrol!" say the patrollers.

"When we fight, we fight great," the patrollers shout in Korean. "When we love, we love hot." They circle up to stretch their legs. The whistle comes out. Tweet. Tweet. Tweeeeeeeet. Switch legs. Then they shout some more.

I ask Pom what they're saying.

"'We open the slopes. We close the slopes. Daemyung patrollers, fighting! Cheer up!'" says Pom.

Afterward, I ask a patroller to open his knapsack. Inside: a few pieces of wood for a splint, a traffic wand like those used to guide

747s across the tarmac, an Ace bandage. And at the bottom, a few tired-looking Band-Aids.

By the time we reach Muju Resort, Korea's largest and highest ski area, I am flagging. Five days of anemic chopstick technique has Pollocked my ski bib with enough chili sauce and ramen noodles to make soup. The best skiers, who once impressed me with their clean carves across blue ice, now only shame me; everyone else terrifies me. In the night's small hours, the echoes of ski patrol whistles direct the unruly traffic of my kimchee-fired dreams.

Muju's centerpiece is the Hotel Tirol, a larch-and-lederhosen hotel that out-Tyrols anything I've ever seen in Tyrolia. I slouch to the bathroom. There, the high-tech Samsung toilet designed to coddle with all manner of lavage and cottony air instead startles me with its hydraulic vigor. I leap up, and a jet of water squirts me in the face.

All of this aside, Muju looks to be the most promising mountain yet, with its two peaks and its claim to Korea's longest and steepest runs and a fenced-off track for snowmobile rides.

The steepest run is closed — "too icy" — so Pom and I try the longest run. Silk Road is a ridgeline stroll that milks its misty Asian mountain-painting panoramas for as long as possible, until a slope designer remembered that people have to get home, whereupon the run corkscrews dramatically. To counter this, crash pads have been stitched together at the most dangerous curves, each emblazoned with warnings in both Korean and English that blur into a sort of guerrilla haiku:

Danger!
Please don't speed Please don't speed Please don't speed Please
    don't speed
Danger! Please don't speed
Danger! Danger! Danger! Danger!

The next morning I pack my bags and walk to the window. The sun is bright and warm. The bull wheel is turning for the beginner's slope below. I watch from my high perch, feeling once again a pathos rising within me for these people, like sap with the warm sun. And then here he comes. Another boy roaring down toward the hotel. I've seen this before. He's actually going to hit the building, I think. He doesn't — barely. He crashes in front of the Edelweiss Terrace.

My peripheral vision, sharpened from five days of heavy use, picks up another skier bearing down on the hotel. He hits the restraining fence that guards a section of the sun deck. The fence trembles but holds him. He doesn't move. No one goes to him.

My window is wide open. I could call out. But now here comes a third. She is almost heat-seeking in her merciless trajectory toward the first. She won't miss. She's going to put a ski tip through his sternum. She crashes at the last moment, however, feet from the hotel's concrete walkway and feet from the first boy.

The girl laughs. The boy whose life she nearly snuffed out laughs. They pick each other up, brush Muju's fake snow from their parkas, and head back up the slope. I leave the window. When I return, the skier in the fence is gone, too.

PATRICK SYMMES

A Peaceful Angle

FROM *Outside*

I SKIPPED a lot of classes in high school, so it wasn't until our soot-streaked Mi-8 helicopter slipped down into the northernmost valley of outermost Mongolia and began whirring us above the Uur River at little more than treetop level that I finally caught up with Hemingway 101.

For three hours, I had been glued to a porthole, watching the wrinkled autumn skin of the earth unveil itself as we flew north, over open desert, into rolling plains, and out toward the Russian border. Each range of hills was steeper than the last, and finally some trees — Siberian larch and pine — began to appear. When we dropped toward the last valley, I saw, flashing below us at a hundred miles an hour, the telltale black circles and twisted thickets left by a forest fire. The fire had been out for several years, but long stretches of gray hillside and tangles of stripped trunks revealed its former rage.

Over the summer I'd been on a sort of literary crack binge, hiding in the cool aisles of library stacks with all the Hemingway stories I was supposed to have read decades ago. But only now, from the Olympian vantage of a Russian helicopter, did I abruptly comprehend one of his most obvious metaphors. The cold fire down below was the same ash-strewn wreckage that greets Nick Adams in the opening sentence of "Big Two-Hearted River," perhaps the prototype for all American fishing tales. In this 1925 story, Adams walks out of that burn, away from his nameless anxieties, carrying a fly rod. Going into the wilderness of Michigan's Upper Peninsula, he finds his "good place," a section of pine forest beside a river marbled with trout. Once the tent was up, "nothing could touch him."

I was having a busy month of discoveries. A late bloomer, I'd gotten married three weeks earlier, my first time on that journey. And now here I was making my first trip to Mongolia, to catch my first taimen, one of the world's most elusive freshwater fish. A massive salmonid once common from Bohemia to Hokkaido, the taimen is making one of its last stands here, in the high, cold, pure rivers of Mongolia's remote watersheds. This rare opportunity is what filled the helicopter with Texas businessmen, doctors, and millionaire factory owners, as well as two New Yorkers: me and James Nachtwey, a legendary globe-trotting photographer for *Time*. We were all here to catch a big fish, maybe the fish of a lifetime.

This was also, unaccountably, my first flight in a helicopter. On the tarmac in Ulan Bator, Mongolia's capital, I had asked Jim for advice. He'd been flying in helicopters for decades, whisking in and out of war zones. Although he didn't say so, Jim had been in Darfur the week before, and the next week, no doubt, it would be some other terrible place. In *War Photographer,* a 2001 documentary about his career, Jim was shown calmly snapping away in burning Balkan villages and shootouts in Palestine. His terrifying pictures from September 11, taken at the feet of the twin towers, open the book *War,* a collaboration of the nine photographers in his agency. Living two miles from ground zero, I only felt like the north tower had fallen on my head; in Jim's case, it nearly had. Despite all this — or perhaps because of it — he had a boyish enthusiasm for adventures like this one, for the innocence of chasing wild fish in wild places. And he loved helicopters.

"They are magic carpets," Jim said, with his usual grin. Jim is a man of few words, and his advice was to the point. "Pee before getting in," he said — there were no toilets. For once, a useful tip.

When we landed and began to unpack, I could not contain my idiotic enthusiasm for my recent discoveries in the field of American literature. I told Jim how I had finally realized, while riding in the Mi-8, that the burned forest in the opening of "Big Two-Hearted Riv —"

"It was the war," Jim interrupted, not looking up from his duffel bag. He kept unpiling his clothes, sorting the fishing gear from the fleece and the socks.

"The fire was the war," he said.

Mongolia is a land of brutal superlatives. With a mean temperature of twenty-eight degrees, Ulan Bator, known as "U.B.," really is the coldest capital in the world. And with fewer than five people per square mile, Mongolia actually does have the lowest population density of any country. Despite a tourism boom — up 50 percent just last year — and a gold-mining rush, half its citizens are still nomadic, husbanding animals over vast spaces of desert and foothill. The place is a synonym for emptiness, the thing beyond the beyond.

Perfect fishing country, in other words. The helicopter had dropped off the Texas doctors in a lower camp, and we were set down sixty miles to the north. This camp, run by a Montana company, Sweetwater Travel, was on the banks of the Uur River, which drains the high timber country east of Lake Hovsgol, Mongolia's biggest, and flows down into the Eg River and eventually on to Lake Baikal, in Russia. The small encampment included five *gers*, the traditional Mongolian tents of thick felt laid over a round frame of willow switches.

There was also a log cabin for dining, and on that late-September night, over a dinner of Mongolian noodles with beef, we met our fellow elect. The guides were both Montanans. Dan Vermillion was a Livingston lawyer who had abandoned the bar to open these waters to catch-and-release fly-fishing a few years ago with his brothers and a Mongolian partner. Charlie Conn was the Candide of the Rockies; upon meeting me he announced that I was about to catch a *big* taimen and never deviated from that faith. His cowgirl wife, Wendy, had flown in with us, as had Bill and Sharon Sumner, irrepressible Texans in their mid fifties. Sharon proved to be a sharp caster, with a game attitude and a balanced personality, which was vital, given that her husband was an angling maniac. Between stints rescuing his plastic-bag factory from one crisis or another, he fished all over the world. He'd tried to break the addiction with golf or hunting, but nothing else worked. Taimen have been known to burst out of the water to swallow prairie dogs neat. Bill had come all the way to Mongolia to see if the world's biggest freshwater salmonid would sate his fish lust once and for all.

Bill wasn't just from Texas; he was from TEXAS. He liked speaking loud, and he liked speaking his mind. About five seconds after we sat down to eat, he asked Nachtwey the question I'd been trying to avoid all day.

"SO, JIM," he bellowed. "I HEARD YOU GOT BLOWED UP IN EYE-RACK. WHAT HAPPENED?"

The first day of fishing was sweet, which should have been a warning. We rolled out in two green johnboats and were soon in warm sunshine along open, sweeping bends in the river. The Uur came out of a canyon here, fast, and made a deep cut into the valley floor. Jim hooked up on his third cast.

In no time he held a thrashing monster in the shallows. It was a mottled, flashing gray and had a disturbingly prehistoric look to it, with a wide mouth, supermodel lips, and rows of sharp-looking teeth. We netted it and photographed it, and I measured it at thirty-six inches. This wasn't quite one of the legendary fish of the Uur, but it was big enough that Jim had trouble holding it out of the water when Dan Vermillion reached in with a blue plastic rivet gun and drove a numbered tag through the dorsal fin. Part of Sweetwater's catch-and-release regimen involves tagging and tracking the taimen, to fill in the gaps about their habits.

Dan used a fishing technique called drop-dragging, which means floating downstream with an anchor tied behind the boat. Taimen fishing requires long, languid casts, each one covering as much water as possible, and slowing the boat helps. We were tossing five-inch poppers with sparkling tails, which landed like old sneakers and threw a wake that screamed *Eat me!* halfway across the valley.

Cast. Cast. Cast. Then cast some more. We'd been warned, repeatedly, that taimen are finicky creatures, hard to find and harder to catch. I'd made 150 casts by lunch, without hooking a thing. In the afternoon the temperature dropped to the forties and the wind picked up. Hurling Chernobyl squirrels into this gale was futile, swinging the heavy rods and lines a sustained torture.

But once you've seen a photograph of a man holding a fish the size of a golden retriever, you believe you will catch one that big yourself. On subsequent days, even Charlie's genetic optimism ("This is the cast . . . OK, I can feel it this time . . .") wasn't enough to summon the taimen. Twenty-inch lenok, a kind of proto-trout,

were there for the taking, but we foolishly ignored them in our re-
lentless hunt for taimen.

Each day the lower reaches of the forest were gilded with more
defectors to autumn, and the upper watershed was soon a golden
brocade woven tightly around the last green holdouts. We experienced all the side effects of wilderness fishing: the ice-cold water
down the back of your underpants; the split thumbs; dogs howling
all night at the wolves; the frosty kiss of an outhouse seat at 4:00
A.M. Jim and I hit the boat at dawn, fished hard all morning and
then all afternoon, floating or afoot.

"Man, this is melancholy," Jim volunteered one afternoon, from
a hunched position in the bottom of the boat, ice coating his boots.
For one of the world's foremost combat photographers, that's really saying something.

People expect photojournalists to twitch and freak, Dennis Hop-
pers of the Apocalypse. But twenty-five years of covering wars had
honed Jim rather than deformed him, stripping away the unnecessary and removing the neurotic. He was full of self-control, a
drinker of club soda who listened carefully and looked where he
stepped. War had rubbed him down into one of the most serene
and sane men I've ever met.

In the log cabin that first night, when Big Bill demanded the
story of what had happened in Baghdad, Jim had paused for a
long moment. Then he gave a barren answer. With all the guides
and clients leaning forward, he said, in a monotone, that someone had thrown a grenade into the Hummer he was riding in. He
had taken some shrapnel in the knee. The *Time* writer with him
had lost his hand. The two soldiers had been discharged for their
injuries.

Everyone sat there, waiting for the rest of the story. But that was
it. Twenty seconds. Just the facts. Jim was a terrible storyteller, probably on purpose. He spoke with his camera.

When we were alone, hiking one day, Jim did finish the Baghdad
story. But it was comedy, not tragedy. He fell into giggles as he related the fallout of that night. Bleeding and stunned, he'd been
evacuated to an American medical unit. But while doctors cut the
shrapnel not just from his knee but from his leg, stomach, face,
hand, and groin, someone had stolen his wallet. It took Jim six
months to replace all the contents. "That's the only thing that re-

ally bothered me," he said, laughing at himself. Blown up by the enemy and then robbed by your own side.

The attack had real consequences. Jim had been laid up for months and still carried a satchel full of medications. Half a year later, he was once again agile as a goat, ready to cover tsunamis and slow-moving social catastrophes. But he couldn't run, and that meant no more assignments to the front lines for the time being. "There hasn't been a war yet where I didn't have to run," he said.

I'd had to run for it a few times myself. For more than a decade I'd covered insurgencies in Colombia, Cambodia, Nepal, and Afghanistan, always at boot level, among the peasant fighters and mad Marxists. I'd grown tired of tear gas and heavily armed teenagers, of having my sources arrested or, in one case, killed, of walking into minefields and tangling with mobs. And yet I'd only glimpsed, as through a curtain, the world where Jim lives almost without pause.

This peripatetic life doesn't lend itself to long-term personal relationships, so, like Nick Adams, I'd begun to walk out of my own burned past, searching, in wilderness and family, for that elusive "good place." I was settling down. In the boat one day, I told Jim about my recent wedding and the fact that my wife was secretly pregnant. We hadn't told anyone, not even our parents, because there had been a miscarriage earlier in the year.

"How old were you when you got married?" Jim asked.

"Forty," I said. Jim is fifty-seven and still a bachelor.

"So," he said. "There's hope for me."

Later, as we drop-dragged through a slow, emerald section of the river, he let slip why he was here. We weren't catching anything, and I was in a black mood, but Jim sailed along, sublimely happy. After yet another cast to a promising spot that produced nothing, he said, "That's why I like fishing. You have this sense of hope." Each cast was a flick toward possibility. A blank slate.

"Palpable hope," he said.

We ate lunch sometimes in a broad meadow, speckled with horses and the ruins of a Buddhist monastery. Dan Vermillion was working with the Tributary Fund, a Montana-based nonprofit devoted to protecting native species by collaborating with indigenous cultures. A local monk, perhaps mindful of the fund's contribution to rebuilding the Dayan Derkh monastery, had ruled that Buddhist sutras condemning the unnecessary harming of animals might be relaxed for catch-and-release fishing if the sport could help protect the species.

Dan was hoping that a Buddhist endorsement would do more than justify a sport fishery. Mongolia's rivers are salted with flakes of alluvial gold, and one mine using cyanide extraction was already operating within earshot of the Uur. There was also proposed placer mining, which would involve ripping up the entire streambed, wiping out the taimen and much else. A "faith-based conservation" movement, as Dan called it, was crucial to stopping the mines and, more important, stopping taimen poaching by Chinese and Russian meat fishermen. Foreigners, too, were having outbreaks of faith. One grateful angler had sent a check for $25,000 to the Tributary Fund; after my visit, the same client contributed another $150,000.

Upstream one afternoon, I hauled in two twenty-inch baby taimen in quick succession, and looked up to see Jim waving at me from the far bank. Dan picked me up in the boat and we went over to find Jim paused over a set of bear tracks in the sand.

"Siberian brown bear," Dan said as we slowly followed the paw prints up from the water's edge, across a beach, and down into a tributary stream. "He better watch out," Dan said. The tracks were heading out of the Uur Valley, toward human settlements. The bear would get shot there and sold in parts for black-market medicine and trophies.

With the Tributary Fund, Dan had arranged for field scientists from the University of Wisconsin and the University of Nevada–Reno to monitor the taimen. Protecting this paradise required some proof of the value of these fish, of the size of their population, of their migration patterns and appeal to sport fishermen. The scientists had their own *ger* camp a half mile from ours and were busy putting radio transmitters into the bellies of captured fish — anesthetizing the taimen, slicing them open, and suturing them back tight. They named each fish before releasing it, so that the river was now dotted with radio-beeping taimen named Snoop Dogg, Pumpkin, and — the very largest, a five-footer weighing in at around one hundred pounds — Anna Nicole. We fishermen had a small role to play; in addition to tagging our catches, Dan had volunteered us as fish herders.

That's how I found myself drinking whiskey in my underwear during the season's first light snowfall. I had roared upriver in an aluminum skiff with Zeb Hogan, a curly-haired Wisconsin fish biologist, and Brant Allen, an experienced taimen researcher from UC Davis. Brant had asked us to help make a "visual survey," which turned out to mean swimming down the Uur, three abreast, trying to drive the fish toward Zeb's Nikonos camera. At a long, gentle curve in the river, we unloaded the boats and started warming ourselves pre-dunk with Johnnie Walker Black and a driftwood fire.

The view encompassed every combination of wild beauty, with steep, snow-dusted mountains in one place and bright sun falling on yellow larch in another. Some scholars believe that our love of spectacular landscapes may be less the product of sentiment than of natural selection. As early as 1.5 million years ago, they argue, our ancestors were genetically imprinted to favor views like this: a valley with hunting grounds; grass to attract animals; a river with clean water; trees for ambush and escape. According to this "woodland-mosaic hypothesis," we are drawn to the patchwork of nature. Just as trout stalk the seam between two currents, we reach for the borders between states of being.

Hopping from foot to foot, we wrestled into dry suits, masks, and snorkels, adding neoprene hoods, booties, and gloves against the cold. We flailed into the Uur and were immediately swept downstream, bobbing like corks and just as helpless. Before I could even gesture at it, the first taimen was gone. But there was another, at once, a silvery juvenile in the lee of a rock. It dropped back warily, looking a bit surprised by my arrival. I lifted a hand to start herding and immediately flipped upside down. By the time I righted myself, I'd spotted another taimen and a pair of lenok.

All week I had angler's blindness: because I caught few fish, I believed there were few fish. But here it became obvious there was a taimen or a lenok for every twenty feet of good river. Brant and Zeb had flushed as many as I had. We got out, laughing for no reason. A few seconds on the bank, in the wind, was enough to send me jogging upstream toward the fire.

As the Dalai Lama might say, torturing a fish ain't kosher. That night, our fifth in camp, I had a nightmare in which my karmic payback was to be reborn as a worm. The next morning Jim looked over from his Mickey Mouse mattress on the far side of the *ger* and said he, too, was sleeping badly, dreaming a lot.

"War dreams?" I asked.

"No," he replied, rolling over. "Those are different."

There was no escaping the world, even here. Jim carried a tiny short-wave radio, but in these high valleys we could hear only Chinese and Russian voices. Fishing is thieving time from that outer world, a way of escaping from responsibilities, news cycles, and the tiny vibrations under the floorboards that signal the approach of some new existential tsunami. Fly-fishing may be an indefensible activity, but play, rest, beauty, and freedom are crucial to sanity and survival. Time, however, doesn't pause just because we do. Charlie had a satellite phone in his tent, and I used it to call home. Normally I preferred my wilderness deep and disconnected, but my expectant wife had been feeling poorly before I left.

The signal bounced off a geosynchronous bird and jingled a receiver in Brooklyn. My wife picked up, in tears. Something was wrong. She was in terrible pain.

The signal coughed and sputtered, making gibberish of the simplest words. "Miscarriage," she said. "The doctors think it might require surgery." In less than a week, perhaps, depending.

For thirteen minutes and forty-six seconds my wife and I talked, and I hung up the phone to the sound of her crying.

The love of remote places, the unreasonable desire to know all of this world, leaves us hostage to fate. My father had been diagnosed with terminal cancer when I was living on another continent. Standing in an airport once, I learned from voice mail that my apartment and everything in it had been destroyed by fire. And now, another lost pregnancy.

Surgery. In days. After I hung up, I said to myself what I had just said to her, in the thirteenth minute: I will be there.

I wanted to go home. Now. But wilderness is unmoved by our needs. That is the point in seeking it, and it is a sharp point. Now, in Mongolia, means three days from now. There was no way out until Monday, when the orange Mi-8 would pick us up shortly after dawn.

I counted the days on my fingers. Friday, Saturday, Sunday, Monday. A lifetime. If I could get out of Ulan Bator by Tuesday, I might reach South Korea Wednesday, Los Angeles the day after that. Then, just maybe, I could make it to New York in time.

In one week the trees had surrendered their colors, the nighttime temperatures had plummeted, and the rivers were shutting down. The taimen vanished from knowledge then. Local lore held that they migrated up the Eg to Lake Hovsgol, or downstream to Lake Baikal, but the scientists' partial evidence indicated that they probably stayed right where they were.

I willed myself to believe that the earth would spin, the river would flow. The aircraft would come. And on Sunday, with one finger left on my calendar, I fished.

Charlie had seen, once, a big taimen resting in a deep bend of the river. We drifted quietly down into it and he pointed out where an old landslide had poured down a bank into the water. "That's where you're gonna catch him," he said.

On the last day of the last week of the brief fishing season on the last river full of taimen, I made one last cast. I dragged an immense black popper across the current, and the hit was so big that I thought Jim had thrown a bowling ball into the water. I hooked, played, and then, after twenty seconds, lost the fish. The mouths of taimen are hard as metal plates, and they throw off a lot of hooks.

The foam fly bobbed to the surface as the blood ran out of my face. Charlie had said a hundred times that taimen will come back around and hit a fly again. Paralyzed, I let the fly ride there, every ounce of attention coiled into my hands, but nothing happened.

Yet luck is made. Second chances are made. I lifted the fly, arced a single false cast, and dropped it back over by the landslide. Nothing. In despair I pulled it in toward the boat, slowly, the way Charlie had taught me. This time the taimen hit with a white-water splash full of teeth, dived back down with a flash of dark tail, and then the fly and the fish came tight on the line, thrashing.

By the time I wrestled it in, my arm was trembling with lactic exhaustion. Taimen are not spectacular fighters, but their size and weight make it a brutal contest. "Thirty-seven inches," Charlie said, looking up from the net. Almost a meter long. This wasn't Anna Nicole, but the fish was fat enough to melt over my fingers like Monterey Jack in a microwave. Holding the sleek gray beast out of the water, posing for photographs, I accumulated some seriously bad karma.

Before releasing it, we studied a deep, round scar in its back. The fish appeared to have survived a stabbing by poachers, who use long wooden tridents. I revived it until my fingers were numbed by the Uur, and the taimen abruptly kicked its way free.

Five minutes later we saw the fish one last time. It was finning slowly against the sandy bottom, down in the black heart of the river. Tired, but still alive. A survivor.

I took Jim's advice and peed before getting into the helicopter, and the magic carpet had us in Ulan Bator by lunch. A veteran of many goodbyes, Jim simply handed me his old copies of *Time* and caught a flight to Beijing. Then Central Asia kicked in: a sudden windstorm shut down the airport, stranding me in the capital, amid broken sidewalks and construction cranes, for more than a day.

The phrase "My wife is in the hospital" can melt the coldest hearts, and once I reached South Korea I was allowed to simply walk onto the next direct flight to New York. We burned up and over the glacial reaches of Alaska, nicked the Arctic Circle at thirty-three thousand feet, and finally, fourteen hours later, dropped into New York, bathed in solar radiation and unwatchable movies the whole way.

From there, everything went terribly, shockingly right. I stumbled into the hospital just as my wife was signing the consent form for anesthesia. When I dropped all my fishing gear, a cloud of Mongolian dust rose into the sparkling room.

The surgery was far worse in anticipation than in the actual event. Twenty brief minutes and a clean bill of health, with walking papers that afternoon. That night we lay in bed, exhausted, infinitely relieved, listening to the elevated train rumble past our brick house and to the vain wailings of car alarms down by the Gowanus Canal.

So that is one last reason to go to Mongolia, to go such a terrible distance away. You have to learn that paradise is not a silver creature in a black stream lined with pine trees. I'd found my good place. Nothing could touch us here.

Speaking of Soup

FROM *The New Yorker*

I TRY NOT TO LET a decade pass without renewing my assault on Spanish, which I keep hearing described as an easy language to learn. In the nineties, in preparation for a trip to northern Spain, I bought myself a videotape Spanish course in the form of a sixteen-episode soap opera — what Latin Americans call a *telenovela* — about a young lawyer who finds love while investigating what happened to her client's first wife. I got so that I could understand the actors fairly well, but when I arrived in Santiago de Compostela I was less successful at understanding people who did not keep repeating, slowly and very clearly, sentences like "Rosario did not die in the war; she escaped that tragedy, thank God." When I decided last winter to regroup my forces, it occurred to me that Ecuador might be a good place to study Spanish this go-around. I had in mind Cuenca, around Holy Week. From what I'd gathered during a previous trip to Ecuador, Holy Week is the only time of year you can get *fanesca* — an exceedingly thick and hearty soup, heavy on the beans. I adore *fanesca,* and, given my record in trying to solve the mysteries of a foreign tongue, I figured that having a particularly appealing fallback made a lot of sense.

Cuenca is a graceful colonial city in the part of the Andes that Ecuadorans call the Southern Highlands. Although it's Ecuador's third-largest city, it wasn't connected by paved road to the rest of the country until the sixties. Among Ecuador's urban-dwellers, Cuencans are thought of as the most traditionalist in matters of religion and culture. I'm a traditionalist myself, at least when it comes to the food associated with various holidays. When Hanuk-

kah arrives, I expect potato latkes. I favor candy corn on Halloween. I am perfectly willing to forgo Christmas fruitcake, but that is
about the extent of my flexibility. (The campaign I carried on some
years ago to change the national Thanksgiving dish from turkey
to spaghetti carbonara was a matter not of straying from a holiday
tradition but of attempting to build a stronger holiday tradition
around a more historically appropriate and, if I may say so, considerably tastier dish.) For years, I went to Brooklyn every New Year's
Day to join some friends from North Carolina in eating Hoppin'
John, the dish that many Southerners serve for good luck every
January 1. Eventually, my North Carolina friends moved away, and
I haven't felt entirely comfortable with a fresh January since. I
knew there was every reason to believe that during Holy Week I
could have expected to find *fanesca* not just in Cuenca but also in
Quito, or even in comparatively secular and cosmopolitan Gua-
yaquil, the port city that serves as the commercial center of Ecuador. Still, it never hurts to be certain.

If I'd had any doubts about my choice of cities, they were erased
as soon as I arrived, ten days or so before Easter. Right down the
street from my hotel, I found a language school that offered one-
on-one instruction, and I took a written placement test on the spot
— a test I thought I'd managed pretty well until I got to a final section on the subjunctive. (I've spent some time since then contemplating the possibility that I might be too old for the subjunctive.)
Both of my teachers turned out to be natives of the city who were as
knowledgeable about local customs as they were about Spanish
grammar. Also, they spoke Spanish as clearly as the lawyer in my
telenovela.

They both assured me that the custom of families eating *fanesca*
on Good Friday remained strong in Cuenca, and that many restaurants would be serving it during the entire week before that. My
first trip to one of Cuenca's markets made it obvious that I was
about as close to the source of *fanesca*'s ingredients as I could get
without living in the middle of a bean patch. All the vegetables and
spices required — corn, for instance, and fava beans and a couple
of kinds of squash — grow in the area, and some of them apparently don't make it as far as Guayaquil, which is only thirty minutes
away by air. That may be because the distribution system seems to
consist largely of indigenous women who come to the market from

the countryside, many of them in the bright-colored flared skirts and high-crowned panama hats that can make even a small woman of some years look rather, well, zippy. In the markets, they sit behind gunnysacks of what their families have grown — ten or twelve kinds of potatoes, or outsized corn kernels of various ages, or a selection of beans so large and potatoes so small that even one of those compulsive veggie connoisseurs who frequent markets like Union Square, in Manhattan, or the Ferry Building, in San Francisco, would have to do some close inspection to make certain that she wasn't on the path to making her signature bean salad out of spuds by mistake.

Cuencans may not be as strict about some Easter customs as they once were — partly, it's thought, because so many of them have in recent years spent time working in somewhat looser societies, like the United States. But many families, I was told by my teachers, still observe the custom of visiting seven churches on the evening before Good Friday, a task that requires devotion but not much walking in the churchy center of the city. Both of my teachers said that as children they were not permitted on Good Friday to wear bright clothes or to play a musical instrument or to listen to music other than sacred music. They were also not permitted to bathe, since an old belief in the area holds that anyone who bathes on Good Friday might be transformed into a fish. I noticed that *Vive Cuenca*, a bilingual booklet of local events that is published each month, finished up its description of this belief by saying, "Take care! Would not be you the first to be converted in one small fish, for not putting care to this myth" — a small witticism that served to give me some idea of how my Spanish must have sounded to my instructors all these years.

Exactly a week before Good Friday, I scored my first *fanesca*, right on schedule, at a small but pleasant restaurant in downtown Cuenca called Ceres. The *fanesca* did not disappoint; it matched the memory I'd preserved of the *fanesca* I had come across half a dozen years before, in the course of a ceviche ramble that, purely by luck, happened to overlap with Holy Week. *Fanesca* has a base of salt cod cooked in milk and thickened with pumpkin seeds. Traditionally, it contains twelve different beans or grains — one for each of the twelve apostles, some people say. Floating on top — or, more likely, lying on top, since this is a marginally liquid bowl of soup — you normally find part of a hard-boiled egg and a miniature empanada or two and often some plantain. My teachers told me that as Good Friday approaches the children of the family often act as assistant peelers and soakers and washers and choppers. Still, when you gaze into a bowl of *fanesca* it is difficult to avoid the suspicion that the mother or grandmother in charge of the kitchen serves it only once a year because once a year is often enough for her to spend all that time preparing a dozen vegetables — just as Jewish mothers of traditional habits may think that once a year is often enough to risk losing bits of knuckle to that potato shredder in the process of making the Hanukkah latkes the old-fashioned way.

When my teachers heard during afternoon classes that after having a *fanesca* for my midday meal I intended to have another one for dinner that evening — at El Maíz, a restaurant that describes its food as Cuencan rather than Ecuadoran — they looked at me the way an American might look at someone who had just announced that he intended to have two Thanksgiving dinners. In a Cuencan home on Good Friday, they explained, a bowl of *fanesca* is a meal in itself, except for something like fruit for dessert, and supper that evening tends to be light. It's true that when I was about halfway through the *fanesca* at Ceres — I'd calculated that I could finish the bowl if I paused for a moment to get my second wind — it occurred to me that this couldn't have been what my mother had in mind when she told me to finish my vegetables. On the other hand, my window of opportunity was not wide. I thought about saying to my teachers, "So many *fanescas,* so little time," but by the time I had constructed that in Spanish the moment had passed.

Being able to say anything I wanted to in Spanish before the moment had passed was what I'd been daydreaming about. I was thinking of the day when my response to a particularly good *fanesca* (the only kind of *fanesca* I've ever experienced) would no longer be limited to "delicious" or "very tasty, thank you." I could envision myself pushing back from the table and making a statement to the waiter that was as complex as the dish itself — something like "I can't take leave of this glorious establishment without saying, in utmost sincerity, that the *fanesca* I've just had the honor of consuming made my heart soar, or at least go pitter-patter, and I want to emphasize that each and every bean had a valiant role to play in

what was, when all is said and done, a perfectly blended and modu-
lated work of art." In that daydream, the waiter is so impressed by
my eloquence that he offers me seconds. I decline, with a short
speech that reminds him of something he once read in a story by
Jorge Luis Borges.

My teachers didn't seem to find it odd that most of my questions in
the first couple of days of classes were about restaurants and local
delicacies. In fact, they appeared to be relieved. One of the difficulties of taking one-on-one conversational Spanish lessons, I remembered from earlier attempts, is that either the teacher or the
student has to come up with something for the conversation to be
about. Right from the start, in that awkward period when both
teacher and student might be wondering where this conversation
could possibly go after they got through the question of where the
student was from and what the weather was like there, we could discuss *fanesca*. We could also discuss *maíz tostados*, which are fried kernels of Andean corn. If you're in luck — which you usually are if
you buy your *maíz tostados* from one of the women sitting behind a
gunnysack in the market — they are kernels of Andean corn that
have been prepared in the same pan as *fritada*, a local specialty that
could be summarized as pork that has been fried just short of forever. *Maíz tostados* are the best thing I've ever come across to nibble on with drinks — so good, in fact, that you don't really need
the drinks. We also had long conversations about *humitas*, which
have some resemblance to tamales. Instead of being dough around
some central element like pork or chicken, though, *humitas* are the
same all the way through — an astonishingly light concoction of
fresh young corn that is ground and mixed with eggs and cheese
and butter and anise and a bit of sugar. If tamales tasted more like
soufflés, they'd taste like *humitas*. In Cuenca, walking through the
market or even down a street, one passes *humita* vendors all the
time — or maybe I should say one comes to *humita* vendors all
the time, since I never actually succeeded in passing one without
stopping.

And my questions in Spanish about *fanesca* did not stop with requests for restaurant tips. One day, I posed the same hypothetical
question to both of my teachers: Let's say that an Ecuadoran soldier has fought valiantly for his country in a war — assume, for in-

stance, that Ecuador invaded France, looking for weapons of mass destruction — and has been gravely wounded. He's sent home, but it is clear that he has only a few weeks to live. His mother asks what she can do for him, and he says that all he wants before he dies is a bowl of her *fanesca*. But it's August. The mother is an observant woman, someone who wears black on Good Friday and visits seven churches the evening before and has never even thought about making *fanesca* any time except during Holy Week. Does she make an exception for her dying son? One of my teachers said definitely yes. The other one reminded me that some of the ingredients in *fanesca* wouldn't be available in August, except perhaps in dried form. If the mother attempted to grant the brave soldier's wish, he might end up with the sort of *fanesca* people eat in Guayaquil.

When we ran out of food talk, I made do for a while by discussing differences in idioms — a subject that has been a staple of my Spanish instruction over the decades. I always get caught up in the fact that, for example, the Spanish equivalent of "You're pulling my leg" is "You're taking my hair" — one of my teachers told me of some demonstrators who, as a symbol of not wanting to be lied to by the government anymore, appeared in front of a government building with shaved heads — or that Ecuadorans who want to leave well enough alone say that they don't want to look for the fifth paw of the cat. I find it fascinating that a carefully raised woman in Ecuador who stubs her toe or gets a paper cut says "*Miercoles!*" ("Wednesday") to avoid saying "*mierda,*" in the same way a similarly raised American in the same situation would say "Sugar!" Yes, I know that I would be much better off studying verb forms instead of collecting idioms, but I can't help it. I use the idioms, even without having mastered the verb forms. On a previous trip to Ecuador, for instance, I'd learned the word *aniñados,* which literally means "childish ones" but in Ecuador refers to spoiled rich people. I now find it hard to believe that I got by in Manhattan for years without having that word in my vocabulary.

As the days went on, either my Spanish improved or I got more desperate for subjects to talk about, because I found myself enlightening my teachers on such American topics as the political impact of soccer moms and the metaphorical use of "white bread," as in "He comes from a very white-bread family." I was concerned that the teachers might use any sustained lull as an excuse to launch an exploration of the subjunctive. Desperation is probably inadequate as an explanation of how one day I came to be telling one of my teachers the plot of *High Noon*. Looking back on this incident, I can say that it followed logically from a discussion of comparative court systems that included the word for "jury," which in Spanish is *jurado*. That led, not unexpectedly, to my mentioning the noted Mexican actress Katy Jurado, who, of course, appeared in *High Noon*, playing the role of what I think could be fairly described as "*la puta con un corazón de oro.*" That led to telling the plot of *High Noon*. Did I do the theme music? You can't tell the plot of *High Noon* without doing the theme music.

On the Monday afternoon before Easter, I found myself with something to make conversation about. "I have to say that the Holy Week traditions of Cuenca are disappearing," I told one of my teachers, disapprovingly, in careful Spanish. The specific tradition I had in mind was serving *fanesca* in restaurants for the week before Good Friday. I had assumed that I might have myself a four-*fanesca* weekend, but the only new *fanesca* outlet I'd found was at the unlikely venue of Trattoria Novecento, an Italian restaurant whose menu items ran toward *mozzarella in carrozza* and chicken Milanese. I'd half expected the waiter to come around and adorn my soup with grated Parmesan and extra-virgin olive oil, but the *fanesca* I got was palpably authentic — proof, I surmised, that the Trattoria Novecento, like so many New York restaurants of whatever ethnicity, had at least one Ecuadoran in the kitchen.

My failure to find more restaurants that were serving *fanesca* didn't mean that I'd gone hungry. For a couple of meals, my alternative turned out to be at one of the market food stands that specialize in roast pig — displayed whole, with his detached head turned back at an impossible angle, as if he'd been lying on his stomach to take the sun and had looked around suddenly to see who was sneaking up behind him. The booths all serve *hornado*, pork pulled off the pig and a couple of crisp pieces of golden-brown skin, accompanied by *mote* (boiled kernels of corn, sometimes compared to hominy) and *llapingachos*, which anybody who was raised in the Midwest is tempted to call potato puffs. *Hornado* — or even a *sándwich de pernil*, which is the same meat, except on a bun — could make some people forget about *fanesca*, but I had kept my focus. I'd counted on getting *fanesca* for Monday lunch at Villa Rosa, widely considered the best restaurant in Cuenca, I told my teacher, but the waiter informed me that they wouldn't be serving it until Wednesday. My account continued with what I'd said to the waiter upon learning how long I'd have to wait for my Villa Rosa *fanesca:* "*Miercoles!*" My teacher burst out laughing. I'd seen it coming — a play on words in Spanish. I would rather have had the *fanesca,* but a play on words in Spanish was definitely progress.

By the following Thursday, I found it hard to believe that I'd ever lamented the absence of *fanesca* in the restaurants of Cuenca. For a couple of days, I'd been having two *fanescas* a day — all delicious, and all heavy enough to make me wonder whether or not I was going to be able to come out of my corner for the next round. I told one of my teachers that I wanted to apologize to the citizens of Cuenca for implying that they were backsliders. OK, I didn't know how to say "backsliders," but there were words to that effect. That evening, rather than seek out a new *fanesca* purveyor to try, I joined the throngs making the traditional visit to seven churches. The streets of Cuenca were jammed, and food vendors were taking advantage of the foot traffic by setting up stands in front of the various churches, selling *humitas* and cotton candy and a sort of shish kebab that Cuencans like and popcorn and homemade chips of potatoes or plantains. Although I started out the evening thinking I might still be full from lunch, I visited at least seven churches, worried that I might otherwise miss the best *humita*-maker. We all have our own way of observing traditions.

I was to spend Good Friday itself in Guayaquil, before flying back to New York, so I phoned Humberto Mata, an American-educated Guayaquileño with whom I'd once consumed a certain amount of ceviche, to see if he could have lunch. Aware of my mission, he said he would endeavor to find another example of *fanesca* — even after I'd felt obliged to tell him that Cuencans had some unkind things to say about the coastal version. I thanked him, and then I said, in English, a sentence I thought I'd never utter: "Humberto, I think I'm all *fanescad* out." That was then. There's nothing I would like now more than a bowl of *fanesca.* By Holy Week, I expect to be desperate.

Contributors' Notes

Chitrita Banerji grew up in Calcutta and received her Master's degree from Harvard University. She is the author of several books on the food and culture of her native Bengal, including *Life and Food in Bengal, Bengali Cooking: Seasons & Festivals,* and *Feeding the Gods* (available in the United States in May 2006). Her articles have appeared in various magazines and journals, including *Granta, Gourmet, Gastronomica, The American Prospect, Calyx,* and the *Boston Globe.* Currently, she is working on a food travelogue titled *Eating India,* to be published by Bloomsbury in 2007.

Michael Behar was born in Seattle, Washington. He is a freelance writer who has been covering adventure travel, extreme sports, the environment, and innovations in science and technology for more than a decade. He is a frequent contributor to *Outside;* his work also appears in *Men's Journal, National Geographic Adventure, Wired, Popular Science, Smithsonian,* and *Discover.* Michael is a graduate of the Medill School of Journalism at Northwestern University. His former posts include a five-year stint at *Wired,* where he was a senior editor, and later as an articles editor for *National Geographic.* He is thirty-seven and lives in Arlington, Virginia, with his wife, Ashley, and rambunctious schnauzer, Sophie.

Paul Bennett writes for *National Geographic, National Geographic Adventure,* and *Architectural Record.* The sailing adventure recounted in his essay left him and his pregnant wife penniless in Europe. He currently divides his time between Paris and Rome, searching for a way home.

Tom Bissell was born in Escanaba, Michigan, in 1974. After graduating from Michigan State University he worked as a Peace Corps volunteer in Uzbekistan and then as a book editor for W. W. Norton and Henry Holt.

He has been a full-time writer since 2001. His first book, *Chasing the Sea,* a travel narrative about Uzbekistan, was published in 2003, and was followed shortly thereafter by a volume of fake DVD commentaries entitled *Speak, Commentary* (written with Jeff Alexander). His short story collection *God Lives in St. Petersburg* appeared in 2005, and for it he was awarded a Rome Fellowship by the American Academy of Arts and Letters. His book *The Father of All Things,* a nonfiction account of his journey to Vietnam with his father, a veteran of the Vietnam War, will be published in early 2007. He currently lives in Rome, and is working on a nonfiction book about early Christianity and a novel set in Michigan's Upper Peninsula. "After the Fall" marks his third appearance in *The Best American Travel Writing.*

Alain de Botton is a London-based essayist. He's the author of eight books to date. Among them are *On Love, How Proust Can Change Your Life, The Art of Travel,* and *The Architecture of Happiness.* He was born in 1969. Further information can be found at www.alaindebotton.com.

Kevin Fedarko is a freelance writer who lives in northern New Mexico and works as a river guide in Grand Canyon National Park. He has been a correspondent for *Time* and now contributes to *Outside, National Geographic Adventure,* and *Men's Journal,* reporting primarily on mountaineering, backcountry skiing, and other aspects of outdoor adventure.

Caitlin Flanagan is a *New Yorker* staff writer, and the author of *To Hell with All That: Loving and Loathing Our Inner Housewife.*

Sean Flynn is a correspondent for *GQ* and has also written for *Esquire,* the *New York Times Magazine, Men's Journal,* and *Golf,* among others. He's written two books, *3000 Degrees: The True Story of a Deadly Fire and the Men Who Fought It* and *Boston D.A.: The Battle to Transform the American Justice System.* He won the National Magazine Award for reporting in 2001 and his work has appeared in *The Best American Sports Writing 2005.*

Ian Frazier writes essays and longer works of nonfiction. His books include *Great Plains, Family, Coyote v. Acme, On the Rez, Dating Your Mom,* and *The Fish's Eye.* "Out of Ohio" appears as a chapter in his most recent book, *Gone to New York.* He lives in New Jersey.

Tad Friend has been a staff writer at *The New Yorker* since 1998, where he writes the magazine's "Letter from California." He is the author of *Lost in Mongolia: Travels in Hollywood and Other Foreign Lands,* a collection of his articles published in 2001. He is married to the *New York Times* food writer Amanda Hesser and lives in Brooklyn.

Pico Iyer is the author of six works of nonfiction and two novels; his books include *Video Night in Kathmandu, The Lady and the Monk, The Global Soul,* and, most recently, *Sun After Dark.* He lives in California, Japan, and, most of all, the spaces between them.

Mark Jenkins writes the monthly adventure column "The Hard Way" for *Outside.* He is the author of three books: *Off the Map,* detailing a coast-to-coast, 7,500-mile crossing of Siberia by bicycle; *To Timbuktu;* and a volume of collected works from *Outside,* entitled *The Hard Way.* Jenkins has been an editor at *Men's Health, Backpacker, Adventure Travel,* and *Cross Country Skier* and his work has appeared in *Bicycling, Condé Nast Traveler, Playboy, GQ,* and many other publications, including *The Best American Travel Writing 2004* and *2005.* He lives in Laramie, Wyoming, with his wife and two children, and is currently at work on his second volume of collected essays.

Heidi Julavits's most recent novel is *The Uses of Enchantment.* She is a founding coeditor of *The Believer.*

Yiyun Li is the author of *A Thousand Years of Good Prayers,* which won both the PEN/Hemingway Award and the Frank O'Connor International Short Story Award. Her stories and essays have appeared in *The New Yorker,* the *New York Times Magazine,* and elsewhere. She lives in Oakland with her husband and their two sons.

Morgan Meis is a cofounder of Flux Factory, an arts collective in New York City. He has a PhD in philosophy from the New School for Social Research and is an editor of 3quarksdaily.com. He writes essays and criticism for a number of different magazines and journals.

P. J. O'Rourke is the author of eleven books, including *Holidays in Hell, Parliament of Whores, Give War a Chance, Eat the Rich, The CEO of the Sofa,* and most recently, *Peace Kills.* O'Rourke was the foreign editor for *Rolling Stone* for fifteen years and has written for such diverse publications as *Automobile, House & Garden, Foreign Policy,* and *Forbes FYI.* He is currently a correspondent for *The Atlantic Monthly* and a contributing editor at *The Weekly Standard.*

Michael Paterniti is the author of *Driving Mr. Albert: A Trip Across America with Einstein's Brain,* which has been published in twenty countries. In addition to awards that include a National Magazine Award and an NEA fellowship, his work has appeared in *Harper's,* the *New York Times Magazine, Rolling Stone, Details, Outside, Esquire,* and *GQ,* where he now works as a correspondent. His next book, a true tale of cheese and murder set in Spain, is due out shortly.

Tony Perrottet is an Australian-born writer living in New York. An aficionado of the history of travel, he is the author of *Pagan Holiday: On the Trail of Ancient Roman Tourists* and *The Naked Olympics: The True Story of the Ancient Games*. He contributes regularly to *Smithsonian, Condé Nast Traveler, The Believer, Outside, Islands,* and *Men's Journal.* He also makes the odd cameo appearance on the History Channel.

Rolf Potts is the author of *Vagabonding: An Uncommon Guide to the Art of Long-Term World Travel.* His travel essays have appeared in publications such as *National Geographic Traveler, Condé Nast Traveler, Outside, Islands, Salon, Slate,* and *The Best American Travel Writing 2000.* Though he keeps no permanent residence, Potts feels somewhat at home in Bangkok, Cairo, Pusan, New Orleans, and north-central Kansas, where he keeps a small farmhouse on thirty acres near his family. Each July he can be found in France, where he is the summer writer-in-residence at the Paris American Academy. His virtual home is www.rolfpotts.com.

Kira Salak is a contributing editor for *National Geographic Adventure,* and in 2005 the National Geographic Society selected her as one of its Emerging Explorers. She is the author of *The Cruelest Journey: Six Hundred Miles to Timbuktu* and *Four Corners: A Journey into the Heart of Papua New Guinea* (chosen by the *New York Times Book Review* as a notable travel book of the year). In 2004, Salak won the PEN Award in Journalism, as well as the Lowell Thomas Gold Award for environmental reporting. Her work has appeared in *National Geographic Adventure, National Geographic,* the *New York Times Magazine, Travel + Leisure, The Best American Travel Writing 2002, 2003, 2004, 2005, Best Women's Travel Writing,* and *Best New American Voices.* Salak holds a PhD in English from the University of Missouri in Columbia.

George Saunders is the author of the short story collections *Pastoralia, CivilWarLand in Bad Decline,* and, most recently, *In Persuasion Nation.* He is also the author of the novella-length illustrated fable, *The Brief and Frightening Reign of Phil* and the *New York Times* best-selling children's book, *The Very Persistent Gappers of Frip* (illustrated by Lane Smith), which has won major children's literature prizes in Italy and the Netherlands. He teaches in the creative writing program at Syracuse University.

David Sedaris is the author of the collections *Dress Your Family in Corduroy and Denim, Me Talk Pretty One Day, Naked, Holidays on Ice,* and *Barrel Fever.* He is a regular contributor to *The New Yorker, GQ,* and National Public Radio's "This American Life."

Sally Shivnan's fiction and essays have appeared in journals including *The Georgia Review, Oxford American, Glimmer Train,* and *Rosebud,* and in the *Washington Post,* the *South Florida Sun-Sentinel, Washingtonian,* and other publications. Her work was also featured in *The Silver Rose Anthology.* She is a senior lecturer in creative writing at the University of Maryland, Baltimore County, and is currently at work on a novel. She lives in Annapolis, Maryland, with two cats and one boyfriend.

Gary Shteyngart was born in Leningrad in 1972 and came to the United States seven years later. His debut novel, *The Russian Debutante's Handbook,* won the Stephen Crane Award for First Fiction and the National Jewish Award for Fiction. It was also named a New York Times Notable Book, a best book of the year by the *Washington Post* and *Entertainment Weekly,* and one of the best debuts of the year by *The Guardian.* His second novel, *Absurdistan,* was published in May 2006. His fiction and essays have appeared in *The New Yorker, Granta, GQ, Esquire, Travel + Leisure,* the *New York Times Magazine,* and many other publications. He lives in New York City.

Christopher Solomon is a former reporter for the *Seattle Times.* He now contributes to the *New York Times, Outside, Ski* magazine, and other publications. He lives in Seattle.

As a contributing editor at *Harper's* and *Outside* magazines, **Patrick Symmes** has traveled with Maoist guerrillas in Nepal, parleyed with both main guerrilla groups in Colombia, profiled drug gangs in Brazil, dirt-biked across Cambodia to visit the Khmer Rouge, and worked his way through the Panama Canal as a deck hand. He is the author of *Chasing Che: A Motorcycle Journey through the Guevara Legend,* which describes a twelve-thousand-mile ride across South America, retracing the journeys and guerrilla campaigns of the revolutionary icon Che Guevara.

A onetime writer for *Time, The New Yorker,* and a current contributor to *The Nation,* **Calvin Trillin** is the author of several collections of essays and three comic novels, including the national bestseller *Tepper Isn't Going Out.* He has also written three previous books on eating: *American Fried; Alice, Let's Eat;* and *Third Helpings;* and the acclaimed memoirs, *Messages from My Father,* a *New York Times* bestseller, and *Family Man.* He's written two books of satirical verse about the Bush presidency: *Obliviously On He Sails* and *A Heckuva Job,* which was published in May 2006.

Notable Travel Writing of 2005

SELECTED BY JASON WILSON

ELISABETH EAVES
   Europe on 600ccs a Day. *Slate.com*, July 1.
   Strange, Strange Socotra. *Islands*, January/February.

DAVID FARLEY
   Of Kings & Cows. *South Florida Sun-Sentinel*, June 26.
KEVIN FEDARKO
   Bad Trip. *Outside*, January.
   Chaos in the Caucasus. *Skiing*, September.
NELL FREUDENBERGER
   Passage to Pondy. *Travel + Leisure*, June.

NICK GALLO
   Acapulco Gold. *mediabistro.com*, August 3.
SAMANTHA GILLISON
   War and Peace. *Condé Nast Traveler*, December.
JULIA GLASS
   Where Icarus Soared. *Gourmet*, August.
ELIZA GRISWOLD
   Medellín: Stories from an Urban War. *National Geographic*, March.
   War's Over, Surf's Up, Gringos Welcome. *National Geographic Adventure*, May.
BOB GUCCIONE, JR.
   Sex, God, and Rock 'n' Roll. *Travel + Leisure*, August.

TOM HAINES
   Retracing Gandhi's Steps. *Boston Globe*, April 3.
   To Think of Leaving Mexico. *Boston Globe*, December 11.
   In Chiapas: On the Edge. *Boston Globe*, December 18.
JOHN HALLMANN
   Traveling Europe in Style with Auckland Dingiroo, Dark Age Tourist and Critic
   of Food and Drink. *McSweeney's.net*, November 16.

PICO IYER
   A Place I've Never Been. *Amazon Shorts*, July.

MARK JENKINS
   Friends Forever. *Outside*, October.

MARK KINGWELL
   The City of Tomorrow. *Harper's*, February.
NICOLE KRAUSS
   Eight Ways of Looking at a Garden. *Condé Nast Traveler*, October.
BENJAMIN KUNKEL
   Boogie Noches. *T: Travel, New York Times Style Magazine*, November 20.

BERNARD-HENRÍ LEVY
   In the Footsteps of Tocqueville. *The Atlantic Monthly*, May-November.

Peter Jon Lindberg
Into the Woods. *Travel + Leisure,* October.

Jessica Maxwell
The Painted Plates of Northern Norway. *Lexus,* no. 1.
Bill McKibben
The Cuban Diet. *Harper's,* April.
Michael McRae
Have You Seen This Croc? *National Geographic Adventure,* March.
Lawrence Millman
Hotties. *Outside,* March.
Pankaj Mishra
Higher Ground. *Travel + Leisure,* August.

Dan Neil
Adventure, Due South. *Los Angeles Times,* November 27.

P. J. O'Rourke
Masters of the Hunt. *The Atlantic Monthly,* July/August.
Lawrence Osborne
Strangers in the Forest. *The New Yorker,* June 13 & 20.

Tony Perrottet
Lost in Space. *Condé Nast Traveler,* December.
Todd Pitock
Open Desert. *Forbes FYI,* October.
Rolf Potts
The Art of Writing a Story About Walking Across Andorra. *WorldHum.com,*
December 30.

David Quammen
In the Kingdom of the Eternal Blue Heaven. *National Geographic Adventure,*
December.
Alan Richman
Close Quarters, *Condé Nast Traveler,* April.

Paul Salopek
Who Rules the Forest? *National Geographic,* September.
Savannah Schroll
Lost in Rural Bavaria. *Hobart,* no. 5.
John Burnham Schwartz
Expatriate Games. *New York Times Magazine,* January 30.
Porter Shreve
Derelicts in the Sinai. *WorldHum.com,* July 25.
Gary Shteyngart
Frontierland. *Travel + Leisure,* September.

JAKE SILVERSTEIN
  Grand Opening. *Harper's,* January.
LEE SMITH
  The Middle of the Middle East. *Travel + Leisure,* January.
  A Talking Tour of Beirut. *Slate.com,* March 11.
ROB STORY (AS TOLD TO)
  Gorillas on the Piste. *Skiing,* November.
THOMAS SWICK
  Slow Down, You Move Too Fast. *South Florida Sun-Sentinel,* January 30.
  Slow Travel Movement: A Primer. *South Florida Sun-Sentinel,* February 6.
PATRICK SYMMES
  The Book. *Outside,* August.

JEFFREY TAYLER
  Travels with Omar. *New York Times Magazine,* January 30.
  Among the Berbers. *National Geographic,* January.
PAUL TOUGH
  The Reawakening. *T: Travel, New York Times Style Magazine,* September 25.

JAMES VLAHOS
  The Incredible Oneness of Shasta. *Skiing,* March/April.

TERRY WARD
  Girl Power in the Land of the Maharajahs. *WorldHum.com,* April 20.
DONOVAN WEBSTER
  Empty Quarter. *National Geographic,* February.
LAUREN WILCOX
  Return of the Cowgirl. *Washington Post Magazine,* March 6.
KYLE WINGFIELD
  A Town, a Man, a Mission. *Wall Street Journal,* March 18.